BECOMING A
MASTER MANAGER

BICENTENNIAL
BICENTENNIAL

1807

⊕WILEY

2007

BICENTENNIAL
BICENTENNIAL

THE WILEY BICENTENNIAL—KNOWLEDGE FOR GENERATIONS

*E*ach generation has its unique needs and aspirations. When Charles Wiley first opened his small printing shop in lower Manhattan in 1807, it was a generation of boundless potential searching for an identity. And we were there, helping to define a new American literary tradition. Over half a century later, in the midst of the Second Industrial Revolution, it was a generation focused on building the future. Once again, we were there, supplying the critical scientific, technical, and engineering knowledge that helped frame the world. Throughout the 20th Century, and into the new millennium, nations began to reach out beyond their own borders and a new international community was born. Wiley was there, expanding its operations around the world to enable a global exchange of ideas, opinions, and know-how.

For 200 years, Wiley has been an integral part of each generation's journey, enabling the flow of information and understanding necessary to meet their needs and fulfill their aspirations. Today, bold new technologies are changing the way we live and learn. Wiley will be there, providing you the must-have knowledge you need to imagine new worlds, new possibilities, and new opportunities.

Generations come and go, but you can always count on Wiley to provide you the knowledge you need, when and where you need it!

William J. Pesce

PRESIDENT AND CHIEF EXECUTIVE OFFICER

Peter Booth Wiley

CHAIRMAN OF THE BOARD

BECOMING A MASTER MANAGER

A COMPETING VALUES APPROACH

FOURTH EDITION

Robert E. Quinn
University of Michigan

Sue R. Faerman
State University of New York at Albany

Michael P. Thompson
Brigham Young University

Michael R. McGrath
Personnel Decisions International

Lynda S. St. Clair
Bryant University

BICENTENNIAL
BICENTENNIAL
1807
WILEY
2007
BICENTENNIAL
BICENTENNIAL

PUBLISHER   Susan Elbe
ASSOCIATE PUBLISHER   Judith Joseph
SENIOR ACQUISITIONS EDITOR   Jayme Heffler
ASSOCIATE EDITOR   Jennifer Conklin
PRODUCTION EDITOR   Nicole Repasky
EXECUTIVE MARKETING MANAGER   Christopher Ruel
DESIGNER   Michael St. Martine
PRODUCTION MANAGEMENT SERVICES   Pine Tree Composition, Inc.
EDITORIAL ASSISTANT   Carissa Marker
SENIOR MEDIA EDITOR   Allie K. Morris
COVER PHOTO   Corbis Digital Stock
ANNIVERSARY LOGO DESIGN   Richard Pacifico

This book was set in 10/12 Adobe Garamond by Laserwords, and printed and bound by R. R. Donnelley/Crawfordsville.
The cover was printed by Lehigh Press, Inc.

This book is printed on acid-free paper. ∞

Library of Congress Cataloging-in-Publication Data

Becoming a master manager : a competing values approach / Robert E. Quinn .. [et al.]. —
   4th ed.
      p. cm.
   Includes bibliographical references and index.
   ISBN-13: 978-0-470-05077-4 (pbk.)
   ISBN-10: 0-470-05077-2 (pbk.)
   1. Leadership. 2. Executive ability. 3. Management. 4. Organizational behavior. I.
Quinn, Robert E.

HD57.7.B43 2006
658.4'092—dc22
                                                     2006046181

INTRODUCTION TO THE FOURTH EDITION

When it was first published in 1990, *Becoming a Master Manager* used as its subtitle "*A Competency Framework*" to emphasize the importance of developing specific management skills. Since that time, a number of new texts have been written that focus on management skills. Although these texts have enriched the field, most lack a compelling theoretical basis for selecting which skills should be identified as being most critical for effective management practice. In contrast, *Becoming a Master Manager* has always focused not only on management practices, but also on organizing those practices in a theoretically valid framework. Research on the competing values model has been used not only to translate theory into practice, but also to use practice to improve theory. To emphasize this aspect of the text, the 4th edition has adopted a new subtitle—"*A Competing Values Approach.*" This does not reflect a change in the fundamental elements of the text—the competing values model has always been central to our approach to developing management competencies. For this edition, however, we decided that it was appropriate to emphasize the competing values approach in the title to help distinguish this text from other management skills books on the market.

The 4th edition also incorporates recent advances from competing values research by emphasizing four critical action imperatives: Compete, Collaborate, Control, and Create. While each of these action imperatives is associated with the historical models that have been used in past editions of the book, this new language is intended to emphasize the proactive character of effective management practice. As in prior editions, this new edition of *Becoming a Master Manager* focuses on the paradoxical nature of management. Despite the apparent contradiction in the action imperatives, effective managers need to emphasize competing *as well as* collaborating *and* controlling *as well as* creating. The competing values approach as presented in this text is designed to help students understand the complex and dynamic nature of the organizational world, as well as to develop their capacity to act confidently, ethically, thoughtfully, and imaginatively in such a world.

A CHANGING WORLD

The theme of a changing world is as apt for this, the fourth edition of the book, as it was for the first three. Paradoxically, along with incessant change we also see a great deal of continuity. For example, concerns raised in the preface to the first edition about how we educate business students continue to be raised. Accrediting agencies for business programs such as AACSB-International continue to revise their standards, focusing attention not only on educational processes but also assurance of learning outcomes. Likewise, this text continues to evolve but retains core elements that have found to be effective in the classroom for educating students about critical management issues and core managerial competencies.

These fundamental issues continue to be relevant for business students because many of the challenges that were present as we wrote previous versions of the text are still present for most organizational leaders. The emergence of the global economy continues to affect public, private, and nonprofit organizations, requiring them to develop new approaches to organization and management. In addition, current political unrest around the globe and ongoing concerns about terrorism have heightened the need for a truly global perspective when evaluating business decisions. New technologies continue to pressure organizations to rethink how they do business. In addition, recent experiences with natural disasters have taught us that technology alone is not the answer. The increasing diversity of the workplace and changing societal expectations continue to present new challenges and opportunities for organizations. On top of all these pressures, recent corporate scandals have eroded the public's trust, so even as their jobs continue to become more complex and challenging, organizational leaders face ever more scrutiny by the media and financial markets. To cope with these changes, organizations must constantly work to develop leaders, women and men at all levels of the organization, who, regardless of title, can take on responsibilities that were previously reserved only for upper-level managers.

In schools of management, faculty continue to experiment with new approaches that focus on helping students develop their capacity to apply knowledge about management and organizations to the work world. In addition, schools of management are experimenting with new modes of delivery. More and more, schools of management are offering courses and other educational experiences that are designed to enhance students' managerial leadership capacities; and leadership is being more broadly defined, recognizing that managers need to be both technically and interpersonally competent. In addition, computing and telecommunications technology have allowed for an increasing number of courses to be conducted outside the traditional classroom setting—in some cases, entire degree programs are available "on-line."

While these changes continue to influence how we think about issues in the field of management education and development, our core values remain the same. In particular, we are committed to a view of management education and development that recognizes our potential not only to inform, but also to transform. To inform is to give the student additional information. To transform is to help the student discover and become a new self, to be more capable of understanding and leading change. Our educational systems have traditionally been devoted to informing. Moving from a primary focus on informing to an approach that values both informing and transforming is not easy, but it is necessary. It requires us to shift our thinking away from either/or approaches that have underlying assumptions that lead us to believe that we must choose between opposites, and to begin to recognize the need to use paradoxical thinking to create both/and approaches. The events that have occurred since our third edition have greatly increased the need to both inform and transform our future leaders. Leadership in every arena is under siege—from the dot.com boom-and-bust to the crisis of confidence in accounting practices and corporate fiduciary principles to the tragedy of September 11, 2001. In the twenty-first century, leaders are being challenged like never before to resolve dilemmas around organizational effectiveness, economic viability, and political and military security with solutions that require both/and thinking.

This text is built around a framework of leadership competency, the *Competing Values Framework,* that is grounded in such paradoxical thinking. It is a framework that forces one to think about the competing tensions and demands that are placed on managers in new ways. Since the early 1980s, the framework has been used in management education programs based in academic settings, as well as in organizationally based management and executive development programs across the nation. It has also been used in a number of international settings, all with impressive results.

OVERVIEW

Chapter 1 of the book explains the *Competing Values Framework.* This theoretical framework integrates four contrasting perspectives on organizing. The four perspectives require managerial leaders to perform eight different managerial roles related to four action imperatives: compete, collaborate, control, and create. To accomplish the productive functions that are necessary in any organization, a managerial leader must play both a director and a producer role, focusing on setting the organization's direction and encouraging productivity and efficiency. On the other hand, to accomplish the human relations functions that are necessary, a managerial leader must play both a mentor and a facilitator role, helping organizational members to grow and develop as individuals, as well as to work together in teams. Although these two sets of roles are highly contrasting, there is another set of contrasts. To accomplish the organizing or stabilizing function that is necessary in any organization, a managerial leader must play both a coordinator and a monitor role, ensuring that workflow is not unnecessarily interrupted and that people have the information they need to do their jobs. In contrast, to accomplish the adaptive function, one must play both an innovator and a broker role, suggesting changes that allow the organization to grow and change and acquire new resources. The framework clarifies the complex nature of managerial work. It also makes clear the bias that most people have for or against the values, assumptions, and theories that are associated with each of the above areas. It makes clear the need to appreciate competing values and the need to master and then to balance and blend competencies from each area. The evolution of the model is traced and developed in Chapter 1.

Chapters 2 to 9 of the book are each dedicated to one of the eight roles. Each chapter is broken into three sections, with each section dedicated to a particular competency associated with the role. In the chapter on the mentor role, for example, the three sections respectively cover understanding self and others, communicating effectively, and developing employees. Each section or competency is presented around a five-step learning model: Assessment, Learning, Analysis, Practice, and Application. To enhance the learning experience throughout the course, we also incorporate a brief "Reflection" following the exercises to encourage further thinking about the issues addressed. The learning model and the benefits of reflection are explained further in the first chapter. Based on student feedback, we included a section on critical thinking in Chapter 1. Previously this information was included as a competency in the monitor role, but students suggested that the framework for presenting arguments was very helpful in working through the competencies throughout the text.

In the first edition of this book, we presented the roles in the historical order suggested in Chapter 1. Based on feedback from colleagues, as well as our own experience, we changed the order of the roles in the second edition to one that we saw as more appropriate to the process of developing one's managerial competencies. More specifically, while we believe that all the roles are important to effective managerial leadership, we see knowing yourself and communicating effectively as two of the most basic skills one needs in order to develop as a leader. We therefore moved the mentor role, which includes these competencies, to the beginning of the book. Feedback on the third edition suggested that we cover the innovator role prior to the broker role, allowing students to first develop an innovation for their organization and then to develop their broker skills by attempting to implement that in their organizations. While there are many reasons why an instructor might desire to present the roles in a different order, we see the mentor role as a good place to start. In the Instructor's Manual, a number of alternatives are explored.

In developing the fourth edition, we have also modified some of the competencies from the first three editions of this book, as well as updated the material within the remaining competencies. As noted earlier, this is a changing world where the nature of managerial work has evolved along with changes in many organizations' external and internal environments. In the paragraphs above we call for greater use of paradoxical thinking, which requires us to recognize that the framework can be simultaneously consistent and changing. That is, while the eight roles remain relevant for managers at all levels of the organizational hierarchy, it is sometimes necessary to reevaluate which competencies are most important for managers in the current organizational environment. We have chosen these competencies based on our understanding of current trends in organizations. As with the order of the chapters, different instructors may very well see other competencies as more important and will decide to focus on different competencies within any one of the roles.

The final chapter of the book returns to the overall model. It provides an integrative perspective and helps the student consider the process of lifelong learning and development. It reminds students that becoming a master manager is a process that will continue as long as they open themselves up to new growth experiences.

Our approach has grown out of over 25 years of research and instructional experimentation. The authors of this text have been involved in doing research that has helped to shape the meta-theory. We have worked with these materials in our university classrooms with undergraduate and graduate students, as well as in management and executive development programs. We have also helped major organizations in both the public and private sectors design large-scale programs to improve the competencies of professional managers. Several thousand professional managers have completed programs that have used the *Competing Values Framework* as an underlying foundation and integrating theme. The results have been gratifying and instructive—gratifying because both our students and we were transformed in the process. We hope that the use of this textbook will lead to similar outcomes for you.

HOW TO USE THIS BOOK

This book may be used in several ways. It can be employed alone as the main text in a course that is specifically designed to develop competencies, or it can be used with a more traditional text to accomplish the same objective. It can accompany more traditional texts in either an organizational behavior or a management principles course. The text has been used in schools of business, as well as in departments and programs of public and nonprofit management. The Instructor's Manual includes several papers written by colleagues in these fields that propose alternative uses of this book. The prospective user may find them to be stimulating in considering new approaches. We would like to thank people who have contributed to the Instructor's Manual with creative and novel essays on alternative teaching methods: Alan Belasen, Meg Benke and Andrew DiNitto, SUNY-Empire State College; Dan Denison, University of Michigan; David Hart, Brigham Young University; Bill Metheny, Montana State University at Billings; Larry Michaelsen, The University of Oklahoma; and Deborah L. Wells, Creighton University. The manual can be accessed at www.wiley.com/college/quinn.

ACKNOWLEDGMENTS

Many of the ideas for this book were originally developed in 1983, and elaborated in 1985, in conjunction with two professional development programs designed for New York State. Funding for those programs and for the first edition of this book was provided by the negotiated agreements between the state of New York and the Civil Service Employees Association, Inc., and the Public Employees Federation, AFL-CIO, and made available through New York State's Governor's Office of Employee Relations, Program Planning and Employee Development Division (now Division for Development Services). We particularly thank Don Giek, former Director of the Division for Development Services. Don truly is a master manager, and we respect and appreciate the enormous efforts he made for us and for so many people in and outside of New York State. Laurie Newman DiPadova was also instrumental in the original development of the first edition of this text, coauthoring the innovator chapter and authoring the original instructor's manual. We are most appreciative of her efforts.

The publishing team at John Wiley & Sons for the fourth edition of this text has been enormously supportive. We would like to express our sincere appreciation to Jayme Heffler, our acquisition editor, and Jennifer Conklin, our associate editor, as well as Carissa Marker and Ame Esterline. Patty Donovan, our project manager at Pine Tree Composition, was also a great help. Despite having a series of impossibly tight deadlines as well as a new coauthor to bring up to speed, they all were generous with their assistance and unflagging in their support. They have our heartfelt gratitude.

We greatly appreciate the time and energy donated by all of the reviewers of Becoming a Master Manager. For the fourth edition, special thanks go to Vijay Mathur, San Jose State University; Michael Shaner, St. Louis University; Robert Sosna, Golden Gate University; and Arnon Reichers, Ohio State University. A number of people were asked to review earlier versions of the book. They are Meg G. Birdseye, University of Alabama; John D. Bigelow, Boise State University; David E. Blevins, University of Mississippi; Allen Bluedorn, University of Missouri; Kent D. Carter, University of Maine at Orono;

Paul D. Collins, Purdue University; Daniel Denison, University of Michigan; Laurie N. DiPadova, University of Utah; Dennis L. Dossett, University of Missouri–St. Louis; Stuart C. Freedman, University of Lowell; Walter Freytag, University of Washington at Bothell; Richard A. Grover, University of Southern Maine; Ester E. Hamilton, Pepperdine University; Steve Inian, California State Polytechnic University; Richard B. Ives, Tarrant County Junior College; Marcia Kassner, University of North Dakota; Kimberlee M. Keef, Alfred University; Gerald D. Klein, Rider University; Mark Lengnick-Hall, Wichita State University; David M. Leuser, Plymouth State College; William E. McClane, Loyola College; Edward J. Morrison, University of Colorado at Boulder; Paula C. Morrow, Iowa State University; Ralph F. Mullin, Central Missouri State University; Joseph Petrick, Wright State University; Gerald Schoenfeld, James Madison University; Tim Schweizer, Luther College; Gregory Stephens, Texas Christian University; William E. Stratton, Idaho State University; David Szczerbacki, Alfred University; Fred Tesch, Western Connecticut State University; Charles N. Toftoy, Golden State University; Barry L. Wisdom, Southwest Missouri State University; Joseph Weiss, Bentley College; and Mark Wellman, Bowling Green State University. We appreciate their many helpful comments and insights.

Many others also contributed to the work of this and/or the earlier editions, and we would like to thank Debbi Berg, Bill Bywater, Chris Dammer, Rachel Ebert, Pauline Farmer, Bruce Hamm, Bill LaFleur, Warren Ilchman, Kary Jablonka, Tom Kinney, Chuck Klaer, Katherine Lawrence, Vicki Marrone, David McCaffrey, Ted Peters, Norma Riccucci, Steven Simons, Onnolee Smith, Eugene Thompson, Ben Westery, Angela Wicks, and John Zanetich. All contributed significantly and we are grateful. Finally we thank our families for their continuous support.

Robert E. Quinn
Sue R. Faerman
Michael P. Thompson
Michael R. McGrath
Lynda S. St. Clair

BRIEF CONTENTS

CONTENTS

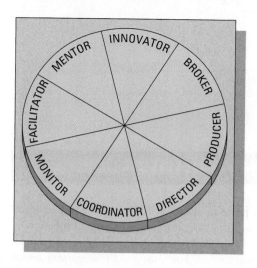

THE COMPETING VALUES APPROACH TO MANAGEMENT

1

■ FOUNDATIONS

The Evolution of Management Models

Action Imperatives: Collaborate, Control, Compete, Create

Organizing the Learning Process

We all have beliefs and we all make assumptions about the right way of doing things. This is certainly true when it comes to managerial leadership. Although our beliefs and assumptions can make us effective, they can sometimes make us ineffective (House and Podsakoff, 1994). When they do make us ineffective, it is hard to understand why. We are not usually very experienced at examining our basic beliefs and assumptions. Nor are we very experienced at adopting new assumptions or learning skills and competencies that are associated with those new assumptions. Often it takes a crisis to stimulate such change. Consider the following case.

I have always seen myself as a man who gets things done. After 17 years with a major pharmaceutical company, I was promoted to general manager in the international division. I was put in charge of all Southeast Asian operations. The unit seemed pretty sloppy to me. From the beginning I established myself as a tough, no-nonsense leader. If someone came in with a problem, he or she knew to have the facts straight or risk real trouble. After three months I began to feel like I was working myself to exhaustion, yet I could point to few real improvements. After six months or so, I felt very uneasy but was not sure why.

One night I went home and my wife greeted me. She said, "I want a divorce." I was shocked and caught off balance. To make a long story short, we ended up in counseling.

Our counselor taught me how to listen and practice empathy. The results were revolutionary. I learned that communication happens at many levels and that it's a two-way process. My marriage became richer than I had ever imagined possible.

I tried to apply what I was learning to what was going on at work. I began to realize that there was a lot going on that I didn't know about. People couldn't tell me the truth because I

1

would chop their heads off. I told everyone to come to me with any problem so that we could solve it together. Naturally, no one believed me. But after a year of proving myself, I am now known as one of the most approachable people in the entire organization. The impact on my division's operation has been impressive.

THE EVOLUTION OF MANAGEMENT MODELS

The man in the preceding story had a problem of real significance. The lives of many people, including subordinates, superiors, customers, and even his family members, were being affected by his actions. He was less successful than he might have been because of his beliefs about what a leader is supposed to do. For him, good management meant tight, well-organized operations run by tough-minded, aggressive leaders. His model was not at all wrong, but it was inadequate. It limited his awareness of important alternatives and, thus, kept him from performing as effectively as he might have.

It turns out that nearly everyone has beliefs or viewpoints about what a manager should do. In the study of management, these beliefs are sometimes referred to as **models.** There are many different kinds of models. Although some are formally written or otherwise explicit, others, like the assumptions of the general manager, are informal. Because models affect what happens in organizations, we need to consider them in some depth.

Models are representations of a more complex reality. A model airplane, for example, is a physical representation of a real airplane. Models help us to represent, communicate ideas about, and better understand more complex phenomena in the real world.

In the social world a model often represents a set of assumptions for, or a general way of thinking about or seeing, some phenomenon. It provides a particular perspective about the more complex reality. Although models can help us to see some aspects of a phenomenon, they can also blind us to other aspects. The general manager mentioned before, for example, had such strongly held beliefs about order, authority, and direction that he was unable to see some important aspects of the reality that surrounded him.

Unfortunately, our models of management are often so tied to our identity and emotions that we find it, as in the preceding case, very difficult to learn about and appreciate different models. Because of the complexity of life, we often need to call upon more than one model; thus we can see and evaluate more alternatives. Our degree of choice and our potential effectiveness can be increased (Senge, 1990).

The models held by individuals often reflect models held by society at large. During the twentieth century a number of management models emerged. Understanding these models and their origins can lead managers to a broader understanding and a wider array of choices.

Our models and definitions of management keep evolving. As societal values change, existing viewpoints alter and new models of management emerge (Fabian, 2000). These new models are not driven simply by the writings of academic or popular writers; or by managers who introduce an effective new practice; or by the technical, social, or political forces of the time. These models emerge from a complex interaction among all these factors. In this section, we will look at four major management models and how they evolved from the conditions in each of the first three quarters of the twentieth century. In doing this, we draw on the historical work of Mirvis (1985). Keep in mind as you read that the emergence of each new model did not mean that old models were swept away. Rather, many people held onto the beliefs and assumptions they had developed under the old model and continued to make decisions based on the old models. Note also that the choice of 25-year periods is arbitrary; we use them to simplify the discussion.

1900–1925: THE EMERGENCE OF THE RATIONAL GOAL MODEL AND THE INTERNAL PROCESS MODEL

The first 25 years of the twentieth century were a time of exciting growth and progress that ended in the high prosperity of the Roaring Twenties. As the period began, the economy was characterized by rich resources, cheap labor, and laissez-faire policies. In 1901, oil was discovered in Beaumont, Texas. The age of coal became the age of oil and, soon after, the age of inexpensive energy. Technologically, it was a time of invention and innovation as tremendous advances occurred in both agriculture and industry. The work force was heavily influenced by immigrants from all over the world and by people leaving the shrinking world of agriculture. The average level of education for these people was 8.2 years. Most were confronted by serious financial needs. There was little, at the outset of this period, in terms of unionism or government policy to protect workers from the demanding and primitive conditions they often faced in the factories.

One general orientation of the period was social Darwinism: the belief in "survival of the fittest." Given this orientation, it is not surprising that *Acres of Diamonds*, by Russell Conwell, was a very popular book of the time. The book's thesis was that it was every man's Christian duty to be rich. The author amassed a personal fortune from royalties and speaking fees.

These years saw the rise of the great individual industrial leaders. Henry Ford, for example, not only implemented his vision of inexpensive transportation for everyone by producing the Model T, but he also applied the principles of Frederick Taylor to the production process. Taylor was the father of **scientific management** (see Theoretical Perspective 1.1). He introduced a variety of techniques for "rationalizing" work and

THEORETICAL PERSPECTIVE 1.1

TAYLOR'S FOUR PRINCIPLES OF MANAGEMENT

1. Develop a science for every job, which replaces the old rule-of-thumb method.
2. Systematically select workers so that they fit the job, and train them effectively.
3. Offer incentives so that workers behave in accordance with the principles of the science that has been developed.
4. Support workers by carefully planning their work and smoothing the way as they do their jobs.

Adapted from Frederick W. Taylor, *The Principles of Scientific Management* (New York: Harper and Brothers, 1911), p. 44.

making it as efficient as possible. Using Taylor's ideas, Henry Ford, in 1914, introduced the assembly line and reduced car assembly time from 728 hours to 93 minutes. In six years Ford's market share went from just under 10% to just under 50%. The wealth generated by the inventions, production methods, and organizations themselves was an entirely new phenomenon.

Rational Goal Model.   It was in this historical context that the first two models of management began to emerge. The first is the **rational goal model.** The symbol that best represents this model is the dollar sign, because the ultimate criteria of organization effectiveness are productivity and profit. The basic means–ends assumption in this approach is the belief that clear direction leads to productive outcomes. Hence there is a continuing emphasis on processes such as goal clarification, rational analysis, and action taking. The organizational climate is rational economic, and all decisions are driven by considerations of "the bottom line." If an employee of 20 years is only producing at 80% efficiency, the appropriate decision is clear: Replace the employee with a person who will contribute at 100% efficiency. In the rational goal model the ultimate value is achievement and profit maximization. The manager's job is to be a decisive director and a task-oriented producer.

Stories abound about the harsh treatment that supervisors and managers inflicted on employees during this time. In one manufacturing company, for example, they still talk today about the toilet that was once located in the center of the shop floor and was surrounded by glass windows so that the supervisor could see who was inside and how long the person stayed.

Internal Process Model.   The second model is called the **internal process model.** While its most basic hierarchical arrangements had been in use for centuries, during the first quarter of the twentieth century it rapidly evolved into what would become known as the "professional bureaucracy." The basic notions of this model would not be fully codified, however, until the writings of Max Weber and Henri Fayol were translated in the middle of the next quarter-century. This model is highly complementary to the rational goal model. Here the symbol is a pyramid, and the criteria of effectiveness are stability and continuity. The means–ends assumption is based on the belief that routinization leads to stability. The emphasis is on processes such as definition of responsibilities, measurement, documentation, and record keeping. The organizational climate is hierarchical, and all decisions are colored by the existing rules, structures, and traditions. If an employee's efficiency falls, control is increased through the application of various policies and procedures. In this model the ultimate value is efficient workflow, and the manager's job is to be a technically expert monitor and dependable coordinator.

1926–1950: THE EMERGENCE OF THE HUMAN RELATIONS MODEL

The second quarter of the century brought two events of enormous proportions. The stock market crash of 1929 and World War II would affect the lives and outlook of generations to come. During this period the economy would boom, crash, recover with the war, and then, once again, offer bright hopes. Technological advances would continue in all areas, but particularly in agriculture, transportation, and consumer goods. The rational goal model continued to flourish. With the writings of Henri Fayol, Max Weber, and others, the internal process model (see Theoretical Perspectives 1.2 and 1.3)

THEORETICAL PERSPECTIVE 1.2

FAYOL'S GENERAL PRINCIPLES OF MANAGEMENT

1. *Division of work.* The object of division of work is to produce more and better work with the same effort. It is accomplished through reduction in the number of tasks to which attention and effort must be directed.

2. *Authority and responsibility.* Authority is the right to give orders, and responsibility is its essential counterpart. Whenever authority is exercised, responsibility arises.

3. *Discipline.* Discipline implies obedience and respect for the agreements between the firm and its employees. These agreements are arrived at by discussion between an owner or group of owners and worker's associations. The establishment of such agreements should remain one of the chief preoccupations of industrial heads. Discipline also involves sanctions judiciously applied.

4. *Unity of command.* An employee should receive orders from one superior only.

5. *Unity of direction.* Each group of activities having one objective should be unified by having one plan and one head.

6. *Subordination of individual interest to general interest.* The interest of one employee or group of employees should not prevail over that of the company or broader organization.

7. *Remuneration of personnel.* To maintain their loyalty and support, employees must receive a fair wage for services rendered.

8. *Centralization.* Like division of work, centralization belongs to the natural order of things. The appropriate degree of centralization, however, will vary with a particular concern, so it becomes a question of the proper proportion. It is a problem of finding the measure that will give the best overall yield.

9. *Scalar chain.* The scalar chain is the chain of superiors ranging from the ultimate authority to the lowest ranks. It is an error to depart needlessly from the line of authority, but it is an even greater one to adhere to it when detriment to the business could ensue.

10. *Order.* A place for everything, and everything in its place.

11. *Equity.* Equity is a combination of kindliness and justice.

12. *Stability of tenure of personnel.* High turnover increases inefficiency. A mediocre manager who stays is infinitely preferable to an outstanding manager who comes and goes.

13. *Initiative.* Initiative involves thinking out a plan and ensuring its success. This gives zeal and energy to an organization.

14. *Esprit de corps.* Union is strength, and it comes from the harmony of the personnel.

Abridged from Henri Fayol, *General and Industrial Administration* (New York: Pitman, 1949), pp. 20–41.

THEORETICAL PERSPECTIVE 1.3

CHARACTERISTICS OF WEBERIAN BUREAUCRACY

Elements of Bureaucracy

1. There is a division of labor with responsibilities that are clearly defined.
2. Positions are organized in a hierarchy of authority.
3. All personnel are objectively selected and promoted based on technical abilities.
4. Administrative decisions are recorded in writing, and records are maintained over time.
5. There are career managers working for a salary.
6. There are standard rules and procedures that are uniformly applied to all.

Adapted from A.M. Henderson and Talcott Parsons (eds.) and Max Weber (trans.), *The Theory of Social and Economic Organizations* (New York: Free Press, 1947), pp. 328–337.

would be more clearly articulated. Yet, even while this was being accomplished, it started to become clear that the rational goal and internal process models were not entirely appropriate to the demands of the times.

Some fundamental changes began to appear in the fabric of society during the second quarter of the century. Unions, now a significant force, adhered to an economic agenda that brought an ever-larger paycheck into the home of the American worker. Industry placed a heavy emphasis on the production of consumer goods. By the end of this period, new labor-saving machines were beginning to appear in homes. There was a sense of prosperity and a concern with recreation as well as survival. Factory workers were not as eager as their parents had been to accept the opportunity to work overtime. Neither were they as likely to give unquestioning obedience to authority. Hence managers were finding that the rational goal and internal process models were no longer as effective as they once were.

Given the shortcomings of the first two models, it is not surprising that one of the most popular books written during this period was Dale Carnegie's *How to Win Friends and Influence People*. It provided some much-desired advice on how to relate effectively to others. In the academic world, Chester Barnard pointed to the significance of informal organization and the fact that informal relationships, if managed properly, could be powerful tools for the manager. Also during this period Elton Mayo and Fritz Roethlisberger carried out their work in the famous Hawthorne studies. One well-known experiment carried out by these two researchers concerned levels of lighting. Each time they increased the levels of lighting, employee productivity went up. However, when they decreased the lighting, productivity also went up. They eventually concluded that what was really stimulating the workers was the attention being shown them by the researchers. The results of these studies were also interpreted as evidence of a need for an increased focus on the power of relationships and informal processes in the performance of human groups.

Human Relations Model.   By the end of the second quarter of the century, the emerging orientation was the **human relations model**. In this model, the key emphasis is on commitment, cohesion, and morale. The means–ends assumption is that involvement results in commitment, and the key values are participation, conflict resolution, and consensus building. Because of an emphasis on equality and openness, the appropriate symbol for this model is a circle. The organization takes on a clanlike, team-oriented climate in which decision making is characterized by deep involvement. Here, if an employee's efficiency declines, managers take a developmental perspective and look at a complex set of motivational factors. They may choose to alter the person's degree of participation or opt for a host of other social psychological variables. The manager's job is to be an empathetic mentor and a process-oriented facilitator.

In 1949, this model was far from crystallized, and it ran counter to the assumptions in the rational goal and internal process models. Hence it was difficult to understand and certainly difficult to practice. Attempts often resulted in a kind of authoritarian benevolence. It would take well into the next quarter-century for research and popular writings to explore this orientation and for managerial experiments to result in meaningful outcomes in large organizations.

1951–1975: THE EMERGENCE OF THE OPEN SYSTEMS MODEL

The period 1951 to 1975 began with the United States as the unquestioned leader of the capitalist world. It ended with the leadership of the United States in serious question. During this period the economy experienced the shock of the oil embargo in 1973. Suddenly assumptions about cheap energy, and all the life patterns upon which they were based, were in danger. By the late 1970s the economy was staggering under the weight of stagnation and huge government debt. At the beginning of this period, "made in Japan" meant cheap, low-quality goods of little significance to Americans. By the end, Japanese quality could not be matched, and Japan was making rapid inroads into sectors of the economy thought to be the sacred domain of American companies. Even such traditionally American manufacturing areas as automobile production were dramatically affected. There was also a marked shift from a clear product economy to the beginnings of a service economy.

Technological advances began to occur at an ever-increasing rate. At the outset of the third quarter of the century, the television was a strange device. By the end of this period, television was the primary source of information and the computer was entering the life of every American. At the beginning of the 1960s, NASA worked to accomplish the impossible dream of putting a man on the moon, but then Americans became bored with the seemingly commonplace accomplishments of the space program.

Societal values also shifted dramatically. The 1950s were a time of conventional values. Driven by the Vietnam War, the 1960s were a time of cynicism and upheaval. Authority and institutions were everywhere in question. By the 1970s the difficulty of bringing about social change was fully understood. A more individualistic and conservative orientation began to take root.

In the workforce, average education jumped from the 8.2 years at the beginning of the century to 12.6 years. Spurred by considerable prosperity, workers in the United States were now concerned not only with money and recreation but also with self-fulfillment. Women began to move into professions that had been closed to them previously. The agenda of labor expanded to include social and political issues. Organizations became knowledge-intense, and it was no longer possible to expect the boss to know more than every person he or she supervised.

By now the first two models were firmly in place, and management vocabulary was filled with rational management terms, such as management by objectives (MBO) and management information system (MIS). The human relations model, however, was also now familiar. Many books about human relations became popular during this period, further sensitizing the world to the complexities of motivation and leadership. Experiments in group dynamics, organizational development, sociotechnical systems, and participative management flourished.

In the mid-1960s, spurred by the ever-increasing rate of change and the need to understand how to manage in a fast-changing, knowledge-intense world, a variety of academics began to write about still another model. People such as Katz and Kahn at the University of Michigan, Lawrence and Lorsch at Harvard, as well as a host of others began to develop the open systems model of organization. This model was more dynamic than others. The manager was no longer seen as a rational decision maker controlling a machinelike organization. The research of Mintzberg, for example, showed that in contrast to the highly systematic pictures portrayed in the principles of administration (see Theoretical Perspective 1.2), managers live in highly unpredictable environments and have little time to organize and plan. They are, instead, bombarded by constant stimuli and forced to make rapid decisions. Such observations were consistent with the movement to develop contingency theories (see Theoretical Perspective 1.4). These theories recognized the simplicity of earlier approaches.

Open Systems Model. In the **open systems model**, the organization is faced with a need to compete in an ambiguous as well as competitive environment. The key criteria of organizational effectiveness are adaptability and external support. Because of the emphasis on organizational flexibility and responsiveness, the symbol here is the amoeba. The amoeba is a very responsive, fast-changing organism that is able to respond to its environment. The means–ends assumption is that continual adaptation and innovation lead to the acquisition and maintenance of external resources. Key processes are political adaptation, creative problem solving, innovation, and the management of change. The organization has an innovative climate and is more of an "adhocracy" than a bureaucracy. Risk is high, and decisions are made quickly. In this situation common vision and shared values are very important. Here, if an employee's efficiency declines, it may be seen as a result of long periods of intense work, an overload of stress, and perhaps a case of burnout. The manager is expected

THEORETICAL PERSPECTIVE 1.4

CONTINGENCY THEORY

Appropriateness of Managerial Actions Varies with Key Variables

1. *Size.* Problems of coordination increase as the size of the organization increases. Appropriate coordination procedures for a large organization will not be efficient in a small organization, and vice versa.

2. *Technology.* The technology used to produce outputs varies. It may be very routine or very customized. The appropriateness of organizational structures, leadership styles, and control systems will vary with the type of technology.

3. *Environment.* Organizations exist within larger environments. These may be uncertain and turbulent or predictable and unchanging. Organizational structures, leadership styles, and control systems will vary accordingly.

4. *Individuals.* People are not the same. They have very different needs. Managers must adjust their styles accordingly.

to be a creative innovator and a politically astute broker (someone who uses power and influence in the organization).

1976–TODAY: THE EMERGENCE OF "BOTH–AND" ASSUMPTIONS

In the 1980s it became apparent that American organizations were in deep trouble. Innovation, quality, and productivity all slumped badly. Japanese products made astounding advances as talk of U.S. trade deficits became commonplace. Reaganomics and conservative social and economic values fully replaced the visions of the Great Society. In the labor force, knowledge work became commonplace and physical labor, rare. Labor unions experienced major setbacks as organizations struggled to downsize their staffs and increase quality at the same time. The issue of job security became increasingly prominent in labor negotiations. Organizations faced new issues, such as takeovers and downsizing. One middle manager struggled to do the job previously done by two or three. Burnout and stress became hot topics.

Peters and Waterman published a book that would have extraordinary popularity. *In Search of Excellence* attempted to chronicle the story of those few organizations that were seemingly doing it right. It was really the first attempt to provide advice on how to revitalize a stagnant organization and move it into a congruent relationship with an environment turned upside down. Like Carnegie's book, long before, it addressed and, in so doing, made clear the most salient unmet need of the time: how to manage in a world where nothing is stable.

As the twentieth century drew to a close, the rate of change rose to new heights. Longstanding political and business institutions began to crumble. The Berlin Wall came tumbling down. A short time later the USSR itself disintegrated. In the United

States some of the most powerful and admired corporations seemed strong one day and in deep difficulty the next. In the new global economy nothing seemed predictable. This was exacerbated by the emergence of the Internet and e-commerce. In the meantime, employees with the right mix of competencies and abilities were in short supply. In 2000, a survey of executives' concerns ("Survey of Pressing Problems," 2000) indicated that the most pressing problems were the following:

- Attracting, keeping, and developing good people
- Thinking and planning strategically
- Maintaining a high-performance climate
- Improving customer satisfaction
- Managing time and stress
- Staying ahead of the competition
- Aligning vision, strategy, and behavior
- Maintaining work and life balance
- Improving internal processes
- Stimulating innovation

These seemingly very different problems are actually all symptoms of a larger problem—the need to achieve organizational effectiveness in a highly dynamic environment. In such a complex and fast-changing world, simple solutions became suspect. None of the four models, discussed earlier and summarized in Table 1.1, offered a sufficient answer. Even the more complex open systems approach was not

TABLE 1.1 Characteristics of the Four Management Models

	Rational Goal	*Internal Process*	*Human Relations*	*Open Systems*
Symbol	💲	△	○	✿
Criteria of effectiveness	Productivity, profit	Stability, continuity	Commitment, cohesion, morale	Adaptability, external support
Means–ends theory	Clear direction leads to productive outcomes	Routinization leads to stability	Involvement results in commitment	Continual adaptation and innovation lead to acquiring and maintaining external resources
Action imperative	Compete	Control	Collaborate	Create
Emphasis	Goal clarification, rational analysis, and action taking	Defining responsibility, measurement, documentation	Participation, conflict resolution, and consensus building	Political adaptation, creative problem solving, innovation, change management
Climate	Rational economic: "the bottom line"	Hierarchical	Team oriented	Innovative, flexible
Role of manager	Director and producer	Monitor and coordinator	Mentor and facilitator	Innovator and broker

sufficient. Sometimes we needed stability, sometimes we needed change. Often we needed both at the same time. The key was to stop assuming that it was an either–or decision, to stop thinking about choosing between the two (Quinn, Kahn, and Mandl, 1994). More and more we needed to learn about both–and assumptions, where contrasting behaviors could be needed at the same time. By the mid-1990s it had become clear that no one model was sufficient to guide a manager and that it was in fact necessary to see each of the four models as elements of a larger model. It is around this notion of a larger, integrated model that this book is organized.

ACTION IMPERATIVES   Collaborate, Control, Compete, Create

A SINGLE FRAMEWORK

At first, the models discussed earlier seem to be four entirely different perspectives or domains. However, they can be viewed as closely related and interwoven. They are four important subdomains of a larger construct: organizational effectiveness. Each model within the construct of organizational effectiveness is related. Depending on the models and combinations of models we choose to use, we can see organizational effectiveness as simple and logical, as dynamic and synergistic, or as complex and paradoxical. Taken alone, no one of the models allows us the range of perspectives and the increased choice and potential effectiveness provided by considering them all as part of a larger framework. As we'll explain soon, we call this larger framework the **competing values framework.**

The relationships among the models can be seen in terms of two axes. In Figure 1.1 the vertical axis ranges from flexibility at the top to control at the bottom. The horizontal axis ranges from an internal organizational focus at the left to an external focus at the right. Each model fits in one of the four quadrants.

The human relations model, for example, stresses the criteria shown in the upper-left quadrant: participation, openness, commitment, and morale. The open systems model stresses the criteria shown in the upper-right quadrant: innovation, adaptation, growth, and resource acquisition. The rational goal model stresses the criteria shown in the lower-right quadrant: direction, goal clarity, productivity, and accomplishment. The internal process model, in the lower-left quadrant, stresses documentation, information management, stability, and control.

To translate these four theoretical models into management practice, we have labeled each quadrant according to the central action focus related to each model: Collaborate for the human relations model, Control for the internal process model, Compete for the rational goal model, and Create for the open systems model. As can be seen in Figure 1.2, some general values are also reflected in the framework. These appear on the outer perimeter. Expansion and change are in the upper-right corner and contrast with consolidation and continuity in the lower-left corner. On the other hand, they complement the neighboring values focusing on decentralization and differentiation at the top and achieving a competitive position of the overall system to the right. Each general value statement can be seen in the same way.

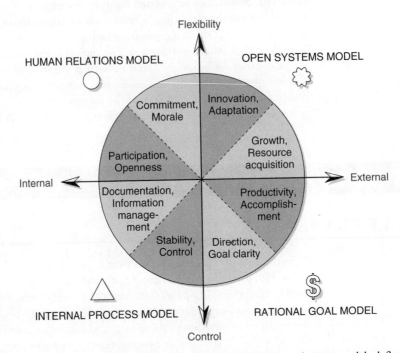

FIGURE 1.1 *Competing values framework: effectiveness criteria.*

Each of the four models of organizing in the competing values framework assumes different criteria of effectiveness. Here we see the criteria in each model; the labels on the axes show the qualities that differentiate each model.

Source: R. E. Quinn, *Beyond Rational Management* (San Francisco: Jossey-Bass, 1988), p. 48. Used with permission.

Each model has a perceptual opposite. The human relations model, defined by flexibility and internal focus, stands in stark contrast to the rational goal model, which is defined by control and external focus. In the first, for example, people are inherently valued. In the second, people are of value only if they contribute greatly to goal attainment. The open systems model, defined by flexibility and external focus, runs counter to the internal process model, which is defined by control and internal focus. While the open systems model is concerned with adapting to the continuous change in the environment, the internal process model is concerned with maintaining stability and continuity inside the system.

Parallels among the models are also important. The human relations and open systems models share an emphasis on flexibility. The open systems and rational goal models share an emphasis on external focus. The rational goal and internal process models emphasize control. And the internal process and human relations models share an emphasis on internal focus.

THE USE OF OPPOSING MODELS

We will use this framework of the four opposing models throughout the book as our management model. We call this framework the **competing values framework** because the criteria within the four models seem at first to carry a conflicting message. We want our organizations to be adaptable and flexible, but we also want them to be stable and controlled. We want growth, resource acquisition, and external support, but we also want tight information management and formal communication. We want an emphasis on the value of human resources, but we also want an emphasis on planning and goal setting. In any real organization all of these are, to some extent, necessary.

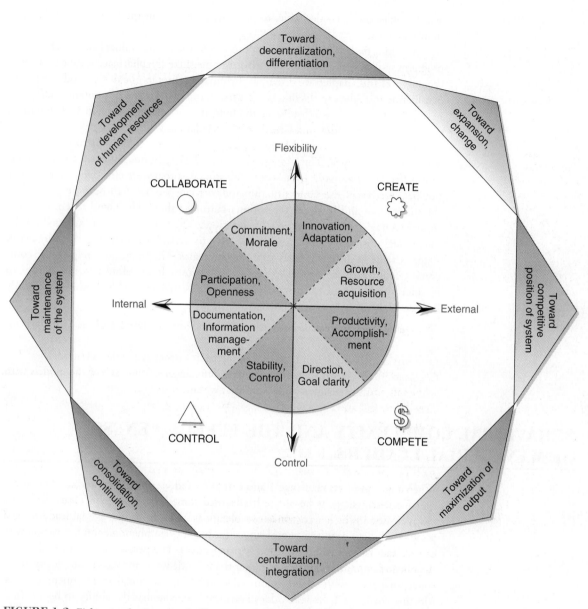

FIGURE 1.2 *Eight general orientations in the competing values framework.*
The eight general values that operate in the competing values framework are shown in the triangles on the perimeter.
Each value both complements the values next to it and contrasts with the one directly opposite it.

Source: R. E. Quinn, *Beyond Rational Management* (San Francisco: Jossey-Bass, 1988), p. 48. Used with permission.

The framework does not suggest that these oppositions cannot mutually exist in a real system. It does suggest, however, that these criteria, values, and assumptions are at opposites in our minds. We tend to think about them as mutually exclusive; that is, we assume we cannot have two opposites at the same time. Moreover, in valuing one over the other we tend to devalue or discount its opposite. As we shall see, however, it is possible—in fact—desirable, to perform effectively in the four opposing models simultaneously.

The four models in the framework represent the unseen values over which people, programs, policies, and organizations live and die. Like the pharmaceutical executive at the outset of this chapter, we often blindly pursue values in one of the models without considering the values in the others. As a result, our choices and our potential effectiveness are reduced. To be effective in the long run, we must engage in Collaborating, Controlling, Competing, and Creating on a regular basis.

For managers the world keeps changing. It changes from hour to hour, day to day, and week to week. The strategies that are effective in one situation are not necessarily effective in another. Even worse, the strategies that were effective yesterday may not be effective in the same situation today. Managers tend to become trapped in their own style and in the organization's cultural values. They tend to employ very similar strategies in a wide variety of situations. The overall framework, based on the four models described here, can increase effectiveness. Each model in the framework suggests value in different, even opposite, strategies. The framework reflects the complexity confronted by people in real organizations. It therefore provides a tool to broaden thinking and to increase choice and effectiveness. This, however, can only happen as three challenges are met.

Challenge 1   To appreciate both the values and the weaknesses of each of the four models

Challenge 2   To acquire and use the competencies associated with each model

Challenge 3   To dynamically integrate the competencies from each of the models with the managerial situations that we encounter

BEHAVIORAL COMPLEXITY AND THE EFFECTIVENESS OF MANAGERIAL LEADERS

When a person meets challenge 1 and comes to understand and appreciate each of the four models, it suggests he or she has learned something at the conceptual level and has increased his or her cognitive complexity as it relates to managerial leadership. A person with high cognitive complexity regarding a given phenomenon is a person who can see that phenomenon from many perspectives. The person is able to think about the phenomenon in sophisticated rather than simple ways. Increased complexity at the conceptual level is the primary objective in most traditional management courses. Meeting challenge 1, however, does not mean someone has the ability to be an effective managerial leader. Knowledge is not enough.

To increase effectiveness, a managerial leader must meet challenges 2 and 3. Meeting these challenges leads to an increase in behavioral complexity. The term *behavioral complexity* was coined by Hooijberg and Quinn (1992) to reflect the capacity to draw on and use competencies and behaviors from the different models. Behavioral complexity builds on the notion of cognitive complexity and is defined as "the ability to act out a cognitively complex strategy by playing multiple, even competing, roles in a highly integrated and complementary way" (p. 164).

Several studies suggest a link between behavioral complexity and effective performance. In a study of 916 CEOs, Hart and Quinn (1993) found that the ability to play multiple and competing roles produced better firm performance. The CEOs with high behavioral complexity saw themselves as focusing on broad visions for the future (open systems model), while also providing critical evaluation of present plans (internal process model). They also saw themselves attending to relational issues (human relations model), while simultaneously emphasizing the accomplishment of tasks (rational goal model). The firms with CEOs having higher behavioral complexity produced the best firm performance, particularly with respect to business performance (growth and innovation) and organizational effectiveness. The relationships held regardless of firm size or variations in the nature of the organizational environment.

In a study of middle managers in a *Fortune* 100 company, Denison, Hooijberg, and Quinn (1995) found behavioral complexity, as assessed by the superior of the middle manager, to be related to the overall managerial effectiveness of the manager, as assessed by subordinates. In a similar study, behavioral complexity was related to managerial performance, charisma, and the likelihood of making process improvements in the organization (Quinn, Spreitzer, and Hart, 1992).

BECOMING A MANAGER: THE NEED FOR NEW COMPETENCIES

The competing values framework integrates opposites. It is not easy to think about opposites. The failure to understand them, however, can hinder the development you need as a managerial leader. We will therefore begin by describing the competing roles managers play in their organization. We will then turn to the specific **competencies** that are embedded in each role. Finally, we will describe a process for developing each of the competencies at the behavioral level.

EIGHT ROLES

The competing values framework is helpful in pointing out some of the values and criteria of effectiveness by which work units and organizations are judged. It is also useful in thinking about the conflicting roles that are played by managers (Quinn, 1984, 1988). Figure 1.3 shows a second version of the competing values framework. The structure of Figure 1.3 is very similar to the structure of Figure 1.1, but this time the figure focuses on *leadership* effectiveness, rather than organizational or work-unit effectiveness. This framework specifies competing roles or expectations that might be experienced by a manager.

Compete: The Director and Producer Roles. In the lower-right quadrant are the director and producer roles. As a **director,** a manager is expected to clarify expectations through processes, such as planning and goal setting, and to be a decisive initiator who defines problems, selects alternatives, establishes objectives, defines roles and tasks, generates rules and policies, and gives instructions.

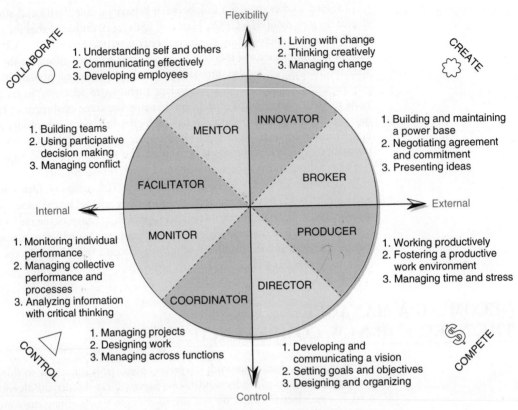

FIGURE 1.3 *The competencies and the leadership roles in the competing values framework.*
Each of the eight leadership roles in the competing values framework contains three competencies. They, like the values, both complement the ones next to them and contrast with those opposite to them.

Source: R. E. Quinn, *Beyond Rational Management* (San Francisco: Jossey-Bass, 1988), p. 48. Used with permission.

When someone is playing the director role, there is no question about who is in charge. Consider, for example, the following statement made about a particularly directive manager:

> *She is everywhere. It seems as if she never goes home. But it is not just her energy; she is constantly reminding us why we are here. I have worked in a lot of organizations, but I have never been so clear about purpose. I know what I have to do to satisfy her and what the unit has to do. In some units around here, the employees really don't care; she has caused people to care about getting the job done.*

When people think about the director role, they often think of a hard-driving person known for a no-nonsense, take-charge attitude. An excellent example is provided by the opening scene of the movie *Patton*. When George C. Scott, portraying General George Patton, addresses his soldiers prior to entering battle, they absolutely know what the objective is and how they are to obtain it. People who excel at the director role are often highly competitive, swift-acting decision makers who make their expectations clear. People walk away knowing exactly what they are to do. These people often argue that there are times when people simply must be kicked around or even removed from their jobs. In such situations directors tend to act decisively.

Patton, and others like him, also tend to serve as excellent examples of the producer role. **Producers** are expected to be task oriented and work focused and to have high interest, motivation, energy, and personal drive. They are supposed to accept responsibility, complete assignments, and maintain high personal productivity. This usually involves motivating members to increase production and to accomplish stated goals. Stereotypes of this role often have a fanatic desire to accomplish some objective. Like Captain Ahab in the novel *Moby Dick*, they drive themselves and their crews unrelentingly toward a stated objective.

Control: Monitor and Coordinator Roles.

In the bottom-left quadrant are the monitor and coordinator roles. As a **monitor,** a manager is expected to know what is going on in the unit, to determine whether people are complying with the rules, and to see whether the unit is meeting its quotas. The monitor knows all the facts and details and is good at analysis. Characteristic to this role is a zeal for handling data and forms, reviewing and responding to routine information, conducting inspections and tours, and authoring reviews of reports and other documents.

Consider, for example, this description of a manager:

She has been here for years. Everyone checks with her before doing anything. She is a walking computer. She remembers every detail, and she tracks every transaction that occurs. From agreements made eight years ago, she knows which unit owes equipment to which other unit. Nothing gets past her. She has a sixth sense for when people are trying to hide something.

A stereotype of the monitor and coordinator roles is the character Radar O'Reilly from the classic TV series *M*A*S*H*. The monitor role suggests a care for details, control, and analysis. The monitor is constantly checking to find out what is really going on. The monitor has a sense of precision and pays attention to measures, reports, and data. Debby Hopkins, the chief financial officer at Boeing, excels in the monitor role, paying attention to every detail. She says she likes "putting my nose into everything," which includes such things as touring factories, changing manufacturing processes, and choosing new advertising agencies. She wants to know every detail.

A real-life example of a coordinator is General H. Norman Schwarzkopf, who, as commander of operations of the U.S. forces during Operation Desert Shield and Operation Desert Storm, assembled 765,000 troops from 28 countries, hundreds of ships, and thousands of planes and tanks in order to defend Saudi Arabia against possible Iraqi invasion in 1990 and then to drive Iraq from Kuwait in 1991. As a **coordinator,** a manager is expected to maintain the structure and flow of the system. The person in this role is expected to be dependable and reliable. Behavioral traits include various forms of work facilitation, such as scheduling, organizing, and coordinating staff efforts; handling crises; and attending to technological, logistical, and housekeeping issues.

Collaborate: The Facilitator and Mentor Roles.

The **facilitator** is expected to foster collective effort, build cohesion and teamwork, and manage interpersonal conflict. In this role the manager is process oriented. Expected behaviors include intervening in interpersonal disputes, using conflict-reduction techniques, developing cohesion and morale, obtaining input and participation, and facilitating group problem solving.

Consider, for example, this description of a public manager:

It is like any company. The finance people and the operations people are always at war. He brings people like that into a room, hardly says a word, and walks out with support from both sides. Same with subordinates—he brings us together, asks lots of questions, and we leave committed to get the job done. He has a gift for getting people to see the bigger picture, to trust each other, and to cooperate.

A particularly outstanding example of the facilitator role is Suzanne de Passe, who served as president of Motown Productions. A highly energetic manager, she was recognized as having many skills, yet the one that stands out the most is her incredible ability for team building. With her, no subject was taboo. Her staff felt free and safe in raising any issue, including the shortcomings of the boss herself. She refused to let any conflict stay hidden. All issues were raised and worked on until there was a resolution and consensus. Her people had a sense of involvement and influence. The level of openness and cohesiveness astounded most newcomers. Many commented that the organization was the only one they had ever seen where the truth was always told and potentially divisive political issues were immediately confronted and resolved. The sense of openness and cohesiveness created an exciting and productive organizational context.

A **mentor** is engaged in the development of people through a caring, empathetic orientation. This might be called the concerned human role. In this role the manager is helpful, considerate, sensitive, approachable, open, and fair. In acting out this role, the manager listens, supports legitimate requests, conveys appreciation, and gives compliments and credit. People are resources to be developed. The manager helps with skill building, provides training opportunities, and plans for employees' individual development. Here we think about a man who was the head of finance in a *Fortune* 100 company. He was known as a master of this role. He would carefully select graduates from the best business schools, bring them into the company, train them, and then watch over every aspect of their career development. To be one of his protégés was to be on the sure track to success.

Create: The Innovator and Broker Roles.

The innovator and broker roles, in the upper-right quadrant of the framework, reflect the values of the open systems model. As an innovator, a manager is expected to facilitate adaptation and change. The innovator pays attention to the changing environment, identifies important trends, conceptualizes and projects needed changes, and tolerates uncertainty and risk. In this role, managers must rely on induction, ideas, and intuitive insights. These managers are expected to be creative, clever dreamers who see the future, envision innovations, package them in inviting ways, and convince others that they are necessary and desirable.

Consider, for example, this description:

In a big organization like this, most folks do not want to rock the boat. She is always asking why, looking for new ways to do things. We used to be in an old, run-down wing. Everyone accepted it as a given. It took her two years, but she got us moved. She had a vision, and she sold it up the system. She is always open, and if a change or a new idea makes sense, she will go for it.

Innovators are usually people with vision. The stereotype is the entrepreneur, such as Bill Gates, who pursues and dreams and builds a great company. Such a person sees a need and a way to fulfill the need. Innovators are willing to take risks in pursuing their vision. A good example is Joy Covey, chief strategist at Amazon.com. She is a high school dropout who is now worth more than $150 million. At Amazon, Covey exhibits a keen ability to foresee future trends and prepare her organization to move in the appropriate direction. She has a creative mind and the ability to communicate her vision.

The **broker** is particularly concerned with maintaining external legitimacy and obtaining external resources. Mary Meeker, an Internet analyst at Morgan Stanley, is seen as a great illustration of the broker role. She has engineered more than 26 IPOs (initial public offerings). She works with bankers and her clients to pursue new ideas and put together deals that will add value for all concerned parties. Image, appearance, and reputation are important. Managers as brokers are expected to be politically astute, persuasive, influential, and powerful. They meet with people from outside the unit to represent, negotiate, and to acquire resources; they market; and they act as a liaison and spokesperson.

THE EIGHT ROLES AT DIFFERENT ORGANIZATION LEVELS

As you think about the eight managerial leadership roles described earlier, you may notice that these descriptions are as applicable to first-level supervisors as they are to executive-level managers of large organizations: The descriptions of the eight roles represent general descriptions of managerial behaviors that are not necessarily tied to a particular level of organizational hierarchy. Indeed, researchers and consultants have used the competing values framework to structure management education, development, and training programs for first-, middle-, and upper-level managers in a wide variety of public, private, and not-for-profit organizations in the United States as well as internationally (Ban and Faerman, 1988; Faerman, Quinn, and Thompson, 1987; Giek and Lees, 1993; Quinn, Sendelbach, and Spreitzer, 1991; Sendelbach, 1993).

Managerial responsibilities do, however, vary across levels of organizational hierarchy. Common sense will tell you that the specific job tasks and responsibilities associated with the first-level manager in the broker role, for example, will likely be starkly different from those of the upper-level manager performing in this role. In some cases, however, while the specific job tasks and responsibilities vary across levels of organizational hierarchy, some of the required competencies for performing in the various roles will remain the same. For example, all managers need to have good interpersonal skills and to have a high level of self-awareness (Kiechel, 1994). Similarly, all managers need to be able to develop plans and to adapt those plans when circumstances change. In this latter case, however, the scope and time frame of planning will likely differ, as will the steps of the planning process. Thus managers may need to learn different competencies to plan at different levels of the organization.

As managers are promoted from one level of the organization to the next, they need to identify which behaviors associated with the various role competencies will generally remain the same, as well as which new behaviors need to be learned and which must be unlearned (Faerman and Peters, 1991). They must also understand how the means to balance the various roles and perform in behaviorally complex ways may change from one managerial position to another. Similarly, human resources managers and those who are mentoring managers as they are promoted need to understand what the similarities and differences in managerial jobs across levels of organizational hierarchy are so that they can help these individuals to grow and develop as they make these transitions (DiPadova and Faerman, 1993).

IDENTIFYING THE CORE COMPETENCIES

The eight roles help us to organize our thoughts about what is expected of a person holding a position of leadership. Although the eight roles are a useful organizing structure, we have not as yet specified what competencies are necessary in order to perform effectively in each of the eight roles. It is to that issue that we now turn.

A group of experts, consisting of 11 nationally recognized scholars and 11 prominent administrators and union representatives, were brought together to identify key competencies associated with each role in the competing values framework (Faerman et al., 1987). Participants were chosen based on their experience and expertise as practitioners or scholars in the field of management. More than 250 competencies were identified and given to this group. Their task was to identify the most important competencies in each of the eight roles. Based on the results of this exercise, a framework was developed. Since it was originally developed, this framework has been used in the instruction of thousands of people. Their feedback has provided valuable insights that have been used to continue to refine the competencies over time as organizational environments and participants continue to change. Table 1.2 shows the eight managerial leadership roles and their key competencies.

Each of the chapters is divided into three sections, and each section is organized around one of the three competencies in the role. Thus the next eight chapters cover 24 key competencies. The competencies are highly consistent with the existing literature (Belasen, 2000; Bigelow, 1991; Boyatzis, 1982; Flanders, 1981; Ghiselli, 1963; Hart and Quinn, 1993; Katz, 1974; Livingston, 1971; Luthans and Lockwood, 1984; Miner, 1973; Mintzberg, 1975; Whetten and Cameron, 1994; Yukl, 1981). Completion of the next eight chapters is likely to greatly broaden your skills and increase your capacities. As you work through the chapters, however, keep in mind that each chapter addresses only one of the eight roles and that the ultimate goal is for you to be able to integrate the competencies that will allow you to operate well in a world of competing values.

It is also useful to recognize that the competing values framework can be used in conjunction with other popular management tools. For example, the balanced scorecard approach (Kaplan and Norton, 1992, 2005) includes measures relevant to three of the four competing values quadrants. Balanced scorecard's internal business perspective fits within the Control quadrant; its financial perspective fits within the Compete quadrant, and its customer and innovation and learning perspectives fit within the Create quadrant. In addition to the areas that the balanced scorecard identifies as key to organizational performance, the competing values framework also recognizes the critical importance of the employees perspective in the Collaborate quadrant.

TABLE 1.2 The Eight Managerial Leadership Roles and Their Key Competencies

Mentor role	1. Understanding self and others
	2. Communicating effectively
	3. Developing employees
Facilitator role	1. Building teams
	2. Using participative decision making
	3. Managing conflict
Monitor role	1. Managing information overload
	2. Analyzing core processes
	3. Measuring performance and quality
Coordinator role	1. Managing projects
	2. Designing work
	3. Managing across functions
Director role	1. Developing and communicating a vision
	2. Setting goals and objectives
	3. Designing and organizing
Producer role	1. Working productively
	2. Fostering a productive work environment
	3. Managing time and stress
Innovator role	1. Living with change
	2. Thinking creatively
	3. Managing change
Broker role	1. Building and maintaining a power base
	2. Negotiating agreement and commitment
	3. Presenting ideas

ORGANIZING THE LEARNING PROCESS

A competency suggests both the possession of knowledge and the behavioral capacity to act appropriately. To develop competencies you must both be introduced to knowledge and have the opportunity to practice your skills. Many textbooks and classroom lecture methods provide the knowledge but not the opportunity to develop behavioral skills.

In this book, we will provide you with both. The structure we will use is based on a five-step model developed by Whetten and Cameron (1994), which takes learning from an instructional approach (an expert giving a lecture) to an instructional–developmental approach (an expert giving a lecture plus students experimenting with new behaviors). We have modified the labels for one of the components in the five-step model and call it the ALAPA model. The components are as follows.

Step 1: Assessment	Helps you discover your present level of ability in and awareness of the competency. Any number of tools, such as questionnaires, role-plays, or group discussions, might be used.

Step 2: Learning Involves reading and presenting information about the topic using traditional tools, such as lectures and printed material. Here we present information from relevant research and suggest guidelines for practice.

Step 3: Analysis Explores appropriate and inappropriate behaviors by examining how others behave in a given situation. We will use cases, role-plays, or other examples of behavior. Your professor may also provide examples from popular movies, television shows, or novels for you to analyze.

Step 4: Practice Allows you to apply the competency to a worklike situation while in the classroom. It is an opportunity for experimenttion and feedback. Again, exercises, simulations, and role-plays will be used.

Step 5: Application Gives you the opportunity to transfer the process to real-life situations. Usually assignments are made to facilitate short- and long-term experimentation.

When initially exposed to these components, students respond in different ways. Some appreciate the structure and invest themselves in the complete learning process. Others may feel that the Assessment exercises are unnecessary; they want to jump directly into the Learning. Still others may think that a particular Practice or Application activity isn't relevant to their current job or career aspirations. Although no textbook can perfectly meet the expectations and needs of every student, we have found that most students only fully appreciate the benefits of the activities *after* they have invested time in them. For example, after completing an exercise on assumptions about performance evaluations, one MBA student wrote, "I never realized my thoughts on performance evaluation until this exercise. Gave me thoughts about how I could change this process at my work." This type of reaction suggests a sixth step for the learning process that can help us move to a higher level of understanding: reflection. Research suggests that reflection can greatly enhance awareness of the impact of self-directed learning (Rhee, 2005) and improve skill development (Argyris, 2002). To encourage reflection, we include a brief comment after most of the exercises throughout the text.

In working with the model, we discovered that the five components, and the methods normally associated with each component, need not be mutually exclusive. A lecture, for example, does not need to follow an assessment exercise and precede an analysis exercise; a lecture might be appropriately combined with a role-play in some other step. The methods can be varied and even combined in the effective teaching and learning of a given competency. In the following chapters, the presentation of each of the 24 competencies will be organized according to the ALAPA model.

Each of the eight roles is presented and illustrated using the competing values framework. Chapters 2 through 9 are each organized around one of the eight roles. In each role there are many competencies. The three sections in each chapter are organized around what we consider to be the three most important competencies in each role.

Before considering the competencies associated with the eight managerial leadership roles, however, we use the ALAPA model to help students develop a critical competency that is vital in all managerial roles: thinking critically.

Core Competency   Critical Thinking

This assessment exercise has two parts. Please complete part 1 before moving to part 2.

Part 1   Think of a topic or issue or situation that you find very upsetting or frustrating. Do a little "ranting" on that issue. That is, write some very strong and emotional statements about this issue or situation. You might begin with "One thing that makes me furious is _____." Try to write four or five sentences.

Part 2   Now imagine that you need to "go public" with your feelings and opinions and convince someone else to share at least some of the intensity you feel about this issue. Is there anything in your ranting that you might convert into an argument, a line of reasoning that another person might find legitimate?

Read and discuss your sentences with a classmate. Talk about why you feel that some of your statements are not good raw material for public reasoning but others might be.

Recruiters want people who can "go public" with their ideas and reactions, quickly and concisely. When you have casual conversations with your friends, you don't always have to support your opinions with evidence. You can just express an opinion. But in the workplace you have to support your claims and proposals in a more systematic and concise way. It's one thing to say that you like the color blue; it's quite another to say that you prefer one brand of cell phone over another. In the first case you are simply expressing a preference whose grounds are wholly personal. Another person can "argue" that green is the best color, but the argument cannot be resolved by recourse to external issues. The preferences here are purely and completely personal.

However, in the second example, in which you state that you prefer this cell phone over another, the grounds for the claim you are making do not depend completely on your own taste. There are external factors you can discuss with another party. There are criteria of design, cost, convenience, and so forth that can be put on the table—"I like the smaller size and lighter weight of the Nokia phone; the user interface on the Nokia makes messages easier to read; the menu has fewer steps for manipulating the functions I use most often; the sound quality is better." True, some of these are personally experienced, but they are criteria that go beyond personal taste. They are shareable, and in some cases impersonal (cost, for example), grounds for having a preference or making a recommendation.

In this section, we're going to examine how managers, and professionals in general, can apply the skills of critical thinking and formulating clear and compelling arguments for the recommendations and evaluations they make.

THINKING ABOUT THINKING

Let's think for a moment about thinking itself as a learned human activity. In what ways has your formal education helped you to "think" more effectively? We're not asking about specific knowledge you've accumulated, but how your ability to handle ideas and marshal evidence has improved. Another way to pose the question is, "How has your formal education helped you to understand the events that you observe and the information you encounter in daily life?" We have asked this question of many MBA students recently. Here are some of the responses we have found most interesting and helpful.

My education has helped me "complexify" my thinking. I have learned that there are seldom simple, single causes for events. There are usually complex, multiple causes that drive events. As an undergraduate, I majored in history. I wrote my senior research paper on the causes of World War I. I can't tell you in one sentence what caused that war; but I *can* tell you what the contributing conditions were and what "trigger events" led to the outbreak of the war. That's what I mean by complex thinking rather than simple, black-and-white thinking.

Some of the tools I've gained from school have helped me approach things in a more systematic way. For example, my study of statistics has really helped me separate the single dramatic cases, the *N* of 1 examples, from patterns of events. The other day, as part of preparing to write a paper on healthcare policy, I watched a person on the C-Span TV network who was testifying before a congressional committee about the quality of healthcare. This person, who couldn't get some important surgery paid for by his HMO (health maintenance organization), had a heart-rending story to tell. But I wanted to know how *representative* this example was. How many people have been in this situation? Is it a one-of-a-kind case, or is it typical? So often, the most dramatic data crowds out the more valid, less dramatic data.

I am a lot better at asking precise questions than I was before I went to college. Even in casual conversation with people, I can learn a lot more and contribute more to a conversation by asking good questions. When someone makes a statement like "I thought that movie was really lame," I follow up with a question like, "What makes you say that?" When someone says "This book was stupid," I want to ask a question like "Was everything in the book stupid, or just part of it?" Sometimes people think I'm weird, but most of the time my questions make the conversations go better.

The students quoted above all realize that issues are often more complex than they at first appear, that the "facts" needed to make a rational decision are not always available to us, and that people often make decisions based on very thin or limited information. They also seem to understand that different people will not always agree on what a "fact" is in a particular case—or perhaps not agree on the meaning or significance of that fact.

The kind of attitude these students demonstrate is appropriate to the role of the manager. Managers spend a lot of time both presenting evidence to support their own ideas and evaluating evidence presented by others. Effective managers are effective thinkers. They don't have to be brilliant, but they need to approach evidence and data with both openness and some healthy skepticism.

MANAGEMENT AND SOUND REASONING: CREATING AND EVALUATING ARGUMENTS

When reasons are put together and presented to one or more people, they form an argument. We are using the term "argument" to mean a train of reasoning, not a quarrel or a disagreement you have with another person. An argument, in this sense, is a case we make for doing, or believing, or recommending something.

Effective managers are good at both framing their own arguments and reacting to the arguments of others. At any given moment, your task as a manager may be to react to someone else's recommendation or to make your own recommendation for doing something. For example, you might make the following suggestion at a weekly staff meeting: "We need to adopt this software application for tracking our financial data because . . ." What comes after that "because" is the support or the gist of your argument. Without that support, your suggestion or proposal would probably not carry much weight. Now, note that reasoning, or critical thinking, as we are describing it, is primarily a process not of creating ideas but of presenting and evaluating ideas and information. (We discuss creating ideas in Chapter 8.) The task of the critical thinker is to make the best decision with the available information in a particular circumstance. The better you are at presenting your own cases and analyzing the cases others put in front of you, the more effective a leader you will be. We're now going to present some tools for mapping arguments and examining evidence clearly and efficiently.

Most arguments, whether simple or complex, have three elements:[1]

1. *The claim* or conclusion of the argument. The claim answers the question, "What's the point here?"

2. *The grounds,* or the facts and evidence that support the claim. The claim can be no stronger than the grounds that support it. The grounds answer the question, "What do you have to go on?" or "What leads you to say that?"

3. *The warrant,* or the bridge between the claim and the grounds. Sometimes this bridge is obvious; sometimes not. The warrant or bridge answers the question, "How does your claim connect to the grounds you've offered" (Toulmin, 1984, pp. 30–38). Now, here we caution you. The warrant is the most subtle of the three elements of argumentation, but if you develop an understanding of it, it will prove a powerful tool for both creating and evaluating arguments.

The following example demonstrates how an implied warrant can be used. The argument is simple because only the claim and grounds are indicated:

> *I see smoke; there must be fire.*

The claim here is "there must be fire." The grounds or evidence on which the claim is based is "I see smoke." Another way to say this is "I see smoke, so there must be fire." But the warrant or bridge that makes the connection between the claim and the evidence is not stated. The warrant is, of course, "where there's smoke there's usually fire." (Notice that the warrant has a qualifier to it: the word "usually." Sometimes there is smoke without fire.)

[1]This approach to mapping arguments is taken from Stephen Toulmin, Richard Rieke, and Allan Janik, *An Introduction to Reasoning.* New York: Macmillan, 1984, pp. 1–59.

Now, examine the following train of reasoning. The elements in this argument are scrambled. Some of the statements below, regarding a patient who was admitted to a hospital emergency room (ER), are warrants, some are grounds, and one is a claim. All the other statements revolve around that claim. After each statement, indicate whether you think it is a claim, a ground, or a warrant.

The patient complains of nausea, which has lasted for over 24 hours.

_____

The patient's examination shows pain and tenderness in his lower-right abdomen.

_____

The patient has a temperature of 101°. _____

Appendicitis is often triggered by a viral flu infecting the gastrointestinal tract.

_____

The patient's pain has migrated over the past 48 hours from the center of the belly to the lower-right abdomen. _____

The pain associated with acute appendicitis often "migrates" from the left side, or the midsection, to the lower-right abdomen. _____

The patient is most likely suffering from acute appendicitis and should be x-rayed and prepared for surgery. _____

The patient's history shows a bad case of viral flu within the past two weeks.

_____

Notice that the warrants are the items that create a bridge between a factual observation and the one claim or recommended action in the list. In the list above there happens to be only one claim. Everything else is either a ground or a warrant. When experts communicate among themselves, they often leave out the warrants behind their reasoning because the warrants are understood. But when they talk to a nonexpert, they need to be more explicit. That means they have to spell out the warrants that connect the claims they are making to the grounds used to support those claims.

For example, a medical intern who had just examined the patient described above might say to the attending physician in the ER,

The patient has a temperature of 101, nausea for the past several hours, migrating pain and tenderness now settled in the lower-right abdomen. The patient says he has also had a recent case of viral stomach flu. I recommend we prep him for surgery on his appendix.

The attending physician might say, "Fine, sounds like an inflamed appendix to me." The warrants, all taken from clinical research, are already understood. But often we need to make our warrants explicit. As our colleague Allen Bluedorn says when teaching this model of reasoning, you need to "show your work" as you do on a calculus homework problem or a chemistry exam. If the attending physician wants to test the logic of the intern's diagnosis, he might ask a question such as, "How does the patient's recent case of the flu support your diagnosis?" The intern would then say that clinical research shows that a viral flu is often the triggering event in causing a person's appendix to become infected. The questions asked by the attending physician require the intern to show his or her work.

In argumentation, you show your work when you expose the bridges or warrants between the evidence you're presenting and the claim(s) that your evidence supports. When people have difficulty following our train of reasoning, the problem is often caused by our failure to make our warrants explicit.

Let's see how we can use this model of argumentation to map some arguments that managers encounter in reports or meetings. Here's an example from a report by a sales manager in a manufacturing company.

We conclude that the 28 percent decrease in unit sales for this quarter was caused by a dramatic deterioration in the quality of service provided during the previous quarter.

The strongest evidence that poor service is the cause of the lower sales is the fact that more than half of our large, regular accounts ordered no new units during the quarter. These are the customers who have a history with our service—some benchmarks for tracking how our service stacks up over time. Now, they apparently have a reason to be dissatisfied and feel that service quality had declined.

On the other hand, sales to new accounts were about average during this quarter. These are customers who have had little experience with the quality of our service work. Further, we suspect that the quality of our service has dropped sharply, because the number of complaint calls recorded in the log, as well as repeat calls requesting service, is about 60 percent higher than during any other quarter on record.

This argument is pretty straightforward:

1. The claim is that a 28 percent decrease in sales last quarter was caused by poor service performance during the quarter that preceded it.

2. The grounds or evidence that the quality of service declined in the previous quarter is threefold.
   - Ground 1: More than half of our large-account customers ordered no new units during the past quarter.
   - Ground 2: Sales to new customers were about average during the quarter.
   - Ground 3: The number of logged complaint calls, as well as repeat calls requesting service, was 60 percent higher than during any previous quarter on record.

3. The warrants, or bridges, that tie the data and claim together are also threefold.
   - Warrant 1: The fact that current, large-account customers ordered no new units indicates some form of dissatisfaction.
   - Warrant 2: We sold an average number of units to new customers. These are people who had no basis of comparison for judging our service.
   - Warrant 3: The complaint call log is our official vehicle for tracking customer satisfaction data. When the calls increase, we assume we have some kind of service problem.

Notice how the author of the report supports his statement that the quality of service has "dramatically deteriorated." He alludes to an official piece of evidence, the service department's log book. Notice that while there is only one major claim, there are several grounds, or pieces of evidence, supporting the claim and a matching number of warrants connecting each ground to the claim. We can draw or map this argument as shown in Figure 1.4.

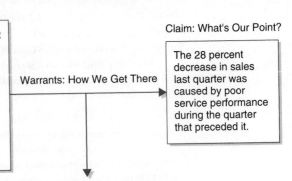

Grounds: What Do We Have to Go On?

Ground 1: More than half of our large-account customers ordered no new units during the past quarter.

Ground 2: Sales to new customers were about average during the quarter.

Ground 3: The number of logged complaint calls, as well as repeat calls requesting service, was 60 percent higher than during any previous quarter on record.

Warrants: How We Get There

Claim: What's Our Point?

The 28 percent decrease in sales last quarter was caused by poor service performance during the quarter that preceded it.

Warrant 1: The fact that current large-account customers ordered no new units indicates some form of dissatisfaction.

Warrant 2: We sold an average number of units to new customers. These are people who had no basis of comparison for judging our service.

Warrant 3: The complaint call log is our official vehicle for tracking customer satisfaction data. When the calls increase, we assume we have some kind of service problem.

FIGURE 1.4 *Basic argument map*

As you work through the exercises in the rest of this text, apply what you have learned about claims, grounds, and warrants. For example, when assessing whether you are a team player (Chapter 3), recognize that your assessment is simply a claim—what grounds do you have to support that claim? By pushing yourself to provide, not just claims, but also grounds and warrants in the exercises throughout this text, you will continue to develop your critical thinking skills. This practice will also be valuable for improving your ability to communicate effectively (see Chapter 2).

ANALYSIS   Argument Mapping

Directions   The following exercise includes two arguments on the same topic. Your job is to read these arguments and analyze them in terms of their plausibility, validity, and persuasiveness.

This can be a group exercise or an individual task. If your instructor prefers to have you work as a group, here are guidelines for the process.

Group Task   Break into groups of four. Two people should analyze one argument together, and the other two people should analyze the other argument together. Take 15 minutes to read and discuss the arguments, and then present your analysis to the other pair of classmates. Evaluate the arguments using the 7-point scale and the evaluation criteria below.[2]

[2]We wish to thank Allen Bluedorn of the University of Missouri for suggesting this exercise and for his helpful advice on teaching critical thinking.

| Scale | Terrible | | 1 | 2 | 3 | 4 | 5 | 6 | 7 | | Excellent |

Argument	*Explicitly Stated Claims*	*Explicitly Stated Grounds*	*Quality of Grounds*	*Explicitly Stated Warrants*	*Overall Quality*
1					
2					

1. Discuss in one page the strengths and weaknesses of the arguments in terms of the major claims being made as well as the grounds and warrants the authors provide to support those claims.

2. Do you find the arguments persuasive and compelling? Why? Why not? Use the 7-point scale above in writing your analysis.

Argument 1

The National Scholarship Achievement Board recently revealed the results of a five-year study on the effectiveness of comprehensive exams at Duke University. The results of the study showed that since the comprehensive exam has been introduced at Duke, the grade point average of undergraduates has increased by 31 percent. At comparable schools without the exams, grades increased by only 8 percent over the same period. The prospect of a comprehensive exam clearly seems to be effective in challenging students to work harder and faculty to teach more effectively. It is likely that the benefits observed at Duke University could also be observed at other universities that adopt the exam policy.

Graduate schools and law and medical schools are beginning to show clear and significant preferences for students who received their undergraduate degrees from institutions with comprehensive exams. As the dean of the Harvard Business School said, "Although Harvard has not and will not discriminate on the basis of race or sex, we do show a strong preference for applicants who have demonstrated their expertise in an area of study by passing a comprehensive exam at the undergraduate level." Admissions officers of law, medical, and graduate schools have also endorsed the comprehensive exam policy and indicated that students at schools without the exams would be at a significant disadvantage in the very near future. Thus, the institution of comprehensive exams will be an aid to those who seek admission to graduate and professional schools after graduation.

Argument 2

The National Scholarship Achievement Board recently revealed the results of a study they conducted on the effectiveness of comprehensive exams at Duke University. One major finding was that student anxiety had increased by 31 percent. At comparable schools without the exam, anxiety increased by only 8 percent. The board reasoned that anxiety over the exams, or fear of failure, would motivate students to study more in their courses while they were taking them. It is likely that this increase in anxiety observed at Duke University would also be observed and be of benefit at other universities that adopt the exam policy.

From R. Petty and J. T. Cacioppo, *Communication and Persuasion: Central and Peripheral Routes to Attitude Change.* New York: Spring-Verlag New York Inc., 1986, pp. 54–55, 57–58. Used with permission.

A member of the board of directors has stated publicly that his brother had to take a comprehensive exam while in college and is now a manager of a large restaurant. He indicated that he realized the value of the exams, since his father was a migrant worker who didn't even finish high school. He also indicated that the university has received several letters from parents in support of the exam. In fact, four of the six parents who wrote in thought that the exams were an excellent idea. Also, the prestigious National Accrediting Board of Higher Education seeks input from parents as well as students, faculty, and administrators when evaluating a university. Since most parents contribute financially to their child's education and also favor the exams, the university should institute them. This would show that the university is willing to listen to and follow the parents' wishes over those of students and faculty, who may simply fear the work involved in comprehensive exams.

PRACTICE Providing Warrants

In groups of three to five people, practice supplying the warrant for each set of claims and grounds listed in the table below. More than one plausible warrant can be given for each set. There is no one, perfectly worded answer. The idea is to provide a bridging statement between the claim being made and the grounds provided to support that claim. We have provided three sample warrants for the first set of claims and grounds.

Claims	*Grounds*	*Warrant(s)*
Southwest Airlines will have a profitable year next year.	The nation's economic growth is predicted to continue at an annual rate of at least 3 percent over the next year. Southwest has enjoyed greater profits than any airline in North America for the past three years.	
I do not believe Gretchen is an ideal choice for supervisor of the customer service department.	She has worked in the department for only eight months. She seems to be rather reclusive—eating lunch by herself and not communicating much with other workers during breaks.	
Our firm needs to invest more resources into new product development in order to remain competitive in the future.	Our sales research shows that 80 percent of our profits over the past three years have been made from products that are more than six years old. We reduced our research and development budget by 28 percent over the past three years. We are living off "the fat of the land."	

APPLICATION   Reflected Best-Self Portrait

Objective   The objective of this exercise is to help you gather evidence about your current skills as a manager. Rather than focusing on your weaknesses at this point, however, we would like you to focus on your strengths. Researchers in the area of Positive Organizational Scholarship (POS) have developed a number of tools for improving leadership skills. This exercise will give you the opportunity to explore some of those tools.

Directions   Making claims is simple: "Susan is a great manager." Substantiating claims, however, requires much more effort. What evidence are we relying on when we claim that Susan is a great manager? What assumptions do we hold about what makes a great manager in the first place? For this exercise, you will be gathering information about your own skills as a manager, from the perspective of your colleagues.

   1. Go to the webpage for Positive Organizational Scholarship at http://www.bus.umich.edu/positive/. Under the POS Teaching and Learning drop down box, select POS Tool. Click on the Purchase and Download link to obtain the Reflected Best-Self exercise. Follow the instructions in the exercise and any additional directions that your instructor may provide so that you can create your own Reflected Best-Self Portrait.

Reflection   Committing to this type of exercise takes courage. Even though the exercise asks for positive examples, it still requires that you open yourself up to hearing what other people think about your performance. Learning to think critically often requires us to let go of old ideas when we discover that the evidence supporting those ideas is weak or non-existent. People who shut down and refuse to accept new ideas and supporting evidence are not only failing their organizations, they are failing themselves.

CONCLUSIONS

People use models that sensitize them to some things and blind them to others. When we act as a managerial leader in an organizational unit, our models greatly affect our level of effectiveness. In this chapter we have traced the evolution of four basic models in management thinking: rational goal, internal process, human relations, and open systems. Each model is based on assumptions that lead to different sensitivities, decisions, and behaviors.

In recent years, world conditions have made it increasingly obvious that there is a need for both–and thinking. As we increase the number of models that we can use to assess a situation, we increase our array of choices and we increase both our cognitive and behavioral complexity.

In this chapter we considered the competing values framework. It suggests that the four basic models of organizational effectiveness can be integrated into a comprehensive whole. The model is called the "competing values" framework because we tend to see the oppositions as conflicts. They are not, however, mutually exclusive. In fact, they need to be complementary. We can use the framework to get out of a single mindset and to increase choice. In becoming a master manager, we seek to use, simultaneously, two or more seemingly opposite approaches. Think, for example, of the leader who practices "tough love." This person is effectively integrating, or making complementary, domains that we normally keep separate.

The competing values framework suggests three challenges: to use multiple mind-sets in viewing the organizational world; to learn to use competencies associated with all four models; and, finally, to integrate the diverse competencies in confronting the world of action. People who meet these three challenges are behaviorally complex and are the most effective managerial leaders.

We use the ALAPA model in presenting these competencies. Although the book allows the instructor to follow traditional instruction methods, it also allows a second phenomenon to occur. It allows you to develop, grow, and internalize new competencies. The emphasis, then, is not on learning traditional social science theory, but on learning how to apply certain aspects of this literature to learning to perform more effectively as a managerial leader.

ASSIGNMENT Course Preassessment

There is an instrument that will allow you to do a preassessment of yourself on the eight roles and the 24 skills in the competing values framework. This preassessment is available in two forms: as a software package and as a written questionnaire. Either may be used. If your instructor wants you to do this preassessment, he or she will direct you in how to proceed.

REFERENCES

Argyris, C. "Double-Loop Learning, Teaching, and Research." *Academy of Management Learning & Education* 1(2) (2002): 206–218.

Ban, C., and S. R. Faerman. "Advanced Human Resources Development Program: Final Impact Report" (unpublished technical report). Rockefeller College of Public Affairs and Policy, University at Albany, SUNY, Albany, NY, 1988.

Belasen, A. T. *Leading the Learning Organization: Communication and Competencies for Managing Change.* Albany: State University of New York Press, 2000.

Bigelow, J. D. (ed.) *Managerial Skills: Explorations in Practical Knowledge.* Newbury Park. CA: Sage Publications, 1991.

Boyatzis, R. E. *The Competent Manager.* New York: John Wiley & Sons, 1982.

Daft, R. L. *Management.* Chicago: Dryden Press, 1988.

Denison, D., R. Hooijberg, and R. Quinn. "Paradox and Performance: Toward a Theory of Behavioral Complexity in Managerial Leadership." *Organization Science* 6(5) (1995): 524–540.

DiPadova, L. N., and S. R. Faerman. "Using the Competing Values Framework to Facilitate Managerial Understanding Across Levels of Organizational Hierarchy." *Human Resource Management* 32(l) (1993): 143–174.

Fabian, F. H. "Keeping the Tension: Pressures to Keep the Controversy in the Management Discipline." *Academy of Management Review* 25(2) (2000): 350–371.

Faerman, S. R., and T. D. Peters. "A Conceptual Framework for Examining Managerial Roles and Transitions Across Levels of Organizational Hierarchy." *Proceedings of the National Public Management Research Conference*, Syracuse, NY, September 20–21, 1991.

Faerman, S. R., and R. E. Quinn. "Effectiveness: The Perspective from Organizational Theory." *Review of Higher Education* 9 (1985): 83–100.

Faerman, S. R., R. E. Quinn, and M. P. Thompson. "Bridging Management Practice and Theory." *Public Administration Review* 47(3) (1987): 311–319.

Flanders, L. R. Report 1 from the *Federal Manager's Job and Role Survey: Analysis of Responses.* Washington, DC: U.S. Office of Personnel Management, 1981.

Ghiselli, E. E. "Managerial Talent." *American Psychologist* 18(1963): 631–642.

Giek, D.G., and P. L. Lees. "On Massive Change: Using the Competing Values Framework to Organize the Educational Efforts of the Human Resource Function in New York State Government." *Human Resource Management* 32(1) (1993): 9–28.

Hart, S., and R. E. Quinn. "Roles Executives Play: CEOs, Behavioral Complexity, and Firm Performance." *Human Relations* 46 (1993): 115–142.

Hooijberg, R., and R. E. Quinn. "Behavioral Complexity and the Development of Effective Managers," in Robert L. Phillips and James G. Hunt (eds.), *Strategic Leadership: A Multiorganizational-Level Perspective*. Westport, CT: Quorum, 1992.

House, R. J., and P. M. Podsakoff. "Effectiveness: Leadership Past Perspectives and Future Directions for Research," in Jerald Greenberg (ed.), *Organizational Behavior: The State of the Science*. Hillsdale, NJ: Lawrence Erlbaum, 1994.

Kaplan, R. S., and D. P. Norton. "The Balanced Scorecard—Measures That Drive Performance." *Harvard Business Review* 70 (1992): 71–75.

Kaplan, R. S., and D. P. Norton. "The Office of Strategy Management." *Harvard Business Review* 83 (2005): 72–80.

Katz, R. L. "Skills of an Effective Administrator." *Harvard Business Review* 51 (1974): 90–102.

Kiechel, W., III. "A Manager's Career in the New Economy." *Fortune* (April 4, 1994): 68–72.

Livingston, J. S. "Myth of the Well-Educated Manager." *Harvard Business Review* 49 (1971): 79–89.

Luthans, F., and D. L. Lockwood. "Toward an Observational System for Measuring Leader Behavior in Natural Settings," in J. G. Hunt, R. Stewart, C. Schresheim, and D. Hosking (eds.), *Leaders and Managers: International Perspectives on Managerial Behaviour and Leadership*. Elmsford, N.Y: Pergamon, 1984.

Miner, J. B. "The Real Crunch in Managerial Manpower." *Harvard Business Review* 51 (1973): 146–158.

Mintzberg, H. "The Manager's Job: Folklore and Fact." *Harvard Business Review* 53 (1975): 49–61.

Mirvis, P. H. *Work in the 20th Century: America's Trends and Tracts, Visions and Values, Economic and Human Developments*, rev. ed. Cambridge, MA: Rudi Press, 1985.

Pauchant, T. C., J. Nilles, O. E. Sawy, and A. M. Mohrman. "Toward a Paradoxical Theory of Organizational Effectiveness: An Empirical Study of the Competing Values Model." Working paper. Laval University, Administrative Sciences, Quebec City, Quebec, Canada, GIK 7P4, 1989.

Quinn, R. E. "Applying the Competing Values Approach to Leadership: Toward an Integrative Framework," in J. G. Hunt, D. Hosking, C. Schriesheim, and R, Stewart (eds.), *Leaders and Managers: International Perspective on Managerial Behavior and Leadership*. Elmsford, NY: Pergamon Press, 1984.

Quinn, R. E. *Beyond Rational Management: Mastering the Paradoxes and Competing Demands of High Performance.* San Francisco: Jossey-Bass, 1988.

Quinn, R. E., and K. S. Cameron. "Organizational Life Cycles and Shifting Criteria of Effectiveness: Some Preliminary Evidence." *Management Science* 29 (1983): 33–51.

Quinn, R. E., J. E. Dutton, and G. M. Spreitzer. "Reflected Best Self Exercise: Assignment and Instructions to Participants." University of Michigan Ross School of Business, Product Number 001B. Ann Arbor, MI, 2004.

Quinn, R. E., J. A. Kahn, and M. J. Mandl. "Perspectives on Organizational Change: Exploring Movement at the Interface," in Jerald Greenberg (ed.), *Organizational Behavior: The State of the Science.* Hillsdale, NJ: Lawrence Erlbaum Associates, 1994.

Quinn, R. E., and J. Rohrbaugh. "A Spatial Model of Effectiveness Criteria: Towards a Competing Values Approach to Organizational Analysis" *Management Science* 29(3) (1983): 363–377.

Quinn, R. E., N. B. Sendelbach, and G. M. Spreitzer. "Education and Empowerment: A Transformational Model of Managerial Skills Development," in John D. Bigelow (ed.), *Managerial Skills: Explorations in Practical Knowledge.* Newbury Park, CA: Sage Publications, 1991.

Quinn, R. E., G. M. Spreitzer, and S. Hart. "Integrating the Extremes: Crucial Skills for Managerial Effectiveness," in Suresh Srivastava, Ronald E. Fry, et al. *Executive and Organizational Continuity: Managing the Paradoxes of Stability and Change.* San Francisco: Jossey-Bass, 1992.

Rhee, K. S. "Self-Directed Learning: To Be Aware or Not to Be Aware." *Journal of Management Education* 27(5) (2003): 568–589.

Robbins, S. P. *Management,* 6th ed. Englewood Cliffs, NJ: Prentice-Hall, 1998.

Roberts, L. M., J. E. Dutton, G. M. Spreitzer, E. D. Heaphy, and R. E. Quinn. "Composing the Reflected Best-Self Portrait: Building Pathways for Becoming Extraordinary in Work Organizations." *Academy of Management Review* 30(4) (2005): 712–736.

Sendelbach, N. B. "The Competing Values Framework for Management Training and Development: A Tool for Understanding Complex Issues and Tasks." *Human Resource Management* 32(1) (1993): 75–99.

Senge, P. *The Fifth Discipline: The Art and Practice of the Learning Organization.* New York: Doubleday Currency, 1990.

"Survey of Pressing Problems 2000: Innovative Solutions to the Pressing Problems of Business." Working paper. University of Michigan, School of Business, 2000. Contact Pauline Farmer at (734) 615–4265.

Whetten, D. R., and K. S. Cameron. *Developing Management Skills,* 3d ed. New York: Harper-Collins, 1994.

Yukl, G. A. *Leadership in Organizations.* Englewood Cliffs, NJ: Prentice-Hall, 1981.

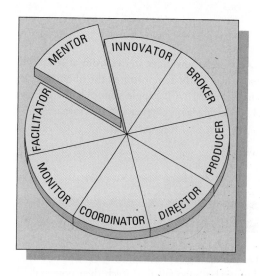

THE MENTOR ROLE 2

■ COMPETENCIES

Understanding Self and Others

Communicating Effectively

Developing Employees

We now turn to the human relations model. In this model the focus is on individuals and groups. Here we recognize that commitment, cohesion, and morale are important indicators of effectiveness. A central belief in this model is that involvement and participation in decision making result in outcomes such as high commitment. The climate emphasized in this model is characterized by teamwork, openness, and strong communication; and the key managerial leadership roles are mentor and facilitator. The task is to establish and maintain effective relationships (Pfeffer, 1994). The action imperative for the human relations model is Collaborate.

In Chapter 1 we pointed out that the **mentor** role might also be called the concerned human role. This role reflects a caring, empathetic orientation. In this role a manager is expected to be helpful, considerate, sensitive, approachable, open, and fair. In acting out the role, the leader listens, supports legitimate requests, conveys appreciation, and gives recognition. Employees are seen as important resources to be understood, valued, and developed. The manager helps them with individual development plans and also sees that they have opportunities for training and skill building. In the mentor role, the manager is also expected to have a high level of self-awareness and to consider how one's actions as a manager influence employees' actions.

In Western society, acts of caring and concern are sometimes seen as soft and weak. Many people think a good leader must be strong, powerful, and in control. Likewise, some individuals find that they have great difficulty with feelings and the expression of feelings. Given such societal and individual orientations, it is tempting to devalue the mentor role. This is a mistake. Great power can derive from attending to the "soft" issues (Nair, 1994). Social science has clearly demonstrated the importance of this role in overall managerial effectiveness (Bass, 1990). People who play the mentor role poorly do not fare well (see Box 2.1). The three competencies in this role are

Competency 1   Understanding Self and Others
Competency 2   Communicating Effectively
Competency 3   Developing Employees

BOX 2.1   THE DERAILED EXECUTIVES

Starting in the early 1980s, researchers at the Center for Creative Leadership began to study "derailed" executives, individuals who had experienced great success in their managerial career but who failed to reach their potential. Since then, a series of studies has shown consistent results regarding characteristics of derailed managers. Interestingly, most of these characteristics were originally strengths that, when taken to an extreme, became flaws.

1. Insensitive to others; abrasive and intimidating
2. Overly demanding
3. Not willing to listen to others
4. Intolerant of dissent—not able to get along with people who have different styles
5. Taking credit for success
6. Blaming others for mistakes
7. Cold, aloof, and arrogant
8. Untrustworthy
9. Dictatorial style

Source: Morgan W. McCall, Jr., *High Flyers: Developing the Next Generation of Leaders,* (Boston, MA: Harvard Business School Press, 1998).

Competency 1   Understanding Self and Others

ASSESSMENT   Anchors and Oars

Objectives   The Anchors and Oars Assessment has two objectives. The first, addressed by Part 1 of the exercise, is to help you identify some of your personal characteristics that are most salient to your own self-image. The second, addressed by Part 2 of the exercise, is to have you learn more about how others see you, as well as to provide you insights into how other people see themselves.

Directions Part 1:   Respond to statements 1a, 1b, and 1c, one at a time. Once you have started on your response to 1b and 1c, do not go back to change any of your previous responses.

1. (a) Write down 10 or more adjectives and nouns that describe who you are now. Examples of nouns that describe you might be *son/daughter, student, manager, musician,* and so on. Examples of adjectives that describe you might be *adventurous, introverted, physically active,*

well-organized, and so on. Think of as many adjectives and nouns as you can; include phrases if you find this helpful.

(b) Now write down 10 or more adjectives and nouns that describe who you were 5 to 10 years ago. Again, write down as many ideas as you have.

(c) Now write down 10 or more adjectives and nouns that describe who you expect to be 5 to 10 years from now. Again, write down as many ideas as you have.

2. Note which items have stayed constant across your life. Note which items have changed from 5 to 10 years ago and which you expect to change over the next 5 to 10 years.

Part 2: Find a partner and write down 10 or more adjectives and nouns that describe that person based on what you know about them. After both of you have finished, exchange lists and talk about the similarities and differences between the list you created for yourself and the one your partner created for you. Are there some characteristics that your partner identified for you that were absent from your own list? Did either of you make assumptions about characteristics of the other person that were not accurate?

Discussion Questions Anchors keep a boat steady, while oars propel a boat forward. All individuals have some personal characteristics that remain constant over time and some characteristics that change. Characteristics that remain constant help keep the individuals steady; those that change allow for development over time.

1. How have your anchors helped you? Are there anchors that have kept you from making important changes?

2. How have different situations in your life encouraged you to make changes?

3. How might you use your current characteristics to help you make the changes you expect to see in yourself over the next 5 to 10 years?

4. How might some of the characteristics that your partner identified but that were not on your own list affect your ability to achieve your personal goals?

Reflection The salience of different personal characteristics can vary greatly across individuals and even across situations. For example, a student's identity as a male may be highly salient in a class that is predominantly female, but much less salient in class that is evenly split between males and females. Identities that derive from group status are likely to be much more salient to members of a minority group than members of the majority group.

Research on social identity theory (Tajfel and Turner, 1985) supports the hypothesis that identity salience is an important variable for understanding attitudes and behavior. For example, Lobel and St. Clair (1992) found that employees who report a high level of career identity salience have higher levels of work effort. They also found that career identity salience had a direct, positive effect on merit increases. Mentors can be more effective if they have a firm grasp on the critical competency of understanding self and others as described in the following pages.

LEARNING Understanding Self and Others

To be a successful mentor, managers must have some understanding of themselves and others. Although all members of a work group have something in common, each individual is also in some way unique. One area where people differ is in their task-related abilities. As a mentor you need to learn about employees' abilities and consider how each person contributes to the organization. Another area where people differ is in their feelings, needs, and concerns. People react differently to different situations, and it is important for managers to be able to perceive and understand these reactions.

As a manager, you need to understand both the commonalities and differences and how these affect how people relate to one another in various ways. By being aware, you can better understand your own reaction to people and their reactions to each other. This understanding should, in turn, make you more effective (Cotton, 1994). In the past decade, many companies have begun to focus on helping managers develop their emotional intelligence (Goleman, 1995, 1998), which involves both personal competence (how we manage ourselves) and social competence (how we handle relationships). Research in this area has shown that emotional intelligence plays a particularly crucial role at higher levels of the organization, where managers spend the vast majority of their day interacting with others.

UNDERSTANDING YOURSELF

We begin this section with a focus on understanding yourself, sometimes referred to as self-awareness. This competency has been shown to be a key factor that differentiates successful managers from those who have derailed (Shipper and Dillard, 2000). There are, of course, many different dimensions of yourself that you could learn about. For example, Peter Drucker (1999), one of world's foremost authorities on management and leadership, argues that in today's economy, given the many choices that people have regarding their work lives, people must manage themselves. He believes that in order to do so, people must be aware of their strengths, their values, and how they best perform. Robert Staub, cofounder and president of Staub-Peterson Leadership Consultants, asserts that "the golden rule of effective leadership [is]: Don't fly blind! Know where you stand with regard to the perceptions of others" (1997, p. 170).

Goleman's (2000) work on emotional intelligence provides three dimensions of self-awareness: emotional awareness, self-assessment, and self-confidence. Emotional awareness involves recognizing your emotions and how they affect you and others. Individuals who have emotional awareness know what they are feeling and why, and they also understand the connection between their feelings and their actions. Self-assessment involves knowing your strengths and limits and being open to feedback that can help you to develop. Individuals who develop this competence are able to learn from experience and value self-development and continuous learning. Self-confidence refers to an awareness of one's self-worth and capabilities. Individuals who possess self-confidence present themselves with a strong sense of self and are willing to stand up for what they believe in, even if this is an unpopular perspective.

In addition to knowing about your emotions, your strengths and limits, and how others perceive you, it is important to know what motivates your behaviors, what influences how you will react in different situations. One major influence on your behavior is your personality. While no one always reacts in the same way under all circumstances, people do have a tendency to feel more comfortable with some behaviors than with others. An individual's personality is generally described in terms of those relatively permanent psychological and behavioral attributes that distinguish that individual from others. The notion that personality is relatively permanent stems from the idea that personality is a trait that can change in adulthood but is mostly formed in childhood and adolescence. Thus, "individuals can be characterized in terms of relatively enduring patterns of thoughts, feelings, and actions . . . [that] show some degree of cross-situational consistency" (McCrae and Costa, 1999, p. 140).

TWO APPROACHES TO PERSONALITY

While there are many different approaches to understanding personality, two of these approaches stand out as being the most widely used in research and in organizational training and development seminars on individual differences in organizations. These are the Five-Factor Model and the Myers-Briggs Type Inventory, which is based on the work of Carl Jung.

As the name would imply, the Five-Factor Model presents five factors, or basic tendencies, that researchers argue encompass most of what has been described as personality (McCrae and Costa, 1990). In the model, each factor is named for one of two ends of a continuum. Of course, most individuals do not fall at the ends of the continua, although people are likely to have a tendency toward one end or the other. As you read the description of each of the traits, you might try to place yourself on each of the continua.

The first factor is referred to as **neuroticism**. Individuals who score high on this dimension tend to worry a lot and are often anxious, insecure, and emotional. Alternatively, those who score low tend to be calm, relaxed, and self-confident. The second factor, **extraversion**, has also been referred to as urgency and assertiveness. This factor assesses the degree to which individuals are sociable, talkative, and gregarious in their interactions with others versus reserved, quiet, and sometimes even withdrawn and aloof. The third factor, **openness to new experiences**, also called intellectance, focuses on the degree to which an individual is proactive in seeking out new experiences. Individuals who score high on this measure tend to be curious, imaginative, creative, and nontraditional. Those who score low tend to be more conventional, concrete, and practical. **Agreeableness**, the fourth factor, focuses on the degree to which individuals are good-natured, trusting of others, and forgiving of their mistakes, as opposed to cynical, suspicious of others, and antagonistic. Finally, **conscientiousness** is associated with individuals' degree of organization and persistence. Those who score high on this continuum tend to be more organized, responsible, and self-disciplined; those who score low tend to be more impulsive, careless, and perceived by others as undependable.

Research has shown extraversion and agreeableness to be positively related, and neuroticism negatively related, to some aspects of leadership, particularly emergent leadership in a leaderless group. This implies that when a group is formed with no explicit leader, the individual who is more extraverted, agreeable, and emotionally stable will likely emerge as the informal leader (Hogan, Curphy, and Hogan, 1994).

The Myers-Briggs Type Inventory (MBTI) is one of several personality assessment instruments based on Carl Jung's theory of psychological types. Jung noticed that people behaved in somewhat predictable patterns, which he labeled types. He noted that types could be described along three dimensions: **introversion–extraversion**, **sensing–intuition**, and **thinking–feeling.** Later, Katharine Briggs and her daughter, Isabel Briggs Myers, added a fourth dimension: **judging–perceiving** (Keirsey, 1998). Their assessment instrument is widely used in organizational workshops to help people understand the different work styles of people in a work unit.

The first dimension, introversion–extraversion, is similar to McCrae and Costa's extraversion factor. It focuses on the degree to which individuals tend to look inward or outward for ideas about decisions and actions. Individuals who are introverted tend to be reflective and value privacy. Individuals who are extraverted tend to like variety and action and are energized by being with people. The second dimension, sensing–feeling, focuses on what we pay attention to when we gather data. Individuals who are sensing types tend to focus on facts and details; they absorb information in a concrete, literal fashion. Intuitive types, on the other hand, tend to try to see the big picture and focus more on abstract ideas.

While sensing–intuition focuses on how we gather data, thinking–feeling focuses on how we use information when making decisions. Thinking types tend to decide with their brains, whereas feeling types tend to decide with their hearts. Thinking types use analytical and objective approaches to decision making. Feeling types tend to base decisions on more subjective criteria, taking into account individual differences. The final dimension focuses on approaches to life and thinking styles. Judging types are task oriented and they tend to prefer closure on issues. They are good at planning and organizing. Perceptive types are more spontaneous and flexible, and they tend to be more comfortable with ambiguity.

The four dimensions of the MBTI can be combined to create different combinations, such as extraverted–sensing–thinking–judging or introverted–sensing–feeling–judging. When you combine all four dimensions, there are 16 different personality types that can be identified. Workshops that focus on people's work styles tend to focus on the combinations because they can help people understand why people approach work tasks in different ways. You might think back to a situation where some people in the group jumped right into the task and others wanted to analyze the nature of the problem first. When you learn about the different styles, you can better understand how to work with others who have different work styles and, if appropriate and necessary, learn to make adjustments in your own work style.

→ INCREASING YOUR SELF-AWARENESS

The importance of having a good understanding of yourself and what motivates or influences your behaviors should be obvious. If you do not understand yourself, it is nearly impossible to understand others. Yet people often find it difficult to learn about themselves. One reason that people find it difficult to learn about themselves is because their friends and colleagues fear being honest because they think such honesty will create conflict or embarrass the other person. Jerry Hirshberg, president of Nissan Design International, Inc., notes that people "have mixed feelings about hearing the truth." He states, "it's like a chemical reaction. Your face goes red, your temperature rises, you want to strike back." He labels this reaction "defending and debating" and argues that people need to fight back the tendency to defend and debate by "listening and learning" (Muoio, 1998).

One key to being able to fight the tendency to defend and debate by listening and learning is to learn how to learn about yourself. Here we present a simple but helpful framework that can help you think about what you do and do not know about yourself. Joseph Luft and Harry Ingham (1955) developed the framework and named it after themselves, calling it the Johari window. As shown in Figure 2.1, it has four quadrants. In the upper left is the open area, which represents the aspects of who you are that are known both to yourself and to others with whom you interact. In the upper right is the blind area. Here are the aspects of you that others see but you do not recognize. In the lower left is the hidden quadrant, sometimes referred to as the façade. These are the things that you know but do not reveal to others. Finally, in the lower right is the unknown quadrant. Here are those aspects of who you are that neither you nor others are yet aware of; they exist but have not been directly observed, and neither you nor those with whom you interact are aware of their impact on the relationship. Later, when they are discovered, it becomes obvious that they existed previously and did have an impact.

The sizes of the four quadrants change over time. In a new relationship, quadrant 1 is small. As communication increases, it grows large and quadrant 3 begins to shrink. With growing trust, we feel less need to hide the things we value, feel, and know. It takes longer for quadrant 2 to shrink in size because it requires openness to honest feedback. Not surprisingly, quadrant 4 tends to change most slowly of all because it requires people to be introspective and to explore things about themselves that are generally taken for granted. While it is often a very large quadrant and greatly influences what we do, many people totally close off the possibility of learning about quadrant 4.

The Johari window provides a useful tool for increasing self-awareness. Yet many people use a great deal of energy in order to hide, deny, or avoid learning about themselves, particularly their inconsistencies and hypocrisies. As a result, quadrant 1 begins to shrink and the others begin to enlarge. When quadrant 1 increases in size, however, the others shrink; and more energy, skills, and resources can be directed toward the

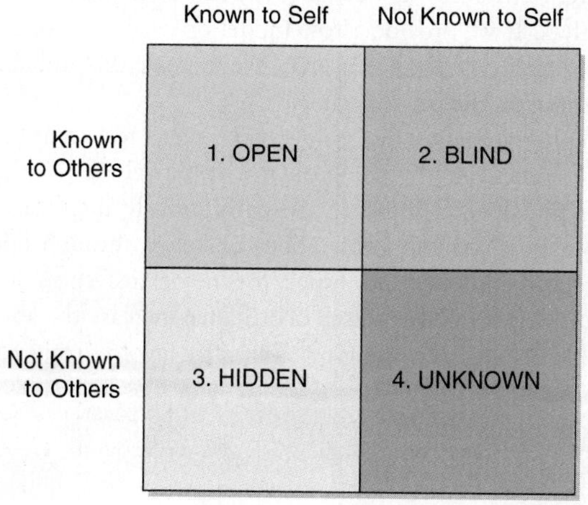

	Known to Self	Not Known to Self
Known to Others	1. OPEN	2. BLIND
Not Known to Others	3. HIDDEN	4. UNKNOWN

FIGURE 2.1 *The Johari window.*

tasks around which the relationship is formed. The more this occurs, the more openness, trust, and learning there is and the more the positive outcomes begin to multiply. Table 2.1 provides some basic guidelines that can help you increase the size of quadrant 1 by asking for feedback.

TABLE 2.1 Guidelines for Asking for Feedback

- Before asking for feedback, make sure you are open to hearing information that may alter your perception. Prepare yourself to hear things that may make you uncomfortable.
- Be aware that the person giving you the feedback is describing his or her own perception of the situation, but realize that his or her feelings are real.
- Check your understanding of the feedback: Ask questions or give examples and share your reaction(s). Clarify issues, explain your actions, and correct perceptions people may have of you, but do not defend and debate.
- Express your appreciation for the person who has given you the feedback. It may have been difficult for that person to be honest with you, and it is important that you show clearly and unequivocally that you welcome the feedback.

UNDERSTANDING OTHERS

The Johari window not only informs us of our own blind, hidden, and unknown areas, but it also makes us aware that these areas exist in others. If we appreciate that others have these three covert areas, then we will realize that they also will likely be defensive about them. And if we point out things in those areas before developing a strong relationship in which feedback is expected, it is likely that they will reject us and that the relationship will grow less trusting.

How, then, do we help others to learn through feedback? How do we build trust? How do we come to better understand others?

The paradoxical problem brings us back to ourselves. A key to positive change lies in focusing not on others but on ourselves. In fact, we need to be sensitive and respectful of others' need for privacy and recognize that their first reaction may be defensiveness. The secret to overcoming defensiveness in others, however, is to overcome defensiveness in ourselves. If we provide a role model of sensitivity, openness, and learning, and ask others for feedback about ourselves, we increase the probability of sensitivity, openness, and learning on the part of others.

To provide such a role model, we need to feel secure enough to be open. Security, however, comes only by being open with ourselves. In other words, the key to understanding and helping others is to continuously increase our own awareness of those things we least want to know about ourselves through openness to external feedback and through sensitivity and respect for the defensiveness of others.

Integrity, security, and self-acceptance increase the ability to practice empathy, the key skill in helping others to grow. **Empathy** involves truly putting yourself in the position of others and honestly trying to see the world as they see it. Table 2.2 lists five rules for helping you to practice empathy.

TABLE 2.2 Rules for Practicing Empathy

Empathy: The Ability to Experience the Feelings of Others

1. You must first examine yourself. If you do not truly want to understand others, if you are insincere, empathy will not work.

2. Communication is more than words. You must be sensitive to times when expressed thoughts and feelings are not congruent. You must read the nonverbal signals as well as the verbal ones.

3. Do not react too quickly to inaccurate statements of fact; listen carefully for the feelings beneath the statement before rushing in to correct facts.

4. You must allow the person to tell the emotional truth, which may include negative feelings about you. You must be ready to openly explore such negative feedback.

5. Use reflective listening (see Competency 2 in this chapter).

ANALYSIS Using the Johari Window to Analyze Behavior

Objective The objective of this analysis is to give you an opportunity to analyze the behavior of others and discuss your observations in class. Because most people are not comfortable analyzing their friends and coworkers publicly, this exercise focuses on analyzing the behavior of fictional characters.

Directions Use the Johari window as a way to analyze the behavior of a character in a television program or movie as you watch it. You may want to watch with other classmates and compare your observations after the show.

Discussion Questions 1. Were there obvious instances of Hidden, Blind, and/or Unknown Areas? If so, how would the course of events change if the character's Open Area was larger?

2. Did any of the other characters attempt to make something in a person's Blind Area known to them? If so, were they successful? Why or why not?

Reflection Just as in real life, characters in popular television shows, movies, and books often behave in ways that either attempt to conceal their true feelings (Hidden Areas) or reflect a lack of self-awareness (Blind and Unknown Areas). Depending on the aims of the writers in fiction-based programs or the reactions of other cast members in reality shows, the results may be comic or tragic, and characters may end up enlightened or disbelieving.

PRACTICE Practicing Receiving Feedback

Objective Increasing your self-awareness requires that you be open to receiving feedback. For many people, however, this is extremely difficult. Often, we tend to shut down and stop listening when someone is trying to give us constructive criticism. Defensiveness is natural, but can be costly—preventing us from learning more about ourselves and improving our personal effectiveness. The objective of this in-class role-play is to give you a chance to experience receiving negative feedback and to think about your responses to it.

Directions   Your instructor will provide you with information for this role-play scenario. Working with a partner, one person should give feedback to the other person. After the first round of feedback, switch partners and have the people who previously gave the feedback receive feedback for the second round.

Discussion Questions   1. How did it feel to give negative feedback to another person? To receive negative feedback?

2. Even though you knew that this was just a role-play, did you find yourself getting defensive or angry as you listed to the negative feedback? If so, why do you think that happened?

Reflection   Sometimes feedback is too vague to be helpful. Critical thinking skills can be used to develop feedback that is more effective. For example, rather than making a general claim such as, "Tom has an attitude problem," describing specific examples of Tom's behaviors and demonstrating why those behaviors are causing problems in the workplace provides more clarity about what Tom needs to do to improve.

APPLICATION   Soliciting Feedback

Objective   Now that you have completed the first four steps of the learning process (assessment, learning, analysis, and practice), it is time to take what you have learned and apply it in the workplace and then reflect upon the results.

Directions   1. Based on the Assessment that you completed at the beginning of this chapter and any additional insights that you have gained from the readings and exercises, write down the key aspects of yourself that you believe are in your Open Area of the Johari window.

2. Choose a friend or coworker that you feel comfortable with and trust. Make sure this is not only a person who knows you well but also someone you think will be honest with you.

3. Explain the Johari window to this person and show him or her what you have in quadrant 1 (Open Area). Explain that you would like to reduce the size of your Blind Area (quadrant 3) and are looking for feedback about your work behaviors, focusing on information that will help you work better with others. You might even develop some specific questions to ask about how you work with others. Try to assure the person that you will welcome feedback that will help you become more aware of your work behaviors. Make sure to show your appreciation to the person for taking a risk.

4. As you listen to the feedback about your Blind Area, pay attention to your feelings. If you begin to feel defensive, take a deep breath, and ask yourself why the information you are hearing is upsetting you. For general comments about your attitudes, ask for behavioral examples to help you understand why you are being seen in a particular way.

Reflection   Soliciting feedback is an important step in the process of understanding yourself, as well as improving yourself. As you continue to work through the competencies in this text, pay attention to your reaction to the different readings and exercises. If something strikes you as "trivial" or "a waste of time," ask yourself why you are reacting the way that you are. Sometimes we reject ideas because they conflict with our existing beliefs, and we don't take the time to think critically about whether our beliefs or the new ideas have stronger supporting evidence.

Competency 2   Communicating Effectively

ASSESSMENT Communication Skills

Objective   The objective of this assessment is to provide you with insights into how you communicate differently with different individuals. Although every interpersonal relationship is unique, we can learn a great deal about our own communication patterns by observing how we communicate with different individuals and people in different positions.

Directions   Assess the communication in two of your relationships: one that is very painful and one that is very pleasant. Next, assess how your communication behavior varies in the two relationships and what areas of communication you might need to work on. Answer the questions by using the following scale.

Scale   Minimal Problem   1   2   3   4   5   6   7   Great Problem

| *Painful* | | *Pleasant* | | |
Other	Self	Other	Self	
___	___	___	___	1. Expresses ideas in unclear ways.
___	___	___	___	2. Tries to dominate conversations.
___	___	___	___	3. Often has a hidden agenda.
___	___	___	___	4. Is formal and impersonal.
___	___	___	___	5. Does not listen well.
___	___	___	___	6. Is often boring, uninteresting.
___	___	___	___	7. Is withdrawn and uncommunicative.
___	___	___	___	8. Is overly sensitive, too easily hurt.
___	___	___	___	9. Is too abstract and hard to follow.
___	___	___	___	10. Is closed to the ideas of the other.
___	___	___	___	Total score

Now go back and reexamine your answers. What patterns do you see?

Discussion Questions   1. How do you think your own communication behavior varies in these two relationships?
2. On what specific problems in the painful relationship do you most need to work?

Reflection   Many people often find it difficult to communicate with people with whom they have a negative relationship. Unfortunately, this can result in a downward spiral, as poor communication results in misunderstandings that may cause the relationship to deteriorate even further. In contrast, learning to communicate more effectively and practicing what you have learned may actually help improve negative relationships and strengthen positive ones.

LEARNING   Communicating Effectively

Interpersonal communication is perhaps one of the most important and least understood competencies that a manager can have—and is vital to playing the mentor role. Knowing when and how to share information requires a very complex understanding of people and situations (Zey, 1990).

Communication is the exchange of information, facts, ideas, and meanings. The communication process can be used to inform, coordinate, and motivate people. Unfortunately, being a good communicator is not easy. Nor is it easy to recognize your own problems in communication. In the exercise you just completed, for example, you may well have downplayed your own weaknesses in communicating and rated yourself more favorably than you rated the other person in the painful relationship.

If, however, you practiced applying the critical thinking tactic described in Chapter 1, identifying the grounds and warrants that support your claim, your assessment is likely to be more accurate than if you simply responded based on your initial impression of your behavior. Although most people in organizations tend to think of themselves as excellent communicators, they consider communication a major organizational problem, and they see the other people in the organization as the source of the problem. It is very difficult to see and admit the problems in our own communication behavior.

Despite this difficulty, analyzing communication behavior is vital. Poor communication skills result in both interpersonal and organizational problems. When interpersonal problems arise, people begin to experience conflict, resist change, and avoid contact with others. Organizationally, poor communication often results in low morale and low productivity. Given that organizing *requires* that people communicate—to develop goals, channel energy, and identify and solve problems—learning to communicate effectively is key to improving work unit and organizational effectiveness.

A BASIC MODEL OF INTERPERSONAL COMMUNICATION

The information exchanged may take a variety of forms, including ideas, facts, and feelings. Despite these many possible forms, the communication process may be seen in terms of a general model (Shannon and Weaver, 1948), which is shown in Figure 2.2.

The model begins with the communicator encoding a message. Here the person who is going to communicate translates a set of ideas into a system of symbols, such as words or numbers. Many things influence the encoding process, including the urgency of the message, the experience and skills of the sender, and the sender's perception of the receiver. The message is transmitted through a medium of some sort. A message, for example, might be written, oral, or even nonverbal. Once it is received, it must be decoded. This means that the person who receives it must interpret the message. Like the encoding process, the decoding process is subject to influence by a wide range of factors.

The model includes a feedback loop between the receiver and the communicator. The **feedback** can take three forms: informational, corrective, or reinforcing. Informational feedback is a nonevaluative response that simply provides additional facts to the sender. Corrective feedback involves a challenge to, or correction of, the original message.

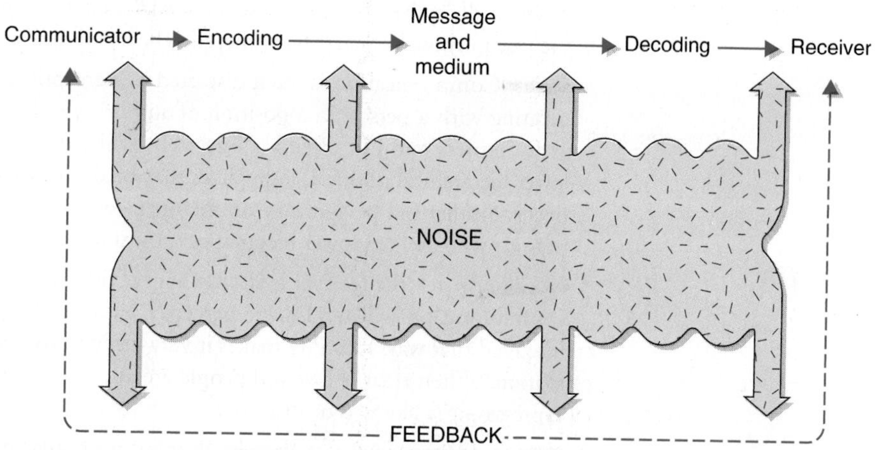

Communicator → Encoding → Message and medium → Decoding → Receiver

NOISE

FEEDBACK

FIGURE 2.2 *A basic model of communication.* Source: *Developed from C. Shannon and M. Weaver,* The Mathematical Theory of Communication *(Urbana: University of Illinois Press, 1948).* Used with permission.

Reinforcing feedback is a clear acknowledgment of the message that was sent. It may be positive or negative.

The final aspect of the model is noise. **Noise** is anything that can distort the message in the communication process. As indicated in Figure 2.2, it can occur at any point in the process. A sender may be unable to clearly articulate the ideas to be sent. In the medium, a document may leave out a key word. In the decoding process, the receiver may make wrong assumptions about the motive behind the message.

BARRIERS TO EFFECTIVE INTERPERSONAL COMMUNICATION

[handwritten margin note: expression / good listener]

Effective interpersonal communication comprises two elements. First, individuals must be able to express themselves. They need to be able to convey to others what they are feeling, what they are thinking, what they need from others, and so on. Second, individuals must be good listeners. They must be open to truly hearing the thoughts and ideas that other people are expressing (Samovar and Mills, 1998).

In organizations, problems can occur in interpersonal communication in either of these elements. They can also occur because the physical environment is not conducive to effective communication. For example, some environments may be too hot or too noisy. Others may provide an inappropriate setting for a particular type of message. Informal messages may be inappropriate in a setting that is highly formal, and formal messages may be inappropriate in settings that are highly informal.

Here we list some barriers to effective interpersonal communication that focus on people's abilities to send and receive messages.

- *Inarticulateness.* Communication problems may arise because the sender of the message has difficulty expressing the concept. If the receiver is not aware of the problem, completely inaccurate images may arise and result in subsequent misunderstandings.

- *Hidden agendas.* Sometimes people have motives that they prefer not to reveal. Because the sender believes that the receiver would not react in the desired way, the sender becomes deceptive. The sender seeks to maintain a competitive advantage by keeping the true purpose hidden. Over time, such behavior results in low trust and cooperation.

- *Status.* Communication is often distorted by perceptions of position. When communicating with a person in a position of authority, individuals often craft messages so as to impress and not offend. Conversely, when communicating with a person in a lower hierarchical position, individuals may be dismissive or insensitive to that person's needs. Similarly, a person may not be open to listening to the ideas and opinions of persons who are in a lower hierarchical position.

- *Hostility.* When the receiver is already angry with the person sending the message, the communication will tend to be perceived in a negative way, whether or not it was intended that way. Hostility makes it very difficult to send and receive accurate information. When trust is low and people are angry, no matter what the sender actually expresses, it is likely to be distorted.

- *Differences in communication styles.* People communicate in different ways. For example, some people speak loudly; others speak softly. Some people provide a great deal of context; others get right to the point and are only interested in "the bottom line." Some of the many differences in communication style are attributable to personal characteristics, such as gender or cultural background. Misunderstandings can develop if people listen less carefully because they are distracted by or uncomfortable with another person's style of communication.

Another important barrier to interpersonal communication stems from organizational norms and patterns of communication that prevent individuals from discussing difficult issues. As discussed in Competency 1 of this chapter, people have defenses that prevent them from receiving messages they fear. All people have some amount of insecurity, and there are certain things they simply do not want to know. Because people in organizations know this, they develop defensive routines (Argyris and Schön, 1996) in which they avoid saying things that might make the other person or themselves uncomfortable. Defensive routines are particularly likely to occur when discussing issues that affect values, assumptions, and self-image.

Chris Argyris of the Harvard Business School refers to the thoughts and feelings that are relevant to a conversation as "left-hand column issues" because of an exercise he uses to discover what they are (Senge, Roberts, Ross, Smith, and Kleiner, 1994). Left-hand column issues include both the things people are thinking but not saying and the things they think the other person is thinking but not saying. Argyris contends that organizations develop left-hand-column issues that keep important issues from surfacing and being discussed. Instead of surfacing these issues, people work around them, avoid them, make things up, and say things they don't mean or believe. Often they go through these pretenses to avoid offending people or having to deal with a difficult situation. But when the list of "undiscussables" becomes larger than the list of "discussables," the organization begins to suffer. Trust erodes and lots of covering up and avoidance make it difficult for people to improve their performance because they have no idea where they stand with one another. Important information is lost or kept concealed.

How does the left-hand-column exercise work? Imagine a conversation you have had or might have with a person at work. The person might be your boss, a coworker, or someone who reports to you. You could probably write down this conversation fairly easily, but before doing so, draw a vertical line down the middle of the paper. Now, in the right-hand column, write down the actual words spoken by you and the other person. In the left-hand column, write down the thoughts, feelings, questions, and concerns that you have but that you would not express out loud. Here's an example of such a conversation:

Left-Hand Column: What Is Thought	*Right-Hand Column: What Is Said*
Terry: I don't want to wait any longer on getting this position filled. We've already waited too long as it is.	**Terry:** Have you had a chance to look at the memo with the list of candidates? If you have any questions or hesitations about who ought to be on the list, just let me know. I want you to be comfortable with the people we bring in to interview.
Troy: I knew Terry wasn't going to add Michelle LaFleur to that list. We talked about it, and he knows I wanted her to be interviewed.	**Troy:** I think it looks pretty good. Have you gotten any feedback from the rest of the team?
Terry: I know what he's thinking: "Does anyone else agree with me that LaFleur should be interviewed?" Why doesn't he just say it? That bugs me.	**Terry:** I haven't heard from anyone yet, but we've got three people out of town until Friday. They may get back to me before then on e-mail. I'd like to interview these people next week. Do you think that's possible?
Troy: Right, another question from the guy who doesn't listen to my suggestions anyway.	**Troy:** I don't see why not. Let's move ahead with it. The last thing we want is to get stuck in a hiring freeze before we get someone in the door.
Terry: I know Troy is miffed about this process. He gets frustrated because we don't follow his proposals, but he keeps putting unqualified people in front of us because he wants to work with them. He's always looking for friends instead of someone to get the work done.	**Terry:** I agree. Thanks, Troy. I think we're making progress.

Clearly, these two people are not saying what they are thinking or feeling, but those feelings are influencing the "deep structure" of their behavior. The conversation on the surface is not as powerful as the silent conversation taking place beneath the surface, in the left-hand column. At the end of the right-hand column conversation that actually took place, both Terry and Troy feel somewhat dissatisfied, but neither one feels comfortable talking about the reason for their dissatisfaction.

People need to be trained to surface left-hand-column issues in ways that are non-punishing and positive. They need to develop the skills to express their concerns in a way that helps the other person want to hear what they have to say. In the mentor role, a manager will often encounter issues that may be sensitive or even threatening to another person. Individuals who develop good communication skills are more effective at surfacing left-hand-column issues.

Of course, it is important to recognize that not all left-hand column issues should always be communicated. One of the important functions of a mentor is to protect protégés, so it would be a mistake to encourage everyone to say exactly what is on their mind at any give time! In the conversation above, for example, it would most likely be helpful for Terry to explicitly state that he considered Michelle LaFleur but did not think that her qualifications fit the position. This might lead to a response from Troy that identified something that Troy had overlooked about Michelle. In contrast, it would not be helpful for Terry to say that he thought Michelle's only qualification was that she was a friend of Troy's, even if that was indeed how Terry felt.

Given the number and intensity of these barriers to effective communication, what should you know to help yourself to communicate effectively? First, you need to develop a few basic skills to express yourself more effectively. Table 2.3 gives seven basic rules for when you are sharing your ideas with others. Most important, always keep in mind the old adage "Think before you speak." An effective speaker who communicates the wrong information can create far more problems than an ineffective speaker who struggles to convey the correct information.

TABLE 2.3 Rules for Effective Communication

1. *Be clear on who the receiver is.* What is the receiver's state of mind? What assumptions does the receiver bring? What is he or she feeling in this situation?
2. *Know what your objective is.* What do you want to accomplish by sending the message?
3. *Analyze the climate.* What will be necessary to help the receiver relax and be open to the communication?
4. *Review the message in your head before you say it.* Think about the message from the point of view of the receiver. Do you need to clarify certain ideas?
5. *Communicate using words and terms that are familiar to the other person.* Use examples and illustrations that come from the world of the receiver.
6. *If the receiver seems not to understand, clarify the message.* Ask questions. If repetition is necessary, try different words and illustrations.
7. *If the response is seemingly critical, do not react defensively.* Try to understand what the receiver is thinking. Why is he or she reacting negatively? The receiver may be misunderstanding your message. Ask clarifying questions.

REFLECTIVE LISTENING

Of all the skills associated with good communication, perhaps the most important is listening. The Stoic philosopher Epictetus, in *The Golden Sayings,* reportedly said, "Nature hath given men one tongue but two ears that we may hear from others twice as much as we speak." This is a good thought to keep in mind, but we should remember that listening is more than hearing what others have to say. Listening requires that we truly try to understand what they are saying. Most people fail to realize just how poorly they tend to listen.

Reflective listening is a tool that is based on empathy (see Table 2.2), which helps us to experience the thoughts and feelings of the other person. In using empathy and reflective listening, instead of directing and controlling the thoughts of the other person, you become a helper who tries to facilitate his or her expression. Instead of assuming responsibility for another's problem, you help that person explore it on his or her own. Your job is not to talk but to keep the other person talking. You do not evaluate, judge, or advise; you simply reflect on what you hear. In fewer words, you descriptively, not evaluatively, restate the essence of the person's last thought or feeling. If the person's statement is factually inaccurate, you do not immediately point out the inaccuracy. Instead of interrupting, you keep the person's flow of expression moving. You can go back later to correct factual errors.

The reflective listener uses open-ended questions, such as "Can you tell me more?" or "How did you feel when that happened?" Evaluative questions and factual, yes-or-no questions are avoided. The key is to keep the conceptual and emotional flow of expression. Instead of telling, the reflective listener helps the other person to discover. Here is an example of reflective listening to help illustrate how it works.

Kathie is the manager of the Training and Development Office in a large public agency. The office has 13 professional employees whose primary job is to conduct training for the agency and 2 secretaries. Allen is a relatively new employee who has been asked to develop new training on "Dealing with Crisis Situations." Kathie is having her first formal meeting with Allen since he was hired two months ago.

Kathie:	Allen, I was wondering how you're doing on the new training program. I had originally hoped that during your first few months we would meet more often, but things have been very hectic. Are you moving along with the project?
Allen:	Well, at first I felt like I was making good progress, but now I'm at an impasse. I'm just feeling frustrated.
Kathie:	Can you tell me why you're feeling frustrated? Is there something about the project that isn't going right?
Allen:	I guess I'm just frustrated with the assignment. I've gathered lots of information, but when I ask the others about what should be included, some say I'm putting in too much information and others say there isn't enough time to practice the new skills.
Kathie:	So are you feeling like you're getting different messages from different people?
Allen:	Yes, and I'm not sure how long the training program is supposed to be. Is it a half-day program, a whole-day program, or a multiday program?
Kathie:	Based on the information you have gathered, how long do you think it should be?
Allen:	Well, I think it should be a two-day program, but I didn't think that I was responsible for making that decision. That's part of my frustration!
Kathie:	I think I understand. Is part of your frustration that you're not sure which decisions you can make on your own and which you need to get approval from others?
Allen:	Yes, that's exactly it. I'm not sure of what the rules are around here and how decisions are made.

To the first-time reader, reflective listening sounds very strange. Experience shows, however, that it can have major payoffs. Trust and concern grow with an ever-deepening understanding of interpersonal issues. More effective and lasting problem solving takes place, and people have a greater sense that their ideas are being listened to by others. In short, communication is greatly improved.

Reflective listening is not, however, a panacea. It is time-consuming to really listen. It requires confidence in one's interpersonal skills and the courage to possibly hear things about oneself that are less than complimentary. There is also a danger that the sender will get into personal areas of life with which the listener is not comfortable and for which a professional counselor would be more appropriate. It is, nevertheless, a vital tool that is seldom understood or employed.

ANALYSIS   Using the Left-Hand Column to Develop Your Communication Skills

Objective   The objective the this analysis is to help you begin to identify gaps between what you say and what you think, as well as to help you understand why those gaps occur.

Directions   1. Think back to a conversation you had with a friend or work colleague involving a problem that you tried to resolve. This may be a problem that has since been solved or one that still does not have a usable solution. Try to identify a difficult problem that involves interpersonal difficulties, such as a conflict about how to do an assignment or a disagreement about who should perform different parts of a task.

Write down the approach that you took to resolve the problem. What did you talk about? What ideas did you have? Did you consider involving others in your problem-solving process?

Using a fresh piece of paper, divide the paper in half and write down the conversation that occurred on the right-hand side of the page. If you cannot remember the conversation verbatim, try to remember the key issues that were raised.

On the left-hand side of the page, write down your thoughts and feelings that were unexpressed during the conversation.

2. Reflect on what you have in your left-hand column. What led you to feel that way? What kept you from expressing your thoughts and feelings? What assumptions did you make about the other person? What do you lose from keeping certain thoughts and feelings to yourself?

3. Think about how you might move some of your thoughts and feelings from the left-hand column to the right-hand column.

Reflection   Sometimes we don't express our thoughts and feelings because we do not feel that we have sufficient grounds for the claims that we would like to make—we don't trust our intuition. But often our reticence is based on a desire to avoid conflict, rather than a lack of solid arguments. Feelings that are not expressed, however, do not simply disappear. Often the best way to minimize conflict is to raise contentious issues early, before they escalate.

PRACTICE   Working in the Left-hand Column: Stacy Brock and Terry Lord

Objective   This practice exercise is designed to help you enhance your ability to surface left-hand column issues and clarify roles and expectations with another person—a boss, peer, or direct report. The two people in this case, Stacy Brock and Terry Lord, have gotten themselves into a box in their working relationship. They have already had one blowup, and they may have another if they cannot handle themselves effectively. Both need some feedback, and both have things they need to say.

Directions   Your instructor will provide you with a role description for either Stacy Brock or Terry Lord. Read the information carefully so you are prepared to play your role from the perspective of your character. Your instructor may have some people role-play the situation in front of the class or may ask everyone to work together in dyads. After you have completed the role-play, respond to the following discussion questions.

Discussion Questions   1. How well were you and your partner (or the individuals who did the role-play in the front of the class) able to communicate?

2. Was it difficult to surface the real issues? Which issues were carefully discussed?

3. Which issues, if any, were undiscussable?

4. What did each person do to make the issues more discussable?

Reflection   For many employees, being labeled "average" is a severe blow to their self-image. To avoid conflict, some managers fail to make any meaningful distinctions among employees on their performance evaluations. This tactic, however, can result in demoralizing exceptional workers. It is also a disservice to employees who could improve with additional mentoring.

APPLICATION   Developing Your Reflective Listening Skills

Objective   It is one thing to practice reflective listening in the classroom, but quite another to apply it in your daily life. The objective is this activity is to help you transfer what you have learned about reflective listening into a habit at work and at home.

Directions   1. Over the next week, practice your reflective listening skills. Whenever you are involved in a conversation, try to gain a better understanding of what the other person is thinking and feeling by asking questions.

2. Keep a journal of your experiences using reflective listening. In your journal note what you said and how the person responded. Note what types of statements elicited strong responses from the other person, and identify ways to continue developing your reflective listening skills.

Reflection   Techniques such as reflective listening are not difficult to understand, but mastering them requires repeated use and reflection. The idea of keeping a journal about your experiences with reflective listening may seem time consuming at first, but it serves to remind you about the need to practice, as well as to increase the effort that you exert developing this important habit.

Competency 3   Developing Employees

ASSESSMENT   Assumptions About Performance Evaluations

Objective   Often we hold unconscious assumptions that keep us from questioning the way things are done. The objective of this assessment exercise is to examine your own assumptions and learn about the assumptions that other people hold concerning performance evaluations.

Directions   Check off the statement in each of the following pairs of statements that best reflects your assumptions about performance evaluation.

Performance evaluation is:

_____   1a. a formal process that is done annually.

_____   1b. an informal process that is done continuously.

_____   2a. a process that is planned for employees.

_____   2b. a process that is planned with employees.

_____   3a. a required organizational procedure.

_____   3b. a process done regardless of requirements.

_____   4a. a time to evaluate employee performance.

_____   4b. a time for employees to evaluate the manager.

_____   5a. a time to clarify standards.

_____   5b. a time to clarify the employee's career needs.

_____   6a. a time to confront poor performance.

_____   6b. a time to express appreciation.

_____   7a. an opportunity to clarify issues and provide direction and control.

_____   7b. an opportunity to increase enthusiasm and commitment.

_____   8a. only as good as the organization's forms.

_____   8b. only as good as the manager's coaching skills.

Discussion Questions

1. As you review your eight answers, do you see any patterns in your assumptions or in the assumptions you did not choose?

2. As you review the statements, can you explain why the performance evaluation process is disliked by most employees in the United States?

3. How would you design an effective process?

4. What characteristics of your performance evaluation process would make it more attractive to employees? Would those characteristics increase or reduce the usefulness of the performance evaluation process for the organization?

Reflection

All performance evaluation systems are not created equal, and even the same system may be evaluated differently by different people. For example, General Electric's performance evaluation system has been praised for its record of developing top-flight talent. It has also been criticized for its requirement that managers must fire those employees who rank in the bottom 10 percent. What characteristics does former GE CEO Jack Welch think are critical to a good performance evaluation system? In his book *Winning*, Welch mentions only four elements: (1) it should be clear and simple; (2) it should focus on relevant, agreed-upon criteria; (3) formal evaluations should be face-to-face, once, or even better, twice annually; and (4) it should include professional development (Welch, 2005).

LEARNING   Developing Employees

In a literal sense, *mentor* means a trusted counselor or guide—a coach. The term derives from a character in *The Odyssey*, the Greek epic poem written by Homer (Bell, 1996). In the poem, Odysseus asks a family friend, Mentor, to serve as a tutor and coach to his son, Telemachus, while he is off at war. In this section we turn to this particular aspect of the mentor role and explore two approaches to developing employees. The first, delegation, focuses on how to develop employees' competencies and abilities by providing them opportunities to take on more responsibility. The second, performance evaluation, focuses on giving employees feedback on their performance. Both of these approaches rely on competencies presented in the two previous sections of this chapter—understanding self and others and communicating effectively.

DELEGATING EFFECTIVELY

One of the best ways for employees to develop their skills and abilities is to work on challenging assignments that push them to go beyond their current level of functioning. As such, delegating tasks and responsibilities to employees provides an excellent opportunity for their growth and development. Nevertheless, some managers resist delegation, using arguments such as "I tried that once and the employee fouled things up royally" or "Delegate my authority? Why? I'm the manager—that's my job—I can do it better myself." Managers who learn to delegate effectively, however, find that it results in a variety of important benefits for themselves and the organization, as well as for employees. Of course, many managers realize that by delegating some of their work, they provide themselves with additional time and thus are able to focus attention on more significant issues. More important for the discussion here, however, is the fact that in delegating tasks and responsibilities to employees, managers give their employees opportunities to develop new skills and abilities, as well as to learn more about the work unit and how it functions. This not only helps employees to be more effective in their work but also strengthens the work unit, thus allowing for a better allocation of organizational resources.

Given the potential benefits of delegation, why do some managers resist delegating tasks to employees? There are several reasons for not delegating. First, many associate delegation with negative managerial behaviors, such as abdicating responsibility for a task or letting someone else—typically those "lower" in the organization—do the dirty work. Some think employees will be offended if their manager asks them to take on a task previously performed by the manager. Second, many managers fear that they will lose control. They are concerned that employees will not do the job as well or exercise the same level of judgment as they would if they did the job themselves. Finally, and perhaps most important, is the fact that many managers have not learned how to delegate effectively; they have not learned that delegation is more than simply giving assignments to employees. Rather, it is the entrusting of a particular assignment, project, task, or process by one individual to another (Schwartz, 1992). As such, it requires a good understanding of what can and cannot be delegated, careful attention to employees' current skill levels, and a good communication process that allows for questions and feedback for both the manager and the employees. It also requires managers to do more than simply tell employees what they want them to do; managers need to share with employees the reasons for the assignment, that is, why the task needs to be done (Klein, 2000). Navy Commander D. Michael Abrashoff, who commanded the *USS Benfold,* a ship that is known for getting tough assignments, argues that it is important for managers in all situations to communicate purpose. He states "getting [crew members] to contribute in a meaningful way to each life-or-death mission isn't just a matter of training and discipline. It's a matter of knowing who they are and where they are coming from—and linking that knowledge to our purpose" (quoted in LaBarre, 1999).

Delegation involves three core elements: responsibility, authority, and accountability. Before delegating, the manager should be aware that he or she is still ultimately responsible for the successful execution of the assignment, project, task, or process. The manager also has the final say, and so should supervise and monitor as appropriate. In delegating, however, the manager must also give the employee certain responsibilities. In particular, the employee should be responsible for achieving intermediate and specific goals and milestones along the way. It is important that managers use the delegation process to clarify the difference between their responsibilities and the employees'. Managers should also make sure that sufficient authority has been transferred to those individuals to whom assignments are delegated to allow them to carry out the task and obtain the resources and cooperation required for its successful completion. Finally, individuals who are delegated assignments should be held accountable for meeting established goals and objectives. Periodic reports and evaluations may be critical here. Here we provide some guidelines for effective delegation.

Keys to Effective Delegation

1. *Clarify, in your own mind, what it is that you want done.* Make sure that you can explain to employees what is to be done, as well as why this assignment is important for the work unit. Writing it down can be helpful.

2. *Match the desired task with the most appropriate employee.* Especially if you are using delegation for the purpose of developing employees, you will want to make sure that this assignment is at the proper level of difficulty, providing the employee some challenge but not so much that he or she becomes frustrated with the assignment.

3. *In assigning the task, be sure you communicate clearly.* Again, it is important that you communicate not only the nature of the task but also your intent. Ask questions to ensure the task is fully understood. Be sure that deadlines and time horizons are clear. To be absolutely certain that employees fully understand the assignment, you might ask them to repeat or feed back their understanding of the delegated assignment.

4. *Make sure that the employee has the time to do the assignment.* If the employee is working on several tasks, make sure that you have clarified the priority of the new task.

5. *Keep the communication channels open.* Make it clear that you are available for consultation and discussion.

6. *Allow employees to do the task the way they feel comfortable doing it.* Show some trust in their abilities. Do not hold such high expectations that they can only fail.

7. *Check on the progress of the assignment, but do not rush to the rescue at the first sign of failure.* Give employees a chance to try solving the problem on their own. Also keep in mind that employees may have initially felt that the assignment surpasses their ability; they may fear being embarrassed by failure but also feel uncomfortable raising this issue. When you show confidence in employees, they often gain the self-confidence necessary to solve the problem. You may be able to avoid this problem at the start by explicitly asking employees how confident they are in their ability to complete the assigned task.

8. *Hold the person responsible for the work and any difficulties that may emerge.* Keep in mind, however, that you are delegating to give the employee an opportunity to develop his or her own knowledge and abilities. Explore what is going wrong, and help the individual to develop his or her own solutions.

9. *Make sure that the person has appropriate authority to carry out the task and obtain the resources and cooperation required for its successful completion.* A classic reason for failed delegation is being given the responsibility for an assignment without being given the authority to complete it or the appropriate discretion in choosing the manner of completion.

10. *Recognize the employee's accomplishments.* Ignoring an employee's efforts can be devastating to motivation. Acknowledge what has been done, and show appropriate appreciation.

THE MANY USES AND PROBLEMS OF PERFORMANCE EVALUATIONS

Now we turn more specifically to coaching, or the notion of developing people by providing performance evaluation and feedback. Feedback on performance is one of the most potentially helpful kinds of information that a person can get. It is critical to improvement, growth, and development. Yet, as implied in Question 2 of the Assessment exercise, performance evaluation is one of the most uniformly disliked processes in organizational America. In fact, a survey of human resources professionals conducted in 1997 by Aon Consulting and the Society for Human Resources Management found that only 5% of the respondents were very satisfied with their performance-management systems (Imperato, 1998). Given the importance of performance evaluation for employee development, it is important to understand why performance evaluation systems so often fail.

In the mentor role, performance evaluation is seen as a tool to facilitate the development of employees, to clarify expectations, and to improve performance. Yet in many organizations, performance evaluations are used for many other purposes. Rather than being used solely as a developmental tool for the individual, it is also an organizational tool (Swanson, 1994). Most often, it is used to make systemwide decisions about rewards such as compensation and promotion. These evaluations generally focus on completing a form rather than on making plans for employee growth and development. Moreover, in many organizations that claim to have annual reviews, performance evaluation is not seen as an important part of the manager's job, and so evaluations are not always completed on a timely basis (Staub, 1997). These conditions do not create an organizational climate that is conducive to constructive feedback and learning.

Performance evaluations may also be used to document negative behaviors in cases of discharge and/or as a data source for developing training and development strategies and staffing plans. Because of the importance of these formal functions, the organization is open to legal challenge. An employee, for example, may sue because of a given promotion decision. Hence issues of accuracy and fairness become increasingly critical, and much of the literature focuses on methods of form design, statistical techniques, and sources of error. The objective, with good reason, is to build a generalized system that fits every situation in the organization and that is fair and defensible. This, of course, is a tall order, and in many organizations, performance evaluation becomes more of a source of high frustration or meaningless game playing than an opportunity to give employees meaningful feedback.

In addition to the organizational problems, many personal pressures make performance evaluation difficult. The process often makes both managers and employees very uncomfortable. How well a person has performed over the past year is seldom as clear as the human resources staff would like to believe it is, and the form is seldom able to capture the complexity of real life. In some cases, employees sense that the quantitative evaluations are really a cover for subjective judgments and challenge what they are told. In other cases, managers and employees may have different views of what a rating means. Darcy Hitchcock, president of AXIS Performance Advisors, talks about one of her first performance evaluations as one of the most painful experiences of her career; she had received a rating of 4 on a 5-point scale. When her boss could not explain why he had not rated her at the highest level, she found herself completely unmotivated (Imperato, 1998).

Not surprisingly, many managers feel uncomfortable admitting that the evaluation process often reduces to subjective judgment, and they usually feel uncomfortable in the role of a "judge." And both managers and employees tend to fear being challenged with questions that they may not be able to answer. Managers often become frustrated when an angry employee becomes hostile or passive. In cases like this, managers may lack the skills to know how to handle the problem. Because conducting effective performance evaluations requires constant observation, recording, and feedback, many managers argue that they simply do not have the time to devote to this activity.

CONDUCTING EFFECTIVE PERFORMANCE EVALUATIONS

In the Assessment exercise at the beginning of this competency, you chose between two options in eight pairs of assumptions about performance evaluation. In each pair of statements, answer *a* reflected traditional control values—those normally associated with the evaluation process. Answer *b*, on the other hand, reflected values rooted in involvement, communication, and trust. In this section we will consider performance evaluation as a two-step process, one that mixes the *a* and *b* views of the world. Although the mixed view presented here differs from what is designed and practiced in most organizations, you may find it to be of some value.

Performance evaluation should start long before the actual evaluation session. If you have the organizational freedom to do so, and if it is situationally appropriate, you might even invite employees to join you in designing a program that will work. Their wisdom may surprise you. You might begin the planning session by discussing what program, if any, is currently in place and what is positive and negative about the system. You might review the value of feedback to individuals and the group and then consider the reasons that most programs fail. With these things in mind, you might as a group specify some guidelines that will work in your situation.

Whether or not you have the opportunity to design a new program, you should consider performance evaluation from the perspective of employee growth and development.

Consider employees' need for feedback. During the time period from one performance evaluation to another, you should engage in frequent conversations with employees. Clearly, feedback should not be a one-time experience. Rather, these conversations should take place at regular intervals and should include specific feedback on employee performance and suggestions for improving performance. Table 2.4 provides some guidelines for giving feedback. These guidelines are useful for both informal conversations and formal performance evaluation sessions.

Giving and receiving feedback requires some self-confidence and trust in employees. As noted in the introduction to this section, many of the skills and competencies discussed in the first two sections of this chapter, especially self-awareness and effective communication, are essential to providing effective feedback. In addition, giving effective feedback requires managers to be aware that they need to regularly observe the performance of employees and make notes of concrete incidents that can provide specific examples of both positive and negative behaviors.

If you do conduct a formal evaluation, you may want to try another unique twist. At some specified time before the evaluation, prepare a written evaluation of yourself to give the employee. Ask the employee to prepare a written evaluation of his or her performance for you. Spend some time reading this self-evaluation and use empathy to put yourself in the person's place. Use this process to prepare yourself for the evaluation session. In scheduling the session, be sure to set aside enough time to fully discuss the employee's self-evaluation. Approach this session as a learning opportunity for both yourself and the employee. Make sure that you have a private setting where you will not be interrupted.

In the actual evaluation, be sure that your own objective is clear. Know what you want to accomplish. Get into an appropriate frame of mind (Krieff, 1996). Ask yourself how you really feel about the person and, most importantly, how you can really help the person. Few managers enter the process in such a frame of mind.

Begin by making sure that the employee is also in an appropriate frame of mind. Remember that the performance evaluation will be most effective if the employee is

TABLE 2.4 Guidelines for Giving Feedback

- Before giving feedback, examine your motivation and make sure the receiver is ready and open to hear you. Ask the person whether or not this is a good time to receive feedback.
- Make sure to give the person feedback in a private place that allows for further dialogue.
- While giving feedback, use "I" statements rather than "you" statements to indicate that these are your perceptions, thoughts, and feelings.
- Provide feedback on both positive and negative behaviors. No one is either all bad or all good. Managers who present only one side lose their credibility for being honest.
- Describe the other person's behavior and your perceptions of it. Present specific examples of behavior that you have observed, rather than generalized statements that describe a demeanor or an attitude.
- Make sure your examples are timely. Giving feedback on a behavior that has long passed is both annoying and difficult to discuss.
- Ask the other person to clarify, explain, change, or correct.
- After giving feedback, give the receiver time to respond.

ready to hear your feedback (Silberman, 2000). Focus first on the positive behaviors. If you have not already asked the employee to write a self-evaluation, ask him or her to list the things that he or she has done well; contribute to the list as much as possible. When you turn to areas that might need improvement, again ask the person to begin; in a supportive way, continue together until you agree on a list. At this point, if you have the skills discussed in the last two sections, you might ask how you as a manager are contributing to this person's problems. For example, you might suggest going through the list and asking what you could do differently. As the person responds, use reflective listening to explore the person's claim in an honest way. Make commitments to change your behavior where possible. In doing so, you are modeling the behavior you would like the employee to practice and develop. After doing this, you might again go through the list and ask the employee what changes he or she might make.

Next, discuss the person's career development plan. Review what progress has been made and what each of you can do to speed progress in the next period. If there is no such plan, one of the assignments should be to write a plan. You may need to help the person here. At the conclusion of the session, summarize what each of you might do differently during the next few months. After this, do an overall review, checking the employee's understanding of each action step. Do a final summary, and set a time for future reviews.

ANALYSIS United Chemical Company[1]

Objective   When faced with our own performance evaluations or those of our subordinates, it is often difficult to separate the people from the issues. The objective of this case analysis and the practice exercise that follows it is to give you the opportunity to analyze how the principles of supportive communication and reflective listening that you have read about in this chapter can be applied to a situation that is "neutral" for you so you can gain a more in-depth understanding of these techniques and how they can be applied.

Directions   Read the case and then answer the questions that follow.

The United Chemical Company is a large producer and distributor of commodity chemicals with five chemical production plants in the United States. The operations at the main plant in Baytown, Texas, include not only production equipment but also the company's research and engineering center.

The process design group consists of eight male engineers and the manager, Max Kane. The group has worked together steadily for a number of years, and good relationships have developed among all members. When the workload began to increase, Max hired a new design engineer, Sue Davis, a recent master's degree graduate from one of the foremost engineering schools in the country. Sue was assigned to a project involving expansion of the capacity of one of the existing plant facilities. Three other design engineers were assigned to the project along with Sue: Jack Keller (age 38, with 15 years with the company), Sam Sims (age 40, with 10 years with the company), and Lance Madison (age 32, with 8 years with the company).

As a new employee, Sue was enthusiastic about the opportunity to work at United. She liked her work very much because it was challenging and offered her a chance to apply much of

[1]Adapted from *Organizational Behavior and Performance*, 3d ed., by Andrew D. Szilagi, Jr., and Marc J. Wallace, Jr. Copyright © 1983, 1980 by Scott, Foresman and Company. Used with permission.

the knowledge she had gained in her university studies. On the job, Sue kept to herself and her design work. Her relations with her fellow project members were friendly, but she did not go out of her way to have informal conversations during or after working hours.

Sue was a diligent employee who took her work seriously. On occasions when a difficult problem arose, she would stay after hours in order to come up with a solution. Because of her persistence, coupled with her more current education, Sue usually completed her portion of the various project stages a number of days before her colleagues. This was somewhat irritating to her, and on these occasions she went to Max to ask for additional work to keep her busy until her fellow workers caught up to her. Initially, she had offered to help Jack, Sam, and Lance with their parts of the project, but each time she was turned down tersely.

About five months after Sue had joined the design group, Jack asked to see Max about a problem the group was having. The conversation between Max and Jack was as follows.

Max: Jack, I understand you wanted to discuss a problem with me.

Jack: Yes, Max. I didn't want to waste your time, but some of the other design engineers wanted me to discuss Sue with you. She's irritating everyone with her know-it-all, pompous attitude. She just isn't the kind of person that we want to work with.

Max: I can't understand that, Jack. She's an excellent worker whose design work is always well done and usually flawless. She's doing everything the company wants her to do.

Jack: The company never asked her to disturb the morale of the group or to tell us how to do our work. The animosity of the group can eventually result in lower-quality work for the whole unit.

Max: I'll tell you what I'll do. Sue has a meeting with me next week to discuss her six-month performance. I'll keep your thoughts in mind, but I can't promise an improvement in what you and the others believe is a pompous attitude.

Jack: Immediate improvement in her behavior isn't the problem—it's her coaching others when she has no right to engage in publicly showing others what to do. You'd think she was lecturing an advanced class in design with all her high-power, useless equations and formulas. She'd better back off soon, or some of us will quit or transfer.

During the next week, Max thought carefully about his meeting with Jack. He knew that Jack was the informal leader of the design engineers and generally spoke for the other group members. On Thursday of the following week, Max called Sue into his office for her midyear review. One portion of the conversation was as follows:

Max: There is one other aspect I'd like to discuss with you about your performance. As I just related to you, your technical performance has been excellent; however, there are some questions about your relationships with the other workers.

Sue: I don't understand—what questions are you talking about?

Max: Well, to be specific, certain members of the design group have complained about your apparent "know-it-all attitude" and the manner in which you try to tell them how to do their job. You're going to have to be patient with them and not publicly call them out about their performance. This is a good group of engineers, and their work over the years has been more than acceptable. I don't want any problems that will cause the group to produce less effectively.

Sue: Let me make a few comments. First of all, I have never publicly criticized their performance to them or to you. Initially, when I was finished ahead of them, I offered to help them with their work but was bluntly told to mind my own business. I took the hint and concentrated only on my part of the work. What you don't understand is that after five months of working in this group I have come to the conclusion that what is going on is a "rip-off" of the company. The other engineers are "goldbricking" and setting a work pace much slower than they're capable of. They're more interested in the music from Sam's radio, the local football team, and the bar they're going to go to for TGIF. I'm sorry, but this is just not the way I was raised or trained. And, finally, they've never looked on me as a qualified engineer, but as a woman who has broken their professional barrier.

Discussion Questions   1. What are the key problems?

2. How would you use the information in this chapter to redesign the meeting between Max and Sue?

3. Do you think Max handled the meeting with Jack effectively? If not, what should he have done differently?

Reflection   In describing the objective of this analysis, we wrote that this was a "neutral" situation. We used quotation marks because, in reality, many people tend to identify with the characters in case studies based on their own past experiences and their social identities. Discussing this case in class can be very productive for surfacing different assumptions that people are making about the characters in the case based on stereotypes rather than based on the limited facts presented in the case.

PRACTICE   What Would You Include in the Performance Evaluation?

Directions   Review the guidelines for giving and receiving feedback that have been presented in this chapter. Then think about the suggestions you had for redesigning Max's midyear review of Sue.

1. Develop a performance evaluation review of Sue. What kind of feedback are you going to give her? What skills will you suggest that she develop?

2. In dyads, role-play Max's midyear performance evaluation review.

Discussion Questions   1. At the conclusion of the role-play, discuss how the performance evaluation went. Did you follow the guidelines for giving and receiving feedback?

2. What did you learn from this role-play?

Reflection   Effectively evaluating performance is a complex task that is made more complicated when we see it as having conflicting objectives. We want to motivate our employees by giving them "positive" feedback. On the other hand, we often need to give them "negative" feedback that they may not agree with and will not be happy to hear. Instead of seeing these as conflicting objectives, emphasizing the goal of employee development helps us transcend this paradox. Employee development focuses our attention less on what has happened in the past and more on what we are working to achieve in the future.

APPLICATION   The Mentor at Work

1. Select a parent, friend, teacher, or other associate with whom you spend time.

2. Think about the areas of life in which this person has been a mentor to you. How well did he or she receive and give feedback? How did he or she help you set personal or work-related goals for developing your skills and abilities? Did he or she delegate work or responsibilities to

you in a way that would help you develop a skill or other ability? What were his or her strengths and weaknesses as a mentor?

3. In a group of four to six students, make two lists. The first list should describe the most important attributes of a mentor. The second list should describe common mentoring mistakes made by people.

4. From the lists you have made, identify difficulties you might have being a mentor as a manager.

5. Develop a personal plan to develop your own mentoring skills so that you can avoid such mistakes.

REFERENCES

Argyris, Chris, and Donald A. Schön. *Organizational Learning II: Theory, Methods, and Practice.* Reading, MA: Addison-Wesley, 1996.

Bass, Bernard M. *Bass and Stodgill's Handbook of Leadership: Theory, Research and Managerial Applications.* New York: Free Press, 1990.

Bell, Chip R. *Managers as Mentors: Building Partnerships for Learning.* San Francisco: Berrett-Koehle, 1996.

Cotton, J. *Employee Involvement. Methods for Improving Performance and Work Attitudes.* San Francisco: Jossey-Bass, 1994.

Drucker, Peter F. "Managing Oneself." *Harvard Business Review* 77(2) (March–April 1999): 65–74.

Goleman, Daniel. *Emotional Intelligence.* New York: Bantam, 1995.

Goleman, Daniel. *Working with Emotional Intelligence.* New York: Bantam, 1998.

Goleman, Daniel. "Leadership That Gets Results." *Harvard Business Review* 78(2) (March–April 2000): 78–90.

Hogan, Robert, Gordon J. Curphy, and Joyce Hogan. "What We Know About Leadership: Effectiveness and Personality." *American Psycholigist* 49(6) (1994): 493–504.

Imperato, Gina. "How to Give Good Feedback." *Fast Company* (Issue 17) September 1998. Retrieved August 22, 2000 (<http://www.fastcompany.com/online/17/feedback.html>).

Keirsey, David. *Please Understand Me II: Temperament Character Intelligence,* Del Mar, CA: Prometheus Nemesis, 1998.

Klein, Gary. "Why Won't They Follow Simple Directions?" *Across the Board* 37(2) (February 2000): 14–19.

Krieff, Allan. *Manager's Survival Guide: How to Avoid the 750 Most Common Mistakes in Dealing with People.* Englewood Cliffs, NJ: Prentice-Hall, 1996.

LaBarre, Polly. "The Agenda—Grassroots Leadership." *Fast Company* (Issue 23) April 1999. Retrieved June 4, 2000 (<http://www.fastcompany.com/online/23/grassroots.html>).

Lobel, S., and L. St. Clair. "Effects of Family Responsibilities, Gender, and Career Identity Salience on Performance Outcomes." *Academy of Management Journal,* 35(5) (1992): 1057–1069.

Luft, Joseph. *Group Processes: An Introduction to Group Dynamics,* 2d ed. Palo Alto, CA: National Press Books, 1970.

Luft, Joseph, and Harry Ingham. "The Johari Window: A Graphic Model of Interpersonal Awareness." *Proceedings of the Western Training Laboratory in Group Development,* University of California, Los Angeles Extension Office, August 1955.

McCall, M. *High Flyers: Developing the Next Generation of Leaders.* Boston: Harvard Business School Press, 1998.

McCrae, Robert R., and Paul T. Costa, Jr. *Personality in Adulthood,* New York: Guilford, 1990.

McCrae, Robert R., and Paul T. Costa, Jr. "A Five-Factor Theory of Personality," in Lawrence A. Pervin and Oliver P. John (eds.), *Handbook of Personality: Theory and Research.* New York: Guilford, 1999: 139–153.

Muoio, Anna. "The Truth Is, the Truth Hurts." *Fast Company* (Issue 14) April 1998. Retrieved August 22, 2000 (<http://www.fastcompany.com/online/14/one.html>).

Nair, K. *A Higher Standard of Leadership: Lessons from the Life of Gandhi.* San Francisco: Berrett-Koehler, 1994.

Pfeffer, J. *Competitive Advantage Through People: Unleashing the Power of the Work Force.* Boston: Harvard Business School Press, 1994.

Rokeach, M. *The Nature of Human Values.* New York: Free Press, 1973

Samovar, Larry A., and Jack Mills. *Oral Communication: Speaking Across Cultures,* 10th ed. Boston: McGraw-Hill, 1998.

Schwartz, Andrew, E. *Delegating Authority.* Hauppauge, NY: Barron's Educational Series, 1992.

Senge, Peter M., Charlotte Roberts, Richard B. Ross, Bryan J. Smith, and Art Kleiner. *The Fifth Discipline Fieldbook: Strategies and Tools for Building a Learning Organization.* New York: Currency Doubleday, 1994.

Shannon, C., and W. Weaver. *The Mathematical Theory of Communication.* Urbana: University of Illinois Press, 1948.

Shipper, Frank, and John E. Dillard, Jr. "A Study of Impending Derailment and Recovery of Middle Managers Across Career Stages." *Human Resource Management* 39(4) (Winter 2000): 331–345.

Silberman, Mel. *PeopleSmart: Developing Your Interpersonal Intelligence.* San Francisco: Berrett-Koehler, 2000.

Staub, Robert E. *The Heart of Leadership: 12 Practices of Courageous Leaders.* Provo, UT: Executive Excellence Publishing, 1997.

Swanson, R. A. *Analysis for Improving Performance: Tools for Diagnosing Organizations and Documenting Workplace Expertise.* San Francisco: Berrett-Koehler, 1994.

Tajfel, H., and H. C. Turner. "The Social Identity Theory of Intergroup Behavior," in S. Worchel and W. G. Austin (eds.), *Psychology of Intergroup Relations,* 2d ed. Chicago: Nelson-Hall, 1985: 7–24.

Torbert, W. R. *Managing the Corporate Dream: Restructuring for Long-Term Success.* Homewood, IL: Dow Jones–Irwin, 1987.

Welch, J. with S. Welch. *Winning.* New York: HarperCollins, 2005.

Zey, M. *The Mentor Connection: Strategic Alliances Within Corporate Life.* New Brunswick, NJ: Transaction, 1990.

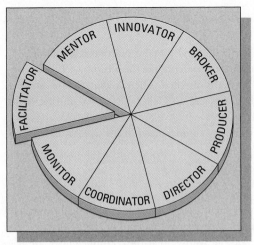

THE FACILITATOR ROLE

3

■ COMPETENCIES

Building Teams

Using Participative Decision Making

Managing Conflict

We have all spent a great deal of time working (and playing) in groups. Some of these groups seem to work very well together, and we sense that the group is able to accomplish something that none of the individuals could have accomplished on his or her own. In these cases, group members tend to identify with the group and may even surprise themselves in what they are able to accomplish individually when working with the group. Other groups, however, seem to function less effectively. In these cases, group members may dread spending time in the group and often feel that they could accomplish the task, or at least their part of the task, much more efficiently if they were left on their own.

Regardless of our past experiences working in groups, the expectation is that we can all expect to be spending a lot more time in groups. Organizational improvement processes, such as total quality management and process reengineering, rely heavily on work teams. In addition, organizations are relying more and more on project teams and task forces, as well as other types of ad hoc, informal work groups, to help solve organizational problems. Increasingly, people from different areas of the organization are being brought together to deal with issues with the expectation that by sharing their differing perspectives they will be able to develop a solution or an approach that none of the individuals could have imagined on their own. The message is clear: Regardless of our job title, whether or not we are labeled as a managerial leader, we must all learn how to increase our skills as members of groups.

In this chapter we will focus on the role of the facilitator. The **facilitator role,** which falls in the human relations model of the competing values framework, focuses on the relationship between a managerial leader and his or her work group. In this role, the

65

manager fosters collective effort, builds cohesion and morale, and manages interpersonal conflict. The facilitator uses some of the same competencies as the mentor, such as listening and being empathetic and sensitive to the needs of others. The role of facilitator, however, centers around the manager's work with groups and the Collaborate action imperative that is central to the human relations model.

In this chapter we will focus on three key competencies of the facilitator:

Competency 1　　Building Teams
Competency 2　　Using Participative Decision Making
Competency 3　　Managing Conflict

Each of these competencies requires the manager to balance individual needs with group needs in order to create and maintain a positive climate in the work group. As you work through this chapter, however, you will see that these competencies are relevant to all group members, not just the individual who is given the title of leader.

Competency 1　Building Teams

ASSESSMENT　Are You a Team Player?[1]

Objective　As we saw in Chapter 2 with the Johari window, sometimes the images that we have of ourselves are not the same as the images that others have of us. One of the objectives of all the assessments in this text is to help you develop a more accurate picture of yourself. The critical thinking technique introduced in Chapter 1 for identifying claims, grounds, and warrants can be an effective tool when completing the assessments in the text.

Directions　The following assessment instrument asks you to examine your behavior as a team member in organizational settings. For each pair of items, place a checkmark in the space in the column that best identifies how you behave in a working group at school, in student or community groups, or on your job.

	Very like me	Somewhat like me	Both describe me	Somewhat like me	Very like me	
Flexible in own ideas		✓			✗	Set in my own ideas
Open to new ideas		✗✓				Avoid new ideas
Listen well to others	✗			✓		Tune out others
Trusting of others				✓	✗	Not trusting of others
Prefer to raise differences and discuss them	✗				✓	Prefer to avoid discussing differences

[1]*Adapted from* training material for Income Maintenance Supervisors, Special Topics Workshop: "Motivation, Teambuilding, and Enhancing Morale," Professional Development Program, Rockefeller College of Public Affairs and Policy, State University of New York at Albany. Used with permission.

	Very like me	Somewhat like me	Both describe me	Somewhat like me	Very like me	
Readily contribute in group meetings	✓	___	___	___	✗	Hold back from contributing in group meetings
Concerned with what happens to others	___	___	✓	___	✗	Not concerned with what happens to others
Fully committed to tasks	___	___	✗	✓	___	Have little commitment to tasks
Willing to help others to get the job done	✓	___	___	___	✗	Prefer to stick to my own task or job description
Share leadership with group	✗	___	___	___	✓	Maintain full control of group
Encourage others to participate	___	___	✗	✓	___	Expect others to participate without encouragement
Group needs come before my individual needs	___	✗	✓	___	___	My individual needs come before group needs

Discussion Questions

1. In what ways do these team behaviors agree with your concept of team membership? How do they differ?

2. What strengths do you think you have working on a team? Weaknesses?

3. Are there times when you have performed more effectively as a team member? Alternatively, have there been times when you did not fully contribute as a team member? If so, what events or circumstances made you behave differently in the different situations?

4. In thinking about your past experiences working in groups, do you think that the people who have worked with you in the past see you as you see yourself? If not, what grounds and warrants would they use to contradict your claims?

Reflection

Two points should be made about this assessment exercise. First, it is not difficult to see that the items on the left are more reflective of team-oriented behaviors than the items on the right. As a result, there is some concern that responses may reflect social desirability bias—the tendency some people have to respond to questions based on what they think the "right" answer is, rather than based on their own opinions or behaviors. Asking respondents to think about the grounds and warrants that they would use to justify their responses may help to increase the accuracy of their responses.

A second important point is to recognize that these assessments are intended as a starting point, rather than an end point. If your assessment suggests that you are not a team player, does that mean that you are doomed to fail in a team-based organization? Of course not! It just means that you may need to focus more attention on developing certain team skills such as trusting others and raising differences in a team setting.

LEARNING   Building Teams

Bill Dyer, an expert on teams, often tells a story about an exchange with an audience of managers. At a conference, he asked approximately 300 managers whether they felt that teamwork and cooperation were essential in their organization and in their work unit. Without exception, managers reported that teamwork was essential. Dyer then asked how many were currently conducting programs to ensure that their team was functioning effectively—fewer than 25 percent responded positively. Finally, Dyer asked how many of their bosses were currently working on developing their team. At the third question, the response fell to below 10 percent. If teamwork is so essential to the proper functioning of the work unit, why do so few managers actively engage in team-building programs?

There are many reasons why managers do not do team building. In some cases, they simply do not understand the potential benefits that can occur from having the work unit function as a team. In other cases, they do not have the knowledge and skills required to turn a work group into a team or may even believe that it is something that "just happens" without any effort. Toward the end of this section, we will look again at barriers to team building and how they can be overcome. First, we will take a closer look at work groups and work teams to see how they function and identify some team building approaches.

WORK GROUPS AND WORK TEAMS

We have all experienced times when we felt that we were working on a "team." That team may have been a sports team, a work-related group, or a group within a community organization. What were the characteristics of that group that made it a team? Probably, the group was well coordinated, everyone had a role to play, and there was a commitment to a common goal. While there is no commonly accepted definition of team, and there are probably as many definitions of teams as there are researchers who study how teams function, there is some consistency in the characteristics generally used to differentiate teams from other types of groups.

First, **the group must be committed to a common goal or purpose.** In *The Wisdom of Teams,* Katzenbach and Smith (1993) focus on having a meaningful purpose as part of the glue that holds the team together. It is the motivation that makes people want to contribute at their maximum ability. Just as important as having a common purpose, these authors assert, is that teams must have specific performance goals that are centered on the team work-product, the results. For example, teams at NASA had to quickly identify and agree to the materials and the design of the space capsules that would be used to bring rock and soil samples from Mars. Even though the conditions the capsule would encounter were uncertain, the engineers had to eventually settle on some final choice. Having an overarching sense of the goals of the project is what allowed the teams to agree on technical specifications without becoming bogged down in personal opinions and disputes (Dahle, 1999).

Second, **members of the group must have clear roles and responsibilities that are interdependent.** One of the key reasons for having people work together in a team is to be able to draw on the different knowledge, skills, and abilities that people bring to the workplace. In building a team, members must understand how they can draw on each other's experience, ability, and commitment in order to arrive at mutual goals. Moreover, task and outcome interdependence can benefit personal work outcomes and motivation (van der Vegt, Emans, and van de Vliert, 1998). Imagination Ltd., a British company that designs customer experiences, brings together teams with skills as diverse as choreography, architecture, and graphic design. These workers know that the most important task is to share information about how they are doing their individual jobs (Fishman, 2000). Everyone does not have to know how to do all the jobs, but everyone should be clear about who is being asked to do what. Perhaps more important, people need to fully understand how their personal efforts contribute to the team work product.

Third, **there is a communication structure that fosters the sharing of information.** The second characteristic indicated that one advantage of bringing people together to work in a team is that they can share the different, and sometimes unique, knowledge, skills, and abilities that they bring to the team. This can only happen, however, if people are willing to share their own ideas and listen carefully to the ideas of others. Larson and La Fasto (1989, p. 56) identify four characteristics of an effective communication structure: (1) The information is easily accessible; (2) the information that is available must be seen as coming from credible sources, (3) in meetings, people must be able to raise issues of concern that may not have been on the formal agenda, and (4) there must be a system for documenting issues that have been discussed and decisions that have been made. A corollary to these four characteristics is that the communication structure must be supported by a climate of trust. People must feel that it is safe to raise controversial or difficult issues without being accused of attacking the other team members. Again, the team cannot benefit from the diversity of ideas if there is no opportunity to openly discuss the different perspectives. Consolidated Diesel has created a communications structure that embodies these characteristics. When holding quarterly meetings with plant employees, one manager decided to switch from two 700-person meetings to fifteen smaller meetings. Such an arrangement encouraged people to ask many more questions, no matter how sensitive (Sittenfeld, 1999).

Finally, **the group must have a sense of mutual accountability.** In many ways, this characteristic flows from the first three. If the team has common goals and members have clear roles and responsibilities, team members will have a sense of commitment to one another. They will see themselves as integral parts of the whole, with each person performing in order for the whole to excel. Moreover, when one member of the team needs help, others are ready to provide that help so that the team can accomplish the goal. An extreme form of this integration is what Lipman-Blumen and Leavitt (1999) call "hot groups." These groups care about the work and center their efforts around the accomplishment of their goals. To that end, they protect the members of the group through thick and thin, in success and failure.

In this fourth characteristic, it is easy to see one of the paradoxes inherent in team functioning—that while each individual must have clear roles and responsibilities, each member must also be willing to take on the tasks of other team members in order to achieve the common performance goals. Thus, when team members are mutually accountable, they do not need to keep an "accounting system" of who has done what for whom. Individuals do not try to take personal credit for their efforts. Rather, they see their efforts as benefiting the team and, by definition, benefiting themselves. When all members understand what it means to be mutually accountable, no one takes advantage of other team members or becomes a free rider, and yet everyone reaps the benefits of the others' efforts.

Each of these four characteristics is essential to the effective functioning of the work team. The question that a managerial leader must ask, however, is: Does my work unit need to function as a team? That is, is it necessary for all members of the work unit to share a common goal or purpose? Does the nature of the work require people to be interdependent? In some sports teams, such as golf teams or gymnastics teams, individuals function quite independently. Although they may practice together and give each other pointers on how to improve their performance, there is no real need for coordination of effort. Other sports teams, such as basketball teams or volleyball teams, require a great deal of interaction and coordination among team members. Players must be in constant communication with each other; each player must be able to "predict" the next player's moves. The same is true of work teams. In some settings, individuals function independently and the work unit would not likely benefit from attempts to turn the work group into a work team. In many settings, however, the work depends on individuals working together and using one another's experiences, abilities, and commitments. In these cases, the managerial leader, in the role of facilitator, must make special efforts to help the work group develop into a work team. In this chapter we will focus primarily on team-building efforts that help team members clarify their roles, responsibilities, and expectations.

ROLES OF TEAM MEMBERS

As was noted earlier in the discussion of the team characteristics, team members usually have specific, and sometimes very specialized, roles. A **role** is a set of expectations held by the individual and relevant others about how that individual should act in a given situation. For example, in basketball, the point guard is expected to bring the ball down the court and set up the play; the center is expected to get under the basket and to rebound. In the workplace, an employee's role is defined by the specific tasks he or she is expected to perform. For example, in a factory there are production managers, machine operatives, and repair persons. In addition, there are health and personnel specialists, accountants and financial managers, maintenance staff, secretaries, and office clerks. Each of these individuals has a specialized role.

In pulling a new team together, people are usually expected to perform somewhat different roles on the team. Therefore, it is important to think about the specific competencies that people can bring to the task. These may be technical competencies, referring to substantive knowledge, skills, and abilities; or they may be personal competencies, referring to qualities, skills, and abilities to help the team work together. Some organizations, such as Context Integration, have developed a Web-based knowledge-management system to help employees identify who can be a resource for solving a technical problem (Salter, 1999).

In addition to the specific or unique competencies that can be used to select team members, team leaders might also consider general characteristics that all team members should possess.

For example, the Mayo Center centers their patient care around teams that are guided by the motto "The best interest of the patient is the only interest to be considered" (Roberts, 1999, p. 156). Teams are assembled and disassembled to achieve this goal, and doctors are paid a set salary to avoid incentives or penalties for referrals or consulting with colleagues. Thus, the team is composed of specialists who know why they are there and what to do. Such an example suggests that whether we focus on technical or personal competencies, unique abilities or general characteristics that everyone on the team should possess, one of the important responsibilities of the manager, as facilitator, is to provide role clarity for his or her employees—to make clear what is expected of each individual performing on the team.

ROLE CLARITY AND ROLE AMBIGUITY

Role clarity implies the absence of two stressful conditions: *role ambiguity* and *role conflict*. Role ambiguity occurs when an individual does not have enough information about what he or she should be doing, what are appropriate ways of interacting with others, or what are appropriate behaviors and attitudes. Consider the following story about four people: Everybody, Somebody, Anybody, and Nobody.

There was an important job to be done and Everybody was asked to do it. Anybody could have done it, but Nobody did it. Somebody got angry about that because it was Everybody's job. Everybody thought Anybody could do it, but Nobody realized that Everybody wouldn't do it. It ended up that Everybody blamed Somebody when actually Nobody asked Anybody.

New employees, who are not familiar with the work unit's norms and procedures, often experience role ambiguity if their manager does not clarify for them what is expected in their job. New managers, making the transition from worker to manager, also often experience role ambiguity because their role expectations have changed.

Role conflict occurs when an individual perceives information regarding his or her job to be inconsistent or contradictory. For example, if manager X tells employee Y to perform task A, and then manager X's boss tells employee Y to stop what he or she is doing and to perform task B, the employee is likely to experience role conflict.

There are several potential sources of role conflict. Role conflict may occur when one or more individuals with whom an employee interact sends conflicting messages about what is expected. It can occur when an individual plays multiple roles that have conflicting expectations. For example, first-line managers represent their organization to their employees, informing them of rules and regulations as well new policies and procedures. Managers, however, are also employees. In the employee role they may disagree with an organizational policy or directive. Role conflict can also occur when an individual's own morals and values conflict with the organization's mission or policies and procedures. For example, an environmentally minded advertising executive might find it difficult to accept a contract with a company that produces toxic or nuclear wastes as a side effect of its primary production of goods. Role conflict may also occur when the expectations for a given role exceed the available time to complete those tasks. This is also sometimes referred to as *role overload* (Coverman, 1989; Katz and Kahn, 1978).

Team leaders sometimes feel role conflict because they have not yet learned the new skills required of team leaders and think they are supposed to behave as "the boss." In traditional organizations, managers were given both authority and responsibility for making decisions. But, as discussed above, the value of using teams results from the team's ability to use the unique knowledge and skills that people bring to the team. Team leaders need to learn how to share power, how to decide when they should be "in charge" and when they should let others take charge (see Competency 2, Using Participative Decision Making, later in this chapter), and that it is reasonable for them to not know everything. Put another way, team leaders need to learn the new set of expectations that employees and the organization have for managers (Dumaine, 1991).

Team-building efforts that focus on clarifying roles help everyone in the work unit or work team understand what others expect. Later in this chapter we will present specific team-building techniques that focus on the clarification of roles. First, however, we discuss three general types of roles that employees play in teams: two that help the team to accomplish its objective and one that hinders the team.

TASK AND GROUP MAINTENANCE ROLES VS. SELF-ORIENTED ROLES

Task and group maintenance roles focus on two necessary components of effective team functioning (Benne and Sheats, 1948; Dyer, 1995). In a task role, one's behaviors are focused on *what* the team is to accomplish. Performing in a task role is sometimes referred to as having a task orientation, or being task oriented. In a group maintenance role, one's behaviors are focused on *how* the team will accomplish its task. Performing in a group maintenance role is sometimes referred to as having a group maintenance, or process, orientation, or being process oriented. Because many maintenance activities focus on the team members and how they interact, some texts refer to people in those roles as being relationship-oriented.

A person may perform several different types of activities when taking on a task role. For example, a person may get the group moving by offering new ideas and suggesting ways to approach a task or a problem, or by simply reminding others that there is a task to be performed. In meetings, persons in the task role may raise or clarify important facts and opinions based on personal knowledge and experiences; encourage others to raise or clarify important facts and opinions based on their knowledge and experiences; pull together the range of ideas discussed in the group and restate them concisely, offering a decision or conclusion for the group to consider; or help the group to assess the quality of its suggestions or solutions, testing to see if the ideas will work in reality. A person in a task role also often brings together, schedules, and combines the activities of others.

Likewise, we can identify different types of activities associated with a group maintenance orientation. People in this role tend to support team members, building cohesiveness and trust among them, alleviating tension, and helping members find ways to see past their differences so that they can continue to work together. They also try to maintain open discussion and encourage others to pursue their ideas and suggestions. People who play this role in a team also often provide the group with feedback on how the group is functioning and suggest processes to ensure that all group members have sufficient opportunities to share their ideas and feelings.

Clearly these types of behaviors are consistent with the four characteristics of teams described above. There is, however, another type of role that some people may try to play in the team that is inconsistent with these team characteristics. This is a self- or individual-oriented role. This role tends to be counterproductive to effective group functioning, drawing attention away from the team to personal needs that are not germane to the team's task or process. People in this role may oppose other members' ideas and suggestions, using hidden agendas to hinder group movement, or try to take over the group by manipulating the group or individual members and by interrupting others. They may also try to draw attention to themselves, either boasting of personal accomplishments, or acting in ways that indicate a feeling of superiority over other team members, or separating themselves from the group and maintaining a distance from other group members.

Sometimes, people take on task and group maintenance roles naturally. You may find that one person consistently tries to bring the group back to its task. Another may be good at making sure that everyone has had an opportunity for input. Yet another may make sure that everyone knows what is to be accomplished by the next meeting and who has specific tasks to perform. The key is to make sure that task and group maintenance roles are appropriately balanced and that self-oriented roles are minimized. If the group tends to find itself completely focused on completing the task, but only a few team members are contributing, team members must ask themselves how they can get one or more people to play the group maintenance role. Alternatively, if the group is always focused on making sure that everyone is getting along, but work is not getting done in a timely manner, the group must think about how it can increase its task behaviors without sacrificing people's commitment to the team. Finally, if the group is not able to accomplish its tasks because it is constantly hindered by one or more individuals who are more concerned about their personal gains or accomplishments, rather than the team's work product, the team must work with these individuals to get them to see how they are hindering the team (see Competency 3, Managing Conflict), as well as to try to get them to accept the team's goals and purpose as their own. In the next section we look at how the appropriate balance between task and group maintenance behaviors may depend on how long the team has worked together in general or on a particular task or problem.

TEAM DEVELOPMENT AND TEAM BUILDING

When a new work group forms, or an established work group undertakes a new task or problem, the group needs to be designed, staffed, structured, and trained before it can transform into a high performance team (Sundstrom, 1999). For example, if team members do not know one another well or have never worked together before, it is important for them to get acquainted and to discuss what competencies each person brings to the team and what types of preferences people have regarding how to approach the task. Alternatively, when an established team takes on a new project, team members are likely to have a good sense of the different competencies people have but still need to discuss various unique perspectives they have on the problem or different approaches that different team members may think are appropriate for the particular project. As you will see, we can identify four stages of team development, each of which requires team members to give different emphasis to the various task and maintenance behaviors discussed above. The leader of a team (and also the team members) must be aware of how the team's needs evolve during these stages of development and encourage group members to perform different aspects of the task and group maintenance behaviors at the different stages.

STAGE 1: TESTING

At stage 1 the goals of the group are established and the task is defined. Group members ask themselves what the purpose of this team is and whether they want to be a member. (Of course, in most work-related situations, group members do not have a choice about their membership.) To create a climate where people can share ideas and feelings and begin to identify and align with a common goal, the group leader should encourage members to offer new ideas and suggest ways to approach the task (task role) and should also make sure everyone's opinion is heard, creating a climate where people feel safe to offer opposing views (group maintenance role).

STAGE 2: ORGANIZING

At stage 2 the group establishes a structure. The group leader must emphasize the common purpose (task role) and establish norms and standards. In addition, the group must clarify issues regarding the sharing of information—how members will communicate with one another and what types of information needs to be shared. If the group has no appointed leader, one of the group members will often emerge as an informal leader in this stage. Sometimes several people are identified as leaders, some focusing more on tasks and others on group maintenance. So that group members may ask more specific questions about what the group will do and how they will do it, the leader should encourage group members to continually question and assess the quality of suggestions and potential solutions (task role) and to resolve differences by helping others understand the differing perspectives that people bring (group maintenance role).

STAGE 3: ESTABLISHING INTERDEPENDENCE

Individual talents are drawn out and used and attention is focused on how to coordinate individual efforts in stage 3. The group leader should focus on member interdependence, discourage competition, and encourage individuals to take on informal leadership roles. The key question group members ask themselves concerns how they can coordinate their individual actions to accomplish the team's goals more effectively. At this stage, focusing on the task, the team needs members to raise and/or clarify important points and differences in perspective, and then to pull together and summarize or synthesize the range of ideas that have been expressed (task roles). Similarly, group maintenance behaviors that help the team to succeed focus on helping members see how the differing perspectives can potentially lead to a more creative or more productive proposal for action, and then encouraging others to pursue different ideas and suggestions.

STAGE 4: PRODUCING AND EVALUATING

If the group has successfully managed the first three stages, by stage 4 it should have transformed into a team and should be working together smoothly. Team members should be committed to a common goal or purpose, have a clear understanding of the different roles and responsibilities of individual team members, have a communication structure that allows for an open sharing of different perspectives, and have a sense of mutual accountability. At this stage, team members begin to evaluate the product of the team effort and also how well the individuals are working together as a team. To solicit input from all group members in evaluating goals, task output, productivity, and team process, the leader should encourage team members to ask questions regarding how it has approached its task and offer suggestions for improving team performance (task role) as well as feedback and observations on the team process (group maintenance role).

Again, one can see how the role that the team leader plays in helping the team develop is both critical and paradoxical. On the one hand, the team leader sets the climate and must be seen as someone with a strong personal vision. On the other hand, the leader must clearly demonstrate a belief in the team's purpose and in the notion that each person's contribution to the team is equally valuable. Thus, team leaders must simultaneously lead and give team members the opportunity to take a leadership role, suggest directions and listen to others' suggestions, and be appropriately involved in the day-to-day work while not micromanaging. In addition, they must find ways to value differences and reward successes, while never allowing some individuals to shine at the expense of the other team members. In the next two sections, we suggest some specific approaches to team building, approaches that build on the notion of maintaining a balance between task and group maintenance focus in the team.

FORMAL APPROACHES TO TEAM BUILDING

Although a team may eventually reach the producing and evaluating stage of its development, it will likely cycle back through the various previous stages as it meets new challenges. Indeed, most work groups experience frequent, if not constant, change. Sometimes these changes are associated with new group members; sometimes they are associated with new tasks and responsibilities. Sometimes the changes are the result of changes in the group's external environment, in which case the group must adjust in order to adapt to a new focus of the organization or new trends in the industry. At this point it is often important to "stop the action" and involve the group in formal team-building activities.

You may have heard the expression, "When you are up to your hips in alligators, you forget that you came to drain the swamp." Sometimes it is important to step out of the swamp and think about what you are doing. Formal team-building activities allow the group to put aside the work of the day, evaluate how well the group is performing as a team, and make any necessary changes. But team-building activities should not be seen as isolated experiences or events. Rather, they should be part of an integrated approach to team building that involves regularly scheduled sessions to allow the team to address whatever issues it is currently facing (Dyer, 1995). At Whole Foods Market, a natural foods grocery chain, teams have clear performance goals and meet at least once a month to share information and solve problems (Fishman, 1996).

When team members are interdependent, there is a need for effective communication among them. Periodic meetings that focus on information exchange may be the most effective way to enhance communication among team members. Many managers hold periodic off-site meetings to help keep employees enthusiastic and energized. The key is to encourage input from everyone regarding problems they are experiencing and questions or concerns they might have. Managers can also bring information about anticipated changes to these meetings. Sometimes it is important to clarify how much and what types of information individuals need in order to perform their jobs effectively. A group meeting to examine current information flows, and whether these flows meet each individual's needs, can enhance team functioning. (The section on Using Participative Decision Making later in this chapter will provide more information on how to conduct effective meetings.)

A fairly simple, but effective, team-building technique involves setting aside a day or two, away from the worksite if possible, to examine three questions: (1) What do we do well? (2) What areas need improvement? (3) What are the barriers to improvement? Starting with an examination of what the team does well reminds the group that while there may be some problems or issues to deal with, the team also has strengths upon which to build. This establishes a positive climate for the team-building session and gets people involved in the discussion. Depending on how much time there is between team-building sessions, the list of areas for improvement may be short or long. This is a good reason to schedule regular team-building sessions. If the list is too long, the team may need to set priorities regarding which issues should be handled first. The last question reminds the team that team building is more than short-term problem solving. It involves taking a larger look at the system and examining specific problems to determine whether they are isolated events or the result of an underlying structural issue. If there is an underlying structural issue, it will likely need to be dealt with before the improvement can be made. The final team product of such a session should be an action plan to deal with whatever problems or issues are raised in the session. The action plan should include a statement of objectives (what the team wants to accomplish with this improvement effort), a time frame for addressing the issue, and a clear assignment of who is responsible for organizing the improvement effort (remember Anybody, Everybody, Nobody, and Somebody!).

As mentioned earlier, one key to effective team functioning is having each team member know his or her role and how that role fits into the larger team effort. Several techniques are available. Role analysis technique (RAT) focuses one by one on the various roles in the group. This technique was first used by KP Engineering Corporation, a manufacturer of welding electronics, and is useful when team members are performing different functions (Dayal and Thomas, 1968). In this activity, the person performing in the role to be analyzed states his or her job as he or she sees it. Other group members then comment on and make suggestions for changes in this job description. The individual in that role then lists expectations of other members who affect how the job is performed.

There is open discussion until agreement is reached on a job description and the associated expectations of others. This process is then repeated until everyone has had his or her job analyzed.

A similar technique is role negotiation (Harrison, 1972). Here all members simultaneously list what expectations they have of others in the work group, focusing on what they feel others should do more of or better, do less of or stop doing, and maintain as is. Lists are exchanged, and individuals negotiate with one another until all team members agree on those behaviors that should be changed and those that should be maintained. A master list of agreements is later circulated to the group.

Responsibility charting (Beckhard and Harris, 1977) involves creating a large chart that lists the group's decisions and activities along the left side of the chart and each employee's name along the top of the chart (see Figure 3.1). Codes indicate whether the individual has the responsibility for the activity or decision (R), has the right to approve or veto a decision (A-V), provides support or resources for the activity or decision (S), or needs to be informed of the activity or decision (I). The chart allows the group to see explicitly whether some members of the group are overloaded and some could be given additional tasks and responsibilities.

FIGURE 3.1
Responsibility chart.

Source: R. Beckhard and R.T. Harris, *Organizational Transitions: Managing Complex Change.* Reading, MA: Addison-Wesley, 1977, p. 78, Figure 6.1. Used with permission.

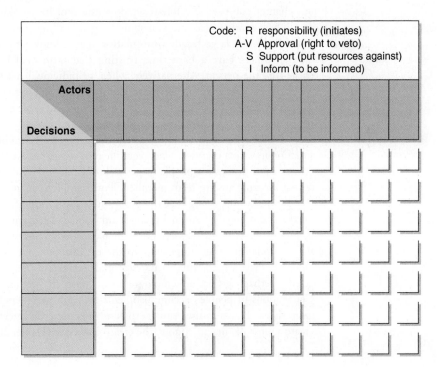

Code: R responsibility (initiates)
A-V Approval (right to veto)
S Support (put resources against)
I Inform (to be informed)

Actors

Decisions

INFORMAL APPROACHES TO TEAM BUILDING

As indicated, team building is not an event, but an ongoing process. In between formal team-building sessions, the team can use informal techniques to encourage team development. Often when people think about team building they assume that it has to do with getting people to like each other, but as Dyer (1995) notes, "The fundamental emotional condition in a team is not liking but *trusting*. People do not need to like one another as friends to be able to work together, but they do need to trust one another" (p. 53, emphasis added). They need to trust that other team members are equally invested in accomplishing the team's goals; they need to trust that other team members will share information appropriately; and they need to trust that other team members will be willing to work out disagreements in a professional manner.

How do you establish trust among team members? First and foremost, team members need to understand that each person's willingness to trust other team members will likely be influenced by that person's observations of the other team members' actions. If team members consistently produce and are willing to help others when they need assistance, trust is likely to develop among the team members. One key element here is ensuring that each person believes in the common goals and so is willing to "go the extra mile" when necessary.

Second, a managerial leader must work to create an atmosphere in which it is safe to trust others. Trust is a behavior that re-creates itself. That is, team members are more likely to trust other team members when they themselves feel trusted—when they feel that others are being open and honest in their communications. In the previous chapter you used the Johari window as a tool for thinking about self-awareness. The Johari window also tells you something about how you relate to others. When an individual has a large façade (information that is known to the self but unknown to others), others have a hard time trusting that individual because they do not feel trusted by the person. Alternatively, when an individual has been candid and sincere with others, that person will more likely be seen as approachable and trustworthy. Thus a managerial leader must begin by trusting the team members and set an example by sharing key information with the team.

Finally, although we indicated that the purpose of team building is not to create a situation in which everyone likes everyone else, we do believe that social interaction can create opportunities for people to get to know each other, thereby creating greater potential for trust among team members. For example, a manager may encourage group interaction by suggesting that the group meet for a meal after work, or during a meal break, where possible. Annual picnics and holiday celebrations, as well as celebrations of personal events, such as birthdays or parenthood, communicate to employees that they as individuals are important to the organization. Christine Rochester, "Ambassador" at Play, a marketing firm, uses small gestures to help her employees feel energized—perhaps giving an employee a car wash or buying milkshakes for a team. Celebrations of people's accomplishments let team members know that their work is appreciated. Play also uses rituals, such as opening every meeting with a drumroll, to create a sense of "magic" among the creative workers (Dahle, 2000).

BARRIERS TO TEAM BUILDING

When we began this section, we noted that team building is not as regularly practiced in many organizations as one might expect, given what we know about the potential for team performance. What we need to ask here is: What are the barriers to team building? How do we overcome them? Of course, one important reason why team-building programs are not more widely used in work organizations is time. Often the need to get the job done leads work groups to focus on specific tasks rather than on planning and coordination. Further, when group members focus on their own parts, they sometimes find it difficult to see the whole picture or to recognize that they are not currently seeing that picture. There is no way to give people more time. Team members and organizational leaders must see the value of team building and recognize that this is a long-term investment. A day or two spent away from the worksite may save the team much more in both time and money in the long run.

A second reason may be a lack of knowledge about how to build a team. Some people assume that "team" is something that does or does not happen. They may not realize the many and varied techniques that can enhance team functioning. It is a manager's responsibility to examine the need for team building in his or her work unit and, if such a need exists, to determine which formal or informal approaches would be most effective.

A final reason—but perhaps the most important one—is organizational culture. Effective team building requires an environment that values differing opinions and open resolution of conflict (see the last competency in this chapter, Managing Conflict). In an organization in which there is mistrust or negative feelings among coworkers, it is difficult to establish a team spirit. In cases such as these, one should consider bringing in an objective outside consultant to do formal team-building or organization development activities.

Similarly, the organization may not reward team behaviors or team-building activities. An organization may prescribe team building for its employees, but if managers are not evaluated on the implementation of such activities, there may be little incentive to take the time to do team building. In a similar fashion, some organizations will hold team-building sessions but then reward employees for their individual performance. If a sales representative is compensated based on individual sales, there is little incentive to share "best practices" with others in the work unit. Here, organizations need to examine their performance and reward systems to ensure that they do not run counter to team-building efforts. Further, upper-level managers need to demonstrate by their own actions their commitment to and support for team-building activities (Dyer, 1995).

ANALYSIS   Stay-Alive Inc.[2]

Objective   Effective managers need to master the use of team-building techniques not only when they are creating a new team, but also when they begin working with an existing team. The objective of this case analysis is to give you an opportunity to identify ways in which the members of Stay-Alive, Inc. applied (or failed to apply) key principles concerning effective team building.

[2]*Adapted from* Judith R. Gordon, *A Diagnostic Approach to Organizational Behavior* (Boston: Allyn & Bacon, 1983), pp. 304–305.

Directions   Read the case study and respond to the questions that follow.

Stay-Alive Inc., a small not-for-profit social service agency, hired Jean Smith to design, implement, and coordinate halfway house living programs for young adults.

When Jean arrived, the agency had an informal organization with little hierarchical structure and extensive participative decision making. The prevailing ideology that shaped virtually all decisions and interpersonal relationships was that a democratic system would be most effective and would lead to a higher level of job satisfaction for workers than would a more rigid hierarchical structure. The staff members attended at least five meetings weekly. Incredibly, the group devoted the majority of time at each one to exploring interpersonal problems.

Most staff were young and had recently finished college. They often remarked that they sought a place to belong and feel accepted. Stay-Alive met that need in many ways: The group acted as a surrogate family for many employees. Even their life outside of work revolved heavily around activities with other Stay-Alive members. Salaries were low, and so the agency hired inexperienced people. Although the employees were bright, enthusiastic, and motivated, some were just beginning to develop the skills needed for effective performance in their jobs. Organizational leaders, therefore, defined success on the job primarily in terms of the employees' ability to relate well to others at work and only secondarily in terms of their ability to work with clients.

Within three months of her arrival, Jean submitted her plan for implementing the program. Her manager praised it, calling it a remarkable piece of work. Soon after the program was implemented, however, it became clear that it was not working. Still, the agency members responded by patting her on the back and telling her what a great job she was doing. Jean soon became frustrated and angry and left the agency.

Discussion Questions   1. Was Stay-Alive Inc. an effective team? Why or why not?

2. How were task and maintenance behaviors being performed in this agency?

3. Rather than leaving, how might Jean have helped Stay-Alive to become a more effective organization?

4. What other suggestions would you give to the management team at Stay-Alive to help them to improve?

5. If you were the director of Stay-Alive, what issues would you want to see addressed in a team-building session?

Reflection   Of the people involved in the Stay-Alive, Inc. case, it is possible that only Jean viewed the problems with the program implementation as a "failure." Look back at the scenario—what evidence is there to suggest that the members of the organization were really interested in making changes to the organization? As we shall see in the Innovator Role (Chapter 8), managing change in an organization depends in part on our ability to understand the existing organization culture.

PRACTICE   "Students-As-Customers" Task Force

Objective   When a group is given an assignment, the members often have a tendency to jump directly into trying to perform the task, rather than spending time in the Testing, Organizing, and Establishing Interdependence stages described in the text. What may appear at first to be a way to save time, however, often turns out to result in a much less efficient process. This exercise gives you a chance to practice the activities described in the first three stages of the team development model. To ensure that everyone will have some expertise to add to the team, the focus of the task force relates to gathering "customer satisfaction" data from university students.

Direction   Divide into groups of approximately six people. Each group will compose a new university task force that is part of the university's total quality management effort. Read the memo from the university president and begin your first meeting according to the suggested agenda provided below. Respond to the agenda questions as if you yourself were attending the meeting. When your task force has completed the two tasks on the agenda, each person should individually respond to the discussion questions. Your instructor will then lead a large group discussion.

Task Force Meeting Agenda

1. Briefly discuss the president's charge.

2. Discuss the following questions:
   (a) What unique skills or abilities does each person bring to the task force?
   (b) What skills do members share in common?
   (c) What specific team or organizational strengths does each person possess?
   (d) What team or organizational weaknesses or areas of discomfort does each person possess?
   (e) How can the team make best use of each individual's skills and abilities?
   (f) How can team members benefit from their time on the task force?

MEMORANDUM

FROM: President Adams
TO: "Students as Customers" Task Force
SUBJECT: Task Force Charge
DATE: January 22, 2006

First, I want to welcome you back to a new semester and thank you for agreeing to sit on this exciting new task force. I think you will find this task force rewarding, and the university will certainly benefit from your input.

As you know, our university has been working since the fall semester with a team of management consultants to develop a total quality management (TQM) program on this campus. As part of this effort, we are beginning to look at "customer satisfaction," recognizing students as our customers. We believe that the best people to help us decide how to gather customer satisfaction data are the students themselves. The members of this task force have been carefully chosen from among our best students. Your charge is to make a recommendation, by the end of this semester, regarding how we might gather such data. You are, of course, free to choose from among many available data-gathering approaches, for example, surveys, interviews, focus groups, and use of existing course evaluation data. You should make your recommendations based on your assessment of how we can get the best information.

I look forward to seeing your recommendations.

Discussion Questions   1. How satisfied were you with the group's discussion? Did you feel comfortable discussing your team and organizational strengths and weaknesses in this first meeting of the group?

2. How well did the task force do at discussing how it could make best use of each person's abilities? Did everyone participate in the discussion?

3. Think about the stages of team development. What elements of stage 1 (testing) did you accomplish in your task force? What elements of stage 2 (organizing) or stage 3 (establishing interdependence) were accomplished? What member behaviors provided support for the team's development?

4. What issues still need to be dealt with to allow this task force to develop as a team?

5. Did a leader emerge? If so, what specific events identified that person as a leader? Who in the group might have emerged as a team leader at a later time?

Reflection   Even when specifically asked to focus on team development activities, some people tend to gravitate toward trying to "solve the problem" rather than focusing on how to *approach* solving the problem. Even for individual decision making, this can lead to jumping to conclusions, but it is especially problematic in team decision making because it may result in decisions that do not reflect the wisdom of all the members of the team.

APPLICATION   Team-Building Action Plan

Objective   Now that you have had a chance to read about team building and practice some team-development activities, it is time to put your learning into practice. The objective of this exercise is to give you a chance to improve the effectiveness of a team on which you are a member.

Directions   Think about a student group, a work unit, a task force, or a committee of which you are currently a member, where you could do some informal or formal team building.

1. Consider carefully which team-building activities are most appropriate. For example, you may feel that the roles and responsibilities of group members are not clear and that you would like to try one of the role clarification techniques. Or you may decide you need to personally practice using task and maintenance roles in group meetings. If you are a group leader, think about whether it is appropriate to meet privately with individuals who have been exhibiting self-oriented behaviors.

2. Write a one to two page memo to your team members describing your concerns about the team. Include a proposed action plan for team-building activities. Remember to use grounds and warrants to justify why you think the team would benefit from participating in these team-building activities.

Reflection   In writing your memo, did you remember to use what you learned about communicating effectively from Chapter 2? Did you leave any "left-hand column" issues unmentioned—what do you think the long-term impact of that decision will be for your team's effectiveness?

Competency 2   Using Participative Decision Making

ASSESSMENT   Meeting Evaluation[3]

Objective   Meetings are a ubiquitous part of organization life. Common as they are, many people find them to be such a bad experience that books, both serious (Doyle and Straub's *How to Make Meetings Work,* [1986] and Steibel's *The Manager's Guide to Effective Meetings [2001]*), more lighthearted (Lencioni's

---

[3]*Adapted from* Frank Burns and Robert L. Gragg, "Brief Diagnostic Instruments," in *The 1981 Annual Handbook for Group Facilitators,* John E. Jones and J. William Pfeiffer (eds.) (San Diego: University Associates, Inc. 1981), p. 89. Used with permission.

Death by Meeting [2004]), and completely rebellious (Adams's *Always Postpone Meetings with Time-Wasting Morons [1994]*), have been written about them. The objective of this assessment is to give you some insight into the effectiveness of the meetings in which you have participated lately.

Directions Think of a meeting of an organization, a study group, or a meeting at work that you recently attended. If you have not recently attended any such meetings, think about the "meetings" of your groups when working on small-group exercises in this or other classes.

Rate the overall effectiveness of the meeting as: very effective (5), moderately effective (4), neither effective nor ineffective (3), moderately ineffective (2), or very ineffective (1). Then respond to the items below using the following scale:

Scale

Strongly Disagree	Disagree	Undecided	Agree	Agree Strongly
1	2	3	4	5

_5_ 1. I was notified of this meeting in sufficient time to prepare for it.

_2_ 2. I understood why this meeting was held (e.g., information sharing, planning, problem solving, decision making, open discussion) and what specific outcomes were expected.

_2_ 3. I understood what was expected of me as a participant and what was expected of the other participants.

_4_ 4. I understood how the meeting was intended to flow (e.g., agenda, schedule, design) and when it would terminate.

_3_ 5. Most participants listened carefully to each other.

_4_ 6. Most participants expressed themselves openly, honestly, and directly.

_4_ 7. Agreements were explicit and clear, and conflicts were openly explored and constructively managed.

_4_ 8. The meeting generally proceeded as intended (e.g., the agenda was followed, it ended on time) and achieved its intended purpose.

_5_ 9. My participation contributed to the outcomes achieved by the meeting.

_3_ 10. Overall, I am satisfied with this meeting and feel that my time was well spent.

Scoring and Interpretation Add your responses to each of the questions and divide the sum by 10. The closer your score was to 5, the more your meeting could be considered very effective; the closer your score was to 1, the more your meeting could be considered very ineffective.

Discussion Questions 1. How close was your initial evaluation of the meeting to your rating based on the questions in the meeting-evaluation scale?

2. Review the meeting-evaluation scale. What were the meeting characteristics that made the meeting more effective? Less effective?

3. What were the specific events at the meeting that made the meeting more effective? Less effective?

4. How can you make your next meeting more effective?

Reflection Meetings are a fact of life so it is important to make sure that they add positive energy rather than negative energy to the workplace. People should not feel that attending meetings is preventing them from getting their work done. Meetings that are planned and run effectively should help us do our work, not detract from getting it completed.

LEARNING Using Participative Decision Making

In the past two decades, there has been increasing attention to a wide variety of techniques and practices that involve employees in organizational decision making. Extending the concept of democracy to the workplace (Weisbord, 1987), participative management techniques are built on the assumption that employees should have the opportunity to have input into decisions that affect their lives. More recently, some researchers have argued that although the participative management approach is consistent with national values of democratic decision making, the more compelling reasons for adopting this type of approach are economic—that organizations employing participative management approaches will have a competitive advantage (Lawler, 1992).

Indeed, largely as a result of global competition and other external pressures, organizations in both the public and private sectors have begun to experiment with a variety of approaches ranging from simply encouraging managers to listen to employees' ideas about work improvements; to creating large-scale participation programs such as quality circles, labor–management quality-of-work-life committees, and self-managed work teams; to implementing organization-wide changes to accommodate new work systems, policies, and procedures. In many cases, organizations that have adopted such changes have found that they have been able to lower costs and raise productivity; produce higher-quality products and services; and respond more quickly, as well as in more innovative ways, to the needs of customers. Moreover, they have found that their employees are more motivated and have a greater sense of organizational commitment (Kirkman and Rosen, 1999). For example, the General Electric jet engine plant in Durham, North Carolina, trusts its employees to make decisions about all aspects of the manufacturing process. With this model they have been able to reduce costs and defects while delivering on time (Fishman, 1999).

Today, few would dispute the notion that involving employees in organizational decisions that affect their lives makes both social and economic sense. The issue at hand is identifying which decisions affect employees' lives. At some level, all organizational decisions that have an impact on organizational performance will affect the lives of the employees. From an organizational perspective, two things are clear. First, in many situations front-line employees are closer to the information necessary to make a decision and should therefore be allowed to make those decisions. This is where organizations can gain competitive advantage by being able to respond more quickly to customer needs. Second, the more organizational information is shared with employees, the greater will be their ability to make decisions that are in the interest of the entire organization. At GE/Durham, workers learn to assemble all parts of an engine and also take turns serving on work councils that make decisions about all aspects of the business. For these roles, they are trained to understand everything from human resources skills to operations management. Thus, workers make decisions based not only on an understanding of how different jobs work but also on an understanding of the welfare of the whole organization (Fishman, 1999).

Nevertheless, there are times when it is unfeasible or inappropriate to involve employees in an organizational decision. Thus, managerial leaders need to be able to decide in specific circumstances whether it is appropriate to involve employees as well what issues need to be considered when involving employees. Although we have talked about the advantages to be gained by using participative approaches, we should be clear that participative decision making is not a single technique that can be universally applied to all situations. As indicated above, there are a wide variety of participation approaches, and managers can involve employees in making decisions in a variety of ways. Which way is most appropriate to use depends on the manager, the employees, the organization, and the nature of the decision itself.

A RANGE OF DECISION-MAKING STRATEGIES

Managers constantly encounter situations in which they must make decisions about their work units and their employees. Most often, the manager has the option of involving or not involving employees in these decisions. Indeed, even team leaders will encounter situations in which a decision must be made about the team and it is not certain that the entire team needs to be involved in the decision. In reality, the choice is not simply between involvement and no involvement. Rather, a wide range of options are available to the manager.

Tannenbaum and Schmidt (1973) were among the first to consider the process of participative decision making. They proposed that decision-making processes vary with respect to the amount of authority held by the boss and the amount of freedom held by employees; an increase in the authority held by the manager, by definition, results in a decrease in the amount of freedom held by employees (see Figure 3.2).

At one extreme of the continuum are processes that are considered to be boss-centered. In these situations, the manager makes the decision and announces it, or maybe

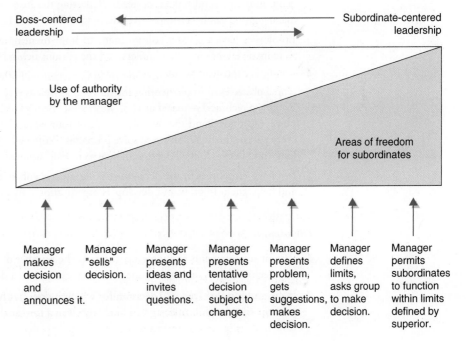

FIGURE 3.2 *Leadership-behavior continuum.*

Source: Reprinted by permission of *Harvard Business Review.* An exhibit from "How to Choose a Leadership Pattern" by Robert Tannenbaum and W. H. Schmidt, March/April 1958. Copyright © by the President and Fellows of Harvard College, all rights reserved. (May–June 1973), p. 164.

tries to sell the decision. At the other extreme are processes that are considered to be subordinate centered. In these situations, employees make decisions, generally within limits set by upper management. Between these two extremes is a series of options by which managers may elicit input from employees, involving them by asking them for ideas and suggestions. Similarly, Lawler (1986, 1992), referring to these two approaches as control oriented versus involvement oriented, discusses both advantages and disadvantages of each approach and indicates that the choice of management approach must be made within a context of sociocultural values, the nature of the work force, the type of product being produced, and the organization's external environment.

Choosing from the range of options available to managers regarding the extent to which employees should be involved in decisions requires a careful examination of the advantages and disadvantages associated with involving employees in the decision-making process as well as an analysis of the particular situation. We begin with a brief examination of the general advantages and disadvantages. Note that some of these parallel the advantages and disadvantages of using team processes discussed in the previous section.

Advantages

1. When more individuals are involved in the decision-making process, there is generally greater knowledge or expertise being brought to bear on the problem. Involving employees in the decision-making process increases the probability that important issues affecting the decision will surface.

2. When employees are involved in decisions, they tend to generate a wider range of values and perspectives, representing the range of issues and concerns at stake in the decision. Increasingly, we are aware that neither the labor force nor the marketplace is homogeneous in background, values, or needs. Reflecting the customer profile in the decision-making group can be a competitive advantage (Cox, 1993, Loden and Rosener, 1991).

3. Employees have a greater commitment to implementing a decision in which they were involved, because they understand the reasons behind the decision.

4. Employees involved in the decision-making process will often be able to identify potential obstacles to implementing the decision as well as ways to avoid them. Kathleen Rhodes, a technical manager at U.S. West, says, "Being a technical manager helps employees to understand the overall concept of [our work]. Plus, they have to tap into every part of the organization to solve problems. People who work in the front row for long enough can do it all because they've seen it all" (quoted in Lieber, 1999).

5. Involving employees in the decision-making process enhances their skills and abilities and helps them to grow and develop as organizational members.

Disadvantages

1. Participative decision making takes time. As the number of people who are involved in a decision increases, so does the time it takes to reach a decision.

2. If the group is involved in a decision for which it does not have the proper expertise, participative decision making will likely result in a low-quality decision.

3. If group meetings are not well structured, individuals with the appropriate expertise may fail to contribute to the discussion, whereas those with little or no knowledge may overcontribute and dominate the discussion.

4. When group members are overly cohesive, they may also become overly concerned with gaining consensus. This is a phenomenon known as groupthink (Janis, 1972). When groupthink occurs, group members avoid being critical of others' ideas and so cease to think objectively about the decision at hand or critically evaluate options.

WHO SHOULD PARTICIPATE—AND WHEN

Given the numerous advantages and disadvantages of participative decision making, how can a manager decide who should participate in which decisions? Vroom and Yetton (1973) created a model that allows managers to examine the questions of *when* to involve employees in the decision-making process; and when they decide to do so, *how* to do it most effectively. The model, shown in Figure 3.3, identifies key problem attributes and five decision-making strategies that can be classified as Autocratic (A), Consultative (C), or Group decision making (G). The five strategies are

AI You solve the problem or make the decision yourself, using information available to you at the time.

AII You obtain any necessary information from subordinates, then you decide on the solution to the problem yourself. In getting the information from them, you may or may not tell subordinates what the problem is. The role played by your subordinates in making the decision is clearly one of providing specific information that you request, rather than generating or evaluating solutions.

CI You share the problem with the relevant subordinates individually, getting their ideas and suggestions without bringing them together as a group. Then *you* make the decision. This decision may or may not reflect your subordinates' influence.

CII You share the problem with your subordinates in a group meeting. In this meeting you obtain their ideas and suggestions. Then, *you* make the decision which may or may not reflect your subordinates' influence.

GII You share the problem with your subordinates as a group. Together you generate and evaluate alternatives and attempt to reach agreement (consensus) on a solution. Your role is much like that of chairperson, coordinating the discussion, keeping it focused on the problem, and making sure that the critical issues are discussed. You do not try to influence the group to adopt "your" solution and are willing to accept and implement any solution that has the support of the entire group (Vroom and Jago 1974, p. 745).

Decision Tree

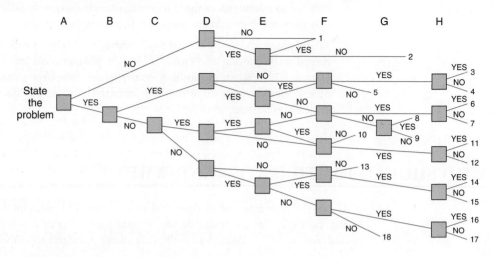

FIGURE 3.3 *Decision-making strategies for group problems.*

From Victor H. Vroom and Arthur G. Jago, "Decision Making as a Social Process: Normative and Descriptive Models of Leader Behavior," *Decision Sciences* (1974), 5, 745. Reprinted by permission of the Decision Sciences Institute, Georgia State University, Atlanta, Georgia.

Alternatives

1. AI, AII, CI, CII, GII
2. GII
3. AI, AII, CI, CII, GII
4. AI, AII, CI, CII, GII
5. AI, AII, CI, CII
6. GII
7. GII
8. CII
9. CI, CII
10. AII, CI, CII
11. AII, CI, CII, GII
12. AII, CI, CII, GII
13. CII
14. CII, GII
15. CII, GII
16. GI
17. GII
18. CII

Selecting the appropriate decision-making strategy requires the manager to ask eight questions about the problem attributes, focusing on (1) the required quality or rationality of the decision, (2) the necessity of group acceptance or commitment to the final decision, and (3) the time available to make the decision. Figure 3.3 shows the decision tree with the labels of the eight questions (A–H) displayed across the top.

QUESTIONS ABOUT PROBLEM ATTRIBUTES

A. Is there a quality requirement such that one solution is likely to be more rational than another?

B. Do I have sufficient information to make a high-quality decision?

C. Is the problem structured?

D. Is acceptance of the decision by subordinates critical to effective implementation?

E. If I were to make the decision myself, is it reasonably certain that it would be accepted by my subordinates?

F. Do subordinates share the organizational goals to be attained in solving this problem?

G. Is conflict among subordinates likely in preferred solutions?

H. Do subordinates have sufficient information to make a high-quality decision?

In deciding which decision-making strategy to employ, a manager asks the eight questions sequentially, following the appropriate path to a set of feasible decision-making strategies. The set of feasible strategies is shown at the bottom of Figure 3.3. Each set of feasible strategies is arrayed so that, reading from left to right, the strategies require an increasing commitment of time and allow for an increasing involvement of subordinates in the process. Thus, if you have great time constraints, you would likely choose the first strategy presented in the feasible set. If you have fewer time constraints, but are concerned about group commitment to the solution and therefore want to maximize input from the group, you should choose from the latter strategies within the feasible set.

In deciding whether to involve employees in the decision-making process, time plays a critical role. You should be careful, however, not to avoid group decision-making strategies because you believe that meetings tend to be inefficient and wasteful of both your own and your employees' time. Although a meeting may take a greater amount of employees' time overall, it may be possible to reach a decision within a shorter time period by bringing everyone together.

Recognizing that participative decision making can lead to better decisions is just one part of the process. It is also important to know how to get the most out of the participants—that requires learning to run meetings effectively.

INCREASING MEETING EFFECTIVENESS

No doubt you have attended some pretty horrible meetings in your life. You have also attended some good meetings. What characteristics differentiate good meetings from bad meetings? First, good meetings accomplish the desired task. Second, in good meetings there is appropriate input from group members, and everyone feels that he or she contributes in an important way.

Note the similarity of these characteristics to the task and group maintenance roles played in transforming a work group into a work team. This is no accident! One key to effective meeting management is the ability to balance the focus between task and group maintenance roles—making sure the group stays on track while ensuring that everyone has an opportunity for appropriate participation. Here are some guidelines for effective meeting management; the guidelines focus on preparing for the meeting, running the meeting, and following up on the meeting. (For more detailed suggestions, see Tropman, 1996.)

Preparing for the Meeting

1. *Set **objectives** for the meeting.* If you are not clear about the purpose of the meeting, it is unlikely that you will feel that you have accomplished something at the end of the meeting.

2. *Select **appropriate participants** for the meeting.* Invite individuals who are affected by, or have an important stake in, the outcome of the decision. Where appropriate, choose participants with the intent of maximizing knowledge and perspective diversity.

3. *Select an appropriate **time** and **place** to meet.* Choosing the appropriate time depends on individuals' work schedules, the amount of time required for the meeting, and what time of day is most appropriate: the fresh early morning or the work-focused

end of day. Choosing an appropriate location depends on how large the group is, whether you will need special equipment (such as a whiteboard, computer projection screen, DVD player, or video conference equipment, etc.), and how much privacy or formality is necessary. Holding a meeting in your office will carry a very different message to your employees than holding the meeting in a conference room.

4. *Prepare and distribute an* **agenda** *in advance.* Like setting the objectives for the meeting, preparing and distributing an agenda in advance increases the likelihood of accomplishing the objectives of the meeting. Include the time and place of the meeting and an estimated time for dealing with each major item on the agenda. Sequence the items so that there is some logic to the flow of topics. This gives participants a better sense of direction for the meeting. It also allows individuals to gather whatever information or resources they may feel will be important for the meeting.

Running the Meeting

1. **Start on time.** Starting on time allows for the best use of everyone's time.

2. *Make sure that someone is taking* **minutes.** Having a record of what decisions were made or were tabled helps ensure that future meetings do not get bogged down in repeating discussions from prior meetings. Minutes are especially valuable to keep everyone informed in case someone has to be absent from a meeting.

3. **Review the agenda** *and check whether there are any necessary adjustments.* Again, this provides a sense of direction for the meeting and will increase the likelihood of task accomplishment.

4. *Make sure that* **participants know each other.** The atmosphere in the meeting will be much more pleasant when people know the others with whom they are meeting.

5. **Follow the agenda.** Pace the meeting. Make sure that each topic is carefully discussed; individuals should not go off on tangents or take the focus away from the item at hand.

6. **Minimize** *(or eliminate)* **interruptions.** Show respect to others in the meeting by keeping telephone calls, papers to be signed, and people walking in with questions to a minimum. After all, if you were away from the office, these interruptions would likely have to wait until you could get to them. Treating your employees and peers as you would a customer demonstrates that you value their input.

7. **Encourage participation by all.** Remember, you selected the participants because you felt they had something to contribute to the decision. If some individuals dominate the discussion, politely ask them to give others an opportunity to contribute. If some are reticent to contribute, try to ask for their opinions or suggestions without embarrassing them.

8. *Conclude the meeting by reviewing or* **restating any decisions** *reached and assignments made.* In order to ensure agreement and to reinforce decisions, it is helpful to review or restate all decisions at the conclusion of the meeting. Clarification of decisions and assignments will increase the likelihood that the next meeting will be productive. You may also want to schedule the next meeting at this time.

Following Up on the Meeting

1. *Distribute minutes in a timely manner.* This reminds people (or informs them, if they were unable to attend the meeting) of what happened in the meeting and what the group accomplished, as well as what their responsibilities are for the next meeting.

2. *If assignments have been made, periodically check with individuals as to their progress.* It is best not to wait until the next meeting to find out that someone has been delayed in completing an assignment.

GROUPWARE—COMPUTER AIDS TO GROUP DECISION MAKING

Earlier we discussed several of the advantages and disadvantages of participative decision making. Implicit in some of the disadvantages was an assumption that participation involved bringing employees together to meet and discuss the issues at hand. Sometimes, however, not everyone who should have input into the decision is available at the same time and/or the same place. As organizations become increasingly reliant on the input of employees in decision-making processes, they also need to find better ways to support employee participation.

Over the past few decades, new approaches to participative decision making have emerged from advances in computing technology in general and the emergence of groupware in particular (Pardo and Nelson, 1994). The term *groupware* generally refers to "any information system designed to enable groups to work together electronically. [It includes] a variety of different products . . . that help groups communicate better, reach faster and better decisions, plan and track a series of actions to reach a goal, and produce reports and other documents as a collaborative effort" (Opper and Fersko-Weiss, 1992, p. 4). Some researchers have extended this definition to include nonelectronic tools as well, suggesting that it is the process, rather than the tool, that is fundamental in enhancing the group's decision making (Johansen et al., 1991). Given our general focus on the potential gains associated with group decision making, here we will assume this broader definition.

One type of groupware that emerged during the 1980s, called *decision conferencing* (Quinn, Rohrbaugh, and McGrath, 1985, Reagan-Cirincione and Rohrbaugh, 1992) or *group (decision) support systems* (Jessup and Valacich, 1993), decreases some of the disadvantages of group decision making by using computer technology and a group facilitator to structure the discussion. These types of meetings range from those that use the computer technology only to track the discussion but otherwise resemble more traditional meetings, to those that allow everyone to "talk" at once through networked personal computers. Users of this latter type of groupware argue that this improves productivity because people have increased opportunity for input. For example, at Boeing users of this type of groupware claim to have "cut the time needed to complete a wide range of team projects by an average of 91%, or to *one-tenth* of what similar work took in the past" (Kirkpatrick, 1992, p. 93, emphasis in original). Managers who use this software also indicate that in addition to each person having more physical (clock) time for input, people often feel freer to contribute since the source of the comment is generally kept anonymous; participants can feel free to disagree with others, even their boss, without the others knowing who is disagreeing.

A useful framework for understanding the potential benefits of groupware builds on the notion that traditional meetings require people to be at the same place at the same time. Stanley M. Davis, in *Future Perfect* (1987), essentially argues that in order to remain viable, organizations will need to shift their thinking from "same time/same place" approaches to organizing to "any time/any place" approaches. That is, in order to meet customer needs more effectively, organizations will need to be unconstrained by time and place; they will need to shorten their production cycles and broaden their geographic boundaries to compete in a global marketplace. The proliferation of Internet retailers who will accept orders from any location at any time offers one example of how organizations have begun to move to an any time/any place manner of thinking. This same logic applies to organizational decision making. Thus, if organizational decision-making processes are to remain viable in this type of environment, they must be able to gather input from employees any time/any place. Tools that support same time/same place meetings include copyboards, PC projection systems, and group decision-support systems. Group decision-support systems can also support same time/different place meetings, as can Internet-based videoconferences using computer video cameras and digital white boards. Tools that support different time/different place (any time/any place) meetings include e-mail and voicemail systems, whereby the use of a distribution list can deliver a message to all meeting participants simultaneously and virtually instantaneously for use when the participants are available.

Ultimately, no matter how we enhance our decision making through the use of technology, the *group* makes the decision. Leaders must be certain that those participating in the decision fully understand others' input and that each person feels that his or her perspective has been heard.

ANALYSIS Decisions by the Group[4]

Objective This exercise asks you to analyze what happened when a plant manager tried to apply the idea of participative decision making in his organization. Be sure to use the tools discussed in the chapter (e.g., Tannenbaum and Schmidt's framework for choosing a leader and Vroom and Jago's participative leadership model).

Directions Read the following story and answer the questions that follow.

John Stevens, plant manager of the Fairlee Plant of Lockstead Corporation, attended the advanced management seminar conducted at a large midwestern university. The seminar, of four weeks' duration, was largely devoted to the topic of executive decision making.

Professor Mennon, one of the university staff, particularly impressed John with his lectures on group discussion and group decision making. On the basis of research and experience, Professor Mennon was convinced that employees, if given the opportunity, could meet together, intelligently consider, and then formulate quality decisions that would be enthusiastically accepted.

[4]*Source:* Reprinted with permission from John M. Champion and John H. Jones, *Critical Incidents in Management* (Homewood, Ill.: Richard D. Irwin, Inc., 1975 ©)

Returning to his plant at the conclusion of the seminar, John decided to practice some of the principles he had learned. He called together the 25 employees of department B and told them that production standards established several years previously were now too low in view of the recent installation of automated equipment. He gave the employees the opportunity to discuss the mitigating circumstances and to decide among themselves, as a group, what their standards should be. John, on leaving the room, believed that the employees would doubtlessly establish higher standards than he himself would have dared proposed.

After an hour of discussion, the group summoned John and notified him that, contrary to his opinion, their group decision was that the standards were already too high, and since they were given the authority to establish their own standards, they were making a reduction of 10 percent. These standards, John knew, were far too low to provide a fair profit on the owner's investment. Yet it was clear that his refusal to accept the group's decision would be disastrous. Before taking a course of action, John called Professor Mennon at the university to ask for his opinion.

Discussion Questions

1. What went wrong?
2. Was John's style of participative decision making appropriate for the situation? Why or why not?
3. What style of participative decision making would you have advised John to use initially? How did you come to this conclusion?
4. What would you suggest that John do now? Be specific in your suggestions!
5. Given the current situation, what advice would you give John about using participative decision making with his employees in the future?

Reflection

As described, John Stevens's experience recalls Alexander Pope's famous line, "A little learning is a dangerous thing. . . ." Unfortunately, many good techniques are often discarded after such a failure. The fault, however, often lies not with the technique itself but with the understanding of the principles upon which the technique is based and the skill of the person using it.

PRACTICE Ethics Task Force

Objective

This group exercise will give you a chance to practice your meeting skills, as well as observe how others behave in meetings. As with any meeting, you will find it helpful if someone is responsible for taking minutes to provide accurate information for the discussion about what took place during the meeting.

Directions

The class will be divided into several small groups to consider an organizational dilemma. In your meeting to discuss the dilemma, think about which participative decision-making skills you can practice.

Directions for the Small Groups

You are members of a task force that has been called in to discuss and make suggestions for policies and procedures to deal with the use of work time and computers for personal business. Recently, some employees have reported to their managers that they feel that some individuals spend a substantial amount of time doing personal business from work and that this affects their workload. A few managers who have confronted employees have indicated that their employees argue that they can only do business with some companies during office hours and that it is not fair to expect them to take personal leave for a few minutes here and there. Other managers have indicated that not enough time is lost to make a big deal about it. Furthermore, they argue, raising the issue will result in negative feelings toward the organization. The division director has asked you to come up with a list of recommendations in which you recognize the need for optimum employee productivity as well as the potential costs, both financial and personal, of monitoring and attempting to change such behaviors.

Discussion Questions

1. What happened during the meeting of the ethics task force?
2. Did you feel prepared for the meeting? If not, what additional information or material would have been helpful?
3. Did all task force members participate in the meeting?
4. Did the discussion stay on track, or was there a tendency to go off on tangents?
5. Did your group discuss any necessary follow-up measures?
6. What suggestions would you make to the meeting chair about running future meetings?
7. What suggestions do you have for yourself for the next time you chair a meeting?

Reflection

Ethical decision making is critical for managers. In the past few years, much attention has been focused on business executives and politicians who have clearly crossed over the line in terms of unethical behavior. In some cases, however, that line is much less clear. When employees receive conflicting messages about what is and what is not acceptable, they may feel that the organization is encouraging them to engage in unethical behavior. Managers who are clear about their values and role model ethical behavior can help employees make the right decisions.

APPLICATION   Meeting Management

Objective

Because people typically have a great deal of experience participating in many meetings, it is easy to fall back into old habits (e.g., sitting quietly when you have an unconventional idea, interrupting when you disagree with someone else). Improving your skills at meeting management requires that you take a step back and observe what typically happens in meetings and think about which actions by participants make the meeting more or less effective.

Directions

During the next few weeks, try to attend and observe meetings of several different groups with which you are involved. In addition to work groups and committee meetings, you might also attend a community meeting or a meeting of a social organization. To help you learn more about both participative decision making and effective meeting mangement, answer the questions below for each of the meetings that you attend.

1. What decisions were made at the meeting?
2. Were these decisions appropriate for group or participative decision making? Why or why not?
3. Who led the meeting?
4. Was an agenda distributed prior to, or at the beginning of, the meeting? Were specific time parameters set for the meeting?
5. Were people properly prepared for the meeting?
6. Was participation of all members encouraged?
7. Did the discussion remain focused on the main issues?
8. Was there proper closure to the meeting (i.e., summarizing accomplishments and allocating follow-up assignments)?
9. If this was a meeting you called, how well did you do at implementing new skills for participative decision making? If it was a meeting called by someone else, what advice can you give the group leader for future meetings?

Reflection   Even experts at managing meetings do not always have totally successful meetings. There will always be variables outside your control when you run a meeting, but to the extent that you incorporate the guidelines for preparing for, running, and following up on meetings, you should find that there are fewer times when your meetings get out of hand or fail to help you meet the objectives that you establish for them.

Competency 3   Managing Conflict

ASSESSMENT   How Do You Handle Conflict?[5]

Objective   Conflict is present in every organization, and not all conflict is bad. Understanding how you generally approach conflict is an important first step in improving your ability to manage conflict productively.

Directions   Think of a friend, relative, manager, or coworker with whom you have had a number of disagreements. Then indicate how frequently you engage in each of the following described behaviors during disagreements with that person. For each item select the number that represents the behavior you are *most likely* to exhibit. There are no right or wrong answers. Please respond to all items on the scale. The responses from 1 to 7 are

Scale	Always	Very Often	Often	Sometimes	Seldom	Very Seldom	Never
	1	2	3	4	5	6	7

5 **2**   1. I blend my ideas to create new alternatives for resolving a disagreement.

2 **3**   2. I shy away from topics that are sources of disputes.

4 **1**   3. I make my opinion known in a disagreement.

5   4. I suggest solutions that combine a variety of viewpoints.

2   5. I steer clear of disagreeable situations.

3   6. I give in a little on my ideas when the other person also gives in.

6   7. I avoid the other person when I suspect that he or she wants to discuss a disagreement.

4   8. I integrate arguments into a new solution from the issues raised in a dispute.

1   9. I will go 50–50 to reach a settlement.

6   10. I raise my voice when I'm trying to get the other person to accept my position.

3   11. I offer creative solutions in discussions of disagreements.

5   12. I keep quiet about my views in order to avoid disagreements.

2   13. I give in if the other person will meet me halfway.

2   14. I downplay the importance of a disagreement.

3   15. I reduce disagreements by making them seem insignificant.

---

[5]*Adaptation of* the Organizational Communication Conflict Instrument (OCCI), Form B, developed by I. L. Putnam and C. Wilson. Reprinted in Wilson, Steven R., and Michael S. Waltman, "Assessing the Putnam-Wilson Organizational Communication Conflict Instrument (OCCI)," Management Communication Quarterly. 1(3), pp. 382–384, copyright © by Sage Publications. Reprinted by permission of Sage Publications, Inc.

    2   16. I meet the other person at a midpoint in our differences.

    5   17. I assert my opinion forcefully.

    6   18. I dominate arguments until the other person understands my position.

    3   19. I suggest we work together to create solutions to disagreements.

    3   20. I try to use the other person's ideas to generate solutions to problems.

    4   21. I offer trade-offs to reach solutions in disagreements.

    2   22. I argue insistently for my stance.

    6   23. I withdraw when the other person confronts me about a controversial issue.

    5   24. I sidestep disagreements when they arise.

    2   25. I try to smooth over disagreements by making them appear unimportant.

    7   26. I insist my position be accepted during a disagreement with the other person.

    1   27. I make our differences seem less serious.

    6   28. I hold my tongue rather than argue with the other person.

    3   29. I ease conflict by claiming our differences are trivial.

    3   30. I stand firm in expressing my viewpoints during a disagreement.

Scoring and Interpretation

Three categories of conflict-handling strategies are measured in this instrument: solution-oriented, nonconfrontational, and control. By comparing your scores on the following three scales, you can see which of the three is your preferred conflict-handling strategy.

To calculate your three scores, add the individual scores for the items and divide by the number of items measuring the strategy. Then subtract each of the three mean scores from 7. The closer your score is to 0, the less likely you are to use that type of strategy; the closer your score is to 7, the more likely you are to use that type of strategy.

Solution-oriented: Items 1, 4, 6, 8, 9, 11, 13, 16, 19, 20, 21   **4.09**

Nonconfrontational: Items 2, 5, 7, 12, 14, 15, 23, 24, 25, 27, 28, 29   **3.33**

Control: Items 3, 10, 17, 18, 22, 26, 30   **2.71**

Solution-oriented strategies tend to focus on the problem rather than the individuals involved. Solutions reached are often mutually beneficial, where neither party defines him- or herself as the winner and the other party as the loser.

Nonconfrontational strategies tend to focus on avoiding the conflict by either avoiding the other party or by simply allowing the other party to have his or her way. These strategies are used when there is more concern with avoiding a confrontation than with the actual outcome of the problem situation.

Control strategies tend to focus on winning or achieving one's goals without regard for the other party's needs or desires. Individuals using these strategies often rely on rules and regulations in order to "win the battle."

Discussion Questions

1. Which strategy do you find easiest to use? Most difficult? Which do you use most often?

2. How would your answers to these items have differed if you had considered someone different from the person you chose?

3. Would your answers differ between work-related and non-work-related situations? Between different types of work-related situations?

4. What is it about the conflict situation or strategy that tells you which strategy to use in dealing with a particular conflict situation?

Reflection   Understanding your preferred conflict-handling style is a first step toward being able to thoughtfully choose an approach to handling conflicts in the future, rather than simply falling into habitual patterns of responding to conflict.

LEARNING Managing Conflict

Over the past three decades, the topics of conflict and conflict management have become increasingly important to managers in organizations of all sizes. In the 1980s, research on organizational conflict indicated that managers were spending between 20 and 50 percent of their time dealing with conflict, with managers at the lower levels of the organizational hierarchy reporting more time spent than managers at the higher levels (Lippitt, 1982). Since then, one might expect these numbers to have increased. Considering the nature of changes that are occurring in organizations as they attempt to adapt to and/or anticipate changes in their external environment, it would seem inevitable that conflict will increase as individuals disagree over how work should be organized, who should participate in various decisions, and what strategies should be used to accomplish organizational goals. Although these statements may at first seem to suggest that organizational anarchy is imminent, you will see in this section that conflict over these types of decisions can potentially lead to stronger organizational performance. When managed appropriately, conflict can be a positive and productive force in decision making.

DIFFERENT PERSPECTIVES ON CONFLICT

Most people in our society see conflict between individuals or groups as harmful. In both work-related and non-work-related situations, people often try to avoid conflict because they believe it will create bad feelings among people that will then lead to a negative atmosphere in which to work or play. In fact, different types of conflict can have either positive or negative consequences. People typically think of relationship conflict, which does often trigger poor outcomes, but task conflict can actually lead to effective decisions (Simons and Peterson, 2000). The key is that group members need to recognize the difference between the two.

Such a view of conflict recognizes not only that conflict is inevitable but also that it should sometimes be encouraged in order to allow new ideas to surface and to create positive forces for innovation and change. As William Wrigley Jr. noted, "When two [people] . . . always agree, one of them is unnecessary" (quoted in Tjosvold, 1993, p. 133). Viewing conflict from this perspective requires us to seek challenges to our thoughts and ideas, to value those challenges over unquestioning acceptance, and to trust those with whom we work (Simons and Peterson, 2000). Jerry Harvey's famous story of the Abilene Paradox (see Box 3.1) provides a clear example of when a challenge can be more valuable than acceptance.

BOX 3.1 THE ABILENE PARADOX

The July afternoon in Coleman, Texas (population 5,607) was particularly hot—104 degrees as measured by the Walgreen's Rexall Ex-Lax temperature gauge. In addition, the wind was blowing fine-grained West Texas topsoil through the house. But the afternoon was still tolerable—even potentially enjoyable. There was a fan going on the back porch; there was cold lemonade; and finally, there was entertainment. Dominoes. Perfect for the conditions. The game required little more physical exertion than an occasional mumbled comment, "Shuffle' em," and an unhurried movement of the arm to place the spots in the appropriate perspective on the table. All in all, it had the makings of an agreeable Sunday afternoon in Coleman—that is, it was until my father-in-law suddenly said, "Let's get in the car and go to Abilene and have dinner at the cafeteria."

I thought, "What, go to Abilene? Fifty-three miles? In this dust storm and heat? And in an unairconditioned 1958 Buick?" But my wife chimed in with, "Sounds like a great idea. I'd like to go. How about you, Jerry?" Since my own preferences were obviously out of step with the rest I replied, "Sounds good to me," and added, "I just hope your mother wants to go."

"Of course I want to go," said my mother-in-law. "I haven't been to Abilene in a long time."

So into the car and off to Abilene we went. My predictions were fulfilled. The heat was brutal. We were coated with a fine layer of dust that was cemented with perspiration by the time we arrived. The food at the cafeteria provided first-rate testimonial material for antacid commercials.

Some four hours and 106 miles later we returned to Coleman, hot and exhausted. We sat in front of the fan for a long time in silence. Then, both to be sociable and to break the silence, I said, "It was a great trip, wasn't it?"

No one spoke.

Finally my mother-in-law said, with some irritation, "Well, to tell the truth, I really didn't enjoy it much and would rather have stayed here. I just went along because the three of you were so enthusiastic about going. I wouldn't have gone if you all hadn't pressured me into it."

I couldn't believe it. "What do you mean 'you all'?" Don't put me in the 'you all' group. I was delighted to be doing what we were doing. I didn't want to go. I only went to satisfy the rest of you. You're the culprits."

My wife looked shocked. "Don't call me a culprit. You and Daddy and Mama were the ones who wanted to go. I just went along to be sociable and to keep you happy. I would have to be crazy to want to go out in a heat like that."

Her father entered the conversation abruptly. "Hell!" he said.

He proceeded to expand on what was already absolutely clear. "Listen, I never wanted to go to Abilene. I just thought you might be bored. You visit so seldom I wanted to be sure you enjoyed it. I would have preferred to play another game of dominoes and eat the leftovers in the icebox."

After the outburst of recrimination we all sat back in silence. Here we were, four reasonably sensible people who, of our own volition, had just taken a 106-mile trip across a godforsaken desert in a furnace-like temperature through a cloud-like dust storm to eat unpalatable food at a hole-in-the-wall cafeteria in Abilene, when none of us really wanted to go. In fact, to be more accurate, we'd done just the opposite of what we wanted to do. The whole situation simply didn't make sense.

Source: Reprinted by permission of publisher, from *Organizational Dynamics,* summer, 1974. All rights reserved.

While we will spend part of the chapter talking about how to encourage or stimulate conflict, we will begin by focusing on conflict that emerges naturally. First, we will present some basic definitions and frameworks for understanding the sources and progression of naturally emerging conflict. We will then look at strategies for managing these conflicts that increase the likelihood that positive outcomes will result. Finally, we will look at a technique for stimulating conflict for the purpose of encouraging innovation (and avoiding unnecessary trips to Abilene).

LEVELS, SOURCES, AND STAGES OF CONFLICT

In order to use conflict constructively, it is important to understand how conflicts arise and how they develop. Although the primary focus in this chapter is on conflicts that arise between individuals or between groups (and that is, in fact, where most conflicts of consequence to organizations arise), it is important to recognize that conflict occurs at all levels of the organization. For example, conflicts may occur between two different organizations, or between units of an organization, when the first organization or unit senses that the second organization or unit is working against the goals or interests of the first.

In addition, individuals often experience internal, or intrapersonal, conflicts. Lewin (1935) identified three types of intrapersonal conflict: (1) those that occur when an individual must choose between two desirable outcomes or courses of action, such as when a manager must choose between two good job candidates; (2) those that occur when an individual sees a goal or outcome as having both positive and negative consequences, such as when one chooses a new job because it potentially has more promotional opportunities, knowing that it also requires leaving the security of one's present job; and (3) those that occur when an individual must choose between two negative outcomes or courses of action, such as during a fiscal crisis when management must decide whether to totally eliminate a single project or program or to cut the budget across the board.

Although this chapter does not discuss at length conflicts at the intrapersonal or interorganizational levels, it is important to be aware of their existence because of their potential impact on interpersonal or intergroup conflicts.

Conflicts in organizations develop for a wide variety of reasons. Often conflicts develop because of individual differences, such as differences in values, attitudes, beliefs, needs, or perceptions. Conflicts also develop between individuals when there are misunderstandings or communication errors, which lead individuals to believe that there are differences in values, attitudes, beliefs, needs, or perceptions. As organizations expand their use of participative decision making, there will be more and more situations in which conflict can arise. In addition, as the work force becomes increasingly culturally diverse, conflict may arise out of misperceptions that are related to differing worldviews held by different cultural groups (Cox, 1993). The tremendous benefits that derive from diverse people bringing differing perspectives to the decision-making process are not likely to occur without conflict over how the decision should be made, who should have input into the decision, how information about the decision should be disseminated, and what the actual decision should be.

Organizational structures may also increase the likelihood of conflict within or between groups. For example, when two or more units perceive that they are in competition with each other for scarce resources, there is likely to be conflict among the units. Similarly, conflicts can arise when two or more units see themselves as having different goals. For example, in large organizations, units associated with cost or quality control, or with setting organizational policies and procedures, often find themselves in conflict with other organizational units. While this appears to be a natural consequence of the differing focuses of the units, of the checks and balances that organizations build into the system, Tjosvold (1993) reminds us that our assumption that conflicts arise out of opposing interests and goals is only partly true and that, most often, conflicts arise out of interdependence. That is, conflicts do not arise because two departments or work units have incompatible long-term interests or goals, but because they disagree on the path or means to accomplish the goal and, more importantly, one cannot accomplish the goal without the other.

STAGES OF THE CONFLICT PROCESS

Regardless of the level or the source of the conflict, conflicts usually follow a set sequence of events or stages. In the first stage, the conflict is latent. Neither party senses the conflict, but the situation is one in which individual or group differences or organizational structures have created the potential for conflict.

When the potential conflict situation is perceived by one or more of the individuals or groups, the conflict moves into the second stage. In this stage, individuals become cognitively and emotionally aware of the differences. Here each of the two parties may attribute intentional and unjustifiable acts to the other. Emotional reactions may take the form of anger, hostility, frustration, anxiety, or pain.

In the third stage the conflict moves from a cognitive and/or emotional awareness to action. It is in this stage that the conflict becomes overt, and the individuals or groups implicitly or explicitly choose to act to resolve the conflict or to escalate it. Actions to escalate the conflict include various forms of aggressive behaviors, such as verbally (or physically) attacking the other persons or group, acting in ways that purposefully frustrate others' attainment of goals, or attempting to engage others in the conflict by getting them to take sides against the other party. Actions to resolve the conflict generally require both parties to take a positive problem-solving approach that allows both of their needs and concerns to be heard and handled. If the two parties believe that they are bound by a common long-term goal, it is more likely that they will take a positive problem-solving approach.

The fourth stage of conflict is the outcome or aftermath. Actions taken in the third stage directly affect whether the outcomes are functional or dysfunctional. Functional outcomes include a better understanding of the issues underlying the conflict, improved quality of decisions, increased attention to the use of creativity and innovation in solving and resolving future problems, and a positive approach to self-evaluation. Dysfunctional outcomes include continued anger and hostility, reduced communication, and a destruction of team spirit. More important, conflicts that result in dysfunctional outcomes often snowball, setting the stage for new conflicts that will potentially be more difficult to resolve because their source will be more complex.

CONFLICT MANAGEMENT STRATEGIES

In the Assessment activity, you identified your preference among three conflict-handling strategies in a particular situation. These three strategies can be represented along two dimensions that show how individuals think and act in approaching situations in which there is conflict (Thomas, 1976). The first dimension represents cooperativeness, or the extent to which you are willing to work in order to meet the other party's needs and concerns. The second dimension represents assertiveness, or the extent to which you are willing to work in order to meet your own needs and concerns. Figure 3.4 shows how these two dimensions define five conflict management approaches. Nonconfrontational strategies are associated with avoiding and accommodating approaches, control strategies are associated with a competing approach, and solution-oriented strategies are associated with collaborating and compromising approaches.

1. *Avoiding approaches.* Avoiding approaches are used when individuals recognize the existence of a conflict but do not wish to confront the issues of the conflict. In avoiding the issues, they work neither to satisfy their own goals nor to satisfy the other party's goals. Individuals may avoid by withdrawing and creating physical separation between the parties or by suppressing feelings and attempting not to discuss the issues of the conflict. This approach is often useful when some time is needed to allow two parties engaged in a conflict to "cool off." In the long term, however, if the conflict is not dealt with, it is likely to surface again. Moreover, avoiding conflict increases the likelihood that important management issues will be similarly avoided. For example, the information leakage that occurs when lower-level managers report only favorable information to their superiors, and screen out information that is less favorable, may result in the avoidance of

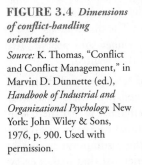

FIGURE 3.4 *Dimensions of conflict-handling orientations.*

Source: K. Thomas, "Conflict and Conflict Management," in Marvin D. Dunnette (ed.), *Handbook of Industrial and Organizational Psychology.* New York: John Wiley & Sons, 1976, p. 900. Used with permission.

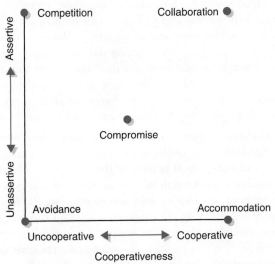

conflict but may also lead to larger problems in the long run. Similarly, the bankruptcy of the Penn Central Railroad has been attributed to mismanagement and a tendency by the company's board of directors to avoid conflict and to not question management's actions (Binzen and Daughen, 1971).

2. *Accommodating approaches.* Accommodating approaches are those for which individuals do not act to achieve their own goals but rather work only to satisfy the other party's concerns. This approach has the advantage of preserving harmony and avoiding disruption. In the short term, this approach is useful when the issue is not seen as very important or when the other party is much stronger and will not give in. In the long term, however, individuals may not always be willing to sacrifice their personal needs in order to maintain the relationship. In addition, accommodating approaches generally limit creativity and stop the search for new ideas and solutions to the problem. Many unnecessary "trips to Abilene" have been taken by individuals believing that they were helping the situation by accommodating.

3. *Competing approaches.* In direct contrast to accommodating approaches, competing approaches (sometimes referred to as forcing) occur when individuals work only to achieve their own goals. In these cases, individuals often fall back on authority structures and formal rules to win the battle. Although competing approaches are appropriate when quick, decisive action is necessary or when one knows that certain decisions or actions must be taken for the good of the group, these approaches often result in dysfunctional outcomes. Competing behaviors set up a win–lose confrontation, in which one party is clearly defined as the winner and the other as the loser. In addition, as with accommodating approaches, the use of competing behaviors generally limits creativity and stops the search for new ideas and solutions to the problem.

4. *Compromising approaches.* Compromising approaches are the first of the solution-oriented strategies. Individuals using these approaches are concerned both with their own interests and goals and with those of the other party. These approaches usually involve some sort of negotiation during which each party gives up something in order to gain something else. The underlying assumption of compromising strategies is that there is a fixed resource or sum that is to be split and that, through compromise, neither party will end up the loser. The disadvantage to this approach, however, is that neither party ends up the winner, and people often remember what they had to give up in order to get what they wanted.

5. *Collaborating approaches.* The second solution-oriented strategy is collaboration. Individuals using collaborating approaches are concerned with their own interests and goals as well as those of the other party. The difference is that there is no underlying assumption of a fixed resource that will force everyone to give up something in order to gain something else. Rather the assumption is that by creatively engaging the problem, a solution can be generated that makes everyone a winner and everyone better off. Clearly these approaches have great advantages with respect to cohesion and morale; the great disadvantage is that they are time consuming and may not work when the conflict involves differences in values.

ADVANTAGES AND DISADVANTAGES OF CONFLICT MANAGEMENT APPROACHES

Each of the conflict management approaches has advantages and disadvantages that make it more or less appropriate for a given situation. Table 3.1 presents the five approaches and the appropriate situations for using each. Clearly your approach will also depend on your own comfort in using the various approaches. Research has shown, however, that collaborating approaches are associated with such positive outcomes as decision-making productivity and organizational performance (Thomas, 1976). In addition, as we discussed in the beginning of this section, recent research suggests that a certain amount of conflict is to be encouraged to allow new ideas to surface and to create positive forces for innovation and change. Collaborating approaches are, in fact, the most effective of the conflict management approaches for allowing new and creative ideas to surface.

HOW TO USE COLLABORATIVE APPROACHES TO CONFLICT MANAGEMENT

As indicated above, collaborative approaches have been found to be most effective, especially in the long run. These solutions fall under the solution-oriented strategies. This should indicate to you that these approaches require the parties to work together to find a solution, or multiple solutions, that meet both sets of needs.

The first step in collaboration is to face the conflict. One party must recognize that a conflict exists, face his or her feelings about the conflict, and be willing to approach the second party to talk about that person's feelings about the conflict. People often find this to be difficult because it requires that they put aside any anger or hostility they are feeling and also that they be willing to face the anger or hostility that may be presented by the other party. Moreover, if there has been a long history of conflict, the second party might not yet be willing to try to collaborate. If you want to try the collaborative approach, you will need to think in advance about how to handle this situation. Decide how to approach the other person. Be persistent, but give the other person whatever time and space he or she needs to agree to collaborate.

It is often a good idea to meet with the other party in a neutral environment. This will promote an atmosphere of willingness to work together on generating positive solutions. When you meet, it is important that you examine your feelings as well as the actual source of the conflict. Each person should state his or her views in a clear, non-threatening way. Make use of the reflective listening techniques presented in Chapter 2.

After both parties have had a chance to surface their personal feelings and views of the conflict, they should move to a mutual definition of the conflict in terms of needs. It is important that both parties share a definition of the conflict before attempting to resolve it; otherwise, you may be focusing on two separate and distinct issues. Again, it is important that you use reflective listening to come to a mutual definition of the conflict.

The next step is to generate potential solutions. Search for solutions that address the needs of both parties. Use creative thinking techniques (see Chapter 8) to increase the

TABLE 3.1 When to Use the Five Conflict Management Approaches

Conflict Management Approach	*Appropriate Situations*
Competing	1. When quick, decisive action is vital.
	2. On important issues where unpopular actions need implementing.
	3. On issues vital to the organization's welfare, and when you know you are right.
	4. Against people who take advantage of noncompetitive behavior.
Collaborating	1. To find an integrative solution when both sets of concerns are too important to be compromised.
	2. When your objective is to learn.
	3. To merge insights from people with different perspectives.
	4. To gain commitment by incorporating concerns into a consensus.
	5. To work through feelings which have interfered with a relationship.
Compromising	1. When goals are important, but not worth the effort or potential disruption of more assertive modes.
	2. When opponents with equal power are committed to mutually exclusive goals.
	3. To achieve temporary settlements to complex issues.
	4. To arrive at expedient solutions under time pressures.
	5. As a backup when collaboration or competition is unsuccessful.
Avoiding	1. When an issue is trivial, or more important issues are pressing.
	2. When you perceive no chance of satisfying your concerns.
	3. When potential disruption outweighs the benefits of resolution.
	4. To let people cool down and regain perspective.
	5. When gathering information supersedes immediate decision.
	6. When others can resolve the conflict more effectively.
	7. When issues seem tangential or symptomatic of other issues.
Accommodating	1. When you find you are wrong—to allow a better position to be heard, to learn, and to show your reasonableness.
	2. When issues are more important to others than to you—to satisfy others and maintain cooperation.
	3. To build social credits for later issues.
	4. To minimize loss when you are outmatched and losing.
	5. When harmony and stability are especially important.
	6. To allow subordinates to develop by learning from mistakes.

Source: Kenneth W. Thomas, "Toward Multi-Dimensional Values in Teaching: The Example of Conflict Behaviors." *Academy of Management Review* 2(3) (1977): 487. Used with permission.

likelihood of finding a solution that meets everyone's needs; avoid making judgments about any of the solutions. Instead of asking yourself "What about this solution will not work?" ask "What about this solution will work?"

After both parties have listed all possible solutions, it is time to select an alternative. Both parties should identify their preferred solutions and think about why these solutions best meet their needs. The two parties should then see if any of the preferred solutions coincide or what sorts of compromises are required to allow them to come to a mutually acceptable agreement.

Once the solution has been identified, decide who will do what and when it will be done. That is, make sure you have an action plan that outlines the steps to carry out the solution. As discussed in the previous section on Using Participative Decision Making, at the end of a meeting everyone should be clear about what decisions have been reached and what assignments have been made. You may also want to identify steps to evaluate your success in implementing your solution. As a final step, it may be appropriate for both parties to identify what they learned from this conflict and what they will do in the future to avoid finding themselves in the same situation again.

When using a collaborative approach, it is important to keep in mind this maxim: Confront the conflict; confront the problem; do not confront the person. That is, if the two parties in conflict can see the problem as their enemy, rather than each other, it will be easier to come to a mutually acceptable solution.

HOW TO STIMULATE CONFLICT AND MANAGE AGREEMENT

In the beginning of this section, we discussed the notion that sometimes unquestioning or unhealthy agreement can be more harmful to the organization than overt conflict. Indeed, as was evident in the case of the Abilene Paradox, unhealthy agreement can lead organizations to "take actions in contradiction of what they really want to do and therefore defeat the very purposes they are trying to achieve" (Dyer, 1995, p. 37).

While there are a number of techniques for stimulating conflict in groups (Faerman, 1996), here we present a technique that divides the larger group into two smaller groups and assigns both groups the task of developing a set of recommendations. The assumption here is that higher-quality decisions will emerge from the juxtaposition of two (or more) opposing sets of recommendations, allowing a synthesis of the best of each set of recommendations. In fact, to stimulate creative solutions, Jerry Hirshberg, founder and president of Nissan Design International, advocates "hiring in divergent pairs"; that is, finding two people who have opposite ways of approaching a situation and thus will create abrasion (Hirshberg, 1999). The following set of guidelines, adapted from Johnson, Johnson, and Smith (1989), who refer to these groups as advocacy groups, provides a way for decision-making groups to structure the discussion to guarantee that differing perspectives will be presented.

Guidelines for Advocacy Groups

1. Groups (two or more) are assigned different positions to adopt.
2. Groups gather data and structure a case for their position and present the case to all other groups.
3. Each presentation is followed by a discussion in which the group is challenged by others who present opposing positions. (It should be noted that these discussions

are referred to as controversy, rather than debate, because the goal is not to win but to hear the different ideas, information, theories, conclusions, etc.)

4. More information is sought to support and refute positions presented as well as to understand others' positions.

5. A synthesis of the different alternatives is sought. This involves creative (divergent) thinking to see new patterns and integrate the various perspectives.

The similarity between this technique and the collaborative method of conflict resolution presented above should be noted. Both require that two groups present differing ideas, defend their ideas, remain open to opposing ideas, and ultimately search for a solution that is mutually beneficial to the different parties. The implication of this similarity, of course, is that most organizational conflicts do not involve a "right" and a "wrong" side, or a "correct" and an "incorrect" way of doing something. Rather, there are numerous alternatives that can be chosen, with the best often being a synthesis of the various possibilities.

ANALYSIS   Zack's Electrical Parts[6]

Objective   Conflicts often can be linked back to multiple causes, not just a single difference of opinion. In analyzing the situation at Zack's Electrical Parts, try to think about how the current conflict developed over time and escalated into a potentially serious problem for this organization.

Directions   Read the following case study and answer the questions that follow.

Bob Byrne's ear was still ringing. Bob was director of the audit staff at Zack's Electrical Parts. He had just received a phone call from Jim Whitmore, the plant manager. Jim was furious. He had just read a report prepared by the audit staff concerning cost problems in his assembly plant.

Jim, in a loud voice, said that he disagreed with several key sections of the report. He claimed that had he known more about the audit staff's work, he could have shown them facts that denied some of their conclusions. He also asked why the report was prepared before he had a chance to comment on it. But what made him particularly angry was that the report had been distributed to all the top managers at Zack's. He felt top management would get a distorted view of his assembly department, if not his whole plant.

Bob ended the call by saying that he'd check into the matter. So he called in Kim Brock, one of his subordinates who headed the audit team for the study in question. Kim admitted that she had not had a chance to talk to Jim before completing and distributing the report. Nor had she really had a chance to spend much time with Dave Wells, who headed the assembly department. But Kim claimed it wasn't her fault. She had tried to meet with Jim and Dave more than once. She had left phone messages for them. But they always seemed too busy to meet and were out of town on several occasions when she was available. So she decided she had better complete the report and get it distributed in order to meet the deadline.

[6]*Reprinted from* Henry L. Tosi, John R. Rizzo, and Stephen J. Carroll, *Managing Organizational Behavior* (New York: Harper & Row), p. 504. Copyright © 1986 Henry Carroll. Used with permission.

That same day, Jim and Dave discussed the problem over lunch. Dave was angry too. He said that Kim bugged him to do the study, but her timing was bad. Dave was working on an important assembly area project of his own that was top priority to Jim. He couldn't take the time that Kim needed right now. He tried to tell her this before the study began, but Kim claimed she had no choice but to do the audit. Dave remembered, with some resentment, how he couldn't get Kim's help last year when he needed it. But the staff audit group seemed to have plenty of time for the study when he couldn't give it any attention. Jim said that he'd look into the matter and agreed that they had been unnecessarily raked over the coals.

Discussion Questions
1. What were the sources of conflict between the staff audit group and the managers in the plant?
2. What were the differences between the interpersonal conflict and the intergroup conflict in this case?
3. How would you describe the conflict in terms of the stages it went through?
4. What should Bob and Jim do now to resolve this conflict?
5. What might Bob do to avoid future conflict situations between the staff audit group and other line managers?

Reflection The auditing function is critical to the control action imperative of the internal process quadrant (see Chapter 4—The Monitor Role and Chapter 5—The Coordinator Role). Not surprisingly, conflict often results when one department is charged with evaluating another.

PRACTICE   Win as Much as You Can[7]

Objective Conflict can emerge in many different settings for many different reasons. After completing this practice exercise, you will be given an opportunity to reflect upon any sources of conflict that emerge during the ten rounds of the activity.

Directions Your instructor will place you in groups of eight (or more). Each of these groups should divide into four smaller groups, trying to keep the small groups evenly balanced. If you have exactly eight, you will be in four dyads; if you have more than eight, you will have some small groups with three or four people. Once you have decided on the small groups, seat yourself so that people in each small group can talk among themselves without being heard by the other small groups.

You will play 10 rounds. In each round, your small group will tell the instructor whether you would like to say X or Y. You will win points based on the configuration of X's and Y's according to the following payoff schedule. Rounds 5, 8, and 10 are bonus rounds. In Round 5, your points are multiplied by 3; in Round 8 they are multiplied by 5; and in Round 10 they are multiplied by 10. The objective of the exercise is to win as much as you can.

[7]*Adapted from* "Win As Much As You Can," by William Gellermann, Ph.D., in *A Handbook of Structured Experiences for Human Relations Training*, Vol. II, Revised, J. William Pfeiffer and John E. Jones (eds.) (San Diego: University Associates, Inc. 1974), pp. 62–67. Used with permission

PAYOFF SCHEDULE

4 X's	Each small group loses 1 point
3 X's	Each small group that said X wins 1 point
1 Y	Small group that said Y loses 3 points
2 X's	Each small group that said X wins 2 points
2 Y's	Each small group that said Y loses 2 points
1 X	Small group that said X wins 3 points
3 Y's	Each small group that said Y loses 1 point
4 Y's	Each small group wins 1 point

In each round, confer within your small group and make a group decision. In rounds 5, 8, and 10, you may confer with the other small groups before making your decision. Use the following scorecard to keep track of your points.

SCORECARD

Round	Time Allotted	Your Choice	Pattern of Choices	Payoff	Balance
1	1½ mins.	__ X __ Y	__ X __ Y		
2	1 min.	__ X __ Y	__ X __ Y		
3	1 min.	__ X __ Y	__ X __ Y		
4	1 min.	__ X __ Y	__ X __ Y		
5	1½ mins.	__ X __ Y	__ X __ Y	× 3	
6	1 min.	__ X __ Y	__ X __ Y		
7	1 min.	__ X __ Y	__ X __ Y		
8	1½ mins.	__ X __ Y	__ X __ Y	× 5	
9	1 min.	__ X __ Y	__ X __ Y		
10	1½ mins.	__ X __ Y	__ X __ Y	× 10	

Discussion Questions

1. Who was "you" in the phrase "win as much as you can"?
2. What does "win" mean in that phrase?
3. What did you assume that your instructor did not say to you?
4. What, if any, conflicts arose within your small group? How did you resolve these conflicts?
5. Does this resemble any real-life experiences you have had? If so, how might you approach this type of conflict differently in the future?
6. Does this exercise tell you that conflict is inherently bad?

Reflection Observing how you (and others) respond to this exercise can be a useful tool for increasing your understanding of self and others, helping to further expand the Open Area in people's Johari window.

APPLICATION Managing Your Own Conflicts

Objective Managing conflict in a controlled setting is one thing. Managing conflict outside the class is another. Several of the techniques that we have covered thus far, however, will be very helpful. Perhaps most obviously, effective communication and reflective listening skills are essential to managing conflict. In addition, however, many of the guidelines for preparing for and managing meetings also come into play. For this application exercise, work on integrating the competencies of both the Mentor and the Facilitator roles.

Directions Select a situation in which you currently are in conflict with someone else.

1. Write a brief description of the conflict that includes

   - The nature of the situation and the underlying issues
   - Your feelings about the situation
   - Your behavior and the behavior of the other party (parties) in the situation, including any conflict management strategies that have been used thus far

2. Develop a plan for resolving that conflict. Your plan should be actionable and should identify:

   - The issues that you plan to address
   - When and where you plan to address those issues
   - What you plan to say and why you plan to say it
   - The type of responses that you anticipate from the other party
   - How you plan to reply to those responses

Reflection It is easier to manage conflict when it does not take you by surprise. Preparation is one of the best prescriptions for managing conflict.

REFERENCES

Adams, S. *Always Postpone Meetings with Time-Wasting Morons.* Kansas City, MO: Andrew McMeel, 1994.

Beckhard, R., and R. T. Harris. *Organizational Transition: Managing Complex Change.* Reading, MA: Addison-Wesley, 1977.

Benne, Kenneth D., and Paul Sheats. "Functional Roles of Group Members." *Journal of Social Issues* 4(2) (1948): 41–49.

Bernstein, James E. "Getting to Know You." *INC* (November 1988): 167–169.

Binzen, P., and J. R. Daughen. *Wreck of the Penn Central.* Boston: Little, Brown, 1971.

Coverman, Shelley. "Role Overload, Role Conflict, and Stress: Addressing Consequences of Multiple Role Demands." *Social Forces* 67 (1989): 965–982.

Cox, Taylor, Jr. *Cultural Diversity in Organizations: Theory, Research and Practice.* San Francisco: Berrett-Koehler, 1993.

Dahle, Cheryl. "Extreme Teams." *Fast Company* (November 1999): 310–326.

Dahle, Cheryl. "Mind Games," *Fast Company* (January–February 2000): 169–180.

Davis, Stanley M. *Future Perfect.* Reading, MA: Addison-Wesley, 1987.

Dayal, I., and J. M. Thomas. "Operation KPE: Developing a New Organization."*Journal of Applied Behavioral Science* 4 (1968): 473–506.

Doyle, M. and D. Straus. *How to Make Meetings Work.* New York: Jove, 1986.

Dumaine, Brian. "The Bureaucracy Busters." *Fortune* (June 17, 1991): 36–50.

Dyer, William G. *Team Building,* 3d ed. Reading, MA: Addison-Wesley, 1995.

Faerman, Sue. "Managing Conflicts Creatively," in James L. Perry (ed.), *The Handbook of Public Administration,* 2d ed. San Francisco: Jossey-Bass, 1996.

Fishman, Charles. "Whole Foods Is All Teams" and "The Whole Foods Recipe for Teamwork." *Fast Company* (April–May 1996): 103–111.

Fishman, Charles. "Engines of Democracy." *Fast Company* (October 1999): 174–202.

Fishman, Charles. "Total Teamwork—Imagination Ltd." *Fast Company* (April 2000): 156–168.

Gordon, Judith R. *A Diagnostic Approach to Organizational Behavior.* Newton, MA: Allyn & Bacon, 1983.

Harrison, Roger. "Role Negotiation: A Tough Minded Approach to Team Development," in W. Warner Burke and H. A. Hornstein (eds.), *The Social Technology of Organization Development.* LaJolla, CA: University Associates, 1972: 84–96.

Hirshberg, Jerry. *The Creative Priority: Putting Innovation to Work in Your Business.* New York: HarperBusiness, 1999.

Janis, Irving. *Victims of Groupthink.* Boston: Houghton Mifflin, 1972.

Jessup, Leonard M., and Joseph S. Valacich. *Group Support Systems: New Perspectives.* New York: Macmillan, 1993.

Johansen, Robert, David Sibbet, Suzyn Benson, Alexia Martin, Robert Mittman, and Paul Saffo. *Leading Business Teams: How Teams Can Use Technology and Group Process Tools to Enhance Performance.* Reading, MA: Addison-Wesley, 1991.

Johnson, David W., Roger T. Johnson, and Karl Smith. "Controversy Within Decision Making Situations," in M. Afzalur Rahim (ed.), *Managing Conflict: An Interdisciplinary Approach.* Westport, CT: Praeger, 1989.

Katz, Daniel, and Robert L. Kahn.*The Social Psychology of Organizations* (2d ed.). New York: John Wiley & Sons, 1978.

Katzenbach, Jon R., and Douglas K. Smith. *The Wisdom of Teams.* New York: HarperCollins, 1993.

Kirkman, Bradley L., and Benson Rosen. "Beyond Self-Management: Antecedents and Consequences of Team Empowerment." *Academy of Management Journal* (February 1999): 58–74.

Kirkpatrick, David. "Here Comes the Payoff from PCs." *Fortune* (March 23, 1992): 93–102.

Larson, Carl E., and Frank M. J. La Fasto. *TeamWork: What Must Go Right/What Can Go Wrong.* Newbury Park, CA: Sage Publications, 1989.

Lawler, Edward E., III. *High-Involvement Management.* San Francisco: Jossey-Bass, 1986.

Lawler, Edward E., III. *The Ultimate Advantage: Creating the High-Involvement Organization.* San Francisco: Jossey-Bass, 1992.

Lencioni, P. M. *Death by Meeting.* New York: Wiley, 2004.

Lewin, Kurt. *A Dynamic Theory of Personality.* New York: McGraw-Hill, 1935.

Lieber, Ron. "Information is Everything." *Fast Company* (November 1999): 246–254.

Lipman-Blumen, Jean, and Harold J. Leavitt. *Hot Groups: Seeding Them, Feeding Them, and Using Them to Ignite Your Organization.* New York: Oxford University Press, 1999.

Lippitt, Gordon L. "Managing Conflict in Today's Organizations," *Training and Development Journal* (July 1982): 67–74.

Loden, Marilyn, and Judy B. Rosener. *Workforce America! Managing Employee Diversity as a Vital Resource.* Homewood, IL: Business One Irwin, 1991.

Opper, Susanna, and Henry Fersko-Weiss. *Technology for Teams: Enhancing Productivity in Networked Organizations.* New York: Van Nostrand Reinhold, 1992.

Pardo, Theresa, and Mark Nelson. "Groupware Technology Testbed," *Center for Technology in Government Project Report* 94-2, Albany, NY: University at Albany, SUNY, 1994.

Quinn, Robert E., John Rohrbaugh, and Michael R. McGrath. "Automated Decision Conferencing: How It Works." *Personnel* (November 1985): 49–55.

Reagan-Cirincione, Patricia, and John Rohrbaugh. "Decision Conferencing: A Unique Approach to the Behavioral Aggregation of Expert Judgment," in George Wright and Fergus Bolger (eds.), *Expertise and Decision Support.* New York: Plenum, 1992.

Reilly, A. J., and John E. Jones. "Team Building," in J. William Pfeiffer and John E. Jones (eds.), *The 1974 Annual Handbook for Group Facilitators.* San Diego, CA: University Associates, 1974.

Roberts, Paul. "The Agenda: Total Teamwork." *Fast Company* (April 1999): 148–162.

Salter, Chuck. "Ideas.com." *Fast Company* (September 1999): 292–307.

Simons, Tony L., and Randall S. Peterson. "Task Conflict and Relationship Conflict in Top Management Teams: The Pivotal Role of Intragroup Trust." *Journal of Applied Psychology* (February 2000): 102–111.

Sittenfeld, Curtis. "Powered by the People." *Fast Company* (July–August 1999): 178–189.

Steibel, B. J. *The Manager's Guide to Effective Meetings.* New York: McGraw Hill, 2001.

Sundstrom, Eric (ed.). *Supporting Work Team Effectiveness: Best Management Practices for Fostering High Performance.* San Francisco: Jossey-Bass, 1999.

Tannenbaum, Robert, and W. H. Schmidt. "How to Choose a Leadership Pattern." *Harvard Business Review* (May–June 1973): 164–197.

Thomas, Kenneth W. "Conflict and Conflict Management," in Marvin D. Dunnette (ed.), *Handbook of Industrial and Organizational Psychology.* Chicago: Rand McNally, 1976: 889–935.

Thomas, Kenneth W. "Toward Multidimensional Values in Teaching: The Example of Conflict Management." *Academy of Management Review* (1977): 484–490.

Tjosvold, Dean. *Learning to Manage Conflict: Getting People to Work Together.* New York: Lexington Books, 1993.

Tropman, John E. *Making Meetings Work: Achieving High Quality Group Decisions.* Thousand Oaks, CA: Sage Publications, 1996.

van der Vegt, Gerben, Ben Emans, and Evert van de Vliert. "Motivating Effects of Task and Outcome Interdependence in Work Teams." *Group & Organization Management* 23 (June 1998): 124–143.

Vroom, V. H. and A. G. Jago. "Decision Making as a Social Process: Normative and Descriptive Models of Leader Behavior." *Decision Sciences* 5 (1974): 743–769.

Vroom, V. H. and P. W. Yetton. *Leadership and Decision-Making.* Pittsburgh: University of Pittsburgh Press, 1973.

Weisbord, Marvin R. *Productive Workplaces: Organizing and Managing for Dignity, Meaning, and Community.* San Francisco: Jossey-Bass, 1987.

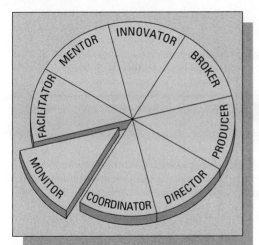

THE MONITOR ROLE

4

INNOVATOR
MENTOR
FACILITATOR
BROKER
MONITOR
COORDINATOR
DIRECTOR
PRODUCER

■ COMPETENCIES

Managing Information Overload

Analyzing Core Processes

Measuring Performance and Quality

The next role we turn to is the monitor role. On the face of it, this role appears less interesting than others in the competing values framework. The word "monitoring" connotes the watchful and intrusive gaze of the bureaucrat or the snooping supervisor. Monitors sound like people who get paid for catching others enjoying their work and putting a stop to it. Monitoring may sound like a controlling and nosy activity, but monitoring, in the way we describe it, is essential to maintaining high performance in both individuals and groups.

The monitor function focuses the manager's attention on internal control issues. For example, a manager might be responsible for managing core processes to ensure consistency. The monitor function is concerned with consolidating and creating continuity. In this chapter we will cover the core competencies of the skilled monitor. These competencies are:

Competency 1   Managing Information Overload
Competency 2   Analyzing Core Processes
Competency 3   Measuring Performance and Quality

We begin with a discussion of information overload. Technological changes have escalated the problem of information overload, not only in our jobs but also in our personal lives as we try to keep up with our faxes, cell phones, laptops, and PDAs.

113

Competency 1 Managing Information Overload

Objective Before we can manage information overload, we need to recognize it. Sometimes we assume that all the information that comes to us is information that we need. This exercise will help you think about the amount and type of data that you receive and how important those data really are to you.

Directions Listed below are some questions about the amount of data and information you routinely have to deal with. A couple of the questions focus on the kind of information you receive on your own performance as a student and employee. Respond to these questions individually and then be prepared to discuss them as a class.

Discussion Questions
1. Has the amount of paper and documents confronting you at school, at work, and in your personal life increased or decreased over the past two years?

2. Do you feel you have become more skillful in sorting, storing, transmitting, and using information?

3. Do you spend hours on the Internet scouring through data, only to log off hours later without an answer to the question that drove you to the Internet?

4. What are your major sources of overload in managing information—e-mail, paper, phone messages, verbal instructions, and requests from others? What are two or three specific things you can do to manage this overload more effectively?

5. Do you often receive information that you don't have any real use for? Do you receive the same information in multiple formats (e.g., e-mail message, paper memo, voice mail message)?

6. How confident do you feel about the information you have on your current performance as an employee? As a student? Do you know where you stand with your supervisor or boss? With your instructors?

7. What additional information would you like to have on these roles?

Reflection Organizational systems are not always designed to provide efficient information flows. "Better safe than sorry" appears to be the motto of much corporate communication. E-mails that are sent to everyone are later followed up with paper copies, "just in case someone doesn't check their e-mail." Memos about scholarship opportunities for children of employees are sent to everyone, regardless of whether they have children. Viewed individually, none of these communications is particularly problematic, but as our in-boxes fill to capacity and our recycle bins are filled to overflowing, they take their toll on organizational performance, as well as employees' feelings of being overwhelmed at work.

LEARNING Managing Information Overload

If managers today agree on anything, it is that the competitive forces in the global economy have made their lives more complex. Information is coming at them at an ever-accelerating rate. Journalist David Shenk says, "Information overload has replaced information scarcity as an important new emotional, social, and political problem (Shenk, 1997, p. 29). Managerial success depends on speed and agility, not just thoroughness and accuracy. In this section we will offer some tools and strategies for converting data into information and managing the flow of that information.

ARE YOU IN DATA OVERLOAD?

Russel Ackoff, an international consultant on managerial problem solving, says that a major problem confronting managers is too much irrelevant information. Managers are surrounded by data that do not tell them what they need to know but that demand attention anyway. The smart managers learn to watch the helpful data and ignore the irrelevant stuff. Less sophisticated managers drown in information anxiety. Richard Wurman, an expert on making information visually accessible, says, "Information anxiety is produced by the ever widening gap between what we understand and what we think we should understand. [It is] the black hole between data and knowledge. It happens when information doesn't tell us what we want or need to know" (Wurman, 2001, p. 14).

See whether you identify with some of these symptoms of information overload as a student or employee:

1. Chronically talking about not keeping up with what's going on around you.

2. Nodding your head knowingly when someone mentions a book, an artist, or a news story that you have actually never heard of.

3. Assuming you must read every e-mail you receive, regardless of who it is from.

4. Thinking that the person next to you understands everything and you don't.

5. Calling something that you don't understand "information." It isn't information if you don't understand it (Wurman, 1989, pp. 35–36).

The fashion of referring to virtually any kind of data as "information" emerged when we started using the word to describe anything that was transmitted over an electrical or mechanical channel (Campbell, 1982). The term "information" meant anything sent by any channel to any receiver, whether the receiver found it informative or interesting or not. "Information" has since become one of the most important terms in our society; however, much of the information we receive is really just unformed data.

We are inundated with bits and pieces of stuff disconnected from any coherent picture, and yet we still feel guilty when we can't assimilate it. Information is probably best thought of as "that which reduces uncertainty." If the information we use is only feeding our uncertainty, it is probably data that have not yet been converted to information. Wurman suggests that most of us need to get beyond the anxiety of not knowing so we can begin to understand. He wants us to relax, feel less guilty about our ignorance, and begin to play with and exploit information instead of being controlled and intimidated by it.

THE ELUSIVE PAPERLESS OFFICE:
TWO STEPS FORWARD, ONE STEP BACK

In 1975 a feature article in *Business Week* predicted a paperless office by the 1990s. But in 1998, paper companies outperformed the skyrocketing Dow Jones stock average by more than 40 percent. The personal computer, the fax machine, and personal digital photography (with the ultimate output usually being on high-quality paper) have all fed our appetite for paper. In fact, research shows that the introduction of e-mail actually increases paper consumption in offices by as much as 40 percent. The availability of e-mail has brought more messages to people than they would otherwise get, and with the messages comes the need to do more printing (Sellen and Harper, 2002). Despite predictions to the contrary, paper consumption has doubled every four years in the United States. In 1995 it was estimated that 95 percent of all documents in organizations were stored on paper with the remaining 5 percent stored digitally. Many experts agree that the proportion of digitally stored documents will continue to increase, but that "paperless office" will remain a myth for many years to come. Paper refuses to disappear from modern offices (Sellen and Harper, 2002, p. 16).

We now know that the goal of completely eliminating paper was unrealistic to begin with. Paper is still an ideal medium of communication and, in some cases, information storage. The problem is that paper tends to be overused.

A better goal than becoming "paperless" is for an office to handle no more paper documents than it really needs to. Most of the written information handled by organizations is still on paper, as is most of the information used by students. Students read books and articles; they write term papers and exams; they take objective tests on machine-read forms; they take lecture notes and trade study notes with other students in study groups. The power of desktop publishing has turned all of us into amateur designers, typesetters, and printers. We spew out documents that then have to be revised and reprinted. Clearly, today's manager must either learn to handle paper or be buried under it.

High technology is finally helping—in some ways. We have made incredible progress in our capacity to store and retrieve data through such methods as optical scanning and "data compression." Nortel Networks' 10-gigabit optical networking platform can transport the entire book collection of the U.S. Library of Congress—4 million titles—from Washington, D.C., to Los Angeles in less than two minutes through one strand of fiber.

Most of you are now conducting research for college papers via the Internet. The search processes are much faster than searching shelves in the library; however, the paper continues to proliferate. The information is available electronically, but much of the information we "extract" has to be printed so that we have a portable record of it.

THE TRAF SYSTEM: TOSS, REFER, ACT, FILE

Good managers review all information, but great managers are able to channel information efficiently. Great managers establish information management habits and systems that force them to do something quickly with every piece of paper and information. Without a system, you may not be able to wade through the insignificant stuff to find the information you need, when you need it. So the first task a monitor must undertake is information management—setting up a system that forces you to do something with every piece of paper that hits your desk. "Traffing," a method recommended by personal efficiency expert Stephanie Winston (Winston, 2004), is the remedy for handling the same piece of paper many times. The metaphor of traffic control is wisely chosen because in order to control traffic we have to give it places to go. Likewise, paper has to be given a few basic routes or streams in which to flow.

The list of items in front of you, all pleading for attention, may be long; however, the number of choices you have for dealing with them is, fortunately, quite short. Winston's advice on Traffing gives you four options:

1. **Toss** papers into the wastebasket or recycling bin (or delete them from your electronic inbox) if they are not immediately valuable. Most of us are too conservative when deciding which things to save. If you throw something out that you later discover you need, you can usually get another copy. For e-mail messages, the electronic version of "tossing" is deleting.

2. **Refer** messages to other people (secretary, staff, colleagues). You should probably set up files for the people you most often refer things to. If you're not using routing slips, start immediately. You can usually save time by using a Post-it note that briefly explains why you're referring the information. You can easily do the same for e-mailed documents by forwarding them with a note from you.

3. **Act** by putting papers requiring your personal action (for example, writing a response letter or a brief report) in an action box or folder. These are the "hot" items you must act on before they get cold. In addition to placing documents in an "act" folder, you should also record the action you need to take on your to-do list. The list is a very efficient reminder of things you need to act on. Most managers do better with a written to-do list than working from memory alone.

4. **File** documents by indicating on the document itself the name of the file into which it should go. Put the paper in a box or file labeled "to file." Keep in mind that reading, in terms of this system, is a form of acting. If a document takes more than five minutes to read, put it in the "act" box. Don't let reading short-circuit your Traffing, or you'll never get the papers sorted. Traffing helps you set priorities and wrap your mind around all the paper and messages you have to deal with. Finally, make a clear distinction between Traffing and acting, and schedule time for doing both.

TAMING THE ELECTRONIC TIGER

So, Traffing, and a little more determination not to get sidetracked by paper, can help you tame the paper tiger; however, as massive as the paper pile is, paper is no longer the major source of information in most managerial jobs today. Most of the messages that confront us are electronic, in one form or another, whether e-mail or voice mail. The volume of digital data pouring into our homes and offices will increase exponentially over the next decade.

And today's managers are more harried than ever before, not only because of all this information coming at them but also because many of them are now working without an assistant. Assistants have traditionally filtered a lot of information and transactions for managers, but many of these support positions have been eliminated from contemporary organizations. Thus, the individual manager has increasingly had to handle the channeling and managing of information.

200 MESSAGES PER DAY

Field research conducted by Pitney Bowes, a global manufacturer of mail systems, reveals that the work of managers and professionals is both aided and interrupted by the constant wash of messages coming to them from the telephone, the Internet, intranets, e-mail, voice mail, and faxes. The messages come about every five minutes, and most managers deal with about 200 messages per day. The volume is a challenge, but the pace and intrusiveness of the messages is a bigger challenge. Managers report that the number of interruptions per hour they must deal with continues to increase ("Message Overload," 1999).

E-mail itself is a current example of how technology can be a burden or a life-saver, depending on how effectively we use it. Because e-mail is so pervasive in both the workplace and the home, we offer a tool that can be used to compose your e-mail messages. This tool can also be used for creating brief and concise voicemail messages for work and for personal use. By using this tool effectively, you can avoid confusing your customers, clients, and coworkers with unclear messages.

THE OABC METHOD: A TEMPLATE FOR COMPOSING CONCISE MESSAGES

The OABC method was developed by William Baker, our colleague and a management communication professor at BYU's Marriott School of Management. Baker drills his MBA students on his OABC method for framing both e-mail and voice mail messages. This acronym stands for Opening, Agenda, Body, and Closing. The OABC method is a great antidote to the rambling and foggy messages that are sent out all over the world every day. This simple method requires you to make a very brief written or mental outline of the message. The outline of the message is usually best ordered in the following way:

1. **Opening:** A quick statement of greeting that sets a positive climate and also identifies you if you are a stranger to your audience.
   - *Example:* "Hi, Chris, it's Karen. Great job on the presentation to the marketing group."

2. **Agenda:** An outline or map of what your message is about. Even brief messages usually need a "frame" or border to go around them.
   - *Example:* "I have two things I wanted to share with you: The first is about the proposal to the Gartner Group, and the second is about a message I got from Kim Lee at the Ford Foundation."

3. **Body:** The "business" message itself, expressed in concrete and simple terms.
   - *Example:* "I think the proposal is solid but it needs more work in the staffing section where we talk about our expertise in data warehousing. I'm attaching a document that gives you more specifics of what I think it should look like.

     Second, Kim Lee at the foundation really needs us to have a representative at the awards luncheon. It's on July 17 at noon. Could you possibly attend in my place? I'll be in Toronto."

4. **Closing:** A concluding statement of what you want the person to do—who does what by when?—and a cordial and efficient ending such as a simple thank-you.
   - *Example:* "Please look at the attachment and share it with the design team. I'll be back on Wednesday to discuss it with you. Also, please let me know by end of the day tomorrow if you can attend the luncheon, and I will call Kim myself from Toronto. Thanks. You've been a better teammate than I've been this week."

This message is more formal than one you might send to a coworker or friend whom you know very well. But notice that it's an easy message to "unpack." It has a pleasant tone and it's coherent and complete. Chris knows exactly what Karen needs from him and when. Make a habit of using the OABC method in any message through any channel.

We have used it with high-level managers and executives who have quickly added it to their toolkit. It can be applied to memos and business letters as well as to e-mail and voice mail.

FACE-TO-FACE MEETINGS STILL ESSENTIAL

We are also making some progress with audio- and videoconferencing software, which allows people to hold meetings without sitting in the same room. They can see and hear one another (most of the time) from remote sites and potentially save thousands of dollars and hours of time by not having to travel to meetings. But, much to the relief of the airline industry, this technology has not rendered face-to-face meetings unnecessary. Teams and work groups can use videoconferencing from time to time once relationships have been established through effective face-to-face interaction. But there is no real substitute for face-to-face meetings, especially during the early stages of group formation. Box 4.1 talks about the importance of physical presence for building relationships.

BOX 4.1   THE VANISHING HUMAN MOMENT

The electronic media we use—faxes, e-mail, voice mail, cell phones, and PDAs (personal digital assistants)—help us communicate more efficiently, but not always more effectively. E-mail, for example, is a very quick way to communicate with someone, but e-mail messages are often impersonal and too crisp to really convey the human element. In our research and consulting in organizations, we see a lot interpersonal conflicts and abrasions caused through the inappropriate use of e-mail.

BOX 4.1   THE VANISHING HUMAN MOMENT
(*Cont'd*)

The cure for the frustrations caused by "electronic hyperconnection" is creating what Edward Hallowell, a psychiatrist who works with business executives, calls the "human moment." The human moment is, in one sense, what businesspeople call "face time," encounters in which people are physically in the same room or place, even for brief periods. But the human moment requires not only our physical presence but also our emotional and mental attention. In the human moment, you are not doing anything but attending to the other person. The human moment, says Hallowell, is disappearing from the workplace, largely because of so much electronic connectivity.

Many managers now lead groups of people who are dispersed geographically, such as sales teams or systems specialists who travel frequently and communicate with each other by e-mail and cell phones. These managers tell us that, from time to time, they must bring their people together so they can reconnect in a human way—to communicate more thoroughly and enjoy each other's company.

The new malady of the workplace, according to Hallowell, is "electronic hyperconnection." The speed and convenience of e-mail and voice mail are great, but when we use them continuously in high-stress settings, they can make our work lives worse, not better. The constant wash of voice mail messages left on our answering systems, the staccato e-mail messages that blip onto our computer screens by the hour—this barrage of information makes most people feel isolated, out of sorts, and defensive.

Ray, a senior systems manager in an investment company, says that he finds himself talking face to face with people less often. Almost all of his communication is "mediated" through some kind of electronic device. Ray has found that, with all its speed and convenience, e-mail has led him into some serious misunderstandings with people. A curt message such as "We could not access this application and need to know why" can be interpreted in many ways. If you're feeling stressed and defensive to begin with, such a message can trigger a very negative response. Ray may read sarcasm or impatience into a message that is not intended. He then fires back an even more defensive or sarcastic response, and the downward spiral begins.

According to Hallowell, the cure for hyperconnectivity is human connection, a human moment, face to face with other people. Human conversations usually go much better in person when we can read the other person's nonverbal cues. Electronic communications, says Hallowell, "remove many of the cues that typically mitigate worry. Those cues—body language, tone of voice, and facial expression—are especially important among sophisticated people (knowledge workers) who are prone to using subtle language, irony, and wit. When all we have is a written message on our computer screen, or a quick voice mail from a coworker, we often misunderstand the other person's intentions, and then start to worry and second-guess the messenger. In person, these exchanges are often fixed before they can go off course."

Hallowell cites the experience of Jack, who founded a real estate development firm in Boston about 10 years ago. Jack discovered, as the years passed and the firm grew larger, that people were less and less connected to each other. There seemed to be more friction and more misunderstanding among the managers. Most of them traveled frequently, and many of them worked out of their homes to save commuting time. Everyone was wired to the office via the Internet, and everyone had cell phones and fax machines. Still, there was a growing sense of isolation.

Jack's solution was not a sophisticated one, but it did wonders for his firm: free pizza every Thursday. People would sit around a big table in Jack's office and talk. There was no agenda, and not everyone could be present every week. But there was always a core of people there who provided continuity. These sessions provided the humor, the contact, and the deeper, richer flow of information the firm needed. Pizza sessions provided the essential human moment.

Source: Adapted from Edward M. Hallowell, "The Human Moment at Work," *Harvard Business Review* (January–February 1999): 58–64.

Our experience in the telecommunications industry, for example, is that the simple conference telephone meeting (where people are linked by audio but not video) has indeed replaced many face-to-face meetings. Nonetheless, air travel and the need to get together in the same room continue to grow. No one travels more than managers working in high technology, the very industry that has produced the videoconferencing technology that was supposed to do away with much of our business travel.

ANALYSIS   Using the Traffing Method to Channel Information

Objective   This in-box exercise gives you a chance to analyze a typical pile of documents that might appear on a manager's desk.

Directions   Imagine that, as the afternoon shift manager in a manufacturing plant, you have received the following documents during the previous few hours. Some are waiting for you in your e-mail inbox. Others are physical documents resting in the in-basket on the corner of your desk. Using the Traffing method, make a note of how you would respond to each document, and then discuss and defend your choices in a group of four or five people. Your own choices reflect how you feel about delegating responsibility and how you prioritize your own work. Don't worry, for the moment, that you lack contextual details on each of these items. Do your best to think through the process of responding to them. See how much agreement your group has in "Traffing."

1. A copy of a report from a quality assurance committee. This report is being circulated to all departments. The document looks interesting, but you're too busy to read it now. You're not even sure why it came to you, but you're intrigued enough to keep it.

2. A quarterly report from the product design unit.

3. A marketing brochure on new office equipment. Your unit will be moved to a new wing in the building, and the "relocation task force" has asked all shift managers to begin making recommendations on what new office furniture to purchase.

4. A memo from the vice president for operations on increases in shop-floor accidents. The number of reported accidents is up 13 percent over last quarter. Two of these resulted in hospitalizations.

5. An invitation to the design unit's holiday party with an RSVP.

6. A list of training films that must be previewed before the end of the month (still haunting your in-basket from last week).

7. Four signed contracts for your final approval.

8. A memo requesting agenda items for the next staff meeting.

9. A sign-up sheet for the next blood drive.

Reflection   In the directions for this exercise, we told you not to worry about the contextual details. In reality, of course, context is very important for deciding the relative priorities of tasks. Taken out of context, a sign-up sheet for a blood drive might seem unimportant, but within the culture of a health organization or the Red Cross, that activity might take on much more importance as a symbolic act in support of the values of the organization.

PRACTICE Monitoring Your Performance by Inviting Feedback

Objective Even straightforward ideas like the Opening, Agenda, Body, and Closing (OABC) approach to communicating require practice, evaluation, and reinforcement. This exercise asks you to work with others on improving your ability to compose messages that are clear, concise, and complete.

Directions In groups of three, practice composing voice mail messages using the OABC method described on pages 118–119. First make a quick written outline of what you want to say in each section, then share the message just as you would leave it over the phone. As a listener, give your classmates some feedback on the clarity and conciseness of the message. Consider the following questions:

Discussion Questions
1. Does the opening set a positive climate both verbally and nonverbally?

2. Does the agenda provide a quick roadmap of what the "body" of the message is about?

3. Is the body clear? If the parts of the body relate, is it clear how they relate? Is there any possibility for misunderstanding? Any ambiguity?

4. Does the closing include action steps—who does what by when—and conclude with a positive tone? Have you included any necessary contact information (e.g., your phone number, stated slowly, clearly, and repeated)?

Reflection If you have ever hung up the telephone after leaving a voice mail and then realized that you failed to mention the reason that you were calling, you'll appreciate the value of the OABC system. If you have ever called to leave a voice mail and been surprised when the other party answered the phone, you may find the OABC system even more useful. When talking on the phone, it is easy to get sidetracked by issues brought up by the other party. If you have gone through the OABC process and made notes about what you want to convey, however, you are less likely to end the conversation without getting your point across to your listener.

APPLICATION Directing Your Own Information Traffic

Objective Think about the channels through which information comes to you, including snail-mail and e-mail, voice mail messages on the phone, reading assignments in your classes, messages from the media (print, visual, and audio), and miscellaneous documents (such as housing contracts, car registrations, and warranty agreements) that you must TRAF.

Directions Evaluate your performance in managing that stack from day to day, week to week. Answer the following questions:

1. Do you use a filing method for important documents?

2. List the five most important documents in your possession and how long it would take you to access them.

3. How could you improve your filing method?

4. How do you "process" your hard-copy mail?

5. How effective is your processing method?

6. Do you lose track of important correspondence or allow mail to pile up unopened?

7. How much time do you think you spend each day looking for documents (including scraps of paper with phone numbers or other bits of information on them)?

8. How effectively do you manage phone time?

9. At your job, what kind of information do you most need to channel and respond to?

10. How could you improve the way you manage information on the job?

Reflection Even managers who are skilled at managing their information traffic sometimes run into road-blocks if there are problems with the underlying communication infrastructure. For example, in late 2005 litigation between Research in Motion (R.I.M.), the maker of the popular BlackBerry wireless e-mail device, and NTP, a patent holding company, heated up, leading to concerns that the BlackBerry system would be shut down. The *Wall Street Journal* reported that, in response, "Information-technology professionals at dozens of big companies—including Citigroup Inc. and Boeing Co.—are drafting contingency plans. Law firms such as White & Case LLP, a New York–based firm, are stockpiling alternative wireless e-mail devices like the Palm Treo 700w. And dozens of government agencies—including the Los Angeles Police Department—are contemplating how they would operate without BlackBerrys, which are currently used to alert police captains in the field about homicides" (Spencer, Vascellaro, and Heinzl, 2006, D1). Having access to too little data, it appears, is still a much greater concern than having access to too much.

Competency 2 Analyzing Core Processes

ASSESSMENT Linking Critical Outcomes and Core Processes

Objective Core processes need to be analyzed to ensure that they are linked directly to the outcomes that we value. How clear are the connections between what you do and what you want to achieve?

Directions Consider your current job. If you are not currently employed, think about your job as a student. Begin by identifying the most critical outcomes of your job—what are you actually trying to accomplish (e.g., sell 10,000 units of a product; create an award-winning advertising campaign; learn how to analyze financial statements; earn an MBA, etc.). Next, think about the activities or processes that you engage in to try to obtain that outcome. Write a memo to your supervisor or your instructor in which you make suggestions for altering the core processes of your job to be more efficient. Be sure to consider the discussion questions listed below.

Discussion Questions 1. Are the main processes that your are currently engaged in clearly linked to the outcome that you are trying achieve?

2. Can you identify some activities that seem to be unnecessary, or even counterproductive, for reaching your goal?

3. Why are those activities part of your job? Are they things you have chosen to do or are they things that your supervisor/instructor has asked you to do?

4. What would happen if you eliminated those activities from your job?

Reflection In his classic article, "On The Folly of Rewarding A, While Hoping for B," Steven Kerr (1975) points out that, despite the fact that people recognize that the behaviors that get rewarded tend to be the behaviors that get repeated, organizations often create reward systems that actually discourage the behaviors they would like to encourage. Faulty reward systems can cause the core processes of an organization to shift away from achieving the stated objectives. Effective monitors work to ensure that reward systems encourage effective performance of the core processes required to accomplish critical outcomes of the organization.

LEARNING   Analyzing Core Processes

WE MONITOR "OUTPUT"—BUT WHAT IS THAT?

Andrew Grove, former chairman of the silicon chip manufacturer Intel Corporation, likes to ask newly promoted managers this question: "What is a manager's output?" He always gets interesting answers. Here are a few (Grove, 1995, p. 39):

- Judgments and opinions given
- Resources allocated
- Decisions made
- Mistakes detected
- Products planned
- Commitments negotiated
- Courses taught

Grove points out that this is really a list of activities—descriptions of what managers do as they attempt to create a final result or output. A surgeon's output is a healed patient living an active life; a fifth-grade teacher's output may be a student prepared with the skills, information, and confidence necessary to move to the next grade. Some activities are vital to achieving outputs, but if we focus too much on activities, they become ends in themselves and we lose sight of outputs. Sometimes, managers lose control of outputs altogether because they are so busy managing activities. A crucial question to ask about any activity in an organization is: "How does this add value to our desired outcomes?"

MONITORING THE VALUE CHAIN: HOW DO WE KNOW HOW WE'RE DOING?

To help businesses distinguish between activities that add value and things that do not, Michael Porter (1985), an expert on business strategy, proposes a model called a *value chain* (Figure 4.1). The value chain is a picture of all the activities a business uses to produce and deliver something its customers will value. Porter lists nine value-creating activities, five of which he calls primary and four of which are support. The five primary activities involve the following:

1. Bringing materials or information into the organization (inbound logistics)
2. Operating on them (operations)
3. Sending them out (outbound logistics)
4. Marketing them (marketing and sales)
5. Servicing them (service)

The four support activities that surround these primary activities and help them operate more effectively are:

1. *Firm infrastructure* (the planning, legal, financial, and accounting transactions used to add value to materials and information)

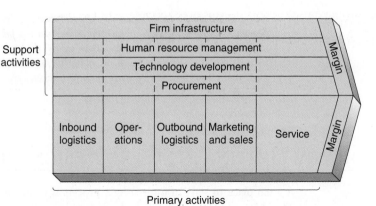

FIGURE 4.1

The generic value chain.

Source: Michael E. Porter, *Competitive Advantage* (New York: Free Press, 1985), p. 37. Porter's figure is cited by Kotler and Armstrong, p. 555.

2. *Human resource management* (the hiring, training, compensating, and socializing of people who do the work)

3. *Technology development* (the equipment, tools, and information that make value adding possible)

4. *Procurement* (acquiring the equipment, tools, ideas, and information necessary to maintain and improve the primary activities)

KEEPING THE BALL IN PLAY: SOME PRINCIPLES OF PROCESS REENGINEERING

Several years ago, two managers at IBM had the task of making the firm's finance department more effective and efficient. Sales representatives would close a deal on the sale of a large computer system and then call the credit department to arrange for financing. The process would sometimes take up to 50 days. In a business that deals with high-ticket items, these delays can be disastrous. Customers can change their minds, the competition can move in, and the customer's initial impressions of the company's commitment and responsiveness can be soured for good.

The managers had a simple but brilliant idea. They pretended they were a credit application form and proceeded to walk themselves through the system. The process usually involved five steps. At each step, the managers asked the person in charge to stop whatever he or she was doing and process the application as usual, only without the delay of having it sit in the pile on the desk. They were astonished to learn that the whole procedure took about 90 minutes! The rest of the time was spent in handing off the form from one department to the next, and having the form sit in various in-baskets. The process was like a baseball game. The game might last nearly three hours, but the ball is actually in play less than five minutes. The job the managers took on was to "reengineer" the system to keep the ball in play.

They replaced their credit specialists—the credit checkers and pricers—with generalists. Now, instead of passing the ball from one department to the next, one person, who is now called a deal structurer, processes the entire application with no handoffs. The major problem with the old system, say Michael Hammer and James Champy, experts on process reengineering, is that it was based on a false assumption *that every bid request was unique and difficult to process, thereby requiring the intervention of four highly trained specialists. In fact this assumption was false; most requests were simple and straightforward. [The managers found that] most of the work the specialists did was little more than clerical. . . . In really tough situations, the new deal structurer could get help from a small pool of real specialists, experts in credit checking, pricing, and so forth. (Hammer and Champy, 1993, p. 38)*

BOILING EGGS:
LOOK FOR THE LIMITING STEP AND DESIGN AROUND IT

A good place to start in improving a process is to understand it in its present form. The things we do every day are loaded with inefficiencies that we may not notice. We can use an example most of us are familiar with: the task of cooking a simple breakfast in a restaurant. Let's assume that the breakfast consists of a three-minute soft-boiled egg, buttered toast, and coffee. The task is to deliver such a breakfast at a scheduled delivery time (within five minutes of the customer's giving us the order), at an acceptable quality level (egg is not hard-boiled or too runny, toast is buttered but not lathered with butter, toast is not burned, etc.), and at the lowest possible cost. The customer wants a good deal; we have to deliver the deal and still do it at a profit over time. Here is how Andrew Grove describes this breakfast-making process from a "manufacturing" standpoint.

> *The first thing we must do is to pin down the step in the flow that will determine the overall shape of our operation, which we'll call the limiting step. The issue here is simple: which of the breakfast components takes the longest to prepare? Because the coffee is already steaming in the kitchen and the toast takes only about a minute, the answer is obviously the egg, so we should plan the entire job around the time needed to boil it. Not only does that component take the longest to prepare, the egg is also for most customers the most important feature of the breakfast.*

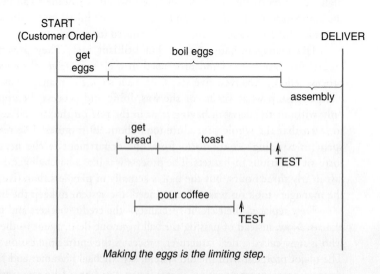

Making the eggs is the limiting step.

What must happen is illustrated in this simple flow diagram. To work back from the time of delivery, you'll need to calculate the time required to prepare the three components to ensure that they are all ready simultaneously.

- *First you must allow time to assemble the items on a tray.*
- *Next, you must get the toast from the toaster and the coffee from the pot, as well as the egg out of the boiling water.*

Adding the required time to do this to the time needed to get and cook the egg defines the length of the entire process—called, in production jargon, the total throughput time.

Now you come to the toast. Using the egg time as your base, you must allow yourself time to get and toast the slices of bread. Finally, using the toast time as your base, you can determine when you need to pour the coffee. The key idea is that we construct our production flow by starting with the longest (or most difficult, or most sensitive, or most expensive) step and work our way back. Notice when each of the three steps began and ended. We planned our flow around the most critical step—the time required to boil the egg—and we staggered each of the other steps according to individual throughput times; again in production jargon, we offset them from each other. (Grove, 1995, pp. 4–5)

Don't let the simplicity of this example deceive you. The idea of a limiting step has very broad application. We have seen more than one manufacturing or service process poorly designed because managers did not either recognize or care about focusing on the limiting step. Grove uses the process of recruiting college graduates to his company, Intel, to illustrate how important it is to design processes around the limiting step. Intel managers visit campuses, interview many candidates (as many as 50), and then invite the most promising ones to visit the company. Intel pays for the candidates' travel and interviews each one in greater detail using managers and other technical people.

After careful consideration, the company offers employment to one or more candidates. Clearly, the limiting step in this process is the students' visit to the plant—because of the cost of travel and the time taken by Intel employees to interview them and show them around. The goal is to have the tightest possible ratio between the number of people invited to visit and the number of people who are offered employment with Intel and accept it. To limit the number of people brought in for visits, Intel managers use phone interviews and correspondence, as well as some follow-up on references to screen the final pool of candidates. This process is difficult and expensive—but far less expensive than bringing too many candidates in for plant visits. The process saves money, increases the ratio of hires per plant visit, and reduces the overuse of the expensive limiting step (Grove, 1985).

Notice that Intel managers also have to use the principle of time offsets here. They have to think backwards and be sure they alert campuses to their visits for interviews, interview as many candidates as possible while on campuses, and build in time to do phone screening and then plant visits with the best candidates—all before graduation.

As you observe various processes, try to notice areas where the system is "soft." Look for bottlenecks and log jams. Look for indications that the process is not centered around the limiting step, or where other processes are not offset but are run in linear fashion, one after the other. Are people boiling eggs and *then* making toast while the eggs get cold, or are they making toast while the eggs are boiling? Further, look for examples of how problems in a process are not found in the low-value stage but only later when time and money have been spent on the process. For analyzing more complex processes, the monitor can benefit by using automated project management tools; we present some of these options in our discussion of the coordinator role in Chapter 5.

You also need to think about what the primary or core indicators are that tell you how effectively a process is operating. What about inventory—the availability and quality of supplies needed? Does inventory stack up, wasting money and space, or do supplies run out, making it impossible to fill orders and resulting in lost customers? What about downtime on equipment? Is vital equipment frequently down because of poor service or old technology? And finally, is the system stable? Does the process produce a product or service within a range of variability that is positive—given the needs of your customers? For example, how many pieces of toast per hundred are burned? How many customers complain about waiting or how many times are waiters corrected by customers in filling orders? Questions such as these can help you decide what to monitor in order to improve the process.

ANALYSIS   Can This Process Be Improved?

Objective   This exercise uses a process that most people are quite familiar with and asks you to analyze it and identify how the process could be improved. Don't forget to pay attention to how "improved" is being defined!

Directions   Read the following case and answer the three discussion questions at the end.

State Automobile License Renewals

Henry Coupe, the manager of a metropolitan branch office of his state's Department of Motor Vehicles, attempted to perform an analysis of the driver's license renewal operations. Several steps are performed in the process. After examining the license renewal process, he identified the steps and associated times required to perform each step, as shown in the following table:

Step	Average Time to Perform (seconds)
1. Review renewal application for correctness	15
2. Process and record payment	30
3. Check file for violations and restrictions	60
4. Conduct eye test	40
5. Photograph applicant	20
6. Issue temporary license	30

Each step was assigned to a different person. Each driver's license application was a separate process in the sequence shown. Coupe determined that his office should be prepared to accommodate the maximum demand of processing 120 renewal applicants per hour.

He observed that the work was unevenly divided among the clerks, and the clerk who was responsible for checking violations tended to shortcut her task to keep up with the other clerks. Long lines built up during the maximum demand periods.

Coupe also found that jobs 1, 2, 3, and 4 were handled by general clerks who were each paid $8 per hour. Job 5 was performed by a photographer paid $8 per hour. Job 6, the issuing of a temporary license, was required by state policy to be handled by a uniformed motor vehicle officer. Officers were paid $12 per hour, and they could be assigned to any job except photography.

A review of the jobs indicated that job 1, reviewing the application for correctness, had to be performed before any other step could be taken. Similarly, job 6, issuing the temporary license, could not be performed until all the other steps were completed. The branch offices were charged $8 per hour for each camera to perform photography.

Henry Coupe was under severe pressure to increase productivity and reduce costs, but he was also told by the regional director of the Department of Motor Vehicles that he had better accommodate the demand for renewals; otherwise "heads would roll."

Discussion Questions   1. What is the maximum number of applications per hour that can be handled by the present configuration of the process?

2. How many applications can be processed per hour if a second clerk is added to check for violations?

3. How would you suggest modifying the process in order to accommodate 120 applications per hour?

Reflection   Sometimes it takes an outside perspective to identify unnecessary activities or the limiting step in a process. When people have been doing a task for a long time, it may be difficult for them to recognize that some aspect of it is no longer necessary.

Source: W. Earl Sasser, Paul R. Olson, and D. Daryl Wyckoff, *Management of Services Operations: Text, Cases, and Readings.* Boston: Allyn & Bacon, 1978.

PRACTICE   A Better Process for Handling Small Business Loan Applications

Objective   This exercise gives you a chance to analyze a business process that focuses on making a decision rather than making a product.

Directions   Read the following case study. Then make any recommendations you believe might improve the loan approval process and meet customer needs for speed, convenience, and accuracy. Although you do not have "profound knowledge" of this process, you will probably have some insights into how it might be improved. Processes such as these grow and change over time by accident, force, individual personality, and other causes. An outsider who has no investment in the status quo and who is looking at the process objectively can usually find ways to improve it.

Work in teams of three people. Try to get "out of the box" and think creatively about some approaches that would save time, reduce the handling of paper as well as the decision time necessary for approval, and make the process flow better. Ask yourselves questions such as the following:

- What are all the steps in the process and how do they relate to each other?
- What steps can be collapsed or completely eliminated?
- During what point of the process does the loan application sit idle in the "value chain" with no value being added?
- What steps of the process require handoffs that take additional time or lead to costly errors?

Please write your recommendations in a simple memo to Chris Fleet, the loan approval team leader of Civic Trust Savings and Loan.

A team of loan officers in the central branch of a regional U.S. bank was given the task of improving the process used by the bank to approve business loans. The bank's leaders were concerned that the number of business loans issued each month by the bank had been steadily declining. (Business loans, as defined by this bank, are for amounts ranging from $250,000 to

$2 million, with a payback period of not more than eight years.) The leaders were not sure what was causing the decline in loan applications. They knew the market for business loans was growing, but their bank was getting a smaller piece of this very lucrative market.

Below is a description of the current procedure for processing business loan applications.

1. Application Form

A customer wishing to apply for a business loan can either pick up the application from a branch office or complete the initial application form on the bank's Web site. When a customer asks a bank employee for a loan application, the employee is expected to refer the customer to a loan officer. A brief chat with the loan officer is very helpful to prospective borrowers. It increases the likelihood that a customer will actually apply for a loan, and it reduces the errors and confusion in the application process.

Last year the bank put its business loan application form on its Web site. This Internet access made the physical application much more accessible to customers; however, the loan officers and secretaries say they receive a lot of calls from borrowers who have difficulty answering the questions on the application. They also find that in some cases borrowers leave important questions blank. (This application for a business loan is more complex and detailed than the form used to apply for an auto loan. The amounts requested are greater, and business loans usually involve more risk than a consumer loan.)

2. Application Assigned to Loan Officer

Local branch loan officers do not evaluate the loan applications. This evaluation is done in the Business Loan Department in the main office in Denver. Every application is sent to Denver.

On the day that a loan application is received at the Denver office, it is assigned by the assistant manager to a specific loan officer. Typically, the assistant manager gathers the applications that have been received during the day and distributes them to loan officers about an hour before the main office closes.

3. Evaluation of the Loan

The loan officer then opens a file on the application and begins collecting from the borrower whatever additional information may be necessary. This requires talking to the borrower, either in person or over the phone. If the borrower lives within 30 miles of downtown Denver, the loan officer tries to make an in-person appointment either at the bank or at the borrower's place of business. For borrowers living farther away, the conversations are held over the phone. As soon as possible, the assigned loan officer calls the potential borrower to ask some questions and "develop a feel" for what the borrower is like and how well he or she knows the business and market in question. These conversations are a vital part of the approval process since the documentation can tell only part of the story. The bank requires the following documentation:

- A record of personal income for the previous three years from the borrower
- A business plan describing the specific use the borrower will make of the loan as a business investment
- A current balance sheet of the business's financial status—cash flow, current debts, and assets—going back three years (for existing businesses with a financial history)

Because the requirements for the business plan and the financial data are listed on the application, about 60 percent of all borrowers include this documentation with their application. This means, however, that 40 percent do not and must either deliver that information to the bank or mail it in later. The process is quite complex. For example, many of these borrowers struggle with the "business plan" section of the application. Others, who have businesses that are already operating, have questions on how to describe their current assets and liabilities.

In cases where all the communicating is done over the phone, the loan officer will need to make at least two calls back to the applicant to clarify information or get information the applicant did not include. The phone and follow-up work may take no more than half an hour in actual discussion time; however, the time taken to actually contact the borrower may range over several days or longer.

4. Credit History Evaluation

The loan officer must also conduct a review of the customer's credit history to verify a good credit rating. In some cases it would save time to run this credit check while the customer is gathering the required documentation on employment and income; however, the bank has found that many customers never follow up on the process after initially submitting an application. So, loan officers, to avoid doing work on loans that never materialize, wait until the customer has submitted all the required documentation before running the credit check. Because the credit-checking process is automated and straightforward, it is now often done by an administrative assistant working with the loan officers.

5. Loan Approval: Yes or No

The loan officer has to verify that the application is complete and that the file contains all the information necessary to run the credit check. This credit check is usually done very quickly (typically 20 minutes) over the Internet through bureaus that provide credit information to lending institutions.

As soon as the file is complete, the loan officer must recommend that the loan be either granted or refused. If the officer recommends that the loan be granted, he or she passes the entire file to the administrative assistant in the loan department who works with the loan approval committee.

6. No? Get Second Opinion

If the officer recommends refusal, that officer must confer with one other officer who either agrees or disagrees with that recommendation. If the two disagree, the file is passed to the assistant branch manager for a decision whether to refuse the loan or pass it on to the committee for approval. If they both agree that the loan should be declined, the customer is notified via a form letter. All applications approved at these levels then go to the loan approval committee.

7. Approval Committee Decision

The approval committee meets once a week on Friday mornings. The committee has five standing members (the branch manager, the assistant manager, and three senior loan officers). Not all five are required to be in attendance for decisions to be made; however, one of the three people in the meeting must be either the branch manager or assistant manager. Typically, the Friday morning sessions last most of the morning. As soon as the committee ends its meeting, the loan officer who handled the file calls the applicant, informs him or her of the committee's decision, and makes an appointment for signing papers in person with the borrower.

The bank's records show that 60 percent of the loan applications are approved at the loan officer level and 40 percent are declined (in less than 3 percent of cases does one loan officer disagree with another that an initially refused loan be accepted). Of all the applications that make it to the committee, about 80 percent are approved.

The flow chart illustrates the primary steps in the process.

Reflection   Using teams to analyze and improve organizational processes can be very useful. Each person looks at the process in a slightly different way, due to their different backgrounds and experiences. For example, a team reviewing the process for handling small business loan applications that includes not only people who have been involved in different stages of that process but also people who are unfamiliar with current processes is likely to come up with more innovative ideas about how to improve the process. Including suppliers or customers in analyzing processes can yield important insights as well.

Loan Application Process

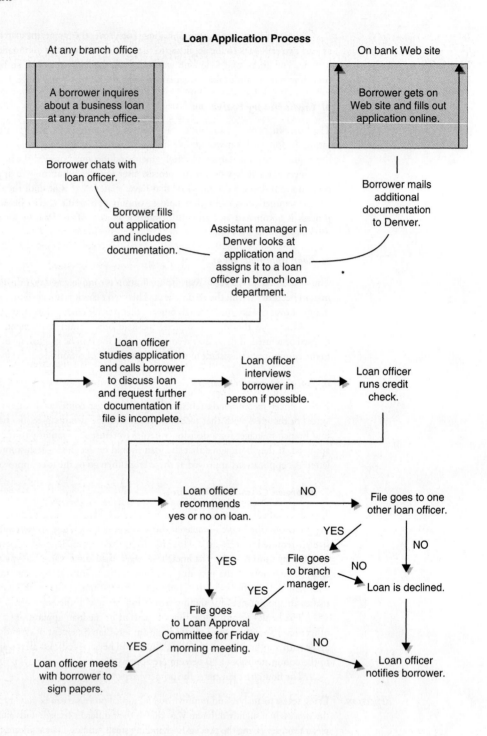

APPLICATION   Mapping and Improving a Process Yourself

Objective Applying process mapping skills in organizations requires having a thorough understanding of what actually happens, not just what is "supposed" to happen. If procedure manuals exist at all, they are likely to reflect old versions of the process or may not include special handling instructions for certain types of transactions. By observing a process firsthand as well as talking to the people involved in the process, this exercise gives you the chance to identify these types of disconnects between what the organization says the process is and how the process actually works.

Directions Select an organization that conducts a process you can map. The organization need not be a formal one. The easiest processes to map are those that recur. Try to observe the process, not just hear about it. Don't be intimidated by the fact that you are not an expert on the process. Your ignorance will be a major resource because it allows you to look at the process with a fresh perspective. Draw a map of the process and discuss how it could be improved. Consider the following suggestions.

- Think about steps that can be collapsed or simply eliminated.
- Look for places in which a product or service sits idle in the "value chain" with no value being added.
- Look for those expensive and time-consuming handoffs and consider ways of eliminating them.
- Look for controls or checks that might be more expensive than they are worth to the process. They take time, and they cost money. Are the costs justified? For example, if you are inspecting all products for quality assurance, can you reduce the inspection to a sample of units? If you are approving the vast majority of applications for credit, do you really need to review all applications with equal care?

Reflection It is important to recognize that some people may resist changes to existing processes. Thus, effective managers also must master the competencies of managing change (Chapter 8: The Innovator Role) and negotiating agreement and commitment (Chapter 9: The Broker Role) to reap the full benefit of their skills at analyzing core processes.

Competency 3   Measuring Performance and Quality

ASSESSMENT   Identifying Appropriate Performance Criteria

Objective In the assessment that you performed for Competency 2, Analyzing Core Processes, we asked you to think about the critical outcomes associated with your job and the core processes/activities that you engage in to achieve those critical outcomes. For this competency, we turn our attention to the metrics that are used to evaluate your performance toward achieving critical outcomes.

Directions Starting with the critical outcomes that you identified previously (either for you as an employee or as a student), think about how the tasks that you are asked to perform are linked to that outcome. Next, identify the points at which you receive feedback about your performance, as well as the types of feedback that you receive. You may find it helpful to construct a simple diagram that incorporates a time line to show when you perform different tasks and when you receive feedback.

Discussion Questions 1. How satisfied were you with your performance feedback prior to completing this exercise?

2. Did assessing the feedback you receive relative to the critical outcomes that you are expected to achieve increase or reduce your satisfaction with that feedback?

3. Did any of the feedback that you receive seem irrelevant to your critical outcomes?

4. How could you revise the feedback that you are given to link it more closely to your critical outcomes?

Reflection Although providing feedback has been linked to better motivation and performance (as we shall see in Chapter 5, Competency 2—Designing Work), lack of timely feedback is still a common complaint in organizations. One solution to the challenge of providing timely feedback is to make performance criteria explicit and provide employees with methods to monitor their own performance. For example, rather than waiting until after the semester is over to get formal student evaluation feedback, some faculty take advantage of web-mediated survey systems to gather student perceptions early in the semester so they can respond to concerns when they arise, rather than after the students have completed the course. Monitoring progress and providing feedback at frequent intervals may add slightly to short-term costs, but the long-term benefits can be very worthwhile.

LEARNING Measuring Performance and Quality

Monitoring in organizations is often associated with some type of measurement. We monitor (count or measure) inventory levels to be certain that we have enough on hand to meet anticipated demand. We monitor patient vital statistics as a measure of the state of their health. We monitor the number and length of telephone calls a customer service representative handles during the course of a day to assess productivity. But are these the things that we should be monitoring?

DECIDING WHAT TO MEASURE AND HOW TO MEASURE IT

What happens when organizations fail to monitor the right outcomes and processes? This, unfortunately common occurrence, can result in situations where we find ourselves "rewarding A while hoping for B," in the words of Steven Kerr (1975). In explaining why reward systems sometimes use inappropriate performance measures, Kerr suggests two issues that are especially relevant to the monitor role. He argues that a fascination with "objective" criterion and an overemphasis on highly visible behavior are two important causes for using inappropriate performance criteria.

WHAT IS RIGHT VERSUS WHAT IS EASY

Both of Kerr's explanations are consistent with the idea that we often measure what is easy to measure, rather than what is important to measure. By honing their understanding of measuring performance and quality, monitors can play an important role helping to identify measures that are most closely linked with the critical outcomes for the organization.

More than 30 years after Kerr's "On the Folly of Rewarding A While Hoping for B" appeared, concerns about what companies are measuring continue to be raised. Walsh (2005) notes that companies often substitute surrogate measures for exact measures of achievement because of the costs associated with the measurement process. For example, surveying customers to learn whether they feel that service quality has improved is more costly than inferring improvements in service quality based on decreasing numbers of customer complaints. Because not all customers who are dissatisfied complain, however, this proxy measure may miss important information.

DEVELOPING A HIERARCHY OF MEASURES

To help organizations develop a comprehensive set indicators that measure progress and achievement, Walsh (2005) outlines a measurement hierarchy. Following Simons (2000), Walsh first classifies measures based on the characteristics of objectivity, completeness, and responsiveness.

- **Objective** measures can be verified independently, in contrast to subjective measures that are dependent on personal judgment.

- Measures that capture *all* of the attributes that are relevant in defining performance are classified as **Complete;** the fewer attributes captured, the less complete the measure.

- Measures are considered **Responsive** if the manager can act to influence the measure; the more direct and powerful that influence, the more responsive the measure.

As an example, share price is an objective measure, but because other factors such as interest rates and investor sentiment also affect share price, it is not a fully responsive measure (Walsh, 2005). Ideally, organizations would define measures that were objective, complete, and responsive. In reality, objective measures often are not complete because they fail to capture important information, particularly for intangibles such as "service quality." To measure service quality, subjective measures drawn from a customer satisfaction survey are likely to convey more useful and accurate information than objective measures of sales volume.

In addition to distinguishing between objectivity, completeness, and responsiveness, Walsh (2005) also considers whether measures focus on outcomes, processes, or initiatives. At the top of Walsh's hierarchy are **Exact Measures of Outcomes.** These are complete measures that cover all the key attributes for the outcome under consideration. Exact measures of outcomes may be objective or subjective and may have different levels of responsiveness.

Next are **Proxy Measures of Outcomes;** proxy measures are used to make inferences about exact measures. For example, an increase in customer referrals may be used to infer that service quality has improved. Proxy measures are incomplete but are often used because they are easier and less expensive to obtain. Both exact measures of outcomes and proxy measures of outcomes are intended to reflect *achievement of strategic objectives* (in the example above, for instance, improving service quality).

Simply measuring achievement/outcomes, however, may not be sufficient. For an organization to improve outcomes, it also needs to understand and measure the processes and initiatives that lead up to those outcomes. Thus, **Process measures** of outputs, activities, and inputs make up the third level. Process measures reflect the *degree of effort being exerted.* Effort alone is not sufficient to guarantee desired outcomes, of course, but it can be an important lever for improvement. The fourth and final level of the hierarchy includes **measures of Initiative progress.** These measures provide information on the *changes being made* by the organization (Walsh, 2005). As with effort exerted, simply making changes may not result in the desired outcomes. Reviewing measures that are currently being used in light of this hierarchy can help to ensure that no important indicators are being omitted.

TAILORING MEASURES TO THE ORGANIZATION AND ITS MISSION

The hierarchy of measures presented above is general enough to be used in any type of organization. The identification of specific measures that should be collected and analyzed will depend on the mission and strategic objectives of the organization. Measuring items for which there are common industry benchmarks can provide a sound basis for comparison, but these measures may not be sufficient, depending on the mission of the organization.

In recent years, many companies have attempted to expand the way they measure performance. For example, the popular balanced scorecard approach (Kaplan and Norton, 1992) includes not only the financial perspective, but also the customer perspective, internal business perspective, and innovation and learning perspective. Incorporating these four perspectives helps to guard against suboptimization (Kaplan and Norton, 1992). More recently, Kaplan (2005) has suggested that the balanced scorecard is the contemporary manifestation of the McKinsey 7-S model (strategy, structure, systems, staff, skills, style/culture, shared values) which gained popularity as a result of Peters and Waterman's (1982) bestseller, *In Search of Excellence.* The balanced scorecard and similar approaches to measuring organizational performance still focus primarily on what is good for the company and ultimately the shareholder. For some, however, that focus is still too narrow.

In recent years there has been a growing interest in measuring organizational performance on more than just operational and financial performance. The concept of the "triple bottom line" gained currency in the late 1990s after the publication of John Elkington's *Cannibals with Forks: The Triple Bottom Line of 21st Century Business* (Norman and MacDonald, 2004). Supporters of the triple bottom line approach argue that organizational success should be measured not only in terms of financial performance, but also with respect to social/ethical performance and environmental performance. Waddock, Bodwell, and Graves (2002) go so far as to suggest that the pressure that stakeholders have put on corporations to be more socially and environmentally responsible has created a new business imperative.

Some business observers and academic researchers have questioned, however, whether changing business models to improve the social and environmental bottom lines might be a poor trade-off (Hayward, 2003). For example, Norman and MacDonald (2004) argue that because no clear, standardized measures exist for social and environmental bottom lines, companies may benefit by adopting the rhetoric of the triple bottom line without actually changing their actions. This brings us back to the key concern for every organization no matter how it defines its mission: What drives organizational effectiveness?

IDENTIFYING DRIVERS OF ORGANIZATIONAL EFFECTIVENESS

As organizations continue to increase in complexity, it becomes more and more complicated to identify the key drivers of organizational effectiveness. Beginning in the mid-1980s, research on enhancing organizational effectiveness began focusing on three main approaches: total quality management (TQM), downsizing, and reengineering

(Cameron and Thompson, 2000). Of these three approaches to enhancing organizational effectiveness, TQM offers the most attention to diverse measures of performance and quality. Despite that fact, in their review of research on TQM Cameron and Thompson (2000) concluded that "the studies that have attempted to evaluate the success of TQM efforts according to some standardized indicators of success do not inspire enthusiasm" (p. 216). Part of the problem appears to be due to inconsistency in applying TQM throughout the organization. One system that takes a comprehensive approach to quality is the Baldrige Criteria for Performance Excellence.

BALDRIGE CRITERIA FOR PERFORMANCE EXCELLENCE

Since 1987, the Baldrige Criteria (the Criteria) have been used by thousands of U.S. organizations to stay abreast of ever-increasing competition and to improve organizational performance practices, capabilities, and results; to facilitate communication and sharing of best practices information for organizations of all types; and to serve as a working tool for understanding and managing performance and for guiding organizational planning and opportunities for learning. The core values and concepts upon which the Criteria are built include "visionary leadership, customer-driven excellence, organizational and personal learning, valuing employees and partners, agility, focus on the future, managing for innovation, management by fact, social responsibility, focus on results and creating value, systems perspective" (NIST, 2005, p. 1).

The Baldrige Criteria go beyond measuring financial performance and incorporate a broad range of constituents. Outcomes continue to be important, but the Criteria also emphasize developing, deploying, and integrating processes that are aligned with the organization's strategic planning process. Outcome measures serve to complete the feedback loop in the strategic planning process.

The connection between quality processes associated with the Baldrige Criteria and outcome measures has been evaluated by the U.S. General Accounting Office (GAO). Looking at data from the 1988 and 1989 Malcolm Baldrige National Quality Awards (MBNQA), the U.S. GAO found that those companies that had been selected as finalists for the quality of their processes also showed improvements in specific outcome measures. Table 4.1 shows the annual percentage improvement for specific outcome measures.

Stock market analyses prepared by the National Institute of Standards and Technology (NIST) generally support a positive association between being a Baldrige winner and stock price. A comparison of stock market returns for Baldrige winners relative to the S&P 500 found that the Baldrige award winners outperformed the S&P return in every year from 1994 through 1999 (NIST, 2000), a finding consistent with an earlier study of the 1988–1996 Baldrige recipients (NIST, 1997). Since 2001, the Baldrige winners did not outperform the S&P (NIST 2003), perhaps because the Baldrige award has expanded to include health care and education organizations and there has been a decline in the number of winners that are publicly traded (NIST 2004).

TABLE 4.1 Results of a U.S. General Accounting Office Study of the Relationships between Quality Processes and Desired Outcomes

Outcome Category Measures	Reported Annual Improvement (%)
Employee-related indicators	
Employee satisfaction	1.4
Attendance	0.1
Turnover (decrease)	6.0
Safety and health	1.8
Suggestions	16.6
Operating indicators	
Reliability	11.3
On-time delivery	4.7
Order-processing time	12.0
Errors or defects	10.3
Product lead time	5.8
Inventory turnover	7.2
Costs of quality	9.0
Customer satisfaction indicators	
Overall customer satisfaction	2.5
Customer complaints (decrease)	11.6
Customer retention	1.0
Financial performance indicators	
Market share	13.7
Sales per employee	8.6
Return on assets	1.3
Return on sales	0.4

Adapted from K. S. Cameron and Michael Thompson, "The Problems and Promises of Total Quality Management: Implications for Organizational Performance," in R. E. Quinn, R. M. O'Neill, and L. St. Clair, *Pressing Problems of Modern Organizations* (New York: AMACOM, 2000), p. 228. Copyright 1999 by AMACOM BOOKS. Reproduced with permission of AMACOM BOOKS in the format Textbook via Copright Clearance Center.

OTHER APPROACHES TO IMPROVING PERFORMANCE

The literature on improving performance and quality is extensive and many organizations have learned from a variety of techniques over the years, including the zero defects and quality is free approaches, TQM, quality circles, kaizen, ISO 9000, the Baldrige Criteria, and Six Sigma (Bisgaard and DeMast, 2006). Recent writings on using enterprise resource planning (ERP) software (Laframboise and Reyes, 2005) with TQM, implementing formal business performance measurement (BPM) approaches (Marr, 2005), applying quality assurance techniques to global supply chain management

(Bandyopadhyar, 2005), and conducting self-assessments with the European Foundation for Quality Management (EFQM) Excellence Model (Benavent, 2006) continue to expand approaches for improving organizational performance. As technology continues to advance and societal expectations for corporations are constantly revisited, the skills and knowledge associated with the monitor role will be critical for organizational success. As Heras (2005, p. 54) notes, "A strategy with no indicators is wishful thinking, and indicators not aligned with strategy are a waste of time and effort."

ANALYSIS Improving Performance in the Health Care Industry

Objective The objective of this exercise is to develop a set of performance metrics for a hospital according to the measurement hierarchy outlined by Walsh (2005) and described in this chapter. This will hone your ability to distinguish different types of measures.

Directions St. Angela's Hospital has decided to adopt the Baldrige Criteria for Performance Excellence to help it meet its mission: providing the highest quality health care in a caring, community setting. You have been asked to head up a taskforce to address Criteria 3.2, part b, related to customer satisfaction and loyalty. Use the abbreviated version of instructions from *2006 Health Care Criteria for Performance Excellence* instrument shown below to prepare a brief report that proposes a set of measures you think are needed to give the hospital the data needed to improve performance with respect to patient satisfaction. (For more detailed information, you can find the entire Criteria at http://www.baldrige.nist.gov/HealthCare_Criteria.htm.)

In that report you need to:

1. Identify where each measure fits in terms of Walsh's (2005) hierarchy (e.g., Exact Outcome, Proxy Outcome, Process, or Initiative Measure).

2. Describe each measure in terms of its Objectivity, Completeness, and Responsiveness.

3. Justify that the combination of measures being recommended will capture the data necessary to meet this Criteria without imposing too high of a cost on St. Angela's hospital.

3.2 b. PATIENT Satisfaction Determination (abridged from the Criteria, see NIST, 2006)

1. HOW do you determine PATIENT satisfaction and dissatisfaction? HOW do you ensure that your measurements capture actionable information for use in securing your PATIENTS' future interactions with your organization, and gaining positive referrals, as appropriate? HOW do you use PATIENT satisfaction and dissatisfaction information for improvement?

2. HOW do you follow up with PATIENTS on the quality of HEALTH CARE SERVICES and transactions to receive prompt and actionable feedback?

3. HOW do you obtain and use information on PATIENTS' satisfaction relative to their satisfaction with your competitors, other organizations providing similar HEALTH CARE SERVICES, and/or health care industry BENCHMARKS?

4. HOW do you keep your APPROACHES to determining satisfaction current with HEALTH CARE SERVICE needs and directions?

Reflection The type of measures that organizations choose to collect and the ways in which data are categorized can convey important messages about organizational values. But often organizations send mixed messages. In health care, high standards of performance are expected, but beliefs that perfection is attainable can result in pressure to cover up mistakes, particularly when investigations of errors focus on blaming individuals rather than identifying problems with organizational systems (Jones, 2002).

PRACTICE Developing Education Performance Metrics

Objective This exercise will give you a chance to develop a set of performance metrics for your own education. Try to identify measures that you think are most critical for meeting your future goals.

Directions 1. Think about what your strategic objectives are for getting an education at this point in your life. As you work on developing a list of objectives, try to think about more than just getting a degree (although that may be one of your strategic objectives) and think about WHY you want to get that degree.

2. For each of the strategic objectives that you listed, identify some key measures that will help you determine whether or not you are on track to achieve that objective. Remember, one objective may require several different measures to adequately capture whether or not that objective has been achieved.

3. Compare the objectives and measures that you have developed. Do you see any objectives that appear to be contradictory? Are there any measures that show up for multiple objectives? How much control do you have over achieving your objectives?

4. Now, consider what the instructor can do to help you achieve your objectives. What measures would be appropriate for assessing the instructor's performance relative to your objectives?

5. Finally, reconsider the situation from the perspective of your instructor. Do you think your instructor has the same objectives that you do? Why or why not? If there are differences between your objectives and the objectives of your instructor, how can those differences be reconciled?

Reflection In many jobs, outcomes are not entirely controllable by the person who is tasked with getting the job accomplished. Doctors who treat patients often must depend on patients to take medications, participate in physical therapy, or avoid certain activities. The desired outcome of a healthy patient is not solely in the hands of the doctor. Likewise, the outcome of an educated student depends not only on the actions of the teacher, but also on the actions of the students, as well as on circumstances beyond the control of either the teacher or students. In situations where there is mutual responsibility, it may be tempting to focus on the performance of the other party, rather than on our own responsibilities. Finding the best balance of performance metrics in these types of situations is doubly difficult, but it is also doubly important.

APPLICATION Developing Performance Metrics for Your Job

Objective In the Assessment for this competency, we asked you to think about the type of performance feedback you receive in your current position. This exercise gives you an opportunity to use the tools we have discussed to develop enhanced performance metrics for your job.

Directions Develop a new performance evaluation form for your job. Be sure that you include measures for Outcomes as well as Processes and Initiatives. Think about how Objective, Complete, and Responsive the measures are, individually and as a set. Discuss your new evaluation form with your supervisor, and then revise them as needed.

Reflection Thinking about your present job and how it is being evaluated currently is one way to improve your performance. Just as important, however, is thinking about where you would like to see yourself in the future. Are there some tasks that you could begin to delegate? As we discuss in more detail in Chapter 7, The Produce Role, delegating can not only help you improve your supervisory skills, it also frees up time for developing skills in new areas. Perhaps you can incorporate some metrics for new initiatives into your performance evaluation to demonstrate your ability to manage change in your organization, a topic that we address in Chapter 8, The Innovator Role.

REFERENCES

Alesandrini, Kathryn. *Survive Information Overload: 7 Best Ways to Manage Your Workload by Seeing the Big Picture.* Homewood, Ill.: Business One Irwin, 1992.

Ashford, Susan J., and Ann S. Tsui. "Self-Regulation for Managerial Effectiveness: The Role of Active Feedback Seeking." *Academy of Management Journal.* 34(2) (1991).

Bandyopadhyay, J. K. "A Model Framework for Developing Industry Specific Quality Standards for Effective Quality Assurance in Global Supply Chains in the New Millenium." *International Journal of Management* 22(2) (2005): 294–299.

Benavent, F. B. "TQM Application through Self-assessment and Learning: Some Experiences from Two EQA Applicants." *Quality Management Journal* 13(1) (2006): 7–25.

Berrger, Warren. "Life Sucks and Then You Fly." *Wired* (August 1999): 156–163.

Bisgaard, S., and J. De Mast. "After Six Sigma—What's Next?" *Quality Progress* 39(1) (2006): 30–35.

Cameron, K. S., and M. Thompson. "The Problems and Promises of Total Quality Management: Implications for Organizational Performance," in R. E. Quinn, R. M. O'Neill, and L. St. Clair (eds.). *Pressing Problems in Modern Organizations.* New York: AMACOM, 2000, pp. 215–242.

Campbell, Jeremy. *Grammatical Man: Information, Entropy, Language and Life.* New York: Simon & Schuster, 1982.

Carlzon, Jan. *Moments of Truth.* New York: Perennial Library, 1989.

Champy, James. *Reengineering Management: The Mandate for New Leadership.* New York: HarperBusiness, 1995.

Cox, Allan. *Straight Talk for a Monday Morning: Creative Values, Vision and Vitality at Work.* New York: John Wiley & Sons, 1990.

Davenport, Thomas H., and Laurence Prusak. *Working Knowledge: How Organizations Manage What They Know.* Boston: Harvard Business School Press, 1998.

Drucker, Peter. "Managing Oneself." *Harvard Business Review* (March–April 1999): 64–74.

Elkington, J. *Cannibals with Forks: The Triple Bottom Line of 21st Century Business.* Gabriola Island BC, Canada: New Society Publishers, 1998.

Gates, Bill. *Business @ the Speed of Thought: Using a Digital Nervous System.* New York: Warner Books, 1999.

Gilovich, Thomas. *How We Know What Isn't So: The Fallibility of Human Reason in Everyday Life.* New York: Free Press, 1991.

Grove, Andrew S. *High Output Management.* New York: Vintage Books, 1995.

Hallowell, Edward M. "The Human Moment at Work." *Harvard Business Review* (January–February 1999): 58–66.

Hammer, Michael, and James Champy. *Reengineering the Corporation: A Manifesto for Business Revolution.* New York: HarperCollins, 1993.

Hayward, S. F. "The Triple Bottom Line." *Forbes,* March 17, 2003, p. 42.

Heras, M. "The State-of-the-Art in Performance Measurement in Spain." *Measuring Business Excellence* 9(3) (2005): 53.

Jones, B. "Nurses and the 'Code of Silence'," in M. M. Rosenthal and K. M. Sutcliffe (eds.). *Medical Error: What Do We Know? What Do We Do?* San Francisco: Jossey-Bass, 2002, pp. 84–100.

Kanter, Rosabeth M., Barry Stein, and Todd D. Jick. *The Challenge of Organizational Change: How Companies Experience It and Leaders Guide It.* New York: Free Press, 1992.

Kaplan, R. S. "How the Balanced Scorecard Complements the McKinsey 7-S Model." *Strategy & Leadership* 33(3) (2005): 41–45.

Kaplan, R. S., and D. P. Norton. "The Balanced Scorecard: Measures That Drive Performance." *Harvard Business Review* (January/February 1992): 71–79.

Kerr, S. "On the Folly of Rewarding A, While Hoping for B." *Academy of Management Journal* 18(4) (1975): 769–783.

Kim, Daniel H. *System Archetypes: Diagnosing Systemic Issues and Designing High-Leverage Interventions.* Pegasus Communications, 1994.

Kotler, Philip, and Gary Armstrong. *Principles of Marketing,* 6th ed. Englewood Cliffs, N.J.: Prentice–Hall.

Laframboise, K., and F. Reyes. "Gaining Competitive Advantage from Integrating Enterprise Resource Planning and Total Quality Management." *Journal of Supply Chain Management* 41(2) (2005): 49–64.

Marr, B. "Business Performance Measurement: An Overview of the Current State of Use in the USA." *Measuring Business Excellence* 9(3) (2005): 56–62.

"Message Overload: Employees Work to Stay Afloat as Message Volume Booms." *Knowledge Management* (1999): 34.

Mitroff, Ian, and Ralph Killman. *Corporate Tragedies: Product Tampering, Sabotage, and Other Catastrophes.* New York: Praeger, 1984.

NIST 1997a. National Institute of Standards and Technology. *Results of Baldrige Winners' Common Stock Comparison.* Accessed online February 19, 2006 at http://www.quality.nist.gov/ Third_Stock_Study.htm.

NIST 1997b. National Institute of Standards and Technology. *Results of 1988–1996 Baldrige Award Recipients' Common Stock Comparison.* Accessed online February 19, 2006 at http://www.quality.nist.gov/Fourth_Stock_Study.htm.

NIST 2000. National Institute of Standards and Technology. "Baldrige Index Beats the Market by Nearly 5 to 1." Baldrige National Quality Program CEO Issue Sheet, December 2000, 1–2. Accessed online February 19, 2006, at http://www.quality.nist.gov/PDF_files/Issue_Sheet_Index.pdf.

NIST 2003. National Institute of Standards and Technology. "Baldrige Beaten by S&P 500 after Nine Winning Years." *NIST Update May 15, 2003.* Accessed online February 19, 2006, at http://www.nist.gov/public_affairs/update/upd20030514.htm#Quality.

NIST 2004. *Baldrige Stock Studies.* Accessed online February 19, 2006, at http://www.quality. nist.gov/Stock_Studies.htm.

NIST 2005. National Institute of Standards and Technology. *Baldrige National Quality Program: Criteria for Performance Excellence* (brochure).

NIST 2006. National Institute of Standards and Technology. *Baldrige National Quality Program: Health Care Criteria for Performance Excellence* (brochure). Accessed online at http://www.baldrige.nist.gov/ HealthCare_Criteria.htm.

Norman, W., and C. MacDonald. "Getting to the Bottom of 'Triple Bottom Line.'" *Business Ethics Quarterly* 14(2) (2004): 243–262.

Perry, Lee, and Eric Denna. *Retrofitting Process Reengineering*. Unpublished manuscript, Brigham Young University, November 1993.

Peters, T. J., and R. H. Waterman Jr. *In Search of Excellence*. New York: Harper & Row, 1982.

Porter, Michael E., *Competitive Advantage*. New York: Free Press, 1985.

Sasser, W. Earl, Paul R. Olson, and D. Daryl Wyckoff. *Management of Services Operations: Text, Cases, and Readings*. Boston: Allyn & Bacon, 1978.

Sellen, Abigail J., and Harper, Richard H. R. *The Myth of the Paperless Office*. Cambridge, MA: MIT Press, 2002.

Senge, Peter. *The Fifth Discipline: The Art and Practice of the Learning Organization*. New York: Doubleday, 1990.

Senge, Peter, Charlotte Roberts, Richard Ross, Bryan Smith, and Art Keller. *The Fifth Discipline Fieldbook: Strategies and Tools for Building a Learning Organization*. New York: Doubleday, 1994.

Shapiro, Eileen C. *How Corporate Truths Become Competitive Traps*. New York: John Wiley & Sons, 1991.

Shenk, David. *Data Smog: Surviving the Information Glut*. New York: HarperCollins, 1997.

Simons, R. *Performance Measurement & Control Systems for Implementing Strategy: Text and Cases*. Englewood Cliffs, NJ: Prentice-Hall, 2000.

Soames, Mary. *The Biography of a Marriage: Clementine and Churchill*. New York: Paragon House, 1988.

Spencer, J., J. E. Vascellaro, and M. Heinzl. "Imagining a Day without BlackBerrys." *Wall Street Journal,* January 25, 2006, vol. 247, issue 20, D1–D4.

Stewart, Thomas A. "Managing in a Wired Company." *Fortune* (July 11, 1994): 44–56.

Tetzeli, Rick. "Surviving Information Overload." *Fortune* (July 11, 1994): 60–64.

Toulmin, Stephen, Richard Rieke, and Allan Janik. *An Introduction to Reasoning*. New York: Macmillan, 1984.

Waddock, S. A., C. Bodwell, and S. B. Graves. "Responsibility: The New Business Imperative." *Academy of Management Executive* 16(3) (2002): 132–178.

Walsh, P. "Dumbing Down Performance Measures." *Measuring Business Excellence* 9(4) (2005): 37–45.

Winston, Stephanie. *Organized for Success: Top Executives and CEOs Reveal the Organizing Principles that Helped Them Reach the Top*. New York: Crown Business, 2004.

Winston, Stephanie. *The Organized Executive: New Ways to Manage Time, Paper and People*. New York: Warner, 2001.

Wurman, Richard S. *Information Anxiety 2*. Indiana, QUE, 2001.

Wurman, Richard S. *Information Anxiety*. New York: Doubleday, 1989.

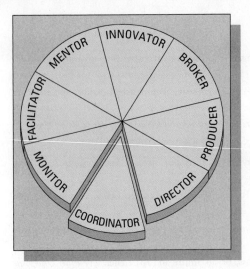

THE COORDINATOR ROLE

5

■ COMPETENCIES

Managing Projects

Designing Work

Managing Across Functions

I n Chapter 1 we discussed the emergence of the Internal Process Model of organizational effectiveness during the first quarter of the twentieth century and indicated that the primary focus of this model is the efficient flow of work and information (with the coordinator primarily responsible for the flow of work and the monitor primarily responsible for the flow of information). When the model first emerged, Henri Fayol's work on the general principles of management articulated a way of organizing work that was believed to result in continuity and stability in the workflow. The scientific management approach, developed by Frederick W. Taylor (1911), argued that work could be accomplished more efficiently if workers performed a minimal number of tasks and managers identified the one best way to perform these tasks. At the time, the Internal Process Model clearly called for routinization of work.

Today, although the Internal Process Model still focuses on the efficient flow of work and information and on stability and continuity in the organization, the underlying principles have changed dramatically. The action imperative of the internal process model is still Control, but computing technology and the globalization of the economy, as well as other economic forces, have changed the nature of work and hence our very understanding of the concept of "efficient flow of work." In 1994, *Fortune* ran a story entitled "The End of the Job." In that article, William Bridges asserted "The job is an idea that emerged early in the 19th century to package work that needed doing in the growing factories and bureaucracies of the industrializing nations. Before people had jobs, they worked just as hard but on shifting clusters of tasks, in a variety of locations, on a schedule set by the sun and the weather and the needs of the day. . . . Now the world of work is changing again: The conditions that created jobs 200 years ago—mass production and the large organization—are disappearing. . . . With the disappearance of the conditions that created jobs, we are losing the need to package work in that way" (1994, p. 64). As this world of work changes, we must look at the role of the coordinator in a new way.

The role of the coordinator involves bringing together the work of two or more employees, work groups, or work units that act interdependently. In today's world coordinators must often bring together groups of organizations to work interdependently as well. In the coordinator role, the manager's task is to make sure that work flows smoothly and that activities are carried out according to their relative importance with a minimum amount of friction among individuals, work groups, and work units. In some cases, the manager may even be required to coordinate across multiple organizations. For example, in 1999, when the New York State Department of Health became aware of the appearance of the West Nile Virus in its state, Dr. Antonia Novello assumed the role of coordinator, bringing together the efforts of federal, state, and local agencies with the goal of containing the virus (see Box 5.1).

BOX 5.1   DR. ANTONIA NOVELLO RESPONDS TO THE EMERGENCE OF THE WEST NILE VIRUS

In August 1999, the West Nile Virus was detected in New York City. As the New York State Health Commissioner, Dr. Antonia Novello assumed the role of coordinator for the project to stop the spread of the life-threatening virus and prevent an epidemic. Dr. Novello was familiar with responses to epidemics from her prior experience as the Surgeon General of the United States, her tenure as a physician in the Public Health Service Commissioned Corps, and time spent as Deputy Director of the National Institute of Child Health and Human Development. In addition, she had experience in coordinating projects and firsthand knowledge of the benefits of governmental agencies sharing resources. Dr. Novello knew that combating the West Nile Virus would be a daunting challenge that would require her to call upon all her prior experience in coordinating people, groups, and organizations.

The West Nile Virus was unknown in the Western Hemisphere until the summer of 1999. How it arrived is still a mystery, but once it got here it spread relatively quickly by transmission through mosquito bites, the primary way in which people can contract the virus. During the summer and fall of 1999, 7 people died from the virus and 62 became infected with it. Additionally, several species of animals, particularly birds, became infected with the virus. Crows seemed to be especially susceptible, with approximately 10,000 dying from the virus in 1999. With birds as a major carrier of the virus, and mosquitoes, after biting infected birds, transmitting the virus to people, a public health crisis loomed large for New York, its surrounding states, and potentially the nation.

Dr. Novello understood that the situation required immediate action. She moved quickly to coordinate the formation of an organization consisting of federal, state, and local health officials. The task facing the participants was to set policies and implement strategies to control the spread of the West Nile Virus. The participants included commissioners and public health directors from the New York metropolitan region, officials in the New York State Department of Health, wildlife and pesticide experts from other New York State agencies, and individuals from the federal Centers for Disease Control.

BOX 5.1   DR. ANTONIA NOVELLO RESPONDS TO THE EMERGENCE OF THE WEST NILE VIRUS (*Cont'd*)

Due to the wide dispersion of organization members and the need for frequent contacts, Dr. Novello implemented meeting and communication techniques for a "virtual organization." As a virtual organization, the coordinated effort would not have a name or a home location. It would exist as a network of people, groups, and other organizations. Within the organization, an electronic information infrastructure was created to support its activities. The participants knew that all the organization's people and resources had to be accessible for frequent and open communication so that information could be shared as soon as it was available.

Several communications methods were established for the organization. An already existent encrypted and secure wide-area network was used for regularly scheduled teleconferencing meetings. Electronic discussion groups were held among participants on the Internet. The Internet was also used for database access and e-mail, both of which became an integral part of the communications system to transfer knowledge and information.

With the infrastructure established for the organization, Dr. Novello successfully created an effective and responsive unit to combat the West Nile Virus. Coordination of the effort was enhanced when, over the winter of 1999–2000, Dr. Novello asked participants and other experts to assist in producing a written plan to battle the virus in the upcoming year. Based on the experience in the summer and fall of 1999, a plan was created for reacting to the West Nile Virus should it reemerge in 2000. When the virus was again identified in the spring of 2000, the plan was used, increasing the coordination among participants. In 2000, there were 2 deaths and 19 people infected with the virus, a substantial reduction from 1999.

Although the West Nile Virus continues to spread along the eastern seaboard, its pace has been slowed through the efforts of Dr. Novello and the organization she created. By coordinating the energies of experts in various areas and from many organizations, Dr. Novello was able to establish a successful organization with a shared sense of purpose and vision. The strategies put in place for West Nile Virus prevention and curtailment through Dr. Novello's coordination continue to abate its progress in New York while offering other states a successful model for coping with the disease.

Sources: Most of this material was taken from: John Zanetich, "Managing Knowledge in the Public Sector: An Intergovernmental Response to the West Nile Virus Epidemic," unpublished manuscript, University at Albany, SUNY, 2001. Used with Permission. Additional material was taken from "West Nile Virus Scare," *Infoplease.com,* October 2001 (http://www.infoplease.com/spot/killerbee1.html). and "West Nile Virus," *Environmental Health Center, Environment Writer,* May 2000 (http://www.nsc.org/ehc/ew/disaster/westnile.htm).

Coordinating work does not mean that the manager makes all the decisions regarding work design and workflow or that the work must be routinized. Instead, it means that it is the responsibility of the coordinator to see to it that the right people are at the right place at the right time to perform the right task, potentially involving employees in any or all aspects of this task as appropriate. Managers performing in this role must be concerned with the resources needed to do the work, including the necessary tools of the job and the physical space where the work is to be done; but they may also give the individual or work team responsibility and authority for carrying out this task. Thus, understanding the principles of participative decision making (see Chapter 3) is critical for effective coordination. Finally, when several people, groups, or organizations are working together, the coordinator is responsible for making sure that the output of one work group is available as input for a second work group when that group is ready. Again, in today's world of work, the coordinator is likely to involve the two work groups in planning how this is to be accomplished.

In this chapter we focus on three interrelated competencies that are key to this new role of the coordinator:

Competency 1 Managing Projects
Competency 2 Designing Work
Competency 3 Managing Across Functions

As you will see in this chapter, these three competencies are vital to accomplishing the organization's work. They are basic to the day-to-day functioning of the organization and the maintenance of its stability and continuity. They do not, however, necessarily assume that stability and continuity need be achieved at the cost of flexibility and adaptability. Rather, in the new world of work, the competencies are concerned with maintaining smooth work processes so that the organization can respond to change in a way that is simultaneously flexible and controlled when necessary.

Competency 1 Managing Projects

ASSESSMENT Project Planning

Objective This exercise is intended to prime your thinking about effective project management by encouraging you to reflect on your past project experiences.

Directions Think about a project or event you have worked on, preferably one in which you had some leadership responsibility. (Note that having leadership responsibility does not necessarily mean that you were the sole project leader.) Think about the planning and coordination, and respond to the questions below.

1. To what extent were goals and objectives made explicit? What role did you play in clarifying goals and objectives?

2. To what extent was the project explicitly segmented into smaller, more manageable activities? Describe the process by which the project was divided up. What role did you play in dividing the project into the smaller activities?

3. To what extent was there a clear understanding regarding a schedule or time line? What role did you play in devising the schedule?

4. To what extent was there a need to coordinate resources (money, equipment, supplies) as well as people? What role did you play in the coordination of resources?

5. Overall, how well was this project or event coordinated? What were the key successes? Where were some needed details overlooked?

Reflection As we noted in Chapter 3 in the Building Teams competency, when a project is assigned there is often a tendency to try to skip over the planning and coordination tasks and to dive directly into working on the project. Effective coordinators recognize that this is a mistake. Looking back at your prior experiences with project work gives you an opportunity to identify any points where coordination broke down and think about how to avoid those problems in the future.

LEARNING Managing Projects

World-class organizations must be adaptable and flexible to succeed. The project management body of knowledge helps organizations to manage change. Project management is used in a variety of business environments to manage nonroutine, complex, one-time processes. Dr. Angela Wicks, the lead examiner for the Malcolm Baldrige Quality Award Programs for the state of Rhode Island and a Massachusetts examiner, notes that project management has been an essential tool in addressing problems as diverse as restructuring the management processes of the United States Army, the reconstruction of California's highway system after an earthquake, new product development, and the reconstruction of New Orleans after Hurricane Katrina. These problems all require planning, directing, and controlling resources to meet the technical requirements, cost targets, and time constraints of a project.

In Chapter 3 we discussed the increasing use of teams in organizations. Project teams are one type of team that have become a necessity in organizations that need to bring specialists from several different organizational areas to work more efficiently on a single, time-limited activity. Although they were originally used primarily in research and development and in construction, changes in the economy, heightened competition, increased complexity in organizational environments, and rapid technological changes have created ideal conditions for project teams to spread to other organizational areas. Project teams are seen as an ideal approach to deal with the need to respond more quickly to changes in the turbulent business environment for several reasons. First, project teams are task focused, thus complementing the way many organizations allocate work—through tasks. Project teams also enable companies to engage the work through the use of cross-functional teams (see Competency 3, Managing Across Functions). Lastly, because project teams make use of resources borrowed from within the firm, and perhaps also from outside the firm, they are flexible and able to act and react quickly to change (Frame, 1999).

In many ways, managing projects is similar to managing long-term programs, and you will find that virtually all the competencies presented in this book are useful to the project manager. There are, however, some specific skills that are associated with the work of the project manager. Many of these specific skills focus on managing the flow of work, and so we include managing projects within the coordinator chapter. We should note that students also find these skills to be useful when coordinating complex group or team projects.

PROJECTS AND PROJECT MANAGEMENT: A DEFINITION

As noted above, there are many similarities between project management and line management. What, then, differentiates the two? Let us start with a definition of the terms *project* and *project management*. Harold Kerzner, considered to be one of the leading authorities on project management, defines a project as:

> *any series of activities and tasks that:*
> - *Have a specific objective to be completed within certain specifications*
> - *Have defined start and end dates*
> - *Have funding limits (if applicable)*
> - *Consume resources (i.e., money, people, equipment)*
>
> *(1998, p. 2)*

Thus projects differ from ongoing programs primarily in that they have a specific end point, in terms of both product and time. Some authors also add that a project should be a unique, nonrepetitive endeavor; that is, it should not be an activity that recurs. Kerzner goes on to define project management as:

> *involv[ing] project planning and project monitoring and includ[ing] such items as:*
>
> - *Project planning*
>   - *Definition of work requirements*
>   - *Definition of quantity of work*
>   - *Definition of resources needs*
>
> - *Project monitoring*
>   - *Tracking progress*
>   - *Comparing actual to predicted*
>   - *Analyzing impact*
>   - *Making adjustments*
>
> *(1998, pp. 2–3)*

The importance of project work cannot be overstated in the current business environment. In a recent article, Tom Peters declared, "In the new economy, all work is project work. And you are your projects!" (Peters, 1999, p. 116). Peters feels strongly that projects should be more than just dreary assignments that are grudgingly accepted. As such, projects are avenues for workers to show their talents and shine, turning the projects into vehicles that make others stand up and take notice—"Wow" projects (Peters, 1999). The tools of project planning and project monitoring are important contributors to making project work a success and making it possible to "Wow" others.

In point of fact, the various tools of project planning and project monitoring are closely tied. Planning clarifies the work to be accomplished and sets priorities for task completion. Planning involves scheduling—establishing timetables and milestones for completion—and resource allocation—developing a budget that forecasts the amount of labor and equipment that will be needed. Alternatively, monitoring tracks progress to see whether the project is proceeding as planned. Is the schedule being adhered to? Are milestones being met? How likely is the project to be completed within, or even under, the projected budget? In the next two sections we will present several key planning and monitoring tools. It should, however, be noted that the monitoring tools will be useful only if the planning has been conducted carefully, with sufficient attention to detail.

PLANNING TOOLS

"Planning is determining what needs to be done, by whom, and by when" (Kerzner, 1998, p. 522). It should make clear the path the project is expected to take as well as the destination. Consequently, the planning process should focus attention not only on the goals and objectives of the project but also on such issues as the technical and managerial approach, resource availability, the project schedule, contingency planning and replanning assumptions, project policies and procedures, performance standards, and methods of tracking, reporting, and auditing (Badiru, 1993). It is thus evident that planning is far more complex than scheduling. Indeed, while scheduling is considered a key element of coordination, it is actually the last step of the planning process and depends on the existence of a precise statement of goals and objectives, accompanied by a detailed description of the scope of work. Below we present some of the key planning tools available to the project manager, with the order of presentation based on the order in which they are likely to be used.

Today, many of these tools can be found in project management software programs such as Microsoft Office's Project Standard 2003 and Enterprise Project Management (EPM) Solution. These types of products incorporate the basic planning tools discussed below and simplify planning, monitoring, and coordinating processes by integrating all data relevant to the project. For example, data can be entered for tasks, working times, schedules, deadlines, people, materials, machines, and so on. During the data entry process, the software can also provide prompts to help establish the order in which work needs to be completed if two tasks are dependent. As data on tasks, times, and schedule are entered, the computer can generate Gantt and PERT charts, as well as other types of reports.

STATEMENT OF WORK

The statement of work (SOW) is a written description of the scope of work required to complete the project. It should include a statement regarding the objectives of the project, brief descriptions of the services to be performed and the products and documents to be delivered, an explanation of funding constraints, specifications, and an overall schedule. Specifications should be included for all aspects of the project and are used to provide standards for determining the cost of the project. The overall schedule should be more general, including only start and end dates and key milestones.

The statement of work may also include brief descriptions of the tasks necessary for project completion as well as a description, where appropriate, of how individual tasks will be integrated into the whole. Alternatively, this information may be included in the work breakdown structure.

WORK BREAKDOWN STRUCTURE

The work breakdown structure (WBS) shows the total project divided into components that can be measured in terms of time and cost. It may be presented in tabular or graphical form, or both (see Figure 5.1). Whether in tabular or graphical form, the WBS divides the project into a series of hierarchical levels; in graphical form it resembles an organizational chart of tasks (rather than positions). The complexity of the project and the degree of control desired during project monitoring will determine the number of levels. Badiru (1993) suggests starting with three levels, with level 1 being the final or total project, level 2 being the major tasks or subsections of the project, and level 3 containing definable tasks or subcomponents of level 2. Again, if the project is very complex, the WBS should include additional levels, until the final level specifies discrete activities that can be examined in terms of the time and cost required to complete the activity.

		ESTIMATED	RESPONSIBLE
	TASK	TIME (DAYS)	PERSON

PROJECT: ORGANIZING THE OFFICE PICNIC

		ESTIMATED TIME (DAYS)	RESPONSIBLE PERSON
TASK 1:	Do invitations and determine number of guests	5	Sam
	Activity 1.1: Get material from last year's picnic		
	Activity 1.2: Edit last year's invitation	.5	Sam
	Activity 1.3: Set up invitation log	.5	Sam
	•		
	•		
	•		
	Activity 1.X: Do final estimate on number of guests	.5	Sam
TASK 2:	Plan and purchase food		
	Activity 2.1: Plan snack food	.5	Marty
	Activity 2.2: Plan main meal	2	Pat
	Activity 2.3: Plan beverages	.5	Chris
	•		
	•		
	•		
	Activity 2.X: Purchase beverages	.5	Chris
TASK 3:	Plan picnic activities		
	Activity 3.1: Do informal poll of activities enjoyed at last year's picnic	5	Linda
	Activity 3.2: Find out where sports equipment is held	.5	Marty
	•		
	•		
	•		
	Activity 3.X: Buy new equipment, as necessary	1	Linda
TASK 4:	Plan and purchase supplies		
	Activity 4.1: Plan food supplies (plates, cups, plasticware, etc.)	.5	Marty
	Activity 4.2: Plan decorations	.5	Chris
	•		
	•		
	•		
	Activity 4.X: Pick up decorations from Picnic Store	.5	Marty

FIGURE 5.1A *Work breakdown structure: Tabular form.*

At the final level, the work breakdown structure should include at least two pieces of information that are needed for coordination of effort: the estimated time to complete the activity and the name of an individual who is responsible for seeing that the activity is completed. Often a third piece of information, the estimated cost of completing the activity, is also included. This allows for better integration of cost and schedule information needed to monitor the project. When cost information is included, people refer to the work breakdown structure as a *costed WBS*. It should be noted that time and cost estimates should be developed by the persons most knowledgeable about

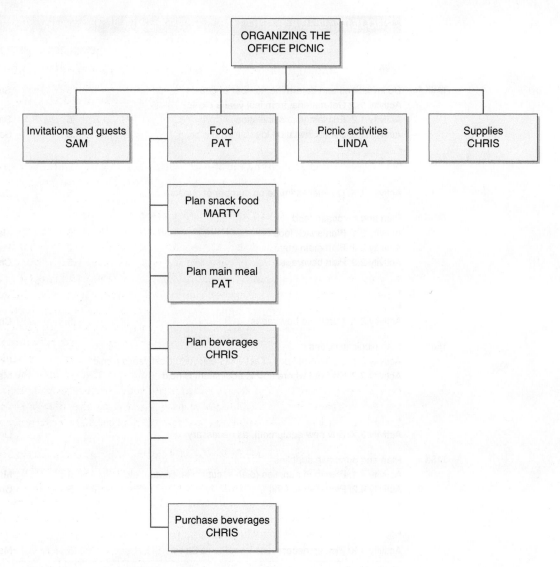

FIGURE 5.1B   *Work breakdown structure: Graphical form.*

those specific activities. Thus, if project team members come from different functional areas, the project manager should likely consult with managers from those different functional areas before making time and cost estimates.

PROGRAM EVALUATION AND REVIEW TECHNIQUE AND CRITICAL PATH METHOD

The WBS provides information on the estimated time of completion for each individual activity, but it does not indicate the order in which the activities can or will take place. It does not indicate whether Activity A must be completed before Activity B can proceed, or whether the two can proceed concurrently. When a project is fairly simple, these interrelationships are not difficult to discern and a schedule can be constructed directly from the WBS by laying out the activities in the order in which they are to be carried out (see the section on Gantt charts, later in this chapter). Alternatively, when a project is complex, it is almost impossible to construct a schedule before the interrelationships among the various activities are made explicit. Network diagrams are graphical tools for making these interrelationships explicit. Until recently, the most popular network diagramming techniques have been *Program Evaluation and Review Technique* (PERT) and *Critical Path Method* (CPM).

PERT was introduced by the Special Projects Office of the United States Navy in 1958 as an aid in planning (and controlling) its Polaris Weapon System, a project that involved approximately 3,000 contractors. At virtually the same time, a similar technique, CPM, was introduced by the DuPont Company. The methods are very similar and essentially show the flow of activities from start to finish. Over the years, the two methods have essentially merged and people often refer to PERT/CPM diagrams and/or analysis. More recently, with the increased use of project management computer software, other similar approaches have been developed and have gained popularity and acceptance (Spinner, 1989). Because the basic logic of network diagramming is essentially the same across the various techniques, we will present the more traditional approaches.

As was implied above, PERT/CPM diagrams allow the project manager to see the flow of tasks associated with a project by showing the interrelationships between activities. They allow the project manager to estimate the time necessary to complete the overall project given the interdependencies among tasks and to identify those critical points where a delay in task completion can have a major effect on overall project completion. In performing the PERT/CPM analysis, one assumes that all tasks or activities can be clearly identified and sequenced and that the time necessary for completing each task or activity can be estimated.

Figure 5.2 shows a simple PERT/CPM diagram. In the diagram, arrows designate activities. The circles at the beginning and end of the arrows are referred to as nodes; they designate starting and ending points for activities. These points in time, called events, consume no time in and of themselves. An activity is referred to as Activity *i,j* or Activity *i-j*, where *i* is the start node and *j* is the end node. Because of the way the diagram is constructed, the PERT/CPM diagram is sometimes referred to as an arrow or activity-on-arrow network diagram. Alternatively, activity-in-node network diagrams, as the name implies, place the activities within the node (usually drawn in boxes) and use the arrows simply to show the necessary ordering of activities. In activity-on-arrow diagrams the numbers along the arrows indicate the expected time for the activity to be completed. Although these numbers may come directly from the WBS, it is customary to calculate an expected time for activity completion (t_e), using a weighted average of an optimistic time (t_o), a pessimistic time (t_p), and the most likely time (t_m) using the following equation:

$$t_e = (t_o + 4t_m + t_p)/6$$

Note that Activity 3,6 has an expected time of zero weeks. This type of activity, called a dummy activity, is used to indicate that Activity 6,7 cannot begin until Activity 1,3 is complete.

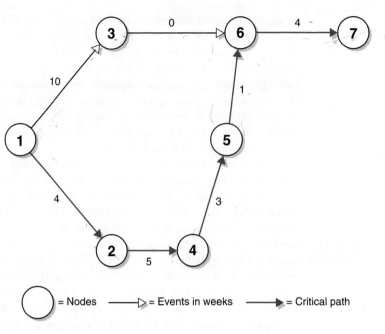

FIGURE 5.2 *PERT network with critical path.*

The critical path is that chain of activities that takes the longest time to proceed through the network. It indicates the least possible time in which the overall project can be completed, and it is the path that needs to be watched most carefully to ensure that the project stays "on track."

To identify the critical path, it is necessary to understand the concept of *slack* or *float*. In Figure 5.2, the critical path, 1-2-4-5-6-7, takes 17 weeks from start to finish. Note, however, that there is another path, 1-3-6-7, which only takes 14 weeks from start to finish. This means that Activity 1,3 could begin three weeks later than Activity 1,2 and the project would still be completed on time, assuming, of course, that the time estimates are fairly accurate. We then say that Activity 1,3 has a total float or slack of 3 weeks. While this is easy to see in Figure 5.2, it requires more effort when the diagram is more complex.

The first step in identifying the critical path is to identify the earliest start and finish times. Start at the first node of the diagram; this has an earliest start time of zero. For the other nodes, the earliest start time equals the earliest finish time of the previous activity. For all activities, the earliest finish time is the sum of the earliest start time plus the estimated time of the activity.

Next, take the largest finish time for the last node and calculate the latest start and finish times by starting at the last node and subtracting the estimated time for completion of that activity from the latest finish time of the previous activity. To identify the critical path, make a list of latest finish times and earliest start times. Time available is then calculated as the difference between the earliest start time and the latest finish time. If available time is equal to the estimated time for completing the activity, there is no float and that activity is on the critical path. Table 5.1 shows the calculations.

TABLE 5.1 Identifying the Critical Path

Activity	Latest Finish Time	(–)	Earliest Start Time	(–)	Time Estimate	(=) Float
1, 2	4		0		0	0*
1, 3	13		0		10	3
2, 4	9		4		5	0*
3, 6#	13		10		0	3
4, 5	12		9		3	0*
5, 6	13		12		1	0*
6, 7	17		13		4	0*

* Critical path
\# Dummy activity—has no time duration

As indicated above, the critical path is important because it is that path that must be most closely monitored. It is the path for which there is no slack, and activities must begin and end on time in order for the project schedule to be met. Activities that are not on the critical path can begin any time between the earliest and latest start dates. The determination is usually made in accordance with the availability of resources, primarily human resources.

Because projects typically require trade-offs among cost, time, and quality, project managers often need to estimate different approaches to the project. Project-crashing analysis can be used to help estimate the trade-offs associated with expediting a particular project by reviewing the costs associated with reducing the amount of time to complete the tasks on the critical path by adding additional resources.

RESOURCE LEVELING

The ultimate purpose of project management is to obtain the most efficient use of resources. Efficient use of resources can be a problem, however, if there are wide swings in resource needs. House asserts, "There will be times when team members feel they can't get enough done. Times when they can't get enough to do. Even when it is carefully planned, a project will not need the same amount of time from the same amount of people throughout" (1988, p. 10). One approach to maximizing the use of people is to use the information from the WBS, together with the information regarding the amount of float, to schedule activities that are not on the critical path.

Kimmons defines resource leveling as "the process of scheduling work on noncritical activities so that resource requirement on peak days will be reduced" (1990, p. 79). Although in this sense *resources* refers to all project resources that are limited within a specified time period, including personnel, equipment, and materials, resource leveling is most often used to allocate personnel to different project activities.

To determine the optimal use of resources, the project manager needs to begin by assuming that all activities will begin at their earliest start dates. Based on this assumption, the project manager can then draw a graph showing the required personnel, by job type (title), over time. This graph will show peaks, times where there is a great amount of work to be done, and valleys, times when there is less work to be done. Using the PERT/CPM diagram and the table that gives the float associated with each activity, the project manager can then level the resources by moving the start dates for some of the activities that have float to a later time (but prior to the latest start date). The process continues until the changes in personnel requirements from one time period to the next are minimized, that is, until the peaks and valleys are evened. Of course, with large, complex projects, the project manager would want to rely on computer software to perform this type of analysis.

✓ GANTT CHARTS

The project manager is now ready to schedule the activities, that is, to set dates on which the various project activities are expected to begin and end. The most popular tool for showing this type of schedule is the Gantt chart, developed by Henry L. Gantt in the early part of the twentieth century. These charts are essentially bar charts that allow you to see at a glance how the different activities fit into the overall schedule.

To develop a Gantt chart, make a list of each of the major activities, grouped as they are in the work breakdown structure and sequenced as they are expected as a result of the PERT/CPM and resource leveling analyses. Construct the Gantt chart by drawing the time line for the project along the horizontal axis of a graph and placing the list of activities along the vertical axis. For each activity, draw a bar showing the time commitment (see Figure 5.3). The Gantt chart is most useful when each activity time is

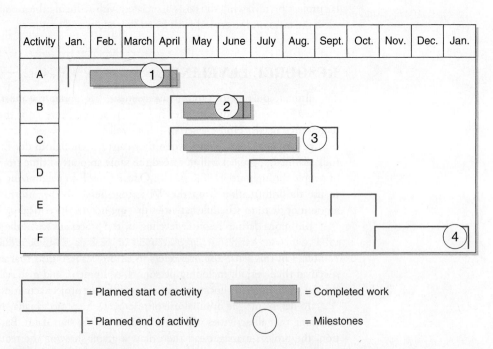

FIGURE 5.3 *Gantt chart.*

commensurate with the units of time drawn on the horizontal axis. That is, if the horizontal axis is drawn in terms of months, most activities should take at least two months. You can also identify specific milestones, or points of accomplishment, within each task by using a circled number within the bar. In Figure 5.3 the milestones could represent first drafts of status reports due at the end of the activity.

Specialized Gantt Charts. Once the Gantt chart is constructed, it can be used to integrate information about projected use of time with information about projected use of other resources. Two types of integrated Gantt charts are commonly used. The first shows personnel task assignments. By listing each individual along the vertical axis, followed by all of the tasks/activities to which that individual is assigned, the project manager can see at a glance which tasks/activities each person is assigned to at each time period of the project (see Figure 5.4). If the task distribution across individuals is uneven or if some individuals were mistakenly given too many work assignments during a single time period, this chart gives the project manager another chance to redistribute task assignments.

The second type of integrated Gantt chart is the Bar Chart Cost Schedule. This Gantt chart simply shows the projected cost of each activity below the bar showing that activity in the overall Gantt chart. This allows the project manager to have some sense of how much money is projected to be spent in each time period. It also allows the project manager to calculate the cost slope by dividing the cost of the activity by

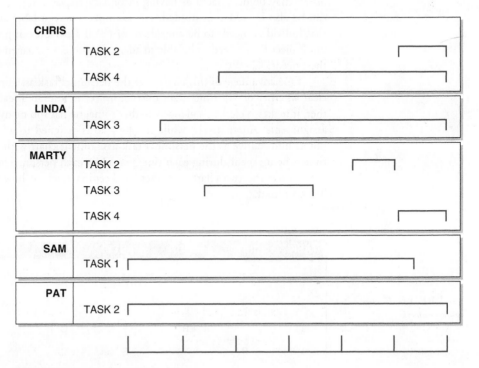

FIGURE 5.4 *Personnel Task Assignments.*

the duration of that activity (in whatever unit of time is being used). Thus, for example, if Activity A costs \$4,500 and is expected to take three weeks to complete, the cost slope in dollars per week is \$1,500. While this piece of information is not interesting in isolation, it becomes interesting when the project manager compares it to the cost slopes of other activities because it gives a sense of the relative cost of activities per time period.

Gantt Charts as Monitoring Tools.   The Gantt chart is also a useful project monitoring tool. By using different colors or different symbols, the Gantt chart can help the project manager track how closely the project is keeping to the planned schedule. When a given task runs over the allotted time, the Gantt chart can be used to determine whether or not the schedule needs to be rethought. Figure 5.3 shows that Activities A and B ran over schedule approximately one week each, whereas Activity C was completed almost one month ahead of schedule.

HUMAN RESOURCE MATRIX

One final planning tool is the human resource matrix. As with the Gantt chart used to show the personnel task assignments, this matrix can be used to see whether workload is evenly distributed across individuals. The human resource matrix lists the tasks/activities along the vertical axis and the names across the top of the matrix (see Figure 5.5). For each task/activity one person is designated as having primary responsibility (P), and others may be designated as having secondary responsibility (S). Other designations can be also be added as needed. For example, one can label an individual as (C) if that individual needs to be consulted, or (B) if a person can provide backup, and so on. Project teams need to be able to adapt the project management tools to best meet their needs.

One advantage of this chart over the personnel task assignment chart is that it is clear whether or not time spent on the project is time in a leadership capacity. Further, it makes it clear at a glance whether someone has too many leadership (primary) assignments. Alternatively, while it tells who is assigned to which task/activity, it is not as informative as the personnel task assignment chart with respect to how much time is being spent during each time period by each person. Therefore, it is probably wise to use the two charts together for keeping track of how human resources are being utilized.

TASK	CHRIS	LINDA	MARTY	PAT	SAM
1				P	
2	S		S	C	P
3		P	S	C	
4	P		S	C	

FIGURE 5.5 *Human resource matrix.*

PROJECT MONITORING

As indicated in the beginning of this section, monitoring is essentially keeping track of progress over the life of the project. There are four primary resources that need to be monitored: time, money, people, and materials. Monitoring involves looking at actual expenditures of resources, comparing actual with estimated, and, where necessary, deciding what adjustments need to be made in the work plan to accommodate discrepancies between actual and estimated.

In the previous section, we gave examples of planning tools that can be used in monitoring the use of human resources and time. Here we will focus on the project budget and time. Note that the tools provided here can be used to look at the total budget or at specific components of the budget, and so they are applicable to monitoring the use of human resources and materials as well.

COST/SCHEDULE INTEGRATION

While project success is generally defined in terms of project completion within constraints of time and cost, and at an appropriate level of performance, Roman argues that, "Often [the project manager] will be rated a success or failure as a project manager according to whether the project comes in under budget, on budget, or over budget" (1986, p. 156). The project manager therefore has good incentives to closely monitor the project budget.

In monitoring the budget, the project manager is concerned with two types of information. The first involves the amount of money budgeted for the work to be performed (budgeted cost of work performed—BCWP) versus the actual cost of performing the work (actual cost of work performed—ACWP). The difference between the two quantities (BCWP—ACWP), called the cost variance, is an indication of how close the estimated costs were to actual costs, with a positive number indicating monetary savings and a negative number indicating a budget overrun. (Again, note that these variances can be calculated for the total budget or by category of expenditure.)

The second type of information involves the amount of money projected to be spent on the actual work performed during the time period (budgeted cost of work performed—BCWP) versus the amount projected to be spent during the time period (budgeted cost of work scheduled—BCWS). The difference between the two quantities (BCWP—BCWS), called the schedule variance, is an indication of whether the money is being spent according to the projected schedule. Here a positive number is an indication that the project is running ahead of schedule—that is, more work is being performed than was originally scheduled—whereas a negative number is an indication that the project is running behind schedule—less work is being performed than was actually scheduled. Alternatively, a negative number could be an indication that some work is being performed out of its scheduled sequence. Harrison (1992) suggests that schedule variance should not be looked at separately from the formal scheduling system; that is, this information should be examined in conjunction with the Gantt chart or PERT/CPM network diagram to determine the actual status of specific activities or milestones.

Cost and schedule variances can be examined graphically or in a table. To examine these variances graphically, the project manager needs to calculate at each time period a cumulative BCWS, BCWP, and ACWP. That is, for each reporting period (usually monthly) the project manager needs to calculate the total projected budget up to that time period (cumulative BCWS), the total projected budget for the work that has actually been performed up to that time period (cumulative BCWP), and the total budget actually spent up to that time period (cumulative ACWP). The three amounts are plotted at each time period along the vertical axis, with time across the horizontal axis. The points are then connected to make a smooth curve (see Figure 5.6). Note that the cumulative BCWS curve extends from the lower-left corner, where no money has been budgeted to be spent before the beginning of the project, to the upper-right corner, where all the money is budgeted to be spent by the end of the project. When the cumulative BCWP curve lies above the cumulative ACWP curve, then the project is running under budget. Alternatively, if the cumulative ACWP lies above the cumulative BCWP curve, the project is running over budget and the project manager needs to understand why. Similarly, if the cumulative BCWS lies below the BCWP, then the project may well be running ahead of schedule. Alternatively, if the BCWS lies above the BCWP, then the amount that the project manager expected to spend up to that time period is less than the amount actually being spent and the project may be behind schedule. In Figure 5.6, the project was initially running under budget but is now running considerably over budget. It was also initially behind schedule, but is catching up.

A *performance analysis report* presents cost and schedule variance in a tabular form. This report is usually generated on a monthly basis, although, depending on the complexity of the project, it could be done more or less often. The report includes two tables, one with information about performance in the current time period and the second with information about cumulative performance. The first table presents five pieces of information for each category of expenditure: the amount budgeted for this time period (BCWS), the amount budgeted for the work performed (BCWP), the amount actually spent in the current time period (ACWP), and the schedule and cost variance. The second table repeats this format, providing cumulative information.

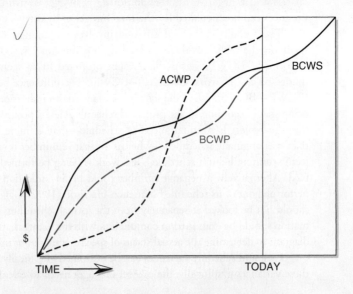

FIGURE 5.6 *Cost/ Schedule Integration Chart.*

Again, the project manager should be concerned when the performance analysis report indicates negative cost or schedule variances. In some cases, project variances may be related to scope creep—the expansion of the project requirements beyond the original plan due to small changes that are made over the course of time. Those seemingly small changes can add up to big differences in the scope of a project, so keeping track of them is essential. In some cases, it may be appropriate to renegotiate the terms of the project, so it is critical for project managers to have solid data to justify any request for changes in resource allocations or deadlines.

THE HUMAN SIDE OF PROJECT MANAGEMENT

As was indicated earlier in this chapter, many of the competencies that are presented throughout this book are relevant to the project manager. In particular, you should be aware that the tools associated with the managerial leadership roles in the human relations quadrant are important to managing a project team. One reason that interpersonal skills are so important in project management is that the project often lies outside of the usual organizational structure. Thus, while projects can be undertaken within a functional area, they are more often undertaken across functional areas in an organization. (Note that the last section of this chapter discusses managing across functions.) Depending on the permanent department structure of the organization, the job of the project manager will have different requirements. Since Chapter 6 discusses the different types of department structures, we will not go extensively into this topic here. It is, however, important to note that the definition of project management includes both projects that are undertaken within a work unit and those that require people to be brought together from across several different work units. Further, while bringing people from different functional areas together makes good sense from a creativity perspective, it may also create priority conflicts if members of the project team are also involved in other work over which the project manager has no authority (Kimmons, 1990). Here it is particularly important for the project managers to have good negotiation (see Chapter 9) and conflict management (see Chapter 3) skills in working with line managers (Thornberry, 1987).

In House's (1988) book, *The Human Side of Project Management,* she discusses interpersonal skills that are needed with clients as well. She argues that internal and external integration (coordination) are two project management tools that are generally given far less attention than the formal planning and control tools. In particular, she argues that when the outcomes of the project are not well defined and/or the project team's experience with project technology is high, there is a greater need to depend on tools of integration than on tools of planning and control. House gives the following rules of thumb regarding the choice of management tools that will most contribute to the project's success:

> *When a project is large and has* well-defined outcomes *but there is only* low experience *behind it, a project manager should expect to depend heavily on formal planning and control techniques.*
> *When a project has* well-defined outcomes *and* high company experience *behind it, [the project manager] should expect to draw heavily on internal integration.*

> *When a project is* large *and has only* loosely-defined outcomes *with* low company experience *behind it, [the project manager] should expect to emphasize external integration, formal planning, and formal control.*
>
> *When a project has* only loosely-defined outcomes *but* high company experience *behind it, the project manager will find . . . people skills at peak demand . . . [and] will rely heavily on external integration and internal integration. (House, 1988, p. 44, emphasis in original)*

While it is of course preferable to have well-defined outcomes, this is not always possible. In this case, it is very important to be in close contact with the client, perhaps even including the client on the project team and communicating on a regular basis, both formally and informally, regarding project progress. In addition, it is important to communicate regularly with key people in your own organization regarding project progress. Similarly, tools of internal integration involve regular formal and informal communication within the project team, using many of the skills of the mentor and facilitator presented earlier in this text.

ANALYSIS PLANNING A TRAINING COURSE

Objective   This exercise asks you to analyze the tasks in a project using the tools that we have discussed.

Directions   Read the following scenario and respond to the questions that follow. Your instructor may have you work individually or in small groups.

Congratulations! You have your first project manager assignment. You were asked to be the project team leader for the team that is going to design a new management training course in your organization. Here is the background information:

Last week your boss found your copy of *Becoming a Master Manager* sitting on your shelf and decided to borrow it. After reading through the book, your boss shared it with the head of the Training and Development (T&D) Unit, and they both agreed that it would provide an ideal foundation for the new management training course that was being discussed. Even though you do not know much about training, they decided that you would be an ideal project manager for the team designing the training since you are familiar with the framework. After receiving the assignment, you met with the head of T&D and agreed on a few basic concepts regarding the training program: (1) The program should run either one week or two; (2) the curriculum should be accompanied by two types of evaluation, one based on participant reaction and one based on the actual changes in work behavior when the participants return to the job; (3) the project team should conduct a needs assessment (i.e., you should interview managers) in the three divisions that will be the heaviest users of the training program to determine what they would like to see included in the curriculum; (4) you should develop some new cases or exercises based on the outcomes of the needs assessment; and (5) you should set up an advisory committee of upper-level managers from across the organization to approve the curriculum and the evaluation instruments.

Fortunately, you have some good people on your team from the training unit and after meeting with them a few times, they volunteered to put together an initial schedule. This morning you found a memo on your desk explaining that they had developed a schedule based on a proposed list of activities with estimated times and a PERT/CPM analysis. The memo indicated that the list of activities, the PERT/CPM network diagram, and a proposed schedule were all attached to the memo, but all you could find was the following list of activities with time estimates:

Activity	Description	Estimated time (in weeks)
1,2	Track literature on evaluation	4
1,4	Set up steering committee	1
1,5	Develop needs assessment questionnaire	2
2,3	Develop reaction evaluation instrument	1
2,10	Dummy activity	0
3,11	Dummy activity	0
4,9	Meet with advisory committee to discuss curriculum	1
5,6	Conduct needs assessment in first division	4
5,7	Conduct needs assessment in second division	2
5,8	Conduct needs assessment in third division	2
6,9	Analyze data and develop cases and exercise	3
7,9	Analyze data and develop cases and exercise	2
8,9	Analyze data and develop cases and exercise	2
9,10	Develop first draft of curriculum	10
10,11	Develop behavior evaluation instrument	3
10,12	Advisory committee reviews curriculum	2
11,13	Advisory committee reviews evaluation instruments	2
12,14	Curriculum revisions based on advisory committee input	2
13,14	Evaluation revisions based on advisory committee input	1
14,15	Conduct two pilot training courses	4

When you tried calling the team members who drafted the memo, you were told that they were away for the next two days at a training conference and no one else knew anything about what they were working on. You have a breakfast meeting scheduled with your boss and the head of the training unit tomorrow morning to discuss the schedule.

1. Based on the list of activities, prepare a PERT/CPM network diagram. What is the critical path?

2. Create a chart of earliest and latest start and finish times. Determine the critical path. What is the shortest time from start to finish?

3. What are your current scheduling concerns? Assuming that you do not have unlimited resources, make a few suggestions for resource leveling and set up a Gantt chart.

4. What concerns do you have about internal and/or external integration? How do you think you should handle these concerns?

Reflection   Manually working through examples may seem unnecessary, given the availability of computer software for project management, but working through problems helps project managers develop a clear understanding of the fundamental planning and scheduling concepts on which the software is based.

PRACTICE The Job Fair

Objective The previous exercise gave you the chance to apply some of the tools of project management, but often it is coming up with the list of tasks that is the most daunting part of the project manager's responsibilities. This exercise asks you to take a step back and figure out on your own what tasks would be required to complete a complex project.

Directions The president of the student association has asked for volunteers to organize a job fair, to be held in conjunction with the annual meeting of the Regional Management Association, and you think this is a great opportunity to try out your project management skills. The job fair was discussed during the last meeting of the student association, and there was a general consensus that:

- The job fair should take place during the first morning of the annual meeting.

- It should provide an opportunity for graduating students to meet potential employers and vice versa. Therefore, potential employers in the private, public, and nonprofit sectors will be invited.

- Organizations (potential employers) will be expected to "rent" a table so they can advertise their organization.

- Students (potential employees) will be expected to submit an updated resume to be placed in a resume book that will be distributed at the job fair to all organizations that rent a table.

The job fair is three months away.

1. Start by thinking about all the activities that need to occur in order to make the job fair a success. (Here are some major tasks to keep in mind: advertising the job fair, contacting potential employers, organizing the résumé book and getting it printed in advance, arranging for the setup of tables. You may think of others.)

2. Create a work breakdown structure.

3. Propose a Gantt chart.

Reflection In addition to the project planning and scheduling tools discussed in this chapter, don't forget to take advantage of other resources—particularly existing knowledge. Although planning a job fair might be a brand new task for you, staff members in the Career Services Office at a college or university are likely to be well versed in organizing these types of events and may be happy to share their knowledge with you over a cup of tea. We will talk more about the value of personal networks for gathering information and assistance in Chapter 9, The Broker Role.

APPLICATION Managing Your Own Project

Objective Now that you have some experience using project management tools and coming up with task lists, it is time for you to tackle your own project.

Directions Choose a complex project or a program in which you are involved at school or work, or in a community organization to which you belong. If you cannot think of any such projects, think about a complex project you would like to undertake, such as organizing a fund-raising event for a nonprofit organization that you think does good work.

Write a proposal designed to convince other people to support your project. Start with a brief description of the project and what you consider to be the most challenging aspects of its planning. Then, using the planning tools presented in this chapter (SOW,

WBS, PERT/CPM, Gantt charts), show how you would plan to complete the project on time and within cost. If there are important issues of internal and external integration that will affect the success of the project, discuss how these issues will be handled.

Reflection Planning a complex project is typically not something that is done in a single session and then cast in stone. Many issues may arise that cause implementation activities to deviate from the original plan. The more complex the project, the more opportunities there are for problems to emerge, so both the monitor and coordinator competencies are essential for effective project management.

Competency 2 Designing Work

ASSESSMENT Your Ideal Work Situation

Objective Everyone has ideas about what an ideal work situation would be like. This assessment will give you a chance to articulate some of the things that are important to you in the workplace. It also serves as a springboard for considering some of the aspects of work that organizational scholars have found to be important for motivating employees.

Directions Write a one- to two-paragraph description of your ideal work situation when you complete your current degree program (if you plan to go on for an additional degree immediately after completing your current degree, write about your ideal work situation when you complete the higher degree). Try to be as realistic as possible; you will not learn much from this exercise if you write that your ideal work situation is one in which you do not have to do any work but get paid large amounts of money.

1. List 5 to 10 characteristics of this ideal work situation.

2. To what extent do the characteristics you have listed focus on the type of work itself, the feelings of accomplishment you will have doing this work, and/or the extent to which you feel the work will give you opportunities to develop personally and professionally?

3. To what extent do the characteristics focus on physical working conditions, such as the physical space, the geographic location, and so on?

4. To what extent do the characteristics focus on work relationships with others, for example, supervisors, coworkers, employees, and customers/clients?

5. To what extent do the characteristics focus on work-related privileges, such as autonomy with respect to what you do, how you do it, and/or when you do it?

6. To what extent do the characteristics focus on financial rewards and/or non-work-related privileges of the work, such as pay and/or bonuses, fringe benefits (health insurance, other types of insurance, education, etc.), or special parking privileges?

7. What other types of characteristics did you use to describe your ideal work situation?

8. Knowing what you know now (assuming you have not yet read the rest of this chapter), what would you tell an upper-level manager about the design of work in today's organizations?

Reflection In responding to the questions above, did you find that there were some things that you didn't even consider when writing about your ideal work environment? Some people focus much more on the job itself while others put more emphasis on the environment or their coworkers. Despite the many differences in the preferences that people express concerning their jobs, as we shall see in the next section, research on job design suggests that there are some basic characteristics that most people find to be important.

LEARNING   Designing Work

In the Assessment exercise, we asked you to describe your ideal work situation. Perhaps your ideal work situation described a specific job within an organization, but there is a good chance that it did not. While in the past most people would have considered the terms "work" and "job" to be virtually synonymous, the world of work is changing. Today more and more people are self-employed and/or have only a temporary or part-time employment relationship with an organization. Even those who have a "full-time job" with an organization are not necessarily spending much time at a centralized worksite (an office) or working what would be considered "regular" hours; they can telecommute through the use of computers and fax machines, working hours that are personally convenient rather than working traditional "9-to-5" hours.

In the introduction to this chapter, we quoted from a *Fortune* article, entitled "The End of the Job," which argued that the world of work is changing and so must our ideas about the way work is packaged. At about the same time, *Business Week* ran a special report, entitled "Rethinking Work" (1994), in which they proclaimed, "The job, certainly, is not dead. There's still a robust need for relationships between employer and employed that rely on stability, security, and shared economic interests. . . . [But t]he relationship isn't what it was" (p. 76). Whether or not the notion of "job" is dead, it certainly is experiencing some profound changes. In particular, changes in the economy and in technology have resulted in the need to think very differently about the nature of work and the relationship between the organization and the employee. In the twenty-first century we can expect workers to be given greater autonomy and more opportunities to design and manage their own work (Cabana and Purser, 1998).

In this section we will explore these issues, focusing on the implications of the changing nature of work for managers who are concerned with the design of work for employees. We begin with a brief history of job design and then explore both individual job and work team approaches to designing work, focusing on two popular techniques: job enrichment and self-managed work teams. While neither of these approaches is new, they both provide means for organizations to rethink how work is organized.

A BRIEF HISTORY OF JOB DESIGN IN THE TWENTIETH CENTURY

As noted in the introduction to this chapter, for most of the twentieth century we have accepted the notion that work is performed most efficiently when large, complex tasks are broken down into smaller, more specialized tasks. In general, this is not an unreasonable assumption (note that this is exactly the process followed in the planning phase of project management), but as the nature of work and the nature of the work force have changed, this notion needs to be reexamined. To some degree this assumption is the legacy of Adam Smith, whose treatise *The Wealth of Nations,* written in 1776, set forth the notions that work could be accomplished more efficiently if it were divided into its component tasks and workers were specialized so that each individual had responsibility for completing only one of the component tasks. In the early 1900s, these principles were reinforced by Frederick W. Taylor and by Frank and Lillian Gilbreth, whose research in the area of scientific management argued that work should be broken down so that workers performed a minimal number of tasks and that, through scientific study, one could determine the one best way to perform each task so that motions that caused fatigue and/or hampered productivity would be reduced to a minimum.

While the notion that dividing up work into specialized tasks has persisted, the assumption that this approach is the most efficient way to do work has been questioned since the 1930s (Lawler, 1992). As the negative effects of task specialization on the individual employee became apparent, efforts to develop techniques to redesign jobs began to appear. In the 1950s and 1960s, various approaches to job design were tried in an effort to improve worker motivation, performance, and satisfaction. Perhaps the best known among these approaches was based on Fredrick Herzberg's (1968) work on employee motivation, which suggested that what motivated people at work was different from what demotivated them.

Herzberg and his associates argued that while the absence of such factors as good pay, supervisory competence, and good working conditions could demotivate employees, the presence of those factors would not necessarily motivate them. Instead, to motivate employees, jobs should be "enriched"; that is, they should be designed so that they are seen as giving individuals opportunities for achievement, recognition, responsibility, and advancement. In organizations such as AT&T, which had been notorious for standardizing and routinizing work processes across the United States (Lawler, 1992), efforts were made to give workers greater responsibility for deciding how the work was to be done and to hold them accountable for how well they did it. Although Herzberg's theory of motivation has often been criticized on methodological grounds, this work laid the foundation for much of the job redesign that was carried out in the 1970s, and we will come back to this approach in the next section. Interestingly, an underlying theme in many approaches to job redesign has been to bring together the work that was previously separated into specialized tasks.

A fundamental issue raised here is: Who controls how work is organized and managed at the lowest levels of the organizational hierarchy—the organization or the employee? The organizational purpose of breaking down work into specialized tasks is to increase organizational efficiency. Lawler asserts, however, that research on job design has shown that these approaches can instead lead to inefficiencies. He argues that when organizations control the design of work processes, there is a tendency to assume "that work should be simplified, standardized, and specialized, and that supervision and pay incentives should be used to motivate individuals to perform their tasks well. In essence, the thinking and controlling part of the work is separated from the doing of the work" (1992, p. 28). In separating the thinking from the doing, workers become inflexible and unable to do any work that does not fit into their narrowly written job descriptions. This can result in loss of productivity when the worker is suddenly unavailable. Not only are the workers inflexible, the entire work process is inflexible, leading to a loss of productivity when the process must be adapted or changed to accommodate changes in economic and/or technological conditions. In addition, the less the workers know about the work process, the more coordination is required to produce the product. When workers are not responsible for an entire product, there tends to be a greater need for quality control.

Alternatively, when employees have greater control over how work is organized and managed, the work tends to be more challenging, interesting, and motivating. When employees are given the opportunity to both think and do, they take ownership of the whole process and therefore are more likely to invest in finding ways to make the process more efficient. In *Crazy Times Call for Crazy Organizations,* Tom Peters gives a variety of examples of employees finding better ways to perform their work, noting "[t]he average employee can deliver far more than his or her current job demands" (1994, p. 71). Later he adds, "if bosses could appreciate the responsibility and pride people take in doing things most of us would be tempted to dismiss as mundane, we'd know how to tap a very profound power" (1994, pp. 83–84).

Over the past few decades, there have been two major streams of effort to redesign work to give employees more control over the process. The first focuses on the individual job and includes efforts to add tasks, responsibility, and/or autonomy. The second stream focuses on redesigning the whole work process to create self-managed work teams. Here we look at these two streams and suggest some guidelines for deciding whether either can be used to redesign the work within a work unit.

JOB DESIGN (REDESIGN): MOTIVATIONAL CRITERIA

As noted above, much of the work on job design has emerged as a result of research on motivation. While the efficiency approach of Adam Smith and Fredrick W. Taylor focused on specific tasks, the motivational approach has focused on the subjective characteristics of the job, or how the individual perceives the job. Again, this assumes that rather than using pay and close supervision as incentives to motivate people to do their work, the work itself could become the incentive. If employees feel positively about the work they are doing, they will not need to be closely supervised; rather, they will manage themselves.

The most frequently used approach to measuring the subjective characteristics of a job derives from a model developed by Hackman and Oldham (1975). The model posits five core job characteristics, or dimensions, that are said to lead to three critical psychological states that influence personal and work outcomes (see Figure 5.7). The five job characteristics are

1. *Skill variety.* The degree to which the job requires the individual to perform a wide range of tasks
2. *Task identity.* The degree to which the job requires completion of a whole piece of work that employees can identify as resulting from their individual effort
3. *Task significance.* The degree to which the job is seen as having an impact on the lives or work of other people

4. *Autonomy.* The degree to which employees have discretion in determining work schedules and procedures

5. *Feedback.* The degree to which the job provides employees with clear and direct information about job performance

The three critical psychological states are

1. *Experienced meaningfulness of the work.* The degree to which the person experiences work as important, valuable, and worthwhile. This is influenced by the degree of skill variety, task identity, and task significance.

2. *Experienced responsibility for outcomes of the work.* The degree to which the employee feels personally responsible for making decisions regarding work processes and work outcomes. This is influenced by the degree of autonomy.

3. *Knowledge of actual results of the work.* The degree to which the employee is able to see, on a regular basis, the effect of his or her performance on the work outcome. This is influenced by the degree of feedback.

As shown in Figure 5.7, the extent to which these five core job dimensions of work influence employees' internal work motivation, work performance, job satisfaction, absenteeism, and turnover is moderated by employees' degree of "employee growth-need strength," or their need for personal accomplishment and individual development. That is, the greater the individual's need for self-actualization through work, the stronger the influence of the job characteristics on personal and work outcomes.

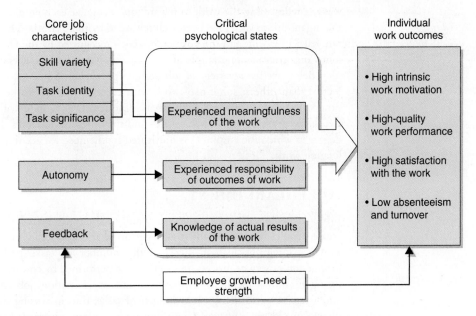

FIGURE 5.7 *Core job characteristics and individual work outcomes in a diagnostic model of job enrichment.*

Adapted from: J. Richard Hackman, and Greg R. Oldham, "Development of the Job Diagnostic Survey," *Journal of Applied Psychology* 60 (1975): 161. Copyright © 1975 by the American Psychological Association and the Authors.

JOB DESIGN STRATEGIES

Over the past few decades, as workers have begun to expect more from their jobs than a paycheck, organizations have increasingly begun to recognize the importance of motivational criteria in job design and have experimented with various techniques that focus not just on increasing job performance but also on increasing employee satisfaction. For example, in 1999 the *Harvard Business Review* ran a story that declared, "the single most important thing on the minds of new MBAs is—not money!—but whether a position will move their long-term careers in a chosen direction" (Butler and Waldrop, 1999, p. 149). Interestingly, while job enrichment techniques were originally seen as primarily applicable to production work, organizations are more frequently applying this approach to white-collar sales and service jobs as well (Lawler, 1992). Indeed, because service workers make up one of the fastest-growing segments of the U.S. labor force, many organizations are finding that one key to their survival is to redesign the work so that the delivery of superior service is a motivator for employees as well as a way of satisfying customers.

Understanding this, the University of Chicago Hospitals (UCH) knew that to survive in the increasingly competitive world of healthcare, it had to implement changes to turn around its low service standards and large employee turnover rate. UCH management found the service quality and staff motivation it wanted to emulate at the Walt Disney World Resort, well known for superior service and motivated staff. To accomplish this transformation, UCH partnered with Disney Industries to learn ways of redesigning the work to reward and recognize each employee's contribution to the organization. UCH has been well rewarded by these efforts. The employee turnover rate fell 33 percent, and the hospital has been recognized by the University Health System Consortium as an example of "best practice" in service excellence (Schueler, 2000).

Below we list a variety of job design approaches. Some are considered more effective than others; some may work with certain types of workers better than with others. Recall that in the Hackman and Oldham (1975) model, the relationship between the five core job characteristics and the outcome variables is moderated by the degree to which the employee is motivated by the need for accomplishment and challenging work.

JOB ENLARGEMENT

Job enlargement increases skill variety and task identity by redesigning the job to increase the number of tasks the person performs. It is also sometimes referred to as horizontal loading, because it increases the number of tasks performed within the production or service process, tasks otherwise performed by coworkers at the same level of organizational hierarchy. Opposite to task specialization, job enlargement requires employees to perform a greater number of tasks, thus increasing their ability to complete a whole piece of work. This approach is often criticized, however, because the work may be no more challenging than when the employee performed only one task. That is, performing many boring tasks may be no better than performing only one boring task if the person has no ability to make decisions regarding how the task will be performed.

JOB ROTATION

Similarly, **job rotation** increases skill variety by allowing individuals to shift among a variety of tasks, based on some time schedule. Like job enlargement, this approach has both advantages and disadvantages. Job rotation can be used to reduce boredom. When there is a monotonous job that must be done, job rotation is one way to share the boredom so that no one employee is assigned solely to that job. Here job rotation, like job enlargement, leads to increased skill variety but not necessarily to increased autonomy or feedback. It thus may have limited ability to influence individual and work outcomes. It can, however, also be used to expose people to different parts of the organization, giving them more knowledge about how the organization is run. Job rotation allows the individual to have a better understanding of the interdependencies among work units and the need for cooperation across units; it also allows managers to see how well a person adapts to the various situations and is therefore sometimes used to test interpersonal skills that may be required for promotion.

JOB ENRICHMENT

Job enrichment is considered the most effective of the various job design techniques in that it can potentially increase all five core job characteristics. Whereas job enlargement and job rotation focus primarily on skill variety and, to a lesser extent, task identity, job enrichment focuses on task significance, autonomy, and feedback as well. That is, instead of merely increasing the number and variety of job activities, job enrichment generally increases the responsibility and decision making for one's work practices as well as enhances the nature of job relationships with managers, coworkers, and clients.

One of the earliest and best-known job enrichment projects was conducted with data entry operators at the Travelers Insurance Companies. In that project, the work of data entry operators was changed to include responsibility for individual corporate accounts, communication with and feedback from the clients, and the completion of a whole piece of work rather than a small part. Measures of job attitudes and productivity indicated that there was a large positive benefit due to the job enrichment changes (Hackman, Oldham, Janson, and Purdy, 1975).

Despite its potential benefits, it was not until the 1980s that American industry, facing a shortage of skilled labor, began to take job enrichment more seriously than it had previously. For example, in 1985 when National Steel lost nearly $150 million, the company struck an agreement with the United Steelworkers Union to consolidate 78 job classifications into 16 and to broaden worker responsibilities and participation (Alster, 1989). Today, as noted above, most organizations in service industries are recognizing that to keep the best service workers they need to create jobs that employees enjoy and find challenging. For example, Microsoft faced a large employee turnover rate for key staff members because so many had been made independently wealthy before turning 40. In an effort to keep these important employees and their knowledge at Microsoft, they were allowed to create their own jobs in order to keep the work a more interesting option than retiring or starting their own companies (Lawler and Finegold, 2000).

There are, of course, other methods for enhancing the nature of jobs. Here we identify several specific approaches to job enrichment.

1. *Forming natural work units.* This means distributing work according to a logic that is based on workflow and completion of a whole job. When natural work groups are formed, jobs have greater task identity and task significance because employees experience their work as a whole rather than seeing only a small piece. (This is similar to the creation of work teams, which will be discussed in the next section.)

2. *Establishing client relationships.* Wherever possible, employees should have direct contact with the ultimate user of the product or service provided. When employees have direct contact, they also need to have the ability to make decisions to help customers (see next item, on vertical loading). At the Ritz-Carlton Hotel chain, every employee, beginning with junior bellhops, is given the authority to spend up to $2,000 to fix a guest's problems (Peters, 1994). At Marriott Hotels, guest service associates (GSAs) perform work that was once done separately by bellhops, doorpersons, front-desk clerks, and concierges. In addition, they can make decisions that they once had to refer up to a supervisor. Says one GSA at the Marriott Hotel in Schaumburg, Illinois, "I have more responsibilities. I feel better about my job, and the guests get better service" (quoted in Henkoff, 1994, p. 110). Thus, direct contact increases the likelihood of feedback as well as increasing skill variety and autonomy.

3. *Vertical loading of jobs.* Vertical loading is simply the redesign of jobs so that employees have greater responsibility and control over work schedules, work methods, and quality checks—and as a consequence have greater autonomy. In the previous item, examples were given regarding employees' ability to make decisions to help customers. Employees also need to be able to make decisions regarding work processes. Therefore, they need to be trusted with the organizational information necessary to make intelligent decisions. Steve Sheppard, CEO of Foldcraft, a restaurant-seating manufacturer, shares financial information with all employees through weekly department meetings. He believes that if employees are to manage for increased profitability, they need to know how money is spent and what the results are of various sales and cost-saving techniques (Peters, 1994).

4. *Opening feedback channels.* Increasing feedback to employees increases their opportunity to adjust and improve their performance. The more frequent the feedback, the greater the likelihood that job performance will improve. Efforts to open feedback channels should focus on job-provided rather than manager-supplied feedback. Many quality programs stress the importance of employees working with their customer(s), whether an internal or external customer. Working with customers increases the likelihood that the employee will value the importance of satisfying them. Thus, while manager-supplied information can be valuable to the employee, job-supplied information is often information provided by the person (work unit) who is actually receiving the product or service. Note also that job-supplied feedback is more accessible when the employee is completing a full piece of work; try to imagine a trip to a restaurant where a different waiter or waitress serves you each course. How would you decide how much tip to leave if the service is inconsistent? Consequently, opening feedback channels also often involves vertical loading and establishing client (customer) relationships.

SELF-MANAGED WORK TEAMS

Self-managed work teams are becoming a more popular and ever-present force in today's business world. In a recent article, Lawler and Finegold state that "organizations are beginning to make the more radical move of abandoning the traditional concept of the job altogether. One factor contributing to the demise of traditional jobs is the growing use of self-managing teams" (2000, p. 6). In support of this fact, the authors state that in a survey of the largest 1,000 U.S. firms, self-managed teams were present in 72 percent of them in 1999 (Lawler and Finegold, 2000).

Historically, self-managed work teams grew out of the sociotechnical approach to work design, which was originally developed in the 1950s at London's Tavistock Institute. The sociotechnical approach was basically built on two assumptions: The first is that the accomplishment of a task requires both a technology, which includes methods and tools, and a social system, which includes the people who work together to get the task done. The second assumption is that these two components need to fit each other if the task is to be done effectively. In contrast to job designs that focus on individual jobs, the sociotechnical approach sees the group as the basic unit of work design. Despite this difference, there is great similarity in the underlying beliefs of these two approaches in that both focus on producing a whole piece of work and both suggest that workers should be given greater autonomy in decision making regarding the work process.

As was the case with participative decision-making approaches discussed in Chapter 3, there is a wide range of decision-making discretion that can be given to self-managing work teams. As a result, they are known by a variety of names besides self-managing work teams, including autonomous work teams, semiautonomous work teams, process teams, and shared-management teams. The name is often based on how much autonomy the team has in decision making (Lawler, 1992). In some cases, work teams are fully responsible for managing the process and have the authority to make decisions on work methods, quality standards, purchasing (dealing directly with suppliers) and inventory, hiring and firing, salaries and bonuses, and so on. In other cases, the team may set production goals and make decisions regarding work methods but does not make human resources decisions. Lawler argues, however, "A team must be given responsibility for enough of the creation of a product or service so that it controls and is responsible for a clear input and a clear output. All the factors that influence how successfully a particular transformation is done should be included within its scope of responsibility" (1992, p. 90).

One issue that must be resolved in order for a work team design to be successful is that of how much cross-training there should be. That is, should team members be trained to perform all the jobs for which the team is responsible or is it expected that each person brings unique skills and responsibilities that are appreciated, but not performed, by others? In some cases, work team designs do indeed call for everybody to be fully able to perform all the tasks required of the work team. For example, work teams in automobile manufacturing plants typically train all members in all aspects of the team's work, but this does not need to be the case.

In Chapter 3 we discussed roles and responsibilities of team members and the notion that people bring unique skills and abilities to work teams and yet are expected to share the work. This issue is particularly important in thinking about work design. In

Reengineering the Corporation, Hammer and Champy talk about process teams— "groups of people working together to perform an entire process" (1993, p. 66)—and discuss the difference between being individually responsible for completing a task and being collectively responsible for a process. They state:

> *Process team workers . . . have a different kind of job. They share joint responsibility with their team members for performing the whole process, not just a small piece of it. They not only use a broader range of skills from day to day, they have to be thinking of a far bigger picture. While not every member of the team will be doing the exact same work—after all, they have different skills and abilities—the lines between them blur. Each team member will have at least a basic familiarity with all the steps in the process and is likely to perform several of them. Moreover, everything an individual does is imbued with an appreciation of the process as a whole. (Hammer and Champy, 1993, p. 68)*

At Kodak, for example, products are designed by teams that include specialists—shutter designers, lens specialists, manufacturing experts, and others. But, as Hammer and Champy note, "A lens designer who used to concentrate strictly and narrowly on lens design now designs lenses in the context of the camera as a whole, which means that he or she inevitably contributes to other aspects of the design and that his or her design will be influenced by what others have to say" (1993, pp. 68–69). Here we again see the paradox of needing to have clearly defined roles and responsibilities while simultaneously asking people to step out of their narrow roles and participate in the full process, of asking employees to contribute their special skills and abilities while expecting them to develop a broader range of skills and abilities.

CHOOSING BETWEEN JOB AND TEAM APPROACHES

If an organization decides to use self-managed work teams, it must make this decision for an entire work unit. While the decision does not have to include the entire organization, it cannot have some people working on teams and others working individually in a given work situation. Thus, an organization must decide whether more traditional, specialized work designs are preferred or whether the organization will choose a work design that gives employees greater responsibility and greater autonomy. To a large degree, this decision should be influenced by the organization's external environment and its technology. If labor costs are low and the environment is fairly stable, a traditional work design may be preferred. If work processes are simple and cannot be made complex, it may not be possible to create enriched jobs, although it may be possible to redesign jobs using job enlargement or job rotation.

Alternatively, if the organization's environment is changing and decisions need to be made quickly, there is a greater need to give employees the ability to make those decisions in a timely fashion. In these cases, the choice between job enrichment and work teams will depend more on the technology. Can an individual take a process from beginning to end or does the process require that a variety of tasks be accomplished simultaneously? In the former case, job enrichment approaches may be preferred because these are often less costly. In the latter case, employees are interdependent and need to be able to interact effectively with others working on the same process. In these cases, work team designs are preferable since the only way for an individual to have a good sense of the full process is to be a member of a team that is given the full responsibility for a whole piece of work.

SOME FINAL CONSIDERATIONS: WORK DESIGN AND KNOWLEDGE MANAGEMENT

Underlying the discussion of work design has been the notion that people will perform their work roles more effectively if they have ownership of the work. Creating an environment in which people have ownership requires that managers value the potential that each person brings to the work environment. In the introduction to this section, we noted that employees are often capable of contributing more than we generally ask of them. At the DuPont Company, there is a famous story about "an hourly worker who responded to an employee survey by writing, 'For some twenty years, you have paid for my hands and you could have had my head for free, but you didn't ask'" (quoted in Gundry, Kickul, and Prather, 1994, p. 35). In designing jobs, organizations need to be more cognizant of workers' capabilities and less focused on the immediate requirements of the task.

Similarly, in designing jobs, organizations (managers) need to consider that job design can (should) be a learning experience. Unfortunately, the core job dimensions do not directly address the issue of challenge, the extent to which a job gives a person the opportunity to try something he or she has never done before. Modern attention to total quality management, however, has also brought attention to the notion of continuous learning and the need for ongoing training and development. While in many cases training and development are an essential part of work team design, this is not always so with individual job design. We would argue that training and development should be an integral part of all work designs and that employees should be evaluated not only on how they currently perform but also on what they do to prepare for future roles. Training and development need not take place within a formal course or workshop; however, the changing nature of work suggests that the new relationship between employers and employees may be based more on a contract of employability than on a promise of job security. As stated in the *Business Week* article mentioned earlier, "job skills, like businesses, are ephemeral, and . . . employees themselves must be continually reinvented. . . . [The organization] has a responsibility to help workers sharpen existing skills or take on new ones" ("Rethinking Work," 1994, p. 86).

Over the next few years, the design of work will focus more and more on learning and knowledge transfer, which are two of the key tasks of work. Consider once again the DuPont employee's comment that the company "could have had my head for free, but didn't ask." In fact, trying to access and document the knowledge that employees have "in their heads" has become a critical strategic business objective for many organizations. The challenge has become how to collect organizational knowledge and transform it into organizational learning. This function is known as knowledge management.

In O'Dell and Grayson's *If Only We Knew What We Know*, knowledge management is defined as "a conscious strategy of getting the right knowledge to the right people at the right time and helping people share and put information into action in ways that strive to improve organizational performance" (1998a, p. 6). Note that this definition emphasizes the interactions among people and the active transfer of knowledge and learning. This is not simply a matter of writing down procedures and having another person learn by reading them.

Influencing this need for interactive transfer of knowledge is the fact that organizational knowledge can be divided into two categories, explicit and tacit. Explicit knowledge is the type of knowledge that organizations are very familiar with collecting and transferring to employees because it can be written down (O'Dell and Grayson, 1998a). Training manuals, corporate policies, procedure books, and the like convey explicit knowledge. On the other hand, tacit knowledge is informal. It does not lend itself to conveyance through formal organizational codification processes (Pfeffer and Sutton, 2000). It is contained in elusive forms such as know-how, judgment, intuition (O'Dell and Grayson, 1998b), and "tricks of the trade." As previously mentioned, most organizations are experts at recording explicit knowledge. It is tacit knowledge that organizations are struggling to have employees share and learn.

To help in the management of tacit knowledge, many companies are looking to a new organizational form called communities of practice. Communities of practice are "groups of people informally bound together by shared expertise and passion for a joint enterprise" (Wenger and Snyder, 2000, p. 139). Each community of practice develops its own structure and methods of interaction. Some may choose to meet for lunch, others may schedule formal meetings during work or at other times. There are also communities of practice that only exist in virtual space, meeting in electronic discussion groups and communicating via e-mail. Whatever form the community of practice takes, it seems to be effective, and many organizations are trying hard to encourage their development. Companies hope that by providing environments that support the formation of communities of practice, that tacit knowledge will be shared through the community's interactions. As companies continue to place a high value on knowledge and learning through knowledge management and communities of practice, there will continue to be changes and improvements in both training and work design.

ANALYSIS   What's My Job Design?

Objective This exercise is intended to help you think about what is important to you in your own job and also to recognize the impact of changing technology on job design.

Directions Think about a job that you currently have or one you had in the recent past. Describe the job design in terms of the five core job characteristics. (If you cannot describe a job of your own, use a job with which you are familiar, such as the job of a family member or close friend.)

Now think about the job outcomes of internal work motivation, quality performance, general job satisfaction, absenteeism, and turnover presented in Figure 5.7 and describe how the five job characteristics affect these outcomes. Is this job a good candidate for job redesign? Why or why not? Is this a job that could be altered to create a work team design? Why or why not?

Think about how (if at all) this job was performed 10 years ago. How (if at all) will it be performed 10 years from now? What caused the changes in the nature of this work over the past 10 years? What are the expected changes that you foresee that influence your perception of the changes to occur over the next 10 years?

Reflection   No job is perfect for everyone. The job characteristics model recognizes this fact by including critical psychological states between the core job characteristics and individual work outcomes. The right amount of autonomy for one person may be far too much for someone else. Individual differences have an important impact on what makes a "great" job!

PRACTICE Redesigning Work

Objective   This exercise gives you an opportunity to practice redesigning a job with a partner.

Directions   For this exercise, work in groups of two. If you described someone else's job in the previous analysis, you may want to find a partner who described his or her own job. Share the results of the previous exercise with your partner. Review the five core characteristics and your responses to the questions regarding redesigning the job or integrating it into a work team design. (For the purpose of this exercise, you should probably choose the one that you agree has the greatest need for change.) Decide on which approach is best and create a new design. Then respond to the following questions:

1. In what ways does the new design give the individual greater opportunity for ownership of the work?
2. What are the personal and/or organizational drawbacks to this design?
3. What about the design would make it difficult to implement in the current organization?

Reflection   Asking you to work with a partner on this practice exercise was a conscious choice about the design of the task. By working with someone else, you were able to get feedback about your ideas. You also used different skills than in the analysis exercise because for the practice exercise you had to communicate with another person. Which activity did you prefer?

APPLICATION Designing the Work Team

Objective   Observing teams in action and talking to members can be a valuable way to learn more about team effectiveness.

Directions   Find an organization that uses work teams to accomplish some of its key tasks. Interview several members of the work team about how decisions regarding work methods, quality standards, purchasing and inventory, hiring and firing, salaries and bonuses, and/or any other key work decisions are made. If you can, observe the team in action. Write a memo to the team describing your findings. Also include any suggestions you might have regarding how to improve the work design of this team.

Reflection   How do you think the team members that you interviewed would respond if you sent them a copy of your memo? If you made suggestions for improving the team, do you think that they would be seriously considered? If not, reconsider how you could present your recommendations so that they would be more likely to be adopted. Be sure to use what you learned in Chapter 1 about critical thinking to provide support for your claims. We will address the issue of making compelling arguments in more detail in Chapter 9 when we discuss the broker role and the competency of negotiating agreement and commitment.

Competency 3   Managing Across Functions

ASSESSMENT   Mapping Your Organization

Objective   The purpose of this exercise is to help you identify where you fit within your organization and how you are connected to other areas.

Directions   1. If you are currently employed, obtain a copy of an organization chart for your employer. If you are not currently employed, find a copy of your school's organizational chart (check with the Human Resource office at your institution). Review the official chart and observe how the structure of the organization is presented. Is there anything that indicates how the different parts of the organization work together? Are differences in the relative power of different departments apparent? If you had to put together a cross-functional team to work on an important project, is it clear who would need to be on the team?

2. Think about your job in the organization (as employee or student) and draw a new chart. Put yourself in the center and draw connections to all the areas in the organization that you need to be effective in your work.

Reflection   The formal structure found in most organization charts is often only a modestly accurate representation of how things actually work. Effective coordinators need to understand not only the official roles and responsibilities in the organization, but also need to recognize the informal networks that can help (or hinder) task accomplishment.

LEARNING   Managing Across Functions

In the previous section, we discussed the design of work from the perspective of the changing world of work. In our discussion, the theme of global competition surfaced as one cause of the need to rethink how we organize work. *Made in America* (Dertouzes, Lester, Solow, and the MIT Commission on Industrial Productivity, 1989), a summary of the report of the MIT Commission on Industrial Productivity, identifies six factors that distinguish U.S. companies that are successful in competing globally from those that are not. They found that the companies that were more successful engaged in simultaneous improvement efforts in quality, cost, and speed; built close ties to customers; built close ties to suppliers; integrated technology into manufacturing and marketing strategies and linked them to organizational changes that promote teamwork, training, and continuous learning; did continual training; and had greater functional integration and less organizational stratification. Three of these factors focus on breaking down barriers that have been created by organizational bureaucracies. They suggest that we not only need to rethink the world of work from the perspective of the individuals who are performing the jobs, but that we also need to rethink work from the perspective of how we allocate work in organizations. They suggest that the separations that are caused by grouping work by functional specialties can result in inefficiencies in communication and coordination, the very functions that hierarchical structures are supposed to support.

In recent years, more attention has been paid to organizational processes that cross functional boundaries (see, e.g., Hammer and Champy, 1993; Rummler and Brache, 1990). One approach that has gained a fair amount of popularity, partly because it can be used without creating excessive disruptions to the current organizational structure, is the *cross-functional team*. Cross-functional teams are made up of specialists from different functional areas, often brought together on an ad hoc basis, to perform some organizational task in a more effective, timelier manner. In the preface to his book on cross-functional teams, Parker notes that, "In many organizations, eight or more disciplines are working together on cross-functional teams to bring a new product to the market, develop a next generation computer system, design a new layout for a factory floor, produce an important new drug, engineer a complex telecommunications network, prepare a long-term corporate strategy, or implement a procedure to upgrade service in a government agency" (1994, p. xii). For example, Web site development companies are making extensive use of what they call cross-functional Web teams. Often these teams start in a company's IT department and then expand to include members from every stage of the business process. The success of these Web site development companies depends largely on the strength of their cross-functional teams (Guenther, 2001). Other dotcom companies believe in the successes of cross-functional teams as well. At drugstore.com, Peter Neupert, CEO, fosters creativity and innovation in his company by bringing staff from unrelated functional areas together to work on projects. Neupert believes so strongly in cross-functional teams that he entrusted one to create the customers' experience on the drugstore.com Web site for its all-important holiday season (Layne, 2000). While cross-functional teams may begin to sound like a panacea, they also pose new challenges for managers who must figure out how to manage a cross-functional team whose members still often report to a functional manager on the organizational chart.

In the next section, we discuss some of the specific challenges that are raised when cross-functional teams are used within traditional work structures. This is followed by an illustrative example of the use of a cross-functional product development team. The chapter concludes with some guidelines for managing cross-functional teams.

CROSS-FUNCTIONAL TEAMS WITHIN TRADITIONAL WORK STRUCTURES

In Chapter 6, one of the competencies focuses on organizational design. Because some of these issues are germane to our present focus on cross-functional management, we briefly present some key concepts and assume that you will explore them in greater depth in the next chapter. We also explore specific challenges for managing cross-functionally in an organization that is more traditionally structured.

Following the principles of Adam Smith and Henri Fayol, organizations have tended to create departments that handle the different functions of the organizations. When departments within a single organization are structured differently so that they can each approach their own task in a way that is most efficient for that particular department, we refer to this as *differentiation*. In traditionally designed organizations, differentiation is accomplished through the creation of specialized jobs and work units that are then organized hierarchically. Thus, individual contributors perform the organization's work. Performance-management and reward systems focus on the individual performer. Job evaluations and job descriptions clearly specify who does what and who reports to whom. Status differentiations are made clear by labels such as "labor" and "management," "bonus eligible" and "bonus ineligible," and so on. Organizational subunits typically consist of individuals with similar expertise performing similar tasks—engineers engineering, marketers marketing, and manufacturing experts manufacturing. Careers are focused on moving up the hierarchy, rather than on adding value to the output of the organization. Budget size and the number of people one manages are symbols of position and power, and may suggest that the organization is more interested in hierarchical control than in the delivery of products or services to a customer (Mohrman, 1993).

When an organization is so differentiated as a consequence of its traditional structure, there is a need for *integration*, or the coordination of work across units. Integration is primarily accomplished by processes inherent in the organizational hierarchy. Processes and procedures are standardized and formalized, specifying how the work is to be done and the sequence by which it is to proceed through the organization. Individual contributors are managed, directed, controlled, and coordinated by middle-level managers who receive strategic guidance from senior-level executives. Galbraith (1973), however, points out that while these types of integrative processes work for relatively simple and static situations, their effectiveness is limited in complex, dynamic, and turbulent environments. The rules of competition and the characteristics of organizations that are successfully competing in today's global market suggest that the current organizational environment is anything but static and simple. Mohrman states that, "complexity and extreme performance pressures" characterize the situation faced by today's organization (1993, p. 113). Consequently, the challenge confronting organizations in the next decade is to "simultaneously" accomplish the following (1993, p. 113):

Achieve multiple focuses (on product, market, customer, and geography) without dysfunctionally segmenting the organization.

Align individuals and groups that are task-interdependent in a manner that fosters teamwork in pursuit of shared overall objectives.

Enable quick, low-cost, high-quality performance while responding to a highly dynamic environment that calls for ongoing change.

Respond to ongoing increases in competitive performance standards by learning how to be more effective.

Attract, motivate, develop, and retain employees who are able to operate effectively in such a demanding organizational environment.

While some organizations are "throwing away their organizational charts in favor of ever-changing constellations of teams, projects, and alliances" (Dumaine 1991, p. 36), many organizations are attempting to manage these challenges within a more traditional structure. The challenge is then to identify processes and devices that are consistent with the complex and dynamic environment that the organization faces, and that allow organizations to integrate and coordinate their efforts within the constraints of what may still be a traditionally designed and structured organizational chart. It is the challenge of trying to create ad hoc structures that both transcend and operate within a traditional organizational design. This is the challenge of managing across functions.

Here we list several specific challenges that are faced by cross-functional project teams. Because many cross-functional teams are formed as a result of a need to respond quickly to competitive pressures, the list focuses on challenges associated with forming a team of strangers (Parker, 1994) to work together in an integrated fashion to produce a product faster than was previously possible when management coordinated the work across the different functional areas.

> The need for a clear charter and consistent support from senior management
>
> The need for a project or product champion, as well as functional champions
>
> The need for early involvement of all relevant functional areas
>
> The need to colocate cross-functional teams
>
> The need for efficient allocation of work across functional areas
>
> The need for speed in the focusing of energy and resources
>
> The need for new and better ways to hear the "voice of the customer"
>
> The need for a clearly defined process for cross-functional decision making
>
> The need for process disciplines and schedule integrity, that is, a need for well-defined, time-based approaches for performing the work

In the next section, these challenges will be illustrated by a specific example of a cross-functional product development team in the late 1980s.

AN ILLUSTRATION OF THE NEED FOR MANAGING CROSS-FUNCTIONALLY: THE STORY OF HEWLETT-PACKARD'S DESKJET PRINTER

In this section we present the story of Hewlett Packard's development of the Deskjet printer to illustrate the potential of a well-managed cross-functional team. The illustration, which draws largely from the chapter on Hewlett Packard in *The Perpetual Enterprise Machine* (Bowen, Clark, Holloway, and Wheelwright, 1994), is a good example of how team members from different functional areas can put aside those differences when they have a clear goal and an understanding that a quick response to competitive pressures requires an integrated focusing of energy and resources.

Prior to 1982, Hewlett Packard (HP), Digital Equipment Corporation, and IBM each sold their printers (along with other peripherals) with their computer systems. In that year, Japanese competitors began to market stand-alone printers; within a few years, one company, Epson, dominated the general-purpose low-end market with 80 percent of the market share. In 1985, prototype inkjet printers hit the market. HP had the edge in this market since the inkjet technology was invented at HP labs, but these printers made little progress because they were more expensive, were not as reliable as impact printers (printers where a lettering device hits the page), and, initially, required special paper. While they offered better resolution and increased flexibility in type style, inkjet printers could not compete against the increasingly sophisticated dot-matrix printers. Shortly after that, laser printers became available and became the best-quality (and highest-cost) option, offering the highest resolution.

In 1979, HP's Vancouver (Washington) division had been formed to build and market impact printers. By 1985, however, given the changing market, the division was facing increasing competitive pressures and profits were steadily declining. That year, the division's charter was expanded to include development of printers using HP's proprietary inkjet technology, and by the end of the year, the division, with the support of group management, embraced a new charter—to focus on the development of a printer for the low-end personal and office market.

The division reacted quickly and placed all its energy and resources on one machine—the Deskjet. The strategic objective was to wedge a niche between lower-priced and lower-quality impact printers and higher-priced, higher-quality laser products by building an inkjet printer with resolution approximating that of a laser printer but with a price that was significantly lower. In fact, the intention was to market the printer at a price that was so low it would essentially eliminate sales of impact and dot-matrix printers for general computer usage. The division was confident that it could accomplish this goal, knowing that (1) the technology had been invented at HP labs; (2) two key managerial leaders in the "puzzle," the Vancouver division R&D manager and the Deskjet project manager, were champions of the technology; and (3) the Deskjet project team had been experimenting with the technology for a few years. Nevertheless, there was still a huge challenge ahead—developing a product that could come close to laser-quality printer standards at a low cost.

The life cycles for printers in the low-end niche of the business were short, averaging about two years. The next generation of printer following the Deskjet would be ready in 15 months; the Deskjet was seen as an interim step in the development of a longer-term strategy for the low-end printer business. Although senior management at HP did not micromanage, they left no doubt that the future of the division was riding on the Deskjet printer. Their charter to the division was to find a path to solid footing in the market. They allowed the project team to identify specific goals. The team formulated one very specific goal that everyone in the division could understand and relate to—create a printer with laser-like quality with a retail price below $1,000. The manager of the division reinforced the group's goal by stating, "If you are not working on Deskjet, then you are just rearranging the deck chairs on the Titanic" (quoted in Bowen et al., 1994, p. 420).

Execution of the project required the most effective management of a cross-functional team. A key component of the product, the print head, required major development work. It was to be developed and manufactured by the components operation in Corvallis, Oregon—a two-hour drive from Vancouver by car. Because of this, the team decided to lower its risks and take as much pressure as possible off the print head effort by assuming additional design tasks in Vancouver. Another major challenge was to cut costs by maximizing the extent to which the product was designed for manufacture. The principal strategy the team adopted for doing this was to minimize the total number of parts in the printer, thereby simplifying assembly, the handling of parts, and purchasing. This meant that manufacturing and suppliers had to be involved early.

Perhaps the greatest challenge that the team faced was confronting a marketplace in which it had virtually no experience. The Deskjet would compete in the fiercely competitive high-volume, dealer-oriented marketplace. If the Deskjet was to accomplish its role in winning the market, the inexperienced marketing team would have to rely heavily on its fellow functions operating in new ways, taking on roles that they had never taken on before. Team members from marketing, R&D, and manufacturing, as well as suppliers would have to operate in a highly integrated cross-functional mode if they were to have any chance of succeeding in this new situation.

Marketing made extraordinary efforts to hear and understand the voice of its potential customers. HP realized that the Deskjet would appeal to ordinary and typical computer users, and so it sought out those customers in an ordinary and typical place—the shopping mall. HP team members actually asked potential customers how they felt about proposed features. While the design engineers were initially reluctant and disbelieving, they became convinced when they went out to the malls themselves and personally talked with potential customers. R&D understood the importance of early involvement of manufacturing and arranged for a dedicated manufacturing engineering group to be assigned only to the Deskjet. From the very beginning, materials engineers had compiled a "materials checklist," which by its presence alone served as a cost focal point for the team, in particular with suppliers.

The team also followed a strict process discipline during the prototyping process. Each month, regardless of whether R&D had completed its share of work on a prototype, manufacturing performed its role—building 50 prototype units. This represented a major cultural shift at HP. In the past, design engineers had dominated the prototyping schedule, allowing themselves to tweak many last-minute changes into a prototype before it was tested. A positive outcome of this new process discipline was that marketing and manufacturing could confidently use the prototyping process to focus on customer needs rather than on the whims of the designers.

Perhaps the most critical aspect of the team's success was its success at integration. From the project's beginning, marketing and manufacturing people were moved into the lab to sit with the R&D engineers. This "colocation" resulted in very strong integration among the three functional teams, something that had previously been atypical at HP, where R&D engineers had typically led the charge alone. In this case, R&D saw itself as the champion for resources for manufacturing. The R&D functional manager occupied a dual role as the manager of the R&D engineers and as a member of the "core group," the key decision-making body that was made up of one person from each of the three functions—R&D, marketing, and manufacturing. While taking a lead role in this group, the R&D functional manager always emphasized the equality of all team members.

Overall, the team had striking drive and energy. The reality that the division's future rested heavily on the project's success or failure generated much commitment and a sense of ownership. There was also a unique synergy between top management and the team regarding the guiding vision of the project. Senior management had provided a clear goal: Steal back market share. But they had also given another clear message: It was the responsibility of the division to make decisions that would cause the goal to become a reality.

KEY GUIDELINES FOR MANAGING CROSS-FUNCTIONALLY

The story of HP's success in developing the Deskjet printer provides several practical lessons regarding key aspects of effectively managing across functions. Here we present a list of guidelines that, although derived largely from other sources (Dumaine, 1991; Meyer, 1993; Parker, 1994), are well illustrated by the story of the Deskjet.

1. *Clarify goals and charter and get team buy-in.* The cross-functional team will generally take the formal charge from senior management, but the team must also feel ownership over the goals. In Chapter 3, we discussed the importance of being committed to a common goal or purpose and indicated that this is the glue that holds the team together. Sometimes the cross-functional team will need to meet with senior management to negotiate the goal or to make sure that there is a shared understanding. In the case of the Deskjet printer, senior management made it clear that they wanted to retrieve market share in the low-end printer market; the product development team then set a more specific goal of creating a printer with laser-like quality with a retail price below $1,000.

2. *Seek to create a critical mass of leadership.* While a single functional unit can generally get by with a single leader, most cross-functional groups cannot. If the ultimate purpose of cross-functional teams is to make optimal use of people from across different functions, each of these functions must have a strong leadership voice. In addition, this is a good time to take advantage of team members' unique talents. Kenan Sahin, president of a software consulting firm in Cambridge, Massachusetts, asserts that in order for organizations to truly take advantage of each person's talents, managers will have to learn how to follow, allowing the person who knows the most about the subject to lead (Dumaine, 1991).

3. *Hold the team and its members accountable for its performance.* Once team members have bought into the goals, they must also buy into the process. Everyone must feel responsible for the team's performance. Team goals should be translated into clear short-term objectives and milestones that are constantly visible and in the forefront of everyone's thinking. While senior management should avoid micromanaging, they should hold the team to standards. When standards are not met, questions should be raised in such a way that team members feel supported rather than attacked.

    At Becton Dickinson, a maker of high-tech medical equipment, a team was given responsibility to develop a new instrument to process blood samples. While the team developed the instrument 25 percent faster than its previous best effort, the CEO felt this was not fast enough. After some research, senior management found the problem in the decision-making structure. Rather than blame the group, they created a new decision-making structure (Dumaine, 1991).

4. *Keep cross-functional teams as small as possible with critical functional representation.* While the purpose of creating a team is to bring together a diverse set of perspectives, years of research on group processes shows that as group size increases, there is a loss of productivity that results from increased time devoted to coordination and communication. One estimate of productivity loss indicates that in groups with as few as five people, between 10 and 30 percent of team members' time is spent

communicating with other team members about the task (Parker, 1994). Alternatively, if there is not sufficient representation of all functional areas from the very beginning, the team will not be able to perform effectively. One solution is to break up the large group into smaller groups, with each small group having representation in a central decision-making group. In the example of the HP Deskjet, the product development team had a small "core group" that made key decisions.

In addition to determining the optimal team size, finding the right mix of people is critical. If all functional areas are represented, but one team member cannot see the value of working on a cross-functional team, size will quickly become a secondary issue.

5. *Provide the cross-functional team with constantly updated and relevant information.* If an organization is to make heavy use of cross-functional teams, it must essentially "rewire" the information system so that cross-functional teams have ready access to the information they need to do their jobs. In the previous section on designing work, we emphasized the notion that in order for employees to make intelligent decisions, they need to have key information that will allow them to make those decisions. The term "informate" has been coined to describe the use of technology to provide people with information that will allow them to make decisions that were once only made by management (Peters, 1994). Again, optimal effectiveness of cross-functional teams will be achieved only if these teams are given what was formerly assumed to be the prerogative of management: authority to make decisions and the information with which to make these decisions in the most reasonable way.

6. *Train members in teamwork and process management.* Operating in cross-functional teams with complex and fuzzy authority and reporting relationships necessitates that members know the core skills of teamwork. In Chapter 3, we presented some of these core skills, including defining roles and responsibilities, managing conflict, using participative decision making, and managing meetings. As was noted in that chapter, teamwork does not develop naturally. There needs to be a conscious effort to develop as a team, and organizations must often be willing to make the investment to give people training in interpersonal skills.

Similarly, people are not inherently knowledgeable about managing processes. As was demonstrated in the HP Deskjet example, a clear understanding of the various processes that must be mastered in the completion of a project or task is critical. Competency 1, Managing Projects, provides an introduction to the key elements of managing processes.

7. *Clarify expectations within and between teams.* Each individual who is part of a cross-functional team has three responsibility perspectives: the team, the function, and the larger organization. Each of these should be clearly articulated before the start of the project. Moreover, leaders of cross-functional teams must have the ability to develop effective relationships with key stakeholders, including leaders of functional departments, senior management sponsors, and other resource people in the organization. Competency 1, Managing Projects, presented the notion of internal and external integration and suggested that regular communication with key project stakeholders is an important element of managing projects. This is even more true if the project is being carried out by a cross-functional team, where the definition of

who is internal and who is external can become somewhat blurred. While it is clear that all organizations have multiple and often competing goals, these competing goals cannot become a barrier to effective cross-functional team management. An organization will be able to use cross-functional teams effectively only if team members and others in the organization identify primarily with the larger organization and only secondarily with their functional units.

One step that is often useful here is the colocation of team members. That is, whenever possible, cross-functional team members should be located as close as possible, "in the same building, on the same floor, and in the same area" (Parker, 1994, p. 78). Physical proximity allows for more regular and more informal interactions. Co-locating team project members also sends a very clear message regarding the importance of the project.

8. *Encourage team members to be willing to step out of their roles.* As a corollary to the previous guideline, we suggest that people must not only be willing to step out of their functional identity to "put on an organizational hat"; they must also be willing to step out of their status or rank identity in order to allow for more optimal use of everyone's unique skills and abilities. As noted in the second guideline, the increasing use of cross-functional teams suggests that more and more, "leaders" on one project will be "followers" on the next. As we discussed in the previous section on self-managed work teams, the most successful teams are ones that are able to manage the paradoxes that are associated with having clearly defined roles and responsibilities, while simultaneously expecting that everyone does everything that needs to be done.

ANALYSIS Errors in the Design?[1]

Objective   When problems occur in organizations, sometimes the most apparent problem is only a symptom of a deeper problem. This analysis asks you to think about how team design, rather than automotive design, might be the real problem for this manufacturer.

Directions   Read the paragraph below. It comes from a real situation encountered in one of the "Big Three" automobile manufacturers. Diagnose the errors that might have been made in managing across the various functional areas that were involved in designing the automobile.

The total amount of electrical power in a vehicle is determined by the capacity of the alternator. The power must serve over twenty subsystems, such as the stereo, the engine, the instrument panel, and so on. These subsystems are developed and controlled by separate "chimney" organizations, and power allocations must be made for each subsystem. The problem was, in this vehicle program, when the requirements of all the chimneys and teams were added up, they equaled 125 percent of the capacity of the alternator. Keith, who had recently taken over as head of this vehicle program (which had made changes in direction and was behind schedule to begin with), called a meeting of the Program Steering Committee designed to resolve this conflict and reach a compromise. However, many of the chimney representatives who were members of the team

[1] *Source:* Denison, Dan, Stuart Hart, and Joel Kahn. "From Chimneys to Cross-Functional Teams: Developing and Validating a Diagnostic Model," Working Paper, University of Michigan, 1993. Used with permission.

came to this meeting with instructions from their bosses [who, incidentally, did their performance appraisals] *not* to make any compromises, but to make certain that their chimney "got what it needed" and "didn't lose out." After Keith presented the group with the problem and the need to reach a compromise solution, their response surprised him: "It's not our problem," they replied, "it's *your* problem."

Questions
1. What advice would you give Keith for dealing with the Program Steering Committee?
2. Which other key stakeholders should Keith deal with? What advice would you give him for dealing with these other key stakeholders?
3. If Keith could "turn back the hands of time," what advice would you have given him at the beginning of this project? Be as specific as possible in your advice.

Reflection
For people who have not experienced the type of situation described above, the story seems almost unbelievable—How could members of the same organization not recognize the importance of coming up with a vehicle design that would actually work? For far too many employees, however, this type of situation rings all too true. Consistent with a sociotechnical systems perspective, organizational structures and processes can result in inefficiency and even divisiveness if people do not understand and respect the interconnections among all functions in the organization.

PRACTICE Student Orientation

Objective
Many events require cooperation across different groups, but special issues often come into play when the groups involved are made up of volunteers. In this exercise you need to think not only about the task issues, but also the people issues given the volunteer nature of the groups who will be participating in the event.

Directions
You are president of the University Students Services Association (USSA). USSA is a student-run organization that coordinates the activities of all other student-run organizations on campus. USSA monitors scheduling of all extracurricular activities, tracks consistency of student organization activities with university policy, and attempts to provide resource support whenever possible.

In the past, each major university organization—such as Academic Support Services, the USSA, the Student Health Services, the Honor Society, and so on—conducted its own new student orientation during the general orientation prior to the beginning of the fall semester. These orientations typically lasted anywhere from one to three hours and included speeches, presentations, videotapes, and workshop-type activities. For most organizational units, these orientations were seen as an opportunity to publicize the way in which they contributed to students' experience of university life. Organizational units spent a great deal of time, effort, and attention in preparing their individual orientations, because they felt it was important for students to learn about how they might take advantage of the services provided. Organizational units took great pride in conducting a professional presentation and paid close attention to the evaluations that students completed. In fact, there was something of an informal competition among the units, with each trying to be the most innovative in its presentation.

This year the provost has decided to try a new approach, declaring that all student orientation sessions will be centrally coordinated and run over a three-day period during the first week of classes. You have been asked to head the team that coordinates this orientation.

Your first task is to prepare a one-page outline of how you will approach this new responsibility. After you have completed the outline, respond to the process questions below.

Process Questions   1. What work- or task-related issues need to be addressed in order to carry out the provost's request?

2. What people-related issues do you foresee?

3. What issues of internal and external integration will need to be addressed in carrying out this task?

4. What was better about the previous format for student orientations? What is better about the new format?

Reflection   Planning, of course, is only the beginning. Before any plan can be implemented, people will need to be convinced to go along with the plan. This is where the competencies of the broker (see Chapter 9) come into play.

APPLICATION   Examining a Cross-Functional Team

Objective   Use what you have learned about managing across functions to improve your own work situation.

Identify a situation that you are currently in at school, at work, or in some other formal organization that has cross-functional elements to it. Analyze the situation in terms of the guidelines presented in this section. In analyzing the situation, find specific ways in which the situation is being managed well, as well as problems. When you identify a problem, try to determine its specific source(s). That is, instead of saying, "Meetings do not accomplish anything," try to determine if the cause of the problem is that goals are not clear, the wrong people are attending the meeting, the person running the meeting has not appropriately organized the meeting, and so on. Suggest ways to improve the "operations."

Reflection   Managing cross-functional teams is complicated by the fact that there are often political, as well as practical, reasons why certain individuals are on the team. Because being left off a team may be considered a slight, cross-functional teams sometimes balloon into large groups. Novices who attempt to reduce the group to a more efficient size, however, may end up making the situation worse rather than better.

REFERENCES

Alster, Norm. "What Flexible Workers Can Do." *Fortune* (February 13, 1989): 62–66.

Badiru, Adedji Bodunde. *Quantitative Models for Project Planning, Scheduling and Control.* Westport, Conn.: Quorum, 1993.

Bowen, H. Kent, Kim B. Clark, Charles A. Holloway, and Steven C. Wheelwright (eds.). *The Perpetual Enterprise Machine.* New York: Oxford University Press, 1994.

Bridges, William. "The End of the Job." *Fortune* (September 19, 1994): 62–74.

Butler, Timothy, and James Waldrop. "Job Sculpting, the Art of Retaining Your Best People." *Harvard Business Review* 77 (September–October 1999): 144–152.

Cabana, Ronald E., and Steven Purser. *The Self-Managing Organization: How Leading Companies Are Transforming the Work of Teams for Real Impact.* New York: Free Press, 1998.

Denison, Dan, Stuart Hart, and Joel Kahn. "From Chimneys to Cross-Functional Teams: Developing and Validating a Diagnostic Model." Working Paper, University of Michigan, 1993.

Dertouzes, Michael L., Richard K. Lester, Robert M. Solow, and the MIT Commission on Industrial Productivity. *Made in America: Regaining the Productive Edge.* Cambridge, MA.: MIT Press, 1989.

Dumaine, Brian. "The Bureaucracy Busters." *Fortune* (June 17, 1991): 36–50.

Frame, J. Davidson. *Building Project Management Competence.* San Francisco: Jossey-Bass, 1999.

Galbraith, Jay R. *Designing Complex Organizations.* Reading, MA.: Addison-Wesley, 1973.

Guenther, Kim. "Creating Cross-Functional Web Teams." *Online* 25(3) (May–June 2001): 79–81.

Gundry, Lisa K., Jill R. Kickul, and Charles Prather. "Building the Creative Organization." *Organizational Dynamics* 22 (Spring 1994): 22–37.

Hackman, J. Richard, and Greg Oldham. "Development of the Job Diagnostic Survey." *Journal of Applied Psychology* 60 (1975): 159–170.

Hackman, J. Richard, Greg Oldham, Robert Janson, and Kenneth Purdy. "A New Strategy for Job Enrichment." *California Management Review* 17(4) (1975): 57–71.

Hammer, Michael, and James Champy. *Reengineering the Corporation: A Manifesto for Business Revolution.* New York: HarperBusiness, 1993.

Harrison, F. L. *Advanced Project Management: A Structured Approach.* New York: Halsted, 1992.

Henkoff, Ronald. "Finding, Training and Keeping the Best Service Workers." *Fortune* (October 3, 1994): 110–122.

Herzberg, Fredrick. "One More Time: How Do You Motivate Employees?" *Harvard Business Review* 46 (January–February 1968): 53–62.

House, Ruth Sizemore. *The Human Side of Project Management.* Reading, MA.: Addison-Wesley, 1988.

Kerzner, Harold. *Project Management: A Systems Approach to Planning, Scheduling, and Controlling,* 6th ed. New York: Van Nostrand Reinhold, 1998.

Kimmons, Robert L. *Project Management Basics: A Step by Step Approach.* New York: Marcel Dekker, 1990.

Lawler, Edward E., III. *The Ultimate Advantage: Creating the High-Involvement Organization.* San Francisco: Jossey-Bass, 1992.

Lawler, Edward E., III, and David Finegold. "Individualizing the Organization: Past, Present, and Future." *Organizational Dynamics* 29(1) (2000): 1–15.

Layne, Anni. "He's Navigating the Dotcom Dustbowl." *Fast Company* (November 2000). (http://www.fastcompany.com).

Meyer, Christopher. *Fast Cycle Time.* New York: Free Press, 1993.

Mohrman, Susan Albers. "Integrating Roles and Structures in the Lateral Organization," in Jay R. Galbraith, Edward E. Lawler III, et al. (eds.), *Organizing for the Future.* San Francisco: Jossey-Bass, 1993, 109–141.

O'Dell, Carla, and C. Jackson Grayson, Jr. *If Only We Knew What We Know.* New York: Free Press, 1998a.

O'Dell, Carla, and C. Jackson Grayson, Jr. "If Only We Knew What We Know, Identification and Transfer of Best Practices." *California Management Review* 40(3) (Spring 1998b): 154–174.

Parker, Glenn M. *Cross-Functional Teams: Working with Allies, Enemies, and Other Strangers.* San Francisco: Jossey-Bass, 1994.

Peters, Tom. *The Tom Peters Seminar: Crazy Times Call for Crazy Organizations.* New York: Vintage Books, 1994.

Peters, Tom. "The Wow Project." *Fast Company* (May 1999). (http://www.fastcompany.com).

Pfeffer, Jeffrey, and Robert I. Sutton. *The Knowing–Doing Gap.* Boston: Harvard Business School Press, 2000.

"Rethinking Work," *Business Week* (October 17, 1994): 74–117.

Roman, Daniel D. *Managing Projects: A Systems Approach.* New York: Elsevier Science, 1986.

Rummler, Geary A., and Alan P. Brache. *Improving Performance: How to Manage the White Space on the Organization Chart.* San Francisco: Jossey-Bass, 1990.

Schueler, Judy. "Customer Service Through Leadership: The Disney Way." *Training and Development* 54(10) (October 2000): 26–31.

Smith, Adam. *The Wealth of Nations.* New York: Random House, 1937. (Original work published 1776).

Spinner, M. Pete. *Improving Project Management Skills and Techniques.* Englewood Cliffs, NJ: Prentice-Hall, 1989.

Taylor, Frederick W. *The Principles of Scientific Management.* New York: Harper & Row, 1911.

Thornberry, Neal E. "Training the Engineer as Project Manager: How to Turn Technical Types into Top-Notch Project Managers." *Training and Development Journal* (October 1987): 60–62.

Wenger, Etienne C., and William M. Snyder. "Communities of Practice: The Organizational Frontier." *Harvard Business Review* 78 (January–February 2000): 139–145.

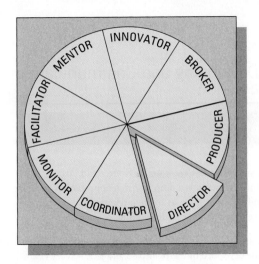

THE
THE
DIRECTOR ROLE

6

■ COMPETENCIES

Developing and Communicating a Vision

Setting Goals and Objectives

Designing and Organizing

The director role in many ways reflects the core of many experts' definitions of "leadership." The competencies we have chosen to frame this role include

Competency 1   Developing and Communicating a Vision
Competency 2   Setting Goals and Objectives
Competency 3   Designing and Organizing

These three competencies can be viewed as a sequence of basic questions that organizational decision makers must continually answer:

- Why should the organization exist? (Developing and Communicating a Vision)
- What do we want it to achieve/accomplish? (Setting Goals and Objectives)
- How can it best achieve/accomplish that? (Designing and Organizing)

Situated in the rational goal quadrant, the action imperative for the director role is Compete. The first two competencies we discuss emphasize the need to be externally focused in order to compete effectively in an ever-changing business environment. The third competency highlights the notion of control through its emphasis on designing systems and processes that help the organization compete effectively.

191

Competency 1 Developing and Communicating a Vision

ASSESSMENT Origins of Personal Vision

ideal & unique image of the future

Objective One definition of vision is "an ideal and unique image of the future" (Kouzes and Posner, 1995, p. 97). An important component of the future, however, is a deep and rich appreciation and understanding of the past and the heritage and legacy it gives us in the present. This exercise will help prepare you for crafting your future by enhancing your understanding of your past.

Directions In preparation for immersion into the competency of Developing and Communicating a Vision, please complete the following "Lifeline" exercise developed by Herb Shepard and Jack Hawley (1974).

1. Draw your lifeline as a graph, with the peaks representing the highs in your life and the valleys representing the lows. Start as far back as you can remember and stop at the present time.

2. Next to each peak, write a word or two identifying the peak experience. Do the same for the valleys.

3. Now go back and think about each peak, making a few notes on why each was a high point for you.

4. Analyze your notes.
   - What themes and patterns are revealed by the peaks in your life?
   - What important personal strengths are revealed?
   - What do these themes and patterns tell you about what you're likely to find personally compelling in the future?

Reflection Please keep your work on this task for use and application within this competency after the Learning section and for use with the other competencies in the director and producer roles. You can also come back to your lifeline to see if your perceptions about peaks and valleys change over time.

LEARNING Developing and Communicating a Vision

Developing and communicating a vision is one of the more glorified competencies that a leader engages in. For many experts on leadership, it is the sine qua non of leadership. Vision is for the leader what mission and values are for the organization—powerful statements of purpose and passion. Gardner (1995) sees the development and communication of vision by leaders as very much a reflection of how they communicate themselves and their "stories":

> *A leader is likely to achieve success only if she can construct and convincingly communicate a clear and persuasive story; appreciate the nature of the audience(s), including its changeable features; invest her own (or channel others') energy in the building and maintenance of an organization; embody in her own life the principal contours of the story; either provide direct leadership or find a way to achieve influence through indirect means; and finally, find a way to understand and make use of, without being overwhelmed by, increasingly technical expertise. (p. 302)*

Bennis and Nanus (1985) identify "attention through vision" as one of four critical strategies for leadership success. They define attention through vision as a means of creating focus on the leader's agenda. In their groundbreaking study of 90 leaders, they found personalities so intent, committed, and absorbed by what they were doing that they exerted an almost magnetic attraction—they did not have to coerce people to pay attention. Their vision was literally "grabbing"—first for the leader him- or herself and then, by virtue of "management of attention," grabbing others and getting them onto the bandwagon heading toward the leader's vision. The visions articulated in the Bennis and Nanus landmark study seemed to engender a confidence on the part of followers— a confidence that translated into a belief that they were capable of performing those acts necessary to realize the vision. Consistent with the assertive "full steam ahead" aura of the director role, these leaders were "challengers," not coddlers, as exemplified by Edwin H. Land, founder of Polaroid, who stated: "The first thing you naturally do is teach the person to feel that the undertaking is manifestly important and nearly impossible. . . . That draws out the kind of drives that make people strong, that put you in pursuit intellectually." Vision "animates, inspirits, transforms purpose into action" (Bennis and Nanus, 1985, p. 30). Bennis and Nanus also remind us of the transactional nature of leader–follower relationships—one cannot exist without the other. They caution us that the leaders in their study "paid" attention as well as catching it. Despite the commanding nature of their subjects, Bennis and Nanus point out that the interaction between the leader and the led is tacitly far more complicated than the simple command—they bring out the best in each other. And the leader and followers are not the only elements in the equation. As Westley and Mintzberg (1989) observe about effective "strategic visions":

> It may be that only with a fit between inner and outer context, between personality and problem, as between the leader and the moment, can the charismatic, empowering response be triggered and the leader thereby be viewed as a "visionary." . . .
>
> Our notion is that strategic visions are complex, novel images that may be more or less conscious, articulate, and realistic. They contain the standard elements of strategy—products, markets, organizational designs, and so on—but contain much more. And they are embedded in contexts: the external strategic contexts of issues and organization, the internal personal context of the life experiences and expectations of the leaders themselves. Visions are contained and expanded in time, tied to the process of evolution itself. Lastly, they are formed by—and in turn, form—a complex structure of justifications by which the visionary explains and makes meaningful his or her vision (to self and others). (pp. 162–163)

While experts disagree on the process by which effective visions are developed and communicated, there is some agreement on critical *elements* of the process, however it may in fact occur. First, there is the *definition, expression, and/or framing* of the vision. There is also the need to attend to the *key content dimensions* of an organizational vision—those elements that must be included in a vision in order for it to "direct" the organization into the future. Ideally, and finally, there is the *empowerment of followers through articulation and communication* of the vision in ways that are compelling to followers (Sashkin, 1989). We will structure our Learning section around these three elements and demonstrate how are they are critical to the complementary competencies in the director role of setting goals and objectives and designing and organizing.

EXPRESSING AND FRAMING THE VISION

framing

There is often a mystical and magical quality attributed to visions and visionary leadership. The imagery of the mountaintop and a bolt of lightning or the comic strip visual of the lightbulb popping out of a character's head are almost inescapable in any discussion of vision. Those who have spent a great deal of time studying vision and visionary leaders have found the reality of visionary expression and framing to be quite different. The metaphors that various authors use to describe the process speak volumes. Westley and Mintzberg (1989) argue that visions that are too specific early on in the process are doomed from the very beginning because the vision(s) get "eaten away" bit by bit as the leader engages in the normal and necessary process of coalition building, trade-offs, and compromises. Effective leaders they cite in their research much more resemble *"garbage collectors"*—individuals who look for useful bits of "rubbish" as they make their daily rounds, seizing on those with potential and building them into their vision as the essential content. Kouzes and Posner (1995) use the "jigsaw puzzle principle" in their explanation of the leader's role in framing visions. No matter how many individuals are involved in the shaping of a vision, followers expect the leader to have the "big picture"— jigsaw puzzle enthusiasts know that it's much easier to put a puzzle together if you can see the picture on the cover of the box! In a typical organizational setting, many individuals have different pieces of the organizational puzzle. Employees may have detailed descriptions of their roles and responsibilities, but in many cases they lack the information about the "big picture," the overall purpose or vision of the organization—the picture on the box cover!

see larger

Kouzes and Posner (1995) also allude to the leader as *"doorman"* or *"concierge"* for vision(s). Visions, in fact, don't typically emerge from lightning bolt strikes fully formed and whole. While past experiences, knowledge, and the current context are the resources that feed intuition, these are not sufficient to produce a vision for the future. Like all gemstones in the rough, they must first be unearthed, polished, and refined so that they can then produce effective ideas. The critical leadership action, then, is "opening the door" of opportunity that presents itself. The leader is not only doorman for the light of opportunity, he or she is also its concierge—helping others see what's ahead of them by having and conveying a focus (Kouzes and Posner, 1995).

doorman/ concierge

KEY CONTENT DIMENSIONS OF VISION

While visions vary greatly in the specificity of their content, there are some core themes that seem to greatly enhance their effectiveness. The first is the case for *change*. Whether it's because of the environment, customer/market demands, products, people, or technology, the need to understand and accept the need for change is a key element in most visions. A second recurring theme is an *ideal goal* or goals— not so specific as to define final outcomes or end-states, but rather related to ideal conditions or processes. A third theme is a focus on *people*, both internal and external organizational stakeholders. While it may seem obvious that visions can be enacted through people, many very elaborate visions fail to address the roles that people play (Sashkin, 1989).

change
ideal goal
people

COMMUNICATING AND OPERATIONALIZING THE VISION

With the leader serving in some capacity as garbage collector or jigsaw puzzle person, and focusing on the key themes of change, ideal goals, and people taking action—how does the leader then proceed to communicate and operationalize the vision? Again, experts disagree on the best process. Sashkin's (1989) framing of the process allows for the broadest and most comprehensive integration of other perspectives. His perspective is that leaders communicate and operationalize the vision by expressing and explaining through words and actions. These words and actions take three forms: strategic, tactical, and personal.

STRATEGIC COMMUNICATION OF VISION

Most organizations attempt to articulate at a strategic level a clear and concise statement of organizational philosophy centered on the specific elements of their visions. Johnson & Johnson has its well-known "credo" (Collins and Porras, 1994, p. 69), which gained worldwide attention when J&J relied on it for guidance on how to respond to the Tylenol tragedy in 1982. During that crisis, J&J took all Tylenol off the shelves across the USA when seven deaths occurred in the Chicago area because someone—not a J&J employee—had laced the capsules with cyanide. The company spared no expense in doing what it thought was right (Collins & Porras, 1994, p. 80). The J&J credo is the core ideology that drives it as a firm. The ultimate purpose for which it exists is "to alleviate pain and disease." The company pursues that purpose through a "hierarchy of responsibilities" that includes *customers* first, employees second, society at large third, and shareholders fourth. J&J strives to be a company where individual opportunity can be optimized and rewards are based on merit and accomplishment. Its approach to designing and organizing is captured in the formula: *Decentralization + Creativity = Productivity.* For J&J, the credo serves as a way of communicating the vision by clearly identifying its underlying values and providing a sketch of the desired organizational culture. Sashkin (1989) points out that the clearer the philosophy, the more potentially useful it can be. It will have greater potential if it speaks to all aspects of the organization that are informed by the vision—namely, adaptation through autonomous action, goal attainment through achieving what the customer wants, and integration of all moving parts through coordinated interpersonal interaction.

TACTICAL POLICIES AND PRACTICES

For the power of a vision to be realized, it must not only be communicated persuasively, but it also must be translated into practices that can be implemented to support the vision. One example of a company that has excelled at moving from vision to implementation is Southwest Airlines. Southwest's record of profitability in the intensely competitive airline industry is often linked with the leadership of founder and former CEO, Herb Kelleher. Kelleher would be the first to insist, however, that one person does not make a successful company. Successful companies depend on "a tremendous mosaic made up thousands of people" (quoted in Gittell, 2005: 56).

In her book, *The Southwest Airlines Way,* Jody Gittell explores ten organizational practices that Southwest has developed to support the company's vision. All 10 practices help to create an environment of "relational coordination" that includes shared goals, shared knowledge, and mutual respect, both within Southwest and with external suppliers and unions (Gittell, 2005).

PERSONAL ACTIONS

Perhaps the most critical and most challenging aspect of visions is leveraging them as powerful incentives to action. Bennis and Nanus (1985) talk about the "grabbing" quality of visions, while Westley and Mintzberg (1989) describe the potential of visions to trigger the "empowerment" response. Kouzes and Posner (1995), however, focus on visions as central to leadership effectiveness:

Shared sense of destiny — enrolling others [handwritten margin note]

> *Leadership isn't about imposing the leader's solo dream; it's about developing a shared sense of destiny. It's about enrolling others so that they can see how their own interests and aspirations are aligned with the vision and can thereby become mobilized to commit their individual energies to its realization. A vision is inclusive of the constituents' aspirations; it's an ideal and unique image of the future for the common good. (p. 124)*

The leader can exert incredible influence with the clear and compelling communication of the vision. Job satisfaction, motivation, commitment, loyalty, esprit de corps, clarity about the organization's values, pride in the organization, and organizational productivity can all be positively affected.

PERSONAL COMMUNICATION OF THE VISION

Every individual has the ability to communicate vision in a way that positively impacts everything from job satisfaction (both of leaders and of followers) to organizational productivity. Berlew (1974) found that excitement among followers is often generated by the opportunity to be "tested," that is, to succeed on one's own; to be part of a social innovation; to demonstrate competence; to do something "good"; and to alter the way things are.

Communications expert Roderick Hart (1984) has identified four categories of words that make up the lexicon used by many leaders:

Realistic / Optimistic / Action / Certainty [handwritten margin note]

1. "Realistic" words portray tangible and concrete objects, such as automobile and highway.
2. "Optimistic" words express hope and possibilities.
3. "Activity" words show motion.
4. "Certainty" words express assuredness.

One of the most famous examples of a leader communicating his vision in a powerful, empowering, and compelling way is Dr. Martin Luther King Jr.'s "I Have a Dream" speech. James Kouzes often uses an audio presentation of Dr. King's speech, after which he asks listeners for their reactions. Their statements convey the kind of response a leader can get when using expressions that are realistic, optimistic, activity-oriented, and confidence- and certainty-generating:

> *"It was vivid. He used a lot of images and word pictures. You could see the examples."*
> *"People could relate to the examples."*
> *"His references were credible."*
> *"He appealed to common bonds."*
> *"He knew his audience."*
> *"He included everybody."*
> *"He began with a statement of the difficulties and then stated his dream."*
> *"He was positive and hopeful—talked about the future"*
> *"He spoke with emotion and passion. It was deeply felt."*
> *"He was personally convinced of the dream."*
> *(quoted in Kouzes and Posner, 1995, pp. 127–128)*

In summary, in order to effectively develop and communicate a vision, leaders must do the following:

- Discover, frame, and evolve a vision that will appeal to a common purpose that engages all followers
- Communicate that vision strategically, tactically, and personally, thereby bringing the vision to life in such a way that people can see themselves in it
- Personally own and believe in the vision so that they can authentically demonstrate that their words match their personal conviction

ANALYSIS Vision During Challenging Times[1]

Objective Conversations about company visions often focus on bright outlooks and positive expectations and include pithy "sound bite" visions. This exercise gives you an opportunity to analyze a company's vision based on a description of its culture.

Directions Read the following case study and answer the questions that follow.

In January 1999, something nearly all PeopleSoft employees thought was impossible happened—a dozen managers met to plan layoffs. When Larry Butler, vice president of human resources, asked attendees at the meeting how they felt, one manager began to outline dismissal strategies, but the boss interrupted him and said, "How do you feel?" Half the room dissolved in tears. Most people thought this could never happen at PeopleSoft—because they were a family. Founded in 1987, PeopleSoft was one of three major competitors in the enterprise resource planning software business—facing off with Oracle and SAP of Germany, both of which are substantially larger than PeopleSoft. When this somber January meeting took place in the winter of 1999, the PeopleSoft family was over 7000 strong.

---

[1]*Adapted from* Quentin Hardy, "PeopleSoft Made Work a Cause, but a Slump Shakes the Faithful," *Wall Street Journal* interactive edition, May 5, 1999. http://interactive.wsj.com/archive/retr.

Even by Silicon Valley standards, PeopleSoft was famous for an aggressively informal and sensitive corporate culture. Its staff routinely worked 70- and 80-hour weeks—and for reasons other than stock options. There was a strong intrinsic payoff to PeopleSoft team members in the company's inside jokes and clubby code language, such as employees being "PeoplePeople," company-funded food being "PeopleSnacks," and corpulent waistlines being "PeoplePounds." PeopleSoft also reveled in the exploits of Dave Duffield, the sometimes flamboyant, always unflappable founder of the company. Being at PeopleSoft was about more than stock options and money—it was about having fun in a place with a lot of "heart."

In a word, PeopleSoft was the kind of company often glamorized and lionized in today's high-tech universe—a highly charged, emotional, empathetic workplace that stands in stark contrast with the industry's highly rational and analytical products (PeopleSoft's major product is their software for managing almost all aspects of human resources management) and often cutthroat tactics. And for a good long run it worked very well. Revenue in 1998 hit $1.3 billion, up more than over 10-fold since 1994, and the price of the company's stock had risen 32-fold over six years before beginning to slide in the summer of 1998. But in the winter of 1999, the 12 managers at the meeting mentioned above, as well as most of the remaining employees, were struggling with suspicion and doubt that their very special place called PeopleSoft was really just another company falling on hard times.

In an interview, CEO Duffield observed that no one in the industry had seen this slowdown coming. The industry-wide slump for enterprise resource planning software was seriously exacerbated by the Y2K problem scenario. Rather than brood about the $2 billion drop in the value of his own PeopleSoft holdings over the previous year, Duffield talked of possible acquisitions and Internet plans. Duffield, whose initials are DAD and whose attitude toward the PeoplePeople often seemed paternalistic, did not want to alarm the family. When news of the search for his replacement jarred some staff members, he assured them that he would still be the "big Kahuna." As PeopleSofts' stock tumbled through the fall of 1998, Duffield still found time to judge a company pumpkin-carving contest. He also told a meeting of about 3,000 employees that the company's new mission was to double the value of the stock in one year.

PeopleSoft as a company is distinct and so are some of its particular problems. In the mid 1980s Duffield, a former IBM sales executive, envisioned the coming boom in so-called client-server systems that tie workers' personal computers to a larger computer serving an entire work unit. Duffield tapped into and enacted that vision by founding PeopleSoft in 1987 along with software designer Ken Morris. By 1989, they had a product just as client-server computing was about to sweep the corporate landscape. They also had worked hard and very successfully at developing a culture that would bind workers to the mission. Duffield leavened the daunting pace with beer blasts and parties at his house. At bigger company bashes, employees wore shirts they had been issued that bore their employee number. Some workers still talk enviously of the "double digits," the pioneers who had joined before there were 100 PeoplePeople. Duffield seemed to have the magic touch and became almost a mythic figure in the company. The PeopleSoft company band named itself the Raving Daves. Employees referred to their offspring as "PeopleBabies"— who received their own numbers. There was shopping at the company "PeopleStore," which offered all sorts of knickknacks with the PeoleSoft logo, including a piece of luggage called a "Duffield bag." In company newsletters, the CEO was called "the legendary Dave Duffield." Duffield stated repeatedly that he did not like the attention but felt it was important for building up a strong company culture: "I will do what's right for the company. If I'm legendary, so be it."

The industry-wide slowdown and the slide in the stock price along with the necessary layoffs were exacerbated by several public and acrimonious lawsuits, embarrassing incidents, and the arrest and civil suit against a PeopleSoft employee for vehicular assault after having had a few drinks at a company-sponsored beer bust. There were also several disappointing acquisitions to roil the waters as well.

Duffield, prior to his departure from the scene, shared some lessons he had learned the hard way: "Growing at 80 percent hides problems." He also regretted his call in the fall of 1998 to double the stock price in a year—it was just a "bad thing to say."

Discussion Questions
1. In the very first paragraph of the Learning section, we quoted Gardner's (1995) observations about the role that a leader's "story" plays in how effectively vision is developed and communicated. Using that quote as an "opening thought," write what you think Duffield's "story" is—evaluate it's strengths and weaknesses and its impact on PeopleSoft.

2. Analyze Duffield's effectiveness in developing and communicating vision, addressing each of the three critical elements:
   - Expressing and framing the vision
   - Key content dimensions of the vision
     - Change
     - Ideal goal
     - People
   - Communicating and operationalizing the vision
     - Strategic communication of vision
     - Tactical policies and practices
     - Personal actions
     - Personal communication of the vision

Reflection
In many ways, Dave Duffield's personality and emphasis on building a strong company culture is reminiscent of Herb Kelleher at Southwest Airlines. In terms of long-term business success, however, their stories are quite different. What are some of the factors that could explain the difference?

PRACTICE   PeopleSoft After the Founder[2]

Objective
This role-play is designed to simulate conversation between a new CEO, a new intern, and a long-term employee about how the new CEO has communicated his vision for the company. In playing your role, keep in mind the concepts we have covered concerning communicating effectively and reflective listening.

Directions
Read the following case study and then perform the role-play that follows. This Practice activity builds on the PeopleSoft discussion in the Analysis section above. It focuses on some of the challenges faced by the leader who succeeded founder Dave Duffield.

In September 1999, Dave Duffield stepped down from his leadership role at PeopleSoft and was replaced by Craig Conway as president and CEO. After a two-year downturn in the company's fortunes, induced by Y2K and a fluctuating Internet strategy, PeopleSoft launched PeopleSoft8, a major upgrade to its flagship enterprise resource planning suite with a completely reformulated code base. The new release was purely browser-based, claimed by officials to improve the product's ease of use and deployment—two problem areas that had dogged the company for years.

In addition to this major new product release, Conway suggested that the world would see and experience a new company that would no longer be content to play second or third to more typically aggressive Oracle, SAP AG, and Siebel Systems. Referring to his rival CEOs,

[2]*Adapted from* Scot Petersen, "PeopleSoft Fights for ERP Ground," *eWeek,* July 17, 2000, Volume 17, Number 29; p. 1, continued onto p. 20.

Conway stated: "These are tough people. In order to be tough externally, we have to be tough internally. We have to be accountable, intense, competitive." Conway's task in many ways was a major course correction that had to address, among other challenges, the recent and abrupt dropping by PeopleSoft of important (from the customer's perspective) service and support programs that had alienated key customers. In an attempt to improve these strained relations, PeopleSoft restored the programs; expanded its sales force by 30 percent in the third quarter of 2000, and created a new consulting group staffed with experts from EDS, KPMG Consulting Inc., and other large consultancies.

The reporter interviewing Conway for the story from which this case is drawn queried: "In addition to the new products, there seems to be a new attitude at PeopleSoft." Conway responded

I think it is a completely different attitude. That's the right word. The demeanor of the company under Dave Duffield was very paternalistic. Confrontation was something Oracle did, both externally and internally. Aggressiveness was not something that was encouraged (at PeopleSoft). The dress was casual, and the attitude was casual. And now the whole world is dressed casually. But I think the whole attitude of the company is much more intense.

When Dave founded the company, he had posters made that had eight values that PeopleSoft was to be known for. And when I came to the company, there were still posters hanging up with those same eight values. When I came to the company, I didn't want to change the culture—a lot about it was very beneficial; it was the reason we were able to attract people and make it a great company. So what I wanted to do was complement the culture with three more values. So I added "intensity, accountability and competitiveness." (emphasis added)

Role-Play

In pairs or triads, engage in the following role-play:

You are just starting an internship at PeopleSoft and are anxious to make a good impression and demonstrate your facility with key knowledge necessary to effectively develop and communicate a vision. You are so proud and pleased with that competency that you even mentioned it on your résumé.

Craig Conway, president and CEO of PeopleSoft, who is always on the lookout for fresh insights and perspectives, happened to see your résumé and has asked you to come to meet with him to share your view on how he's done developing and communicating vision in his new role.

If you are in a dyad, your partner will improvise the role of Craig Conway. If you are in a triad, the third person will play the role of "everyPeople," a long-term employee.

Take a few minutes to outline your pitch to Conway and, when told to do so by your instructor, begin the role-play.

Reflection   In December 2004, PeopleSoft agreed to be acquired by Oracle in response to a hostile takeover battle that had lasted a year and a half. Dave Duffield, who had left the company in 1999, returned to the company in October 2004 to try to prevent the takeover (Bank, 2004). Why do you think that the three additional values Conway added—intensity, accountability, and competitiveness—were not sufficient to prevent a takeover of PeopleSoft by Oracle?

APPLICATION   Crafting Your Personal Vision Statement

Objective   This application exercise gives you a chance to think back on the lifeline graph that you prepared at the beginning of this chapter and use it as a starting point for crafting your personal vision statement.

Directions   Inevitably, sooner rather than later, someone will want to hear about who you are and what your "vision" (story) is. It may not come out in exactly those words, but that will be the reality of the experience.

It may be part of a question or series of questions during a job interview, it may come from a counselor or family member during a conversation about your career and future, or it may be part of an early conversation you have with someone with whom you are establishing a new relationship.

But it will come. So be prepared. Take the time and script out your personal vision statement. Be sure to attend to and include all facets that are relevant from the Learning section.

After you've revised it a few times and it truly reflects your passion and energy, try presenting it to a friend.

Reflection Presenting your vision statement to someone else takes courage, but has two important benefits. First, it gives you practice communicating a vision, something you will need to do more and more frequently as you progress in your career. Second, it also helps you to refine your personal vision. If you haven't been able to excite the interest of your listener, then perhaps you haven't truly identified your core passion that will give your vision the energy that you need to achieve it.

Competency 2   Setting Goals and Objectives

ASSESSMENT   Personal Goals

Objective Goals and objectives for both our personal lives and our professional lives are extensions of the visions we develop for ourselves and of the professions and organizations that we choose. This exercise will prepare you to strengthen the connections between your visions and your actions.

Directions List *at least* one goal (but do not restrict yourself to one) that you have in each of the following four categories.

1. Personal relationships
2. Academic/scholastic accomplishments
3. Career/job interests
4. Your financial future

Reflection These questions will help you focus on basic aspects of goal-setting processes in your personal and professional or school life. There are several keys to making *any* goal-setting process effective, and we discuss those throughout the Learning section that follows. Our intent is to get you thinking about goal setting as it relates to your academic, personal, and professional life.

Please check to see whether your goals are consistent with your "story" from the Application activity in Competency 1.

You will be referring back to these goals throughout discussions and activities related to the director role and competencies included under the producer role in Chapter 7.

LEARNING   Setting Goals and Objectives

Moving forward logically from the development and communication of vision, we come to the formulation of specific organizational plans, goals, and objectives aimed at realizing the vision. Broader (i.e., organizational) goals then (ideally) get translated into various subgoals at the divisional, functional, or other business-unit level and then ultimately cascade down the organization to relevant departments, units, teams, and individuals. Again, as an ideal. Goal setting goes back to the earliest attempts at directing the efforts of individuals and sets of individuals toward a common end. The idea of assigning employees a specific amount of work to be accomplished, a specific task, a quota, a performance standard, an objective, or a deadline can be found as far back as the turn of the twentieth century. When Frederick W. Taylor was defining the appropriate amount of pig iron to be handled by a single man in a single day, he was engaging in classic goal setting for blue-collar workers. This was a fine-grained process that clearly defined and delineated every aspect of the task: how it was to be performed, expected outcomes, and rewards for accomplishing it.

In the 1960s, a white-collar, managerially focused version of goal-setting emerged in "management by objectives" (discussed below). While much has changed about individuals—the work they do and the settings in which they do it—goal setting is alive and well in the new economy.

Our plan in this section is to review the key lessons learned about goal setting from the past, get a clear understanding of how work environments in the new economy impact goal-setting effectiveness, and gain a fuller appreciation of the relationship among developing and communicating a vision and setting goals and objectives.

GOAL SETTING—THE BASIC BUILDING BLOCKS

What is goal setting, and why should the manager be concerned about it? Experts tell us that various forms of planning and goal setting have been used by managers since the turn of the twentieth century. Hundreds of research studies on goal setting have been conducted, with 90 percent of them reporting positive benefits. These results suggest that a median improvement of 16 percent in performance (with minimum and maximum ranging from 2 percent to 58 percent) can be attained through the use of goal-setting techniques (Locke and Latham, 1985, p. 6). Latham and Wexley (1994) cite several research studies that conclude that whenever one group of employees is required to set and pursue specific goals, members of that group invariably increase their productivity substantially over that of groups that do not set goals. They cite studies of employees whose professional diversity varies from engineers and scientists to loggers.

Goal setting takes place at all levels in an organization. The focus, purpose, and kinds of activities that take place as part of the process, however, vary with the level of the organization in which they take place. At the most senior levels of managerial leadership, for example, goal setting tends to be focused primarily around what Latham and Wexley (1994) refer to as the organization's superordinate goal—namely its *vision*. That focus tends to be strategic and directional. It involves an organization's most basic and fundamental decision: the choice of missions, strategies, and major allocations of resources. These strategic/visionary choices, taken together, will generally shape the organization's overall future.

At lower managerial and supervisory levels, goal setting tends to be more tactical, with a primary emphasis on *implementing* and carrying out decisions made as part of strategic visioning or directional planning. Here, the process involves the following:

1. Formulating specific objectives, targets, or quotas that need to be achieved by a certain time.

2. Developing an action plan to be followed and identifying specific steps to be taken in order to meet or exceed those objectives.

3. Creating a schedule showing when specific activities will be started and/or completed.

4. Developing a "budget" (including any type of necessary resources).

5. Estimating or projecting what will have happened at certain points during the life span of the plan.

6. Establishing an organization to implement decisions.

7. Setting standards against which performance will be evaluated.

LESSONS LEARNED FROM GOAL-SETTING RESEARCH AND PRACTICE[3]

Independent of the specific level, perspective, or application of goal setting, research and practice have yielded the following 10 lessons:

1. *Specific, challenging goals tend to result in better performance than vaguely specified, easily attained goals.* Goal setting is more effective when goals are clearly defined in terms of what needs to happen, how often, in what quantity, and by when. Clear, specific goals reduce the probability of miscommunication or misunderstanding and provide a clearer "target" to work toward. Generally, more challenging goals result in higher levels of performance—within certain constraints. Goals should be perceived as attainable given a reasonable "stretch" of effort.

2. *Feedback on progress in goal attainment enhances the process.* Feedback on progress toward the desired objective is essential. When individuals are told how well they are performing against some expected standard, they can make changes in their efforts, if necessary, or continue unchanged if their actions have proven to be effective. The source of feedback and its timing are also important variables.

3. *Goals should be prioritized if there are more than one.* Using the relative importance of a goal or objective to rank it enables individuals to direct their actions and efforts in proportion to the importance of each goal. This ranking also serves to verify both the manager's and the subordinates' expectations.

---

[3]*Adapted from* E.A. Locke and G.P. Latham, *Goal Setting: A Motivational Technique That Works.* Englewood Cliffs, NJ: Prentice-Hall, Inc., 1984. Used with permission.

4. *Informal competition among employees produced by goal setting and feedback can enhance the benefits of the process.* Informal competition often arises spontaneously when performance is evaluated and fed back to individuals in quantitative terms. Excitement, challenge, and pride in accomplishment can result from constructive peer pressure. However, too much "formal" competition can lead to unproductive rivalry.

5. *Goal accomplishment and performance should be rewarded.* These incentives cover the gamut from monetary incentives to various forms of nonmonetary reward.

6. *Goal setting can be an important part of performance management.* Performance appraisal processes serve several intended and sometimes unintended functions in organizations. Ideally, appraisals lead to the identification of strengths and weaknesses in individual performance and, consequently, improved individual and hence organizational performance. Some performance appraisal processes, however, lead to a decline in performance when individuals are criticized and respond defensively. One key way to avoid this unintended outcome is to evaluate a person's performance against preset goals.

7. *Individuals need to develop action plans to carry out their goals.* Action plans detail the specific tasks and schedules required to accomplish goals. The development of an effective plan presupposes that the goal or objective has been clearly defined.

8. *Organizational policies need to be reviewed for consistency and complementarity with goal accomplishment.* Organizational policies exert a tremendous influence over the effectiveness of goal accomplishment. Typically, policies related to decision-making processes and speed, communication, and productivity have the greatest impact.

9. *The climate within which goal setting occurs should be a supportive one in which managers help and encourage their employees to succeed.* Results suggest that individuals whose managers behave supportively during goal-setting processes accept or set much higher goals than those whose managers are nonsupportive. Managerial support gives people confidence and trust, which leads to higher levels of performance.

10. *Depending on how they are used, goals can decrease or increase the amount of stress perceived by subordinates.* The goal-setting process generates negative stress when goals are too difficult (have a high risk of failure) or when there is goal overload, goal conflict, or goal ambiguity. The process can reduce or prevent negative stress by making certain expectations are clear.

These 10 lessons on planning and goal setting suggest that the processes involved, although only a part of the manager's function, are tied to and intimately relate to almost all aspects of management and organization. They have an *impact* on subordinate understanding and communication, motivation, performance appraisal processes, and reward systems. The 10 lessons also suggest that planning and goal-setting processes are *affected by* broader organizational policies and processes as well as the specific "climate" within which those processes take place.

While it is typically called by different names in different organizations, one classic management tool/process that embodies and illustrates all of the lessons from goal setting research and practice is management by objectives.

USING GOALS AND OBJECTIVES AS A MANAGEMENT TOOL: MBO-TYPE APPROACHES

Management by Objectives (MBO) is a term used to describe a broad array of systems, procedures, and programs. What may be called MBO in one organization may not exactly match what you find called by that name in another organization. But, generally speaking, all MBO programs share the following characteristics:

Characteristics of MBO-Type Processes[4]

1. Joint goal setting between members of two consecutive levels of supervision.
   - Managers provide subordinates with a framework reflecting their own goals and objectives.
   - Subordinates propose objectives for themselves.
   - Managers and subordinates discuss, sometimes modify, and eventually agree upon a set of objectives for the subordinates.

2. Periodic measurement and comparison of actual performance against agreed-upon goals and objectives.
   - Subordinates review their own progress and describe it periodically (as agreed) to their managers.
   - This sequence is repeated as necessary.

3. Objectives, whenever and wherever possible, are stated in quantifiable terms such as units, dollars, percentages, and so on.

WHAT MAKES A GOOD MBO

Well-written and formulated goals and objectives can serve as the cornerstone of an MBO system. There is, however, an art and science to the process. Take New Year's resolutions as an example. Many individuals will identify as one of their top two or three resolutions: "I want to lose some weight this year." Consider this personal example of an objective for its utility in an MBO-type system. In and of itself, the objective of "losing" weight is not very informative. It gives no indication of how much weight (quantity), no sense of how fast the weight is to be lost (time), and no indication of the "processes" to be used in losing the weight (quality). It also gives no indication of attainability (thus not allowing for any health challenge) or any sense of flexibility to allow for changes or midcourse corrections.

Consider some examples that are work related:

- Work on my interpersonal skills
- Purchase a computer-based system
- Improve the filing system

[4]*Adapted from* A.C. Filley, R.J. Houser, and S. Kerr, *Managerial Process and Organizational Behavior,* 2d ed., Glenview, IL: Scott, Foresman, 1976.

- Reduce daily entry error rate
- Make better decisions

How can we improve these goals and objectives to make them more useful in an MBO-type system? Doran[5] has suggested that meaningful objectives are "smart"—that is:

Specific	A specific area of improvement is targeted.
Measurable	Some indicator of progress is established
Assignable	Ability to specify an individual or group who will be responsible to accomplish the goal.
Realistic	Given available resources, state what can realistically be achieved.
Time Related	Specification of when the result(s) can be achieved.

WRITING AN MBO

Let's revisit the weight-loss example already cited and apply what we have just presented.

Old Objective	Lose weight this year.
New Objective	Lose 30 pounds by June 15 so that I can wear a size 39 suit to my 20th high school reunion.
Action Steps	To accomplish this, I must

1. Cut my calories to 1,500 per day.
2. Eliminate beer from my diet beginning immediately.
3. Eat fruit or nothing between meals beginning next week.
4. Reduce consumption of sweets to one serving per week beginning in two weeks.
5. Begin a regular exercise program (alternating jogging and aerobics).

SPECIAL CHALLENGES FOR SETTING GOALS AND OBJECTIVES IN NEW ECONOMY ORGANIZATIONS

In many ways, new economy, Internet-based organizations do not easily lend themselves to the assumptions of hierarchy and chain of command. In the new economy, information is ubiquitous and voluminous—and it is power. Very rapid change is in many ways its currency. All organizations are experiencing dramatically increased pressures for performance from all of their stakeholders—employees, customers, and shareholders. New innovative products and services are expected faster, at higher quality, and with lower cost. The dynamic flexibility, adaptability, responsiveness, and constant realignment these factors require have led many organizations to focus "laterally" as well as hierarchically when setting goals and objectives. As we discuss elsewhere, cross-functional teams are being used at many different levels and in many types of organizations. Regardless of the nature of the team or teams, their existence substantially impacts the setting of goals and objectives.

[5]"There's a S.M.A.R.T. Way to Write Management's Goals and Objectives," by George T. Doran, Nov. 1981, from *Management Review*. Reprinted, by permission of publisher, from *Management Review*, November/1981 © 1981. American Management Association, New York. All rights reserved.

SETTING GOALS AND OBJECTIVES IN THE NEW ECONOMY ORGANIZATION

Mohrman, Cohen, and Mohrman (1995) proposed the model below as a realistic and pragmatic way to address the process of goal setting in team-focused organizations. Team-based/lateral organizations are very much dependent on the organization's direction being widely known throughout the organization. There must be a similar and comprehensive understanding of the direction so that issues within and between teams can be resolved and complex trade-offs that require cross-functional input can be made.

ACTION STRATEGIES FOR SETTING GOALS AND OBJECTIVES IN NEW ECONOMY ORGANIZATIONS[6]

Define a Strategy, Communicate It, and Operationalize It at All Systemic Levels. This action strategy assumes we have done our job developing and communicating vision (mission), strategies, and plans. The challenge in team-based/lateral organizations is the need to know both the general business stategy and the strategy for the specific team's product or contribution to the process. Imperative for the first-line product or process team is the articulation of its particular microstrategy. This is not to be done unilaterally; rather, members of the various teams should be given an opportunity to provide input. It then becomes management's responsibility to ensure that both the macro- and microstrategies are clearly articulated, broadly shared, and understood as well as that those strategies reflect both appropriate member input and information from the external environment.

Align Goals Vertically and Laterally. Various performing units—individuals, teams, product lines, or process owners—have goals, and these goals are often nested within each other as well as interrelated within the organization as a whole. All of these various goals in combination must "add up" to the business goals. It is imperative that there be an alignment between higher and lower levels of the organization (systemic levels) and between units at the same level within a larger unit (e.g., different teams at the same level within a single unit). This necessitates goal setting that is both vertically and laterally sensitive.

Choose Goals that Are Measurable. Having measurable goals at every level of performance—especially the team level—increases unit and organizational effectiveness. Examples include performance outcomes/targets such as cost, quality, schedule, revenue, and profit. Lateral examples include reusing a certain amount of software code, earning a particular percentage of revenue from new products or new customers, and achieving an order of a certain magnitude from a particular new customer. These goals have SMART attributes as we described earlier.

---

[6]*Adapted from* S.A. Mohrman, S.G. Cohen, and A.M. Mohrman Jr., *Designing Team-Based Organizations.* San Francisco: Jossey-Bass, 1995, pp. 172–179.

Assign Rewards in Accordance with Organizational Goals. What organizations reward sends a powerful signal to organizational members about what is really valued in the organization—that is, those behaviors that senior leadership really wants and that move all stakeholders forward. Rewarding someone for individual performance without acknowledging the performance of the team of which he or she is a member will likely cause continued focus on individual efforts only.

Do Not Assume That Direction Precludes Empowerment. In our discussion of the producer role in Chapter 7, we spend a good deal of time focusing on the role empowerment plays in determining individual and work unit productivity. When it comes to goal setting, there is often trepidation about direction being in conflict with empowerment. In fact, direction, appropriately framed, is critical for empowerment to occur. It is direction that provides broad knowledge of where the organization is headed, the strategy for getting there, and the criteria and priorities that result. It is the translation of that broad direction into local goals that aligns the various performing units of the organization and the individuals within teams.

Plan Collectively. The fact that involvement in decision making increases ownership and commitment to the process and outcomes is crucial in the setting of goals and objectives. Involvement of individuals in the setting of team or unit goals and objectives takes advantage of the ability of members to develop performance strategies that are flexible, that they can control, and that they believe will work. A frequent lament is, "We understand the need for stretch goals—tell us what they are but give us leeway in determining how we accomplish them!"

Facilitate Flexibility and Responsiveness. The setting of goals and objectives in the new economy is an ongoing, dynamic, and frequently changing process. In knowledge-work settings, goals, plans, and even strategies change frequently, requiring objective- and goal-setting processes that provide for periodic reviews, renegotiating, and updating. This ongoing process attends to the changes that arise as clients and customers initiate changes consistent with their own needs.

ANALYSIS   MBO Is Not for Me[7]

Objectives   The following case can be analyzed in a number of different ways. Although we have included it within the "setting goals and objectives" competency, it can also be used for analyzing the mentoring and communication skills of the manager and the communication skills of the employee.

Directions   Read this case of Don Smith's objection to objectives, and then answer the questions that follow.

You are Nancy Stuart, plant personnel manager for Countrywide Manufacturing Company's local plant in Jamestown, Ohio, a city of about 17,000 people. The plant is the principal employer in the area.

[7]"Don Smith's Objection Objectives" from *Behavior in Organizations: An Experiential Approach,* 5th edition, by J.B. Lau and A.B. Shani, 1992, pp. 356–357. Reprinted by permission of Richard D. Irwin Inc. and the authors.

During the past two years, the personnel division (see Figure 6.1 for the organization chart) in the central headquarters of Countrywide has been quite successful in helping line managers learn and implement a new management by objectives (MBO) program throughout the company. The vice president for personnel of Countrywide was recently embarrassed when the company president asked him, "If MBO is improving effectiveness in the line divisions throughout all the plants, why haven't you used it more in your own personnel area?" This resulted in a directive to you and all plant personnel officers to come up immediately with a five-year plan applying the MBO approach. You wrote a memorandum to your branch

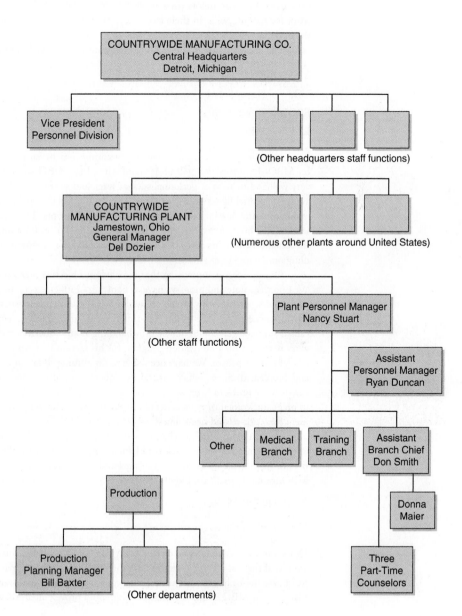

FIGURE 6.1
Organization chart for the Countrywide Manufacturing Company.

chiefs asking them to submit a first draft of a plan to include objectives and how they are to be implemented and evaluated. This would provide data for a planning conference of your branch chiefs.

Don Smith is the chief of your counseling branch. He was hired two years ago to replace an employee who was retiring. Don was right out of college, having completed a master's in counseling. He has proved himself to be highly successful in getting the line managers in the plant to use counseling services. The quality of his branch's service is recognized throughout the plant. Last year, Don recruited Donna Maire, who had just completed her graduate work. Don has trained her well, and the two of them are a great team. In addition, Don employs on a part-time basis three counselors (they work full time for the public health office, but are allowed to work for Countrywide in their free time). Don and Donna are the only regular employees in the branch.

The following is an informal memorandum you received from Don in answer to yours:

MEMORANDUM

TO: Nancy Stuart

FROM: Don Smith

RE: MBOs

I am scheduled to leave on my two-week vacation tonight, so I am writing you about my views on MBO. I am sure you will understand when I say MBO seems to apply to production areas very well and to areas of personnel such as wage and salary administration, but it really does not apply to counseling services. Last week, Donna and I saw a total of 25 employees for counseling and had 8 interviews with managers about problem people. The three part-time counselors each worked two hours last week, and their caseload was 4 each, for a total of 12. Compare this with the situation two years ago when I came aboard and the one-person counseling service was handling only 4 to 5 cases a week.

Our business is so pressing that the obvious objective is to get another full-time counselor. We find that more and more we have to book appointments for a week or two ahead. The people who need several sessions with a counselor because of the seriousness of their cases are being assigned whenever possible to the part-timers from Public Health. We are getting more and more calls from managers asking for help in handling nonproductive employees. One has asked us to work with him on a motivation program for his section that would help raise the production of all eight of his people. We have been able to do nothing so far on the program to help alcoholics and problem drinkers, which central headquarters thinks we should be doing. I am really not sure this is a problem here; we have had no referrals. Managers seem more interested in problems of pregnant women than social drinkers. We ought to also get started on a policy guidance statement for work-related stress illness.

Do you agree with me when I say that in a service area like counseling the main objective is to get enough qualified counselors to handle employee problems that already exist? So the objectives of my branch are (1) more personnel and (2) a bigger budget. If you need anything else on MBO for our branch, ask Donna. She knows our work as well as I do.

See you in two weeks,

Don Smith

Don's answer is the first you receive from your branch chiefs. You are a little taken aback and wonder if the rest of your team is going to be as flippant, and apparently perplexed, in trying to formulate their objectives. The chiefs of your medical training branches were making snide remarks about MBO at lunch yesterday. This could prove embarrassing because the vice president of personnel is the executive who brought MBO programs into the organization. You become vaguely aware that you are not sure how Don should go about defining his objectives.

Discussion Questions
1. Why did Nancy's approach to the MBO program generate such a negative reaction? What should she have done differently, based on the principles of effective MBO systems?

2. Assume that Nancy decides to try writing Don's objectives herself because he is on vacation. What can she do to help get herself started? What are some objectives that you think would be appropriate for Don?

3. What does the fact that neither Don nor Nancy seem to have a clear idea of what Don's objectives should be tell you about the vision for the organization?

Reflection Depending on the culture of the organization where you work, you may never receive a response from an employee that is as brash as the one provided by Don Smith. In many organizations, most of Don's comments would have remained hidden in his "left-hand column" (recall Chapter 2—the section titled Communicating Effectively), reflecting a more avoidant approach to managing conflict. Avoidant strategies might include just ignoring the request or sending back a polite memo saying "I'll get to this after vacation" but then never follow up. Because effective MBO systems depend on consistency throughout the organization as well as commitment to the objectives that are identified, it is critical that collaboration or at least compromise be used to come to agreement on what objectives should be.

PRACTICE   Creating an Implementation Plan

Objective This exercise gives you an opportunity to practice developing an implementation plan for a specific goal.

Directions In the Assessment for Competency 2, you were asked to identify goals in four categories (personal relationships, academic/scholastic accomplishments, career/job interests, and financial future). Select whichever of these goals is the most important to you. Develop an implementation plan for achieving your goal.

Discussion Questions
1. Did you include SMART objectives in your plan and identify the specific steps necessary to achieve your goal?

2. Are there any outside factors that might affect your ability to achieve your goal?

3. How confident do you feel about achieving this goal now that you have identified the steps you need to take to reach it?

Reflection Sometimes we set goals that are unrealistic. By specifying the specific steps required to accomplish our goals, we may find that we need to modify our goals, perhaps by extending our timeline for achieving a particular goal or by reducing its scope.

APPLICATION   Writing Your Own MBO

Objective The objective of this exercise is to apply what you have learned about setting goals and objectives to your own life.

Directions 1. Select one of the following options:

A. If your company does not use MBO, develop your own objectives based upon what you know about the company's mission and your role within the organization.

B. If your company uses MBO, review your current objectives relative to the mission of the organization and your unit.

C. If you are not currently employed, use your personal vision and goals and work on developing objectives for yourself that connect your goals for your personal relationships, academic accomplishments, career interests, and financial future.

2. Discuss your MBO with someone who can give you constructive feedback on the consistency of your objectives and the vision of the organization (or your personal vision).

Reflection   Sharing your MBO with people who can help you achieve your objectives (e.g., your boss, partner, family, etc.) may not only improve the quality of your objectives, but also may help reinforce your commitment to meeting them.

Competency 3   Designing and Organizing

ASSESSMENT   Assessing Organizational Culture

Objective   This exercise is designed to give you some insight into the culture of your organization. It is drawn from the Organizational Culture Assessment Instrument* (Cameron and Quinn, 2006). The interpretation is included later in this chapter.

Directions   Review the following four statements and indicate how well each statement reflects your organization by dividing 100 points across the four statements.

_____ *The organization is a very personal place. It is like extended family. People seem to share a lot of themselves.*

_____ *The organization is a very dynamic and entrepreneurial place. People are willing to stick their necks out and take risks.*

_____ *The organization is very results-oriented. A major concern is with getting the job done. People are very competitive and achievement oriented.*

_____ *The organization is a very controlled and structured place. Formal procedures generally govern what people do.*

_100_ *Total Points to Be Allocated*

Reflection   This simplified assessment of organizational culture only taps the surface of the many ways that organizations differ. Research suggests that there is no one "best" organizational culture. Similarly, different individuals may feel more comfortable in different organizational cultures.

LEARNING   Designing and Organizing

Traditional organization theory focuses on the role of an organization's *strategy* and the *environment* in which it operates in determining the most effective way to design and organize. Structural contingency theory suggests that organizations be designed and structured along some continuum of mechanistic to organic, depending on the complexity and

Adapted from K. S. Cameron and R. E. Quinn, Diagnosing and Changing Organizational Culture Based on the Competing Values Framework (San Francisco: Jossey-Bass, 2006). Used with permission.

turbulence of the environment within which they exist. The basic rule is that the more complex and turbulent the environment, the greater the need for a more organic structure and design. Organizations in the new economy, however, are confronted with an even more challenging environment. It contains sophisticated and demanding customers, wanting an incredible variety of options at an unprecedented pace. It is also characterized by an unprecedented breadth and depth of change accompanied by almost unattainable expectations regarding speed and the very mixed blessing of the most ubiquitous and advanced information technology in the history of humankind. These environmental circumstances will almost certainly continue to drive the evolution of organizational structural metaphors from the now seemingly simplistic "mechanistic" and "organic" to the more recent ones, including "horizontal," "lateral," and "virtual."

Petzinger (1999) captured the essence of the evolution of mental models (i.e., paradigms) of organizations and their structures in *The New Pioneers*. Petzinger's (1999) work on mental models focuses on their evolution in the realm of organizations and their structures. Simplistic mechanical metaphors like machines and clocks have been replaced by more organic and dynamic ones like organisms and ecologies. Metaphors for organizational strategy have migrated from emphasizing predictability to adaptation while those for leadership have evolved from command and control to articulation of vision and autonomy of employees.

Central metaphors	Machines, clocks	*to*	Organisms, ecologies
Strategic objectives	Optimum design Predictability	*to*	Adaptation, continuous improvement
Leadership implications	Command and control	*to*	Articulation of vision, autonomy of employees
Sources of value	Land, materials, energy/fuel	*to*	Knowledge, information
Management objective	Economies of scale	*to*	Unity of purpose
Structure	Hierarchies	*to*	Self-organizing teams
Organizing principles	Division of labor	*to*	Synthesis of minds

Petzinger's metaphors and models of today's organizations are very consistent with our framing of the core competencies of the director and producer roles. In providing direction, the key implication for the leader is no longer command and control, but rather the articulation of vision, as discussed above. Productivity of employees is no longer attained in Frederick Taylor's world, where "all possible brain work" is removed from the workplace, but rather in a work environment characterized by autonomy of employees, creativity, adaptation, and continuous improvement.

Designing and organizing, then, is driven by the vision and strategy articulated. No design is perfect; each has relative strengths and weaknesses. The vision and strategy set the criteria for choosing among trade-offs of various designs. Galbraith (1995) has suggested the "star model" as a framework for designing organizations. The star model identifies five categories or elements to consider in the design process:

- Strategy
- Structure

- Processes
- Rewards
- People

Strategy.   As defined by Galbraith, strategy is the organization's "formula for winning"—it specifies the goals and objectives to be achieved as well as the values and mission that will drive the organization. Strategy, as Galbraith frames it, includes two of the three core competencies that make up the director role—developing and communicating a vision and setting goals and objectives. For Galbraith, strategy in the design process is aimed at setting out the basic direction of the organization.

Structure.   In Galbaith's model, structure determines the placement of power and authority in the organization. The classic elements of stucture include specialization (division of labor), span of control, distribution of power (centralization vs. decentralization), and departmentalization (i.e., functions, products, workflow processes, markets, and geography). In many cases, discussions of organizational design often emphasize how the company is currently structured and how a "structural change" would impact effectiveness. We include a review and discussion of the classic elements of structure below.

Processes.   Galbraith utilizes biological metaphors when he compares an organization's structure to anatomy and its processes to physiology or functioning. Processes, in Galbraith's framework, broadly include information and decision processes that span the breadth and depth of the organization's structure. They include management processes, which are both vertical and horizontal. Examples of vertical processes include business planning and budgeting processes. Horizontal, or lateral, processes are designed around the work flow, as we discuss in more detail in our treatment of cross-functional processes.

Rewards.   In any organizational setting, the outcome hoped for from reward systems is the alignment of the goals of individual employees with the goals of the organization. There has been much change in this area as the impact of lateral processes, increasingly team-based organizations, and the centrality of nonmonetary rewards has increased. We will discuss rewards in great detail in our treatment of the producer role in Chapter 7.

People.   Galbraith's definition of "people" in the context of his model includes the human resource policies that relate to the attraction, recruitment, selection, development, and rotation of employees. These policies, when combined and aligned appropriately, produce the talent pool that is necessary to the strategy and structure of the organization.

We have already covered much of what Galbraith includes under his rubric of "strategy" in our discussion of the director competencies of developing and communicating a vision and setting goals and objectives. Rewards will be covered extensively in our discussion of the producer role competencies in Chapter 7. Here we will focus primarily on the classic "skeleton" for organizational design—structure—and then address the remaining two of Galbraith's design elements—people and processes—in a discussion of organizational culture and change as an alternative model for designing and organizing.

STRUCTURE AND ORGANIZING: CORE CONCEPTS AND PRINCIPLES

Once organizational and work unit plans are set, a manager must decide how to allocate and coordinate organizational resources in order to accomplish goals. **Organizing** is the process of dividing the work into manageable components and assigning activities so as to most effectively achieve the desired results. Said in another way, if planning provides the tools for deciding "where you want to go and how best to get there," organizing provides the tools to actually "get you there."

At the organizational level, organizing involves designing the organizational structure so that the work can be efficiently and effectively allocated across the different departments and work units. At the work unit level, organizing involves designing jobs and allocating tasks so that the work unit can effectively accomplish its goals in support of the overall organizational mission. In this section we will examine both organizational and job design, focusing on current tools and techniques of organizing that have evolved from ideas first written about by Adam Smith in 1776.

EFFICIENCY AS AN ORGANIZING PRINCIPLE

In *The Wealth of Nations,* written in 1776, Adam Smith (1937) established two management principles that still stand today as guiding principles for organizations. Writing about the manufacture of straight pins, Smith noted that if (1) the work were divided into its component tasks and (2) workers were specialized so that each individual had responsibility for completing only one of the component tasks, the overall job would be accomplished far more efficiently than if each worker performed all tasks associated with the job.

More than 200 years later, the process of organizing is still very much influenced by the principles of **division of labor** (that work should be divided into component tasks) and **specialization** (that each person should be assigned only a small piece of the total job). Although current management thought on how to design organizations and jobs effectively no longer focuses exclusively on efficiency, it remains an important building block in the process of organizing.

Small organizations often remain informal with respect to rules and procedures. They have little need for standardization of jobs and specialization—when a job needs to be done, people share in the work. Large organizations, however, require rules and procedures. Without standardization and specialization there would be chaos. Organizing, then, serves several important functions.

1. Organizing clarifies *who* is supposed to perform which jobs and *how* those jobs should be divided among organizational members.
2. Organizing clarifies the *lines of authority,* specifying who reports to whom.
3. Organizing creates the *mechanisms for coordinating* across the different groups and levels of the organization.

DESIGNING ORGANIZATIONS THROUGH DEPARTMENTATION

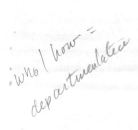

At the organizational level, dividing jobs among organizational members is called **departmentation.** Here employees are grouped into departments according to some logic. Three pure forms of departmentation are departmentation by function, departmentation by division, and departmentation by matrix.

BY FUNCTION

Departmentation by function creates departments based on the specific functions that people perform. For example, financial management offices, engineering departments, and legal offices are grouped by function. All people in these offices perform similar functions.

Organizing by function increases organizational efficiency by having people with similar expertise working together to perform similar functions. Conversely, it decreases organizational efficiency because the structure creates barriers between departments that generally result in increased time to respond to interfunctional problems.

BY DIVISION

Departmentation by division creates departments based on services, clients, territories, or time differences. For example, AT&T reorganized its computer-oriented division from a functional structure to a divisional structure in order to increase coordination. IBM organizes its marketing by geographic region, both domestic and worldwide. In the United States, IBM has two marketing divisions: North–Central and South–West.

Organizing by division increases organizational efficiency because the departments can be more responsive to specific client or regional needs. Conversely, it often leads to duplication of effort and makes it more difficult for people who are doing the same type of work, in different departments, to share their ideas and learn from each other.

BY MATRIX

Departmentation by matrix, or matrix organization, attempts to reap the advantages and overcome the disadvantages of functional and divisional organizational forms by combining the two. In matrix organizations, employees are assigned (1) to a functional department and also (2) to a cross-functional team that focuses on specific projects or programs. They report to the heads of both the functional department and cross-functional team. For example, an engineer in a manufacturing firm that is organized in matrix form will report to the head of the engineering department and also to the product manager, who also manages marketing, production, and finance specialists assigned to that project or product. Such diverse service and manufacturing organizations as Prudential Insurance, General Mills, and Caterpillar Tractor are organized in matrix form.

CHOOSING A FORM OF DEPARTMENTATION

As discussed previously, each of the pure forms of departmentation has advantages and disadvantages. In choosing a form of departmentation, organizations often organize according to a mix of these forms. For example, because of the greater flexibility and ability to respond to client needs, many corporations are organized by division with respect to the specific products or services they provide, but they are organized by function with respect to personnel/human resources management, financial management, and legal offices. Similarly, some organizations are organized by division with respect to regions but by function within each region. Hospitals and psychiatric institutions may have matrix structures for providing services, but they maintain a functional structure for such activities as records management, building maintenance, and nutrition and dietary services.

LINES OF AUTHORITY

In addition to defining how the organization's work is to be divided, departmentation defines the organization's authority relationships—who reports to whom. In designing authority relationships, we often rely on three efficiency principles. First, each person should report to one and only one manager. This is referred to as the **unity-of-command principle.** The principle ensures that employees know from whom they should expect job assignments and reduces the potential for conflicting job assignments. Note that, by definition, matrix organizations violate the unity-of-command principle. In fact, the advantages of matrix organizations are considered to be sufficient to warrant this violation. Managers in matrix organizations, however, should monitor job assignments and communication patterns to check that employees are not receiving conflicting messages from their two bosses.

Building on the principle of unity of command, the **scalar principle** states that there should be a clear line of command linking each employee to the next higher level of authority, up to and including the highest level of management. When the lines of authority are clear, it is easier to know who is responsible for the completion of each job.

Finally, the principle of **span of control** states that a person can effectively manage only a limited number of employees. How many, then? The answer is not clear and may vary with the individuals involved. But the principle recognizes that as the number of individuals reporting to a manager increases, the more difficult it is to coordinate and control individual efforts.

The size of the span of control influences the organization's structure. For a given number of employees, as the span of control decreases, the number of levels in the organizational hierarchy increases. More managers are needed and, hence, the greater the number of layers in the hierarchy. Conversely, the greater the span of control, the fewer the number of managers needed and, hence, the fewer the number of layers in the hierarchy.

Organizations with many levels in the hierarchy are referred to as **tall organizations;** organizations with fewer levels in the hierarchy are referred to as **flat organizations.** In general, tall organizations tend to operate less efficiently than flat ones. Recent trends in both industry and government have been to reduce the number of levels in the hierarchy and to increase the span of control.

CONFLICTS AMONG ORGANIZING PRINCIPLES

The five principles of organizing—specialization, division of labor, unity of command, scalar chain, and span of control—often contradict one another (Simon, 1976). There will always be situations in which adherence to one principle of efficiency will result in violation of a second principle. In these situations, trade-offs will be required across different types of efficiency. To decide which trade-offs to make, return to the overall mission of the organization and determine which principle of efficiency serves this mission most efficiently.

DIFFERENTIATION AND INTEGRATION

When the environments and technologies within a single organization differ, there is greater need for **differentiation** across departments. That is, departments should be structured differently so that they can approach their tasks differently. Departments can be differentiated according to time, goal, and interpersonal orientation.

1. *Time orientation.* Some tasks, such as paper processing, require a shorter time orientation than others, such as planning or research.

2. *Goal orientation.* Even when organizations have a single organizational mission, the goals of the individual work units will differ to some degree. For example, organizational units closely associated with the organization's mission pursue different goals than do organizational units associated with maintaining the organization's structure (personnel, financial management, etc.).

3. *Interpersonal orientation.* To the extent that the degree of interdependency among employees varies across organizational tasks, patterns and styles of interaction will differ across work units.

Thus, organizational subsystems that must be more responsive to their environments should be organized to allow for greater response. Organizational subsystems that have more uncertain environments must be organized to allow for greater flexibility and adaptability to sudden changes. And organizational subsystems that have more uncertain technologies should be organized to accommodate the greater need for interaction among people.

Returning for a moment to the organizational level, think about the organizational implications of maintaining a highly differentiated organization. If each subsystem is structured differently, the potential exists for the organization to become a "disorganization." In fact, the greater the differentiation across units, the greater the need for **integration**, or coordination across units (Lawrence and Lorsch, 1967). Various mechanisms are available to the organization to achieve effective integration, ranging from basic tools (such as rules and procedures, referral of problems up the hierarchy, and planning) to more complex tools (such as liaison roles, task forces and interunit teams, and matrix organization designs). An in-depth discussion of these mechanisms is beyond the scope of this chapter. Suffice it to say that rules, procedures, and the referral of problems up the hierarchy tend to work best when the need for integration is low. Alternatively, when departments that are highly differentiated have high needs for integration, task forces, teams, and matrix structures are most effective.

ORGANIZATIONAL CULTURE AS A FRAME FOR DESIGNING AND ORGANIZING

Given the challenges of the new economy, we began our discussion of designing and organizing by noting that the classical principles of organization structure almost seem too slow and cumbersome to reflect current organizational realities, which are marked by unprecedented customer expectations; rapidly changing, ferociously competitive, and turbulent environments; and the revolutionary impact of advances in information

technology. Nadler and Tushman (2000), in a recent article trying to anticipate "the organization of the future," observed that in recent years it has become evident that "values,
culture, and shared goals are replacing the formal structures as the glue that holds organizations together" (p. 58). With the increasing role that culture seems to be playing in organizational life, it seems only logical that it should get more of our attention as we
consider the design and organization of companies. This assertion is supported by a great
deal of recent research suggesting that many initiatives aimed at organizational improvement often fail because of inattention to the role and impact of organizational culture.
Studies of downsizing, total quality management, and reengineering have found that
when they were implemented independent of a change in culture, they were often unsuccessful because when the organization's culture, values, orientations, definitions, and goals
stay constant—even when procedures and strategies are altered—organizations return
quickly to the status quo. (Cameron, 1995; Cameron, Freeman, and Mishra, 1993).

Galbraith (1995) suggests that the five elements of design that make up his star
model are levers that leaders control that can affect organizational performance and
culture, but only by acting "through" the design levers that affect behavior. We would
like to suggest that the environment of the new economy is such that Galbraith's sequence of effects can be turned around (see Figure 6.2) and that culture can be used as
a lead variable (i.e., lever) in understanding and leveraging (or changing) current organization design.

The competing values (CV) culture framework (Denison & Spreitzer, 1991;
Cameron & Quinn, 1999) emerges from the juxtaposition of the same two dimensions
that make up the CV leadership framework (see Figure 6.3). The horizontal dimension
reflects the competing demands created by the internal organization and the external

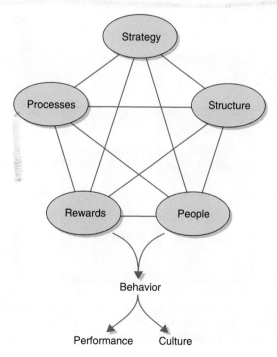

FIGURE 6.2 *Culture as a framework for understanding and diagnosing organizational design.*

environment. One end represents a focus on buffering to sustain the existing organization, while the other represents a focus on adaptation, competition, and interaction with the environment. This dimension is respectively analogous to our discussion of integration and differentiation. The vertical dimension reflects the competing demands of change and stability. One end represents an emphasis on flexibility and spontaneity, while the other represents a complementary focus on stability, control, and order. This dimension is analogous to the distinction we made above about structures varying from mechanistic to organic forms.

The four culture types that result (see Figure 6.3) are templates of our four CV leadership quadrants. In the upper-left quadrant, mirroring the human relations model, is group culture (also known as the "clan"). In the lower-left quadrant, mirroring the internal process model, is hierarchical culture. In the lower-right quadrant, mirroring the rational goal model, is the rational culture (also known as the "market" or "firm"). In the upper-right quadrant, mirroring the open systems model, is the developmental culture (also known as "adhocracy").

The Group Culture ("Clan"). The culture mirroring the values of the human relations model, the group or clan, has a primary concern with shared values and goals, cohesion, participativeness, individuality, and a sense of "we-ness"—more like extended families than an economic vehicle. The ultimate purpose of organizations that emphasize group culture tends to be group maintenance. Core values include belonging, trust, and participation. Primary motivational factors include attachment, cohesiveness, and membership. Leaders in a group culture tend to be supportive, considerate, participative, and facilitative of interaction through teamwork. Effectiveness criteria include the development of human capital and the commitment of individual members.

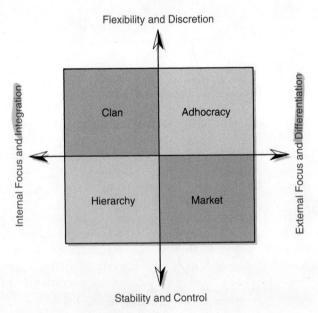

FIGURE 6.3 *Competing Values Culture Framework.*

The Hierarchy Culture. The culture mirroring the values of the internal process model, the hierarchy, has a primary concern with internal efficiency, uniformity, coordination, and evaluation. Typically, organizations with a strong hierarchical culture emphasize the execution of policies and regulations. Primary motivational factors include security, order, rules, and regulations. Leaders in a hierarchy culture tend to be conservative, cautious, and very attentive to technical issues. Effectiveness criteria include control, stability, and efficiency.

The Rational Culture ("Firm"). The culture mirroring the values of the rational goal model, the rational culture or "market"/"firm", has a primary concern with productivity, performance, and goal achievement. This culture is oriented toward the external environment instead of internal affairs. It is primarily focused on transactions with external constituencies such as customers, suppliers, and so forth. Typically, the driving purpose of organizations with a rational culture emphasis tends to be the pursuit and attainment of well-defined objectives. Primary motivating factors include competition and the successful achievement of predetermined ends. Leaders in a "market" culture tend to be directive, goal oriented, instrumental, and functional. These leaders are constantly vigilant about providing productivity and structure. Effectiveness criteria include planning, productivity, and efficiency.

The Developmental Culture ("Adhocracy"). The culture mirroring the values of the open systems model, the developmental culture or "adhocracy," is primarily concerned with flexibility and change but maintains a primary focus on the external environment. Cultures that are strongly characterized by adhocracy emphasize growth, resource acquisition, creativity, and adapting and responding to the external environment. A central purpose is often to maximize individuality, risk taking, and anticipating the future. Primary motivating factors include growth, stimulation, creativity, and variety. Leaders in an adhocracy tend to be entrepreneurial and idealistic, with a willingness to take risks and an ability to develop a vision of the future. Effectiveness criteria include growth, the development of new markets, and resource acquisition.

Diagnosing Organization Culture. The assessment that you completed at the beginning of this competency asked you to allocate 100 points across four descriptions of organizations. The first description is consistent with the clan culture, the second with the adhocracy, the third with the market/firm culture, and the fourth with the hierarchy culture. More detailed versions of the competing values assessment instruments can provide a more fine grained diagnosis of your organization culture, but for our purposes this broad brush approach provides a starting point for thinking about the connection between organization culture and design.

Aligning Culture and Design. Each of the four cultural types has a perceptual opposite. The "clan," concerned with cohesion, morale, and the development of human resources, starkly contrasts to the "market," with its pursuit of market share, goal achievement, and vanquishing competitors. The "hierarchy," with its passion for efficiency, timeliness, and smooth functioning, contrasts with the "adhocracy," looking for fulfillment in cutting-edge output, creativity, and growth. Yet while they exist as "polar opposites," they share a common focus—the clan and the adhocracy share an emphasis on flexibility, the adhocracy and the market share an external focus, the market and the hierarchy share the value of control, and the hierarchy and the clan share an internal focus.

Two key assumptions underlie the competing values culture framework. The first is that each of the four should be viewed as ideal types defined by the competing values model. Organizations functioning in the real world are very unlikely to reflect only one of the four culture types. Typically, organizations reflect some level of all four, with one or two more dominant than the others. The second key assumption of the competing values culture framework is the critical importance of balance. When one of the four models is overused or overemphasized, an organization may become ineffective and the positives of the quadrant may become weaknesses. The framework also stops short of the normative and prescriptive bias that the most effective culture is one that has incorporated the attributes of all four types.

Cameron and Quinn (1999) have articulated a process involving the "profiling" of an organization's perceived current culture, identification of desired future states based on strategy and the current state of the organization, and necessary changes and actions aimed at altering the culture appropriately. Their process facilitates several types of comparisons important in understanding an organization's current culture and its impact on design and performance. Some of those comparisons that are useful in understanding the effectiveness of a given organizational design include the *type* of culture (i.e. market, adhocracy, etc.) that characterizes an organization, *discrepancies* between the current and the desired future culture, the *strength* of the culture type that seems to dominate, and the *congruence* of culture profiles generated on different attributes by different subsets of individuals in organizations.

Type is critical since organizational effectiveness and success depend to a great extent on the match between an organization's culture and the various demands that the relevant competitive environment makes. If organization X is operating in a viciously competitive and aggressive industry within a rapidly changing and turbulent environment, it may not survive with a culture that is very strong on the group/clan aspect and relatively weak on market culture orientation. Discrepancies identify the disconnects between the state of the organization now and where the organization thinks it needs to be in order to be effective. These discrepancies help focus on the right elements of organizational design to use as levers to resolve the discrepancies. Strong cultures typically reflect homogeneity of energy, focus, efforts, and performance in environments where unity and shared vision are required. Depending on the nature of the challenge(s) the organization is facing, the desired culture may be stronger or weaker than the current culture. For example, a firm with a very strong and homogeneous culture may try to find opportunities to become more "flexible" and pliable when it needs to be heavily involved in alliances and multiorganizational partnerships. The notion of congruence implies that various aspects of an organization's culture are in fact aligned and consistent. That is, each of the five elements of Galbraith's star model—strategy, structure, processes, rewards, and people—would tend to emphasize the same set of cultural values. A simple sports example of incongruence would be to pay each member of a professional basketball team based only on the number of points he or she individually scores. Such a reward system would be very incongruous with the required strategy, structure, and process required for winning basketball games (Cameron and Quinn, 1999)!

In our discussion of this competency, we suggested that the nature, pace, and complexity of the new economy require a knowledge of the classic lessons about designing and organizing—derived mostly from work on organizational structure—as well as the ability to apply and leverage that knowledge in a way that makes it more usable working at Internet speed. The solution we have suggested is the use of organizational culture as a lens to help understand and diagnose the effectiveness of an organization's design as well as a lever to help improve an organization's effectiveness and performance.

Every organization, even the most mundane and ubiquitous, is very much a function of its design. The experience that key stakeholders have with an organization—be they customers, employees, suppliers, partners, shareholders, and so forth—will be enhanced or diminished by the appropriateness of the organization's design to its situation and environment.

ANALYSIS Designing and Organizing as a Result of Changing Technology[8]

Objective   This case provides you with an opportunity to consider the dynamic relationship between a company's environment and its strategy, design, and organization.

Directions   Read the following case study and answer the questions that follow.

Steve Ellis, a Wells Fargo senior vice president known as a talented maverick, had been at the bank for 12 years. Before that he had obtained an MBA from the University of Oregon as well as been the proprietor of a tavern in the city of Portland, Oregon.

In the spring of 1999, Ellis decided to bet his career on an idea. During his 12 years at the bank, he had specialized in corporate banking, successfully helping to manage areas ranging from problem real estate loans to cash-management and Treasury operations. Ellis became uncomfortably aware that the Internet was beginning to remake the entire world of finance.

Ellis attended a conference of bankers in Atlanta that April, and one of the keynote speakers was Scott McNealy, chairman and CEO of Sun Microsystems. After McNealy delivered one of his typically electrifying presentations about the online economy, Ellis's response was: "I got Internet religion—I came home and pulled five people off their jobs. Then we brought in an Internet consulting firm and drafted a high-level strategic plan about how Wells Fargo should organize around the Internet channel."

Soon, Steve Ellis began shopping and circulating his "brash and almost taunting views" in a white paper. He believed that the bank needed to create a strong Internet team for wholesale banking that cut across all existing business lines. The 148-year-old institution symbolized by the stagecoach would have to rethink the basic ways that it worked with its customers. And it needed to do so very quickly. Ellis's lobbying soon became a crusade and gathered enough momentum that he was asked to make a presentation of his ideas to Wells Fargo commercial and corporate banking executives at a company off-site meeting. This was a "make or break" moment for him, since the president and CEO of the entire bank, Richard Kovacevich, was a surprise guest in the audience. Ellis's aggressive

[8]*Adapted from* George Anders, "Power Partners," *Fast Company* (September 2000): 146–158.

lobbying and blunt talk paid off. Senior executives at Wells Fargo decided that Ellis was onto something very important and very big and that he was the person to make it real.

Ellis's vision was the creation of an electronic-procurement service as fast as possible. The service would allow corporate customers to run purchasing departments online. Wells Fargo would realize small commissions on the transactions—but more important, the bank would establish the Wells Fargo Web site as a vital part of its customers' workday.

There was a problem, however. This was July of 1999—the year of the now infamous Y2K problem. Because of anxiety about possible computer snags associated with Y2K, regulators insisted that banks could not do massive software upgrades after September 15, 1999. That gave Ellis slightly less than two months to build the foundation required for his vision to become a reality. Ellis obviously needed a partner—the fastest, smartest Silicon Valley startup that knew how to do e-procurement. Ellis chose RightWorks, a San Jose–based company founded in 1996 by Vani Kola, 36, an engineer from India. Ellis and his colleagues told Kola that if her team could deliver the entire e-procurement framework before the Y2K drop-dead date, they would give RightWorks the Wells Fargo contract. With six weeks to deliver, RightWorks accepted.

Discussion Questions

1. What aspects of the case above are issues of designing and organizing?

2. Describe issues related to strategy, structure, and the role of the Internet.

3. What kind of departmentation do you think you would find if you were to spend a week reviewing organization charts for all of Wells Fargo's operations?

4. What culture types do you think characterize Wells Fargo bank? Why?

5. What culture types do you think might be reflected in RightWorks? Why?

6. What aspects of the case do you think bode well for success?

7. What aspects of the case do you think increase the likelihood of failure?

Reflection

Decisions about organization design always need to take into account the technology available. Some organizations, like Wells Fargo, prefer to be on the cutting edge of technology; other organizations prefer to wait to see how new technologies perform before undertaking significant redesign processes.

PRACTICE   Designing a Collaborative Relationship

Objective

The Wells Fargo scenario not only portends significant changes in design and organization within the company, but it also depends on Wells Fargo's relationship outside the company with RightWorks. This exercise gives you an opportunity to try your hand at designing a relationship between these two organizations.

Directions

Building on your analysis of Wells Fargo's plan to create an electronic procurement service, create an action plan that incorporates as many principles as are appropriate and relevant to the design of a successful collaboration between Wells Fargo and RightWorks.

Discussion Questions

1. How might the five elements of Galbraith's star model be used to ensure that this relationship works effectively?

2. What types of liaisons between these two organizations will be needed?

3. How will the cultures of these organizations affect their ability to work together?

Reflection

Many organizations are finding they need to collaborate closely with suppliers and customers to operate effectively, making the design of effective interorganizational relationships critical to their success.

APPLICATION Understanding the Design and Organization of Your Company

Objective The objective of this application activity is to improve your understanding of the design and organization of your company.

Directions Select an organization that you have extensive knowledge of. Ideally, this would be the organization you currently work in or very recently worked in. It could be a school-related organization or some other one that you have been extensively involved with. Using that organization as a focal point, complete the following:

1. Secure the formal organization chart (if available) of that organization. Review it and conduct an analysis of its use of efficiency as an organizing principle, its intended structural configuration, its line of authority, and any available information on the nature of differentiation and integration.

2. Review the discussions of cultural types and the competing values cultural framework. As best you can, try to "profile" the primary cultural type(s) reflected in your organization.

3. Consider the environment in which your organization is currently operating. Given your analyses from questions 1 and 2, decide whether the current structure and culture should be redesigned so the company could compete more effectively. Be sure that you can justify your claims regarding improvements to the organization design using grounds and warrants based on the principles of design and organization discussed in this chapter.

4. Interview the leader of the organization and query that person as to his or her perceptions of the effectiveness of the organization relative to its current design. Ask what might make the organization more effective.

Reflection In theory, when an organization's structure does not fit well with its current strategy and environment, the obvious solution is to redesign the organization. In reality, making significant structural and cultural changes to organizations is extremely difficult. Because of the complexity of organizations, it is often not clear what structure would best fit the current circumstances. In addition, because of the dynamic pace of change, it is often not clear how long current circumstances will continue. As a result, organizational structures often continue to exist even after they become dysfunctional.

REFERENCES

Anders, George. "Power Partners." *Fast Company* (September 2000): 146–158.

Bank, D. "New Code: After 18-Month Battle, Oracle Finally Wins over PeopleSoft." *Wall Street Journal* (December 14, 2004): A.1.

Bennis and Nanus. *Leaders: Strategies for Taking Charge.* New York: Harper & Row, 1985.

Berlew, D.E. "Leadership and Organizational Excitement." *California Management Review* 17(2) (1974): 21–30.

Cameron, Kim S. "Downsizing, Quality, and Performance," in Robert E. Cole (ed.), *The Fall and Rise of the American Quality Movement.* New York: Oxford University Press, 1995.

Cameron, Kim S., Sarah J. Freeman, and Aneil K. Mishra, "Downsizing and Redesigning Organizations," in George P. Huber, and William H. Glick, (eds.), *Organizational Change and Redesign.* New York: Oxford University Press, 1993.

Cameron, K.S., and R.E. Quinn, *Diagnosing and Changing Organizational Culture.* San Francisco: Jossey-Bass, 2006.

Collins, James C., and Jerry I. Porras. *Built to Last.* New York: Harper Collins, 1994, p. 69.

Denison, D.R., and G.M. Spreitzer, "Organizational Culture and Organizational Development: A Competing Values Approach." *Research in Organizational Change and Development* 5, (1991): 1–21.

Galbraith, J.R. *Designing Organizations.* San Francisco: Jossey-Bass, 1995.

Gardner, H.E. *Leading Minds: An Anatomy of Leadership.* New York; Basic Books, 1995.

Gittell, J.H. *The Southwest Airlines Way: Using the Power of Relationships to Achieve High Performance.* New York: McGraw-Hill, 2005.

Hardy, Quentin. "PeopleSoft Made Work a Cause, but a Slump Shakes the Faithful." *Wall Street Journal* (May 5, 1999): 1–7.

Hart, R.P. *Verbal Style and the Presidency.* San Diego: Academic Press, 1984.

Kouzes, J.M., and B.Z. Posner. *The Leadership Challenge.* San Francisco: Jossey-Bass, 1995.

Latham, Gary P., and Ken N. Wexley. *Increasing Productivity Through Performance Appraisal,* 2d ed. Reading, MA: Addison-Wesley, 1994.

Lawrence, Paul R., and Jay W. Lorsch. *Organization and Environment: Managing Differentiation and Integration.* Boston: Division of Research, Graduate School of Business Administration, Harvard University, 1967.

Locke, E.A., and G.P. Latham. "Organizational Goal Setting Questionnaire Interpretive Guide," Organization Design and Development, Inc. Copyright 1985.

Mohrman, S.A., S.G. Cohen, and A.M. Morhman, Jr. *Designing Team-Based Organizations.* San Francisco: Jossey-Bass, 1995.

Nadler, D.S., and Tushman, M.L. "The Organization of the Future: Strategic Imperatives and Core Competencies for the 21st Century, *Organizational Dynamics,* vol. 27, published by American Management Association International NY, NY, pp. 45–60.

Petzinger, Thomas Jr. *The New Pioneers: The Men and Women Who Are Transforming the Workplace and Marketplace.* New York: Simon & Schuster, 1999.

Sashkin, Marshall. "The Visionary Leader," in Jay Conger (ed.), *Charasmatic Leadership.* R.N. Kanungo and Associates. San Francisco: Jossey-Bass, 1989.

Shepard, H.A., and J.A. Hawley. *Life Planning: Personal and Organizational.* Washington, DC: National Training and Development Service Press, 1974.

Simon, Herbert A. *Administrative Behavior.* New York: Free Press, 1976.

Smith, Adam. *The Wealth of Nations.* New York: Random House, 1937. (Original work published 1776.)

Westley, Frances R., and Henry Mintzberg. "Profiles of Strategic Vision: Levesque and Iacocca," in Jay Conger (ed.), *Charismatic Leadership.* San Francisco: Jossey-Bass, 1989.

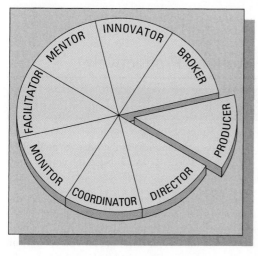

THE PRODUCER ROLE

7

■ COMPETENCIES

Working Productively

Fostering a Productive Work Environment

Managing Time and Stress/Balancing Competing Demands

The rational goal's complement to the director role is the producer role. Effectively enacting the producer role is reflected in individual managerial leaders being personally "productive"—motivated, empowered, and committed, consistent with the Compete action imperative. It is also reflected in the environment that the individual managerial leader creates for his or her employees and associates: does it result in their being motivated, empowered, and committed, that is, is it an environment in which *they* can work productively and competitively. Effective execution of the producer role also requires individual managerial leaders to achieve and maintain a balance between push for effort and productivity and maintenance of overall health and effectiveness for themselves individually and for their people. In this chapter we frame the producer role with the competencies:

Competency 1 Working Productively
Competency 2 Fostering a Productive Work Environment
Competency 3 Managing Time and Stress/Balancing Competing Demands

Competency 1 Working Productively

Objective   Many times we fall into work habits without stopping to consider whether they are productive. This exercise asks you to reflect on your recent work experience and to begin the process of assessing the effectiveness of your work habits.

Directions   Take five minutes to think about a situation during the last few months when you felt you worked very productively and were very motivated. Write a short, one-paragraph description of that situation. In it be sure to explain *why* you were able to work so productively. Also, as part of your paragraph, identify which of your reasons were under your *direct and personal* control and which were not. Conclude your paragraph with a statement about whether the situation you described is an exceptional one or a typical one.

Reflection   In the situation you described, your high level of productivity and motivation was very likely a consequence of a large number of factors. The ones you identified as being under your direct and personal control likely reflect your own underlying sources or catalysts for working productively (i.e., our first competency of the producer role—Working Productively). While these factors vary from person to person, there is a growing body of literature and research on what helps individuals work productively and with a high degree of motivation. We will turn our attention to these below in the Learning segment.

Those factors you identified as not being within your direct and personal control may very well be those that fall within the scope of our second competency, Fostering a Productive Work Environment. These factors are often heavily influenced by the management and leadership philosophy, along with the human resource programs and practices of the organizations we work in.

Some of the factors you identified as not within your direct and personal control could also fall in the vast gray space between the two. They may reflect your awareness and ability to balance and prioritize the levers under your control and effective strategies for pulling those levers. We will address these in our last competency, Managing Time and Stress/Balancing Competing Demands.

Productivity is a key measure of individual, group, and organizational effectiveness. The nature of organizations and the competitive environment within which they operate have made high productivity and superior performance at all levels of endeavor imperative. However, in the new economy of the Internet, information and services—where intellectual capital has superseded natural resources and other forms of capital and technology has turbocharged almost every aspect of work—no measure is more complicated or controversial. While tangible assets such as factories and other forms of capital easily lend themselves to evaluation according to accounting and economic metrics, human capital presents challenges on many dimensions.

We will examine the competency of working productively through the lenses of several relevant frameworks. Our discussion of personal peak performance includes a focus on Csikszentmihalyi's (1990) work on optimal experience. In anticipation of our discussion of the second key competency in the producer role, fostering a productive work environment (which takes a primarily external or extrinsic perspective on motivating productivity), we will also review a framework for understanding and leveraging our primary "intrinsic" motivators as springboards for working productively. We will then weave each of those perspectives together through the construct of "empowerment" as a bridge between working productively (as an individual) and fostering a productive work environment (for others and the organization).

OPTIMIZING INDIVIDUAL PERFORMANCE

Garfield (1986) examined individual performance in an attempt to understand what contributes to superior productivity or performance, focusing on a construct he refers to as "personal peak performance." Garfield studied individual high achievement in a wide array of endeavors. The results were truly encouraging for all individuals because the conclusions reached suggest that personal peak performance does not result from a specific innate talent or trait. Nor does it result from a particular set of behaviors. Rather, personal peak performance seems to result from an overall pattern of traits or attributes. Garfield found that peak performers in his study were *results-oriented* because of a sense of *personal mission,* able to display the dual capacities of *self-management* and *team mastery,* and capable of making course corrections and *managing change.* He found that peak performers most value internal goals and intrinsic rewards and that they care a great deal about the tasks they perform. They also need an appropriate level of challenge—a consistent search for reasonable risks and opportunities to pursue "stretch" goals.

Another perspective on optimal performance is represented by the work of Mihaly Csikszentmihalyi (1990), who examined endeavors in both the work and leisure arenas that contribute to the attainment of optimal performance, which he refers to as "flow." Csikszentmihalyi identified four useful practices integral to the attainment of optimal performance—that is, the "flow" state:

1. *Setting goals.* Focusing attention on a few options or challenges makes setting goals absolutely essential. These goals define a direction or course of action and in the process suggest skills required for the accomplishment of the goals. Individuals then compare the results of their efforts to the identified goals. It is also critical that the choice of goals be under the control of the individual—not externally imposed. There must be personal ownership. (See Chapter 6 for more on setting goals.)

2. *Becoming totally engaged in and immersed by the activity.* Those experiencing the flow state and optimal performance typically beome completely engrossed in the activity. They are at once preoccupied, fascinated, and engaged by the focus of their efforts. This immersion is typical of those individuals who both excel at what they do and enjoy themselves in the process. This intense involvement is aided by the ability to focus and concentrate

3. *Being hypersensitive and aware of the activity as it is occurring.* Those individuals who attain the flow state of optimal performance are not easily distracted. They are engaged and involved in the activity. Anyone who has watched an Olympic athlete

competing in an event has seen this degree of attention, but it is also characteristic of individuals involved in artistic and interpersonal endeavors. This intense focus helps diminish self-consciousness, which is the most common and troublesome source of distraction.

4. *Becoming adept at enjoying the immediate experience in real time.* The combination of goal setting, deep involvement, and strict focus and attention allows individuals to enjoy the activity whether the circumstances are ideal or very poor. The sense of personal control and mastery over the situational factors allows the realization of pleasure in the most minute aspects of the activity and experience.

INTRINSIC MOTIVATION AS A LENS FOR UNDERSTANDING AND A SOURCE OF WORKING PRODUCTIVELY

For the better part of the last century, psychologists of all stripes researched motivation in the workplace. As in many other research areas, there was much competition, conflict, and controversy over theories and explanations, often accompanied by conflicting research results. A fundamental distinction made in literature on motivation is between *extrinsic* and *intrinsic* sources. Extrinsic sources are forces that are external to the person and have a concrete reality (e.g., food, money, or praise from another individual). Intrinsic sources are forces that are generated by the individual him- or herself (e.g., sense of accomplishment). A fundamental theme in the study of motivation is that human behavior is motivated by a set of "needs." A need is an internal state in an individual that causes clusters of objects or outcomes to be sought. Abraham Maslow (1954) proposed that there are a series of needs that operate hierarchically from lower-order needs (e.g., physical safety) to higher-order needs (autonomy, achievement, and "self-actualization"). Maslow and other need theorists believed that once a need or level of needs was satisfied, it was no longer a "motivator." Maslow also theorized that the lower-order needs can only be satisfied by outcomes that are extrinsic (external) to the individual and that the higher-order needs could only be satisfied by outcomes that are intrinsic (internal) to the individual. These higher-order needs are also to some extent an exception to the principle that a need once sated is no longer a motivator. Maslow and others believed that the need for self-actualization or growth seemed to be insatiable—the more individuals obtain outcomes that satisfy the need, the more important it becomes and the more of it they desire.

David McClelland's (1961) theory of motivation focused on three critical motives/needs: the need for achievement (nAch), defined as the imperative to strive, succeed, and achieve against a set of goals or standards; the need for power (nPow), defined as the need to compel others to behave in ways in which they would otherwise not have behaved; and the need for affiliation (nAff), defined as desire for close and amicable interpersonal relationships. Other need theorists, most notably Frederick Herzberg (1968), suggested that pay and other such extrinsic rewards can never be motivators, only a source of dissatisfaction—factors he referred to as "hygienes." Factors that Herzberg saw as motivators included achievement, recognition, the nature of the work itself, responsibility, advancement, and growth. Hackman and Oldham's (1980) job characteristics model, also an intrinsic motivation–based model, describes the impact of

Review the characteristics pg 168 169

five dimensions of a job's design: *skill variety, task identity, task significance, autonomy,* and *feedback*. Hackman and Oldham believed that intrinsic motivation occurred when three psychological states were present: experienced meaningfulness, experienced responsibility for outcomes of the work, and knowledge of actual results of the work. Application of the job characteristics model—through, for example, job "design"—could then theoretically make work more motivational by making it more likely to result in the psychological states of meaningfulness, responsibility, and knowledge of results.

There has recently been a resurgence of interest in intrinsic motivation and how it is manifested in the workplace, both in the continued evolution and refinement of original research on need theories of motivation (Thomas, 2000) and in new work on the process of "empowerment" (Spreitzer, DeJanasz, and Quinn, 1997). We will review the work of Thomas and that of Spreitzer and colleagues as part of laying a foundation and building a toolkit for both this competency, Working Productively (focused on what's under the control of the individual) and the competency Fostering a Productive Work Environment (focused on what's typically not under the individual's control). All these authors have a common understructure to their work; their contributions complement each other and provide us with a diagnostic approach that will help with both competencies. We will conclude this chapter with a review of self-management as formulated by Robert E. Kelley, since his framework serves as a natural bridge between the individual emphasis of working productively and the organizational emphasis of fostering a productive work environment.

EMPOWERMENT AND INTRINSIC MOTIVATION

Those who have studied the psychology of empowerment define it as *intrinsic motivation* reflected in four psychological states related to an individual's orientation to his or her work role (Thomas and Velthouse, 1990):

Empowerment

- *Meaning.* The innate worthiness of the task or pursuit; the value or significance of the mission/purpose that drives an individual (grounded in one of the job characteristics identified above—experienced meaningfulness)

- *Competence.* Confidence in one's ability to perform the task or pursuit skillfully, to not only "get the job done" but to get it done well

- *Self-Determination.* The discretion, autonomy, and choice involved in initiating, maintaining, and regulating one's actions in the pursuit of the task ("tell us what to do, but not how to do it")

- *Impact.* The degree to which an individual can influence strategic, administrative, or other outcomes at work; a sense of advancement related to one's purpose

Taken together, these four psychological states suggest an *active* rather than a *passive* orientation to one's role at work. Individuals who are empowered do not perceive their role and situation as a given or a constraint, but rather something that is capable of being shaped by their own actions (Spreitzer, 1992). Research has also demonstrated that the four psychological states combine into an overall construct of psychological empowerment (Spreitzer, 1995).

The concept of empowerment, as we have framed it, takes the perspective of the individual him- or herself. It is grounded in intrinsic motivation and is under the control of the individual. Bowen and Lawler (1992) have defined empowerment from an organizational perspective as follows:

> sharing with frontline employees four organizational ingredients: (1) information about the organization's performance, (2) rewards based on the organization's performance, (3) knowledge that enables employees to understand and contribute to organizational performance, and (4) power to make decisions that influence organizational direction and performance. (p. 32)

We will revisit the organizational perspective in Competency 2, Fostering a Productive Work Environment.

PRACTICING SELF-MANAGEMENT TO LEVERAGE INTRINSIC MOTIVATION

The new economy has made self-management more necessary, appropriate, and desirable for both individuals and organizations. The increased complexity and demands of the new economy make close monitoring and supervision impractical and inappropriate, hence individuals need to be more self-managing, which requires more individual initiative and commitment grounded in the deeper motivations of intrinsic rewards.

The core elements of self-management very much mirror the elements of traditional external managerial control models that focus on the individual or the organization as a whole: Start with the very highest level of analysis (i.e., vision/mission); articulate a strategy for pursuing the vision/mission (specific initiatives, activities); implement the strategy (execute the initiative, activities); and then evaluate progress made toward realization of vision/mission as well as the quality of the implementation of the initiatives/activities. Thus self-management at the individual level involves (1) *committing* to higher-level purpose (vision/mission), (2) *choosing* what to do to realize this purpose (initiatives/activities), (3) *executing* the activities, and (4) *monitoring* for how well we accomplished them (competence, quality) and for progress toward the ultimate purpose. Thomas (2000) has suggested that for the individual, these steps of committing, choosing, executing, and monitoring each can be linked to a particular intrinsic reward and examined for maximum leverage of that reward in the process. If we take each of the psychological states related to each of the intrinsic motivators identified by Thomas and Velthouse (1990) and link them to a part of the self-management process, we will be better able to understand how to better leverage or rebalance the impact of each on our personal productivity.

- *Meaning.* Selecting and committing to a purpose will increase our sense of experienced meaningfulness
- *Self-Determination.* Choosing what initiatives/activities to perform in order to realize the purpose will increase our sense of experienced self-determination or choice
- *Competence.* Executing and monitoring/evaluating the quality of the initiatives/activities increases the sense of experienced competence
- *Impact.* Monitoring/evaluating the amount of progress toward realization of the ultimate purpose articulated contributes to a sense of efficacy and impact

Thomas (2000) proposes a set of strategies for shoring up and reinforcing the leverage of each of the four intrinsic rewards (i.e., building blocks):

Meaning and Leading for Meaningfulness

1. Providing a noncynical climate
2. Clearly identifying passions
3. Providing an exciting vision
4. Ensuring relevant task purposes
5. Providing whole tasks

Self-Determination/Choice and Leading for Choice

1. Delegating authority
2. Demonstrating trust in workers
3. Providing security and allowing for honest mistakes
4. Providing a clear purpose
5. Providing information

Competence and Leading for Competence

1. Getting the knowledge you need
2. Getting the positive feedback you need and listening
3. Recognizing your own skills
4. Managing challenge in your own work
5. Setting high, noncomparative standards for yourself

Impact/Progress and Leading for Progress

1. Building collaborative relations
2. Developing your own milestones
3. Taking the time to celebrate successes
4. Making contact with customers
5. Measuring improvements and tracking intrinsic motivation

ANALYSIS   When Are Your Colleagues the Most Productive and Motivated?

Objective   Now that you have read about different theoretical approaches to motivation, you are in a better position to analyze how closely the situations described by you and others as being highly productive fit with those theoretical frameworks.

Directions   Refer back to your description in the Assessment activity of the situation in which you were most motivated and productive. In groups formed by your instructor, consider and respond to the following questions. Appoint a spokesperson in your group to present a five-minute summary to the class.

Discussion Questions   1. What common factors exist across your descriptions of personal productivity and motivation?

2. Do any of the examples reflect the four useful practices for attainment of the "flow" state identified by Csikszentmihalyi?

3. Which of the four psychological aspects of empowerment (meaning, competence, self-determination, and impact) seem most related to productivity and motivation in your examples?

4. Are there any surprising or unexpected themes or relationships reflected in the various examples?

5. Brainstorm a list of "principles" or lessons learned from the examples discussed in your group. Compare the list to the strategies for reinforcing the intrinsic motivators identified by Thomas. Are there Similarities? Differences?

Reflection   In discussing highly productive experiences with others, you may have been surprised to hear some people talk about attaining a state of "flow" while doing tasks that you never considered very interesting or important. Individuals can have very different ideas about what goes into making up the basic building blocks of meaning, choice, competence, and impact!

PRACTICE   Feeling Dead-Ended[1]

Objective   This exercise asks you to both analyze an employee's productivity and motivation and then practice identifying ways that she could work to improve her own intrinsic motivation.

Directions   Read the following case study and answer the questions that follow.

Margaret Jardine was sure when she completed her associate's degree in business at Wagner Community College, more than eight years ago, that she would go places in her career in the public sector. She had graduated with honors from WCC with an emphasis in finance and accounting. She passed the Audit Clerk exam the first time with a grade of 92; she was second on the list and was hired within six months. Within the next 14 months she had taken and passed the Senior Audit Clerk exam. It took two years to be selected from the list.

She felt she had truly made the right decision because she moved so quickly within the first four years. She felt that the Civil Service system was large enough to allow for movement into a variety of areas considering her two-year degree, her good work performance, and her ability to do well, it seemed, on exams.

She felt that she had been successful in her first four years because she had been able to work closely with good people. She was a hard worker and a fast learner.

Margaret waited almost two years to take the Principal Audit Clerk (grade 11) exam and failed it with a grade of 68. She couldn't believe it. She went to the review to determine what she had done wrong. The answers, though tricky, seemed so clear when the monitor explained them.

[1] *Adapted from* an exercise used in *Getting Work Done Through Others: The Supervisor's Main Job*, Advanced Human Resources Development Program, New York State Governor's Office of Employee Relations and CSEA, Inc., 1987.

Now she had to wait between two and three years for the next exam, depending on the need to fill positions. She felt thoroughly discouraged.

What distressed her even more was that she worked with a grade 11 Principal Clerk who "didn't know beans about the work." Margaret was the one who got all the difficult assignments because her accuracy rate was so high and she always met her deadlines.

Margaret felt that given her ability and recent responsibility, she should really be in charge of the unit, regardless of her grade on the test. Recently, she began to wonder about her future in the Tax and Finance Department. She even wondered about staying with government service. She was feeling almost dead-ended and didn't know how or where to move. It seemed, suddenly almost, that there was little or no movement within her area of expertise.

In her years with state government, she felt that she had done well with fairly regular pay increases, promotions, the degree of responsibility held, and the expertise gained. Now, however, she felt that she had lost some of her motivation. Now if she put in extra time, it was only out of the need to get something done that *had* to be done. It certainly was not voluntary.

Margaret felt trapped, pigeonholed in some way. She felt like she had no idea where she was going in the state. Others who had come when she did all seemed to be on their way to their goal, so to speak. She thought that perhaps they had chosen a broader, more diversified career path, situations that were easier to promote from. She felt that her work was very good and highly valued, but her salary increases were getting smaller and her options were becoming more limited. Recently, Margaret had turned down a very attractive offer from Northwestern Security and Exchange, a small finance company in Salem, near Albany, New York, because she thought there would be too little opportunity for advancement. Now she wondered if it would have been better to take the opportunity.

Still, Margaret was confused about her feelings about the state. She felt that a move elsewhere might not be wise because she'd lose what seniority she had, her retirement benefits, and so on.

After dialing Northwestern's number, only to hang up before it rang, Margaret decided that she would put off any decision for at least a month so she could have plenty of time to think over her situation.

Discussion Questions

1. How would you describe Margaret's personal productivity and motivational level at the present time? Are any of the conditions that stimulate personal peak performance present? Are any of the psychological aspects (meaning, competence, self-determination, and impact) of empowerment present?

2. What factors contributed to this present situation?

3. What can Margaret do to clarify her options and choices? Are any of the strategies Thomas identified for shoring up the four intrinsic motivators (i.e., his "building blocks") relevant? How could they help Margaret?

4. What specific steps would you suggest to her?

5. Do you see any similarities between Margaret's situation and situations you have gone through? Explain.

6. With your answers to Question 5 in mind, what actions can you identify that would help renew enthusiasm, increase productivity, and boost motivation?

Reflection

As we noted in the Assessment that began this chapter, motivation and productivity are influenced by many factors. In addition to Margaret's lack of intrinsic motivation, she is also suffering from a sense of inequity which is lowering her motivation and productivity. Rather than setting high, noncomparative standards for herself as Thomas (2000) suggests for building up intrinsic motivation, Margaret is focusing on comparing herself to others which has the effect of reducing even further her sense of competence.

APPLICATION   Creating Your Own Strategy for Increasing Personal Productivity and Motivation

Objective   Throughout this section you have had the opportunity to assess and explore your personal productivity and motivation level and the factors that influence and affect them. In this Application activity, you will have a chance to plan ways to maintain or increase your personal productivity and motivation using those ideas and skills discussed so far.

Directions   Please answer the following questions as specifically as you can. Although some responses (e.g., Questions 1, 4, and 5) may be voluntarily shared, this information will be seen only by you.

1. What are the major forces contributing to productivity and motivation in your life? (Consider your work at school, or at a job, or any extracurricular activity in which you're involved.)

2. What are the principle blocks or impediments to these forces?

3. Are any of these forces related to Csikszentmihalyi's "flow state" conditions or the psychological aspects of empowerment?

4. What can you do to enhance the positive forces contributing to your productivity and motivation?

5. How can you neutralize the blocks or impediments to these forces?

6. How will you know that you are successful?

Reflection   Maintaining a high level of motivation and productivity is not the result of a one-time exercise. Because our lives and situations are constantly changing, we need to revisit the issue of motivation and productivity on a regular basis. Naturally no one can expect to be operating at peak performance levels all of the time, but taking time for regular motivation and productivity "checkups" certainly helps.

Competency 2   Fostering a Productive Work Environment

ASSESSMENT   Factors Contributing to a Productive Work Environment

Objective   For the past several years, *Fortune* magazine has published a list of the "100 Best Companies to Work For"® in America. For 2006, the top three companies were Genentech, Wegmans Food Markets, and Valero Energy (Colvin, 2006). *Fortune* uses both employee survey data collected by the Great Place to Work® Institute, as well as their own evaluation of the policies and cultures to the company.

Directions   Review the factors below from the Great Place to Work® Institute's web page, http://www.greatplace-towork.com/great/model.php, and evaluate how well you think your company fares in terms of these categories.

- Credibility—Communications are open and accessible; competence in coordinating human and material resources; integrity in carrying out vision with consistency

- Respect—Supporting professional development and showing appreciation; collaboration with employees on relevant decisions; caring for employees as individuals with personal lives

- Fairness—equity: balanced treatment for all in terms of rewards; impartiality: absence of favoritism in hiring and promotions; justice: lack of discrimination and process for appeals

- Pride—in personal job, individual contributions; in work produced by one's team or work group; in the organization's products and standing in the community

- Camaraderie—ability to be one's self; socially friendly and welcoming atmosphere; sense of "family" or "team"

Reflection   Although it may seem paradoxical, some of the companies that are rated the best companies to work for are also know as having pressure-packed, grueling jobs according to *Fortune* magazine's Matthew Boyle (2006). Two factors help explain the paradox. One is providing excellent rewards for employees who are high achievers. Perhaps even more important, however, is selecting the right employees in the first place—those who thrive on the stress created by a high performance workplace. As Boyle notes, "At the best companies to work for, pressure is in the eye of the beholder."

LEARNING   Fostering a Productive Work Environment

As we have indicated many times previously in this book, the competitive challenges confronting organizations today are unlike any that came before. Customers are more demanding than ever, competition has never been keener, and employees have never expected more from their organizations and their leaders. The upshot of all this is that it has never been more critical or more difficult to maintain a productive work environment with motivated people in it.

In this section, we will review two critical aspects of fostering a productive work environment. First we will review the central lessons of the literature on reward systems, with an eye toward the context of the new economy. Then we will examine the process of motivating others—specifically, the application of motivation theory to understanding the needs of organizational members.

THE CHALLENGES OF REWARD SYSTEMS IN THE NEW ECONOMY

One of the most challenging aspects of the new economy is the fundamental shift in the nature of the psychological contract between employer and employee. Historically, the contract had a paternalistic framework: If you are loyal, work hard, and do as you are told, the organization will "take care of you," including provision of a secure job, steady pay increases, and financial security. The drastic downsizings of the late 1980s and early 1990s, however, destroyed any notion of "safety." The paternalistic contract was replaced by one that many viewed negatively, essentially a crisis contract: If you stay, you can do your job plus someone else's and get the same pay and be part of a reactive crisis-oriented company. Not exactly the type of contract most employees are excited to sign.

Today, more and more organizations are approaching the psychological contract with their employees from a starting point that acknowledges the importance and value of human capital. This contract is best described as an "employability" contract: If you develop the skills we need, apply them in ways that help the company succeed, and behave consistently with our new core values (new for most organizations), we will provide a challenging work environment, support for your development, and rewards commensurate with your contribution. All concerned share membership in a high-performance organization (Lawler, 2000).

The changing nature of the employer–employee relationship, which is accelerated by the new economy, is also reflected in the increasingly stiff competition for recognition as one of America's "best places to work." The criteria that we asked you to consider in the Assessment exercise of this competency are critical ingredients in what has become a fierce competition. The selection process is very much employee-driven. Two-thirds of the scoring process is based on answers provided by employees to 57 questions that determine the Great Place to Work® Trust Index®, a survey created by the Great Place to Work® Institute in San Francisco. The areas measured by the survey parallel the content of the criteria we introduced to you in the Assessment above. The remaining one-third of the scoring process is a function of the materials that competing companies submit to substantiate their case for being rated among the best places to work. Among the more influential components of this third are the Great Place to Work® Culture Audit®.

Despite the stiff rivalry for recognition as one of the best places to work, intense global competition has forced even the best companies to revise their techniques for engaging and retaining their employees. For example, Colvin (2006) reports that the number of top 100 companies covering 100 percent of employee health benefits dropped to only 14 in 2006, down from 33 in 2001. Defined benefit plans are offered by only 27 of the 100 companies; down from 40 three years ago. In place of these types of costly benefits, companies are finding more creative ways to provide a supportive environment for employees. One enormous area of growth is telecommuting (only 18 of the top 100 companies allowed telecommuting in 1999; in the 2006 *Fortune* list 79 companies include telecommuting as an option) (Colvin, 2006). Flexibility is also showing up with compressed workweeks (up from 25 in 1999 to 81 in 2006) and personal-concierge services to help time-strapped employees with routine chores (Colvin, 2006).

As valuable as these types of extrinsic benefits are, they are also easily imitable—so by themselves they won't keep a company in the top 100. Consistent with research on intrinsic motivation, the keys to winning employees' hearts and enthusiasm for the long term depends on making employees feel that they are trusted, recognizing employee accomplishments and efforts, and helping employees find meaning in their work (Colvin, 2006).

We next turn to an extended discussion of expectancy theory because it provides the most comprehensive process approach to the task of motivating others. We then revisit the topic of empowerment from the organizational perspective (i.e., what organizations can do to foster empowerment) and conclude with a review of effective reward strategies that take into account the challenges of empowerment in the new economy and the broader challenge of fostering a productive work environment.

MOTIVATING OTHERS: APPLYING THE EXPECTANCY APPROACH TO MOTIVATION

Writing about motivation theory fills literally thousands of books and journal articles. As always, it is our concern to discuss theory only as it informs practice. One of the most comprehensive theories of motivation in use today is **expectancy theory,** which is

amt effort
perfi
outcomes

a motivational theory based on the relationships among the amount of effort exerted on a job, performance on the job, and outcomes of that performance. The expectancy framework incorporates the central elements of need theory—as outlined in Competency 1, Working Productively—and key process variables. Victor Vroom (1964) was the first to conceptualize expectancy theory with the following equation:

Motivation = expectancy × valence × instrumentality

or

$$M = E \times V \times I$$

Figure 7.1 graphically depicts expectancy theory.

Vroom's formulation of the theory has been expanded to take into account multiple outcomes (Nadler and Lawler, 1977). The expanded equation becomes:

$$\text{Motivation} = E \rightarrow P \times \Sigma[(P \rightarrow 0) \times (v)]$$

or

Motivation = effort to performance × the sum of [(performance to outcomes) × (valence)]

Note that the fundamental linkages are the same, but the expanded equation allows the consideration of multiple outcomes. Consider the following example: Anne Johnson is the project leader of a group of computer programmers and systems analysts who have been charged with the task of creating a new MIS for one of her company's largest divisions. Johnson is a little disappointed at the rate at which progress has been made. She is considering working on the project during the entire holiday weekend that is coming up.

Applying the multiple outcomes version of the expectancy theory, we can analyze Anne's level of motivation regarding working over the holiday weekend. Let's begin with the effort to performance linkage (i.e., expectancy). Here, the consideration is whether or not working over the holiday weekend (the "effort" to be expended) will result in her completing the new MIS more quickly. Anne can estimate the probability of this using a number between 0 and 1. If she believes that she personally can be productive and move the project along over the holiday weekend, then she will likely estimate this probability as being relatively high—say 0.9.

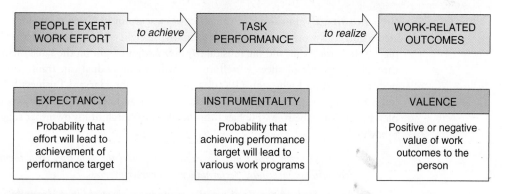

FIGURE 7.1 *Elements in the expectancy theory of motivation.*

Source: John R. Schermerhorn Jr., Management for Productivity, 3rd ed., New York: John Wiley & Sons, 1989, p. 365. Used with permission.

Let us now turn to the instrumentality, or performance-to-outcome linkage. Here, the concern is what the probability is that if she does indeed complete the project more quickly, it will lead to certain outcomes. Those outcomes could include a promotion, increased responsibility, a special recognition award, a spat with her husband and family about not being at home over the holiday, exhaustion, fatigue, and so on. Johnson could estimate a probability for *each* of these (e.g., What is the probability that if I complete this project quickly, I will get a promotion?). Johnson must then determine the valence (attractiveness, value) each of these has to her and then include those valences into the equation (using a $-1 \ldots 0 \ldots +1$ scale for each outcome, with -1 being extremely undesirable and $+1$ being extremely desirable).

With the multiple outcomes version of the expectancy formulation, Johnson can weigh, balance, and make trade-offs among the various outcomes and their valences.

How can you, as a manager, apply expectancy theory? There are three ways for you to apply the three components of the expectancy theory:

1. Tie effort to performance.
2. Link performance to outcome(s).
3. Understand valences for desired employee outcomes.

TIE EFFORT TO PERFORMANCE

Employees might ask themselves, "If I work hard (exert a certain level of effort), can I attain the level of performance expected by my manager?" Managers can respond in two ways to tie an employee's effort to performance:

1. They can increase the employee's estimate of the effort-to-performance probability by involving the subordinate in defining what "performance" is. This implies the existence and use of MBO-type processes and performance evaluation systems (see the discussion of Using Goals And Objectives As a Management Tool: MBO-Type Approaches in Chapter 6.)

2. They can utilize the power of positive expectations with subordinates (see "Be a *Positive* Pygmalion," below).

Be a Positive Pygmalion. Pygmalion was a sculptor in Greek mythology who created a gorgeous woman who was subsequently brought to life. George Bernard Shaw's play of the same name and the musical *My Fair Lady* are built on the same theme—that through the power of sheer self-effort and will, an individual can transform another person. J. Sterling Livingston (1969), a professor at the Harvard Business School believes that supervisors, managers, and executives at all levels in organizations can also play Pygmalion-type roles. He bases this belief on research of his own that suggests the following:

1. *What managers expect of their subordinates and the way they treat them largely determine subordinates' performance and career progress.*

2. *A unique characteristic of superior managers is their ability to create high performance expectations that their subordinates fulfill.*

3. *Less effective managers fail to develop similar expectations, so, as a consequence, the productivity of their subordinates suffers.*

4. *Subordinates, more often than not, do what they believe they are expected to do.*

Being a positive Pygmalion is one of the single most important ways in which a manager can motivate subordinates. It does not require large amounts of money or other types of extrinsic rewards. It does not require dealing with the complexities and contingencies of job design. It is under the complete control of the manager. But it is not easy. Being a positive Pygmalion for your subordinates goes to the very heart of your assumption about people and your own managerial style. It also requires that you be a positive Pygmalion for yourself—that is, believing that you are capable of being a peak performer, achieving the "flow" state, and maximizing your experience of the intrinsic rewards of meaning, competence, self-determination, and impact as we discussed in Competency 1.

LINK PERFORMANCE TO OUTCOME(S)

Employees might ask themselves, "If I, in fact, perform at the level expected by my manager, what is the likelihood that certain outcomes will result?" The manager can address this concern by making certain that employees are aware of all the possible outcomes that will result from performance. Regular and consistent use of performance appraisals and MBO-type discussions such as those discussed in Chapter 6 are again the most effective means of accomplishing this.

UNDERSTAND VALENCES FOR DESIRED EMPLOYEE OUTCOMES

Employees can evaluate all possible outcomes and the attractiveness or value (i.e., positive or negative) each has to them. Managers can address this component by making certain that they know what "outcomes" are important to their employees. There's no substitute for knowing your employees. Depending on the size of your group, you can obtain this information either through one-on-one conversations or, if the group is too large, through employee attitude surveys.

LEVERAGING INDIVIDUAL AND ORGANIZATIONAL MOTIVATIONAL APPROACHES TO OPTIMIZE REWARD STRATEGIES IN THE NEW ECONOMY

As we discussed in Competency 1, Bowen and Lawler (1992) have articulated the organizational framework of empowerment. Considering the four levers—information, rewards, knowledge, and power—that Bowen and Lawler identify, how can organizations best leverage desirable extrinsic rewards (i.e., those with high valence); individual organizational members' search for ways to maximize their experience of empowerment; and the intrinsic rewards of meaning, competence, self-determination, and impact?

The challenges of the new economy make the application of all rewards a greater challenge than ever. Companies can directly provide a great variety of rewards such as recognition, fringe benefits, cash, status titles, and many others. The array of rewards potentially offered by corporations today is incredibly diverse, as evident in our earlier discussion of companies recognized as "best places to work." But just how appealing are these rewards, relative to their monetary cost? We discussed the issue of how appealing rewards are in our discussion of valence as part of expectancy theory. There are, however, some key lessons about the use of various rewards. In the analysis below, the prickly issue of how much money is enough or not enough is examined. Research, unfortunately, gives us no precise answer to this. Typically, the amount of money needed to engender motivation is best thought of as a percentage of the amount somebody already possesses. For example, in order to determine how significant a $500 bonus will be to a group of individual employees, one must consider the amount of their current base salaries. If $500 is less than 1 percent of their annual salary, it will likely not be enough to have an impact on motivation. But if the amount is 5 percent or more of annual salary, it may have an impact on motivation. However, 5 percent should not be taken as an amount that will always serve as a motivator. Although 5 percent is probably enough to be significant to the typical individual, in most cases, 10, 15, or even 20 percent or more may sometimes be required, depending on how large an effect the organization desires to have on the motivation of a given individual (Lawler, 2000).

One should not, however, conclude that small amounts of money are never motivating. Small amounts of money, when used and framed symbolically, can be very motivating. A small stuffed animal dressed and decorated to resemble the recipient is presented monthly to the staff member in a corporate university who works "above and beyond" the call of duty. An invitation to dinner with the CEO and president of the company for members of an engineering team who beat schedule and budget on a critically important project can be coveted. These are but a few of the thousands of examples of how small amounts of money can serve as powerful motivators. The following are some critical characteristics of these types of rewards:

- The rewards are presented and bestowed publicly. The recognition factor and its impact on our sense of competence make publicity critical.
- The rewards in question are given at the right periodic intervals (i.e., not too frequently). The influence on meaning and impact diminishes if the rewards are provided too often. The uniqueness and sense of being special and having status are lost as the reward degenerates into an everyday occurrence and the sense that "if enough time passes, I'll get one, too."
- The process of selecting reward recipients has credibility. Those who make the selection must be highly respected individuals with access to accurate information about the accomplishments and performance in question.
- The rewards are linked to winners. The importance and status of symbolic rewards increase when early winners are universally perceived as being of high status and are well respected.
- The culture of the organization makes the rewards particularly meaningful. A big boost to the visibility and meaningfulness of the reward is gained if the symbol or artifact has great cultural significance (Lawler, 2000).

CONCLUSIONS

Fostering a productive work environment requires attention to the entire universe of potential workplace factors. The importance and impact of these factors are very much a function of the specific context and the specific individuals involved. While fostering a productive work environment is very much a function of the control organizations have over information, knowledge, rewards, and power—that is, how empowering an environment they create—the power of understanding and knowing how to leverage the intrinsic motivators of meaning, competence, self-determination, and impact cannot be underestimated.

In Competency 3, Managing Time and Stress/Balancing Competing Demands, we review the vast body of knowledge related to understanding and managing the pushes and pulls of the desire to be personally productive in the pursuit of our own personal goals and adequately supporting and contributing to those of the organization. We will study time and stress management within the context of balancing the competing demands these two dynamics generate.

ANALYSIS   The Case of Michael Simpson[2]

Objective   This exercise gives you the opportunity to analyze a common human resource management issue, salary compression/inversion, which occurs when market forces push salaries for new hires up faster than salary increases for existing employees. Salary compression refers to a shrinking differential in the pay received by continuing employees relative to new hires. Salary inversion occurs when the salaries of new hires exceeds the salaries of current employees.

Directions   Read the case of Michael Simpson, and answer the questions that follow.

Michael Simpson is one of the most outstanding managers in the management consulting division of Avery McNeil and Co. He is a highly qualified individual with a deep sense of responsibility.

Simpson obtained his MBA two years ago from one of the leading northeastern schools. Before being graduated from business school, Simpson had interviewed with a number of consulting firms and decided that the consulting division of Avery McNeil offered the greatest potential for rapid advancement.

Simpson was recently promoted to manager, making him the youngest manager at the consulting group. Two years with the firm was an exceptionally short period of time in which to achieve this promotion. Although the promotion was announced, Simpson had not yet been informed of his new salary. Despite the fact that his career had progressed well, he was concerned that his salary would be somewhat lower than the current market value that a headhunter had recently quoted him.

Simpson's wife, Diane, soon would be receiving her MBA. One night over dinner Simpson was amazed to hear the salaries being offered to new MBAs. Simpson commented to Diane, "I certainly hope I get a substantial raise this time. I mean, it just wouldn't be fair to be making the same amount as recent graduates when I've been at the company now for over two years! I'd like to buy a house soon, but with housing costs rising and inflation following, that will depend on my pay raise."

[2]*From* David Nadler, M. Tushman, and N. Hatvany (eds.), *Managing Organizations.* Boston, Little, Brown, 1982. Used with permission from the authors.

Several days later, Simpson was working at his desk when Dave Barton, a friend and a colleague, came across to Simpson's office. Barton was hired at the same time as Simpson, and had also been promoted recently. Barton told Simpson, "Hey, Mike, look at this! I was walking past Jane's desk and saw this memo from the personnel manager lying there. She obviously forgot to put it away. Her boss would kill her if he found out!"

The memo showed the proposed salaries for all the individuals in the consulting group that year. Simpson looked at the list and was amazed by what he saw. He said, "I can't believe this, Dave! Walt and Rich are getting $2000 more than I am."

Walt Gresham and Rich Watson had been hired within the past year. Before coming to Avery McNeil, they had both worked one year at another consulting firm.

Barton spoke angrily, "Mike, I knew the firm had to pay them an awful lot to attract them, but to pay them more than people above them is ridiculous!"

"You know," replied Simpson, "if I hadn't seen Walt and Rich's salaries, I would think I was getting a reasonable raise. Hey listen, Dave, let's get out of here. I've had enough of this place for one day."

"Okay, Mike, just let me return this memo. Look, it's not that bad; after all, you are getting the largest raise."

On his way home, Simpson tried to think about the situation more objectively. He knew that there were a number of pressures on the compensation structure in the consulting division. If the division wished to continue attracting MBAs from top schools, it would have to offer competitive salaries. Starting salaries had increased about $3500 during the last two years. As a result, some of the less-experienced MBAs were earning nearly the same amounts as others who had been with the firm several years but who had come in at lower starting salaries, even though their pay had been gradually increased over time.

Furthermore, because of expanding business, the division had found it necessary to hire consultants from other firms. In order to do so effectively, Avery McNeil found it necessary to upgrade the salaries they offered.

The firm as a whole was having problems meeting the federally regulated Equal Opportunity Employment goals and was trying especially hard to recruit women and minorities.

One of Simpson's colleagues, Martha Lohman, had been working in the consulting division of Avery McNeil until three months ago, when she was offered a job at another consulting firm. She had become disappointed with her new job and, on returning to her previous position at Avery McNeil, was rehired at a salary considerably higher than her former level. Simpson had noticed on the memo that she was earning more than he was, even though she was not given nearly the same level of responsibility. Simpson also realized that the firm attempted to maintain some parity between salaries in the auditing and consulting divisions.

When Simpson arrived home, he discussed the situation with his wife. "Diane, I know I'm getting a good raise, but I am still earning below my market value—$3000 less than the headhunter told me last week. And the fact that those two guys from the other consulting firm are getting more than me shows that the firm is prepared to pay competitive rates."

"I know it's unfair, Mike," Diane replied, "but what can you do? You know your boss won't negotiate salaries after they have been approved by the compensation committee, but it wouldn't hurt to at least talk to him about your dissatisfaction. I don't think you should let a few thousand dollars a year bother you. You will catch up eventually, and the main thing is that you really enjoy what you are doing."

"Yes, I do enjoy what I'm doing, but that is not to say that I wouldn't enjoy it elsewhere. I really just have to sit down and think about all the pros and cons in my working for Avery McNeil. First of all, I took this job because I felt that I could work my way up quickly. I think that I have demonstrated this, and the firm has also shown that they are willing to help me achieve this goal. If I left this job for a better paying one, 1 might not get the opportunity to work on the exciting jobs that I am currently working on. Furthermore, this company has time and money invested in me. I'm the only one at Avery that can work on certain jobs, and the company has several lined up. If I left the company now, they would not only lose me, but they would probably lose some of their billings as well. I really don't know what to do at this point, Diane. I can either stay with Avery McNeil or look for a higher paying job elsewhere; however, there is no guarantee that my new job would be a fast track one like it is at Avery. One big plus at Avery is that the people there already know me and the kind of work I produce. If I went elsewhere, I'd essentially have to start all over again. What do you think I should do, Diane?"

Discussion Questions

1. What are the motivational drivers of Simpson's dilemma?

2. Using expectancy theory, define the dilemmas.

3. Given the limited information in the case, what evidence do you see that Avery McNeil possesses the qualities of one of Levering and Moskowitz's "best places to work"?

4. If you were Simpson's manager, and he approached you with this problem, how would you respond? Could you use this opportunity to apply any of the principles of expectancy theory? Intrinsic motivation? Empowerment?

Reflection

In one way, Mike Simpson's situation is similar to Margaret Jardine in the Competency 1 Practice exercise, "Feeling Dead-Ended." Both Mike and Margaret feel a sense of inequity or injustice in the workplace when they compare their situations to the situations of other employees. Pay compression is likely to become an even bigger problem when the economy is growing and demand for talent is strong. In commenting about the proportion of organizations that have pay compression problems, one compensation consultant recently commented, "It's an overwhelmingly large number, whether they [organizations] admit it or not" (J. Fox, chair of Fox Lawson & Associates LLC, quoted in Ladika, 2005).

PRACTICE The Same Old Job[3]

Objective

This exercise puts you in the position of a manager with an unmotivated employee. In contrast to Michael Simpson, Helen Ames presents a different type of motivation challenge, one that can't be solved by increasing her pay.

Directions

Read the following case study and answer the questions that follow.

Helen Ames awoke this morning with another headache. This was the second time in three days. She hadn't been sleeping well for the past four months or so either. When she awoke, a feeling of dread overpowered her again; she thought about going to work. As she sat on the edge of the bed, she thought about the good working conditions, the decent pay, and the people with whom she worked. But it didn't seem to matter.

She'd been thinking a great deal recently about how tired and bored she'd become. She'd been on the job now three and a half years, and all the excitement was gone. There was plenty of work to do, but it all seemed routine now. She didn't even get upset or excited about the problems that arose because she felt like "she'd heard it all before."

[3]*Adapted from* an exercise used in *Getting Work Done Through Others: The Supervisor's Main Job,* Advanced Human Resources Development Program, New York State Governor's Office of Employee Relations and CSEA, Inc., 1987.

She was tired of doing "the same old thing, day in and day out." Even though the assignments were different, the tasks seemed almost identical: writing reports, checking quotas, giving the same directions over and over again to the same people—the same problems in the same areas. She could almost describe what would happen every day for each situation.

Helen's friends and family told her how lucky she was to have a job at which she did well and that offered security. Some had begun to ask her what it was that she would really like to do or what it was that would make her happy. They suggested that she take some time to think about what was wrong and what she could do about it.

She decided to request three days off.

Discussion Questions

1. How would you describe Helen's personal motivation level?

2. What personal conflicts exist for her?

3. If you were supervising Helen Ames and had all this information, how would you try to motivate her? Which of the principles of intrinsic motivation and empowerment could be used to increase Helen's personal motivation?

Reflection

Researchers Morgan and Feldman (2000) would likely classify Helen Ames as "underemployed." They suggest that underemployment is a serious problem that affects approximately 25 percent of the U.S. workforce. Underemployment, working at a job that does not fully utilize employee skills, is not simply a problem for those employees who are bored with their work—although those employees certainly need and deserve support from their managers. It is also a problem for their organizations, resulting in increased turnover and absenteeism. Organizational climate may also be negatively affected (Morgan and Feldman, 2000). Thus, managers who work with employees like Helen to help them find more challenge and meaning in their work are acting both as mentors and as producers in their organizations.

APPLICATION   Understanding Organizational Reward Systems

Objective

The diagnostic framework that follows will be helpful to you in assessing the overall motivation potential and reward systems in potential job areas.

Directions

If you are currently employed, use the questions below as a guide for evaluating how effective your organization's current motivation and rewards system is for creating a productive work environment. If you are not currently employed or are looking for a new job, use the questions below as a starting point for interviewing potential employers about how they motivate their employees and what their reward systems are.

Motivation and Reward Systems: A Diagnostic

1. What are the rewards offered by your organization that are useful in getting individuals to pursue organizational objectives?

   - Consider economic incentives such as pay and benefits.
   - Consider symbols of prestige and status.
   - Consider informal job content incentives such as freedom, recognition, and interesting work.
   - Consider the characteristics of those places identified as "best places to work" by Levering and Moskowitz.

2. How is each reward listed in question 1 obtained?

   - Is it a function of individual performance?
   - Is it a function of group performance?
   - Is it a function of fixed membership (the reward is automatically awarded to all organization members)?
   - Is each primarily an extrinsic or intrinsic reward?

3. How do individuals decide to join this organization and what keeps them here after they have joined?

4. What does the organization do to ensure that employees continue to experience the workplace as productive?

Reflection   Organizations cannot survive by providing only intrinsic rewards, but the more effectively they create an environment that is intrinsically motivating, the better off they will be. Unfortunately, the impact of extrinsic rewards often diminishes over time. Employees may begin to feel entitled to the reward, rather than motivated by it. Just as significantly, research as summarized by Gagne and Deci (2005) suggests that in some cases providing extrinsic rewards to individuals for doing a task may actually reduce their intrinsic motivation.

Competency 3   Managing Time and Stress/Balancing Competing Demands

ASSESSMENT   Organizational Stressors

Objective   This exercise asks you to identify aspects of your current situation that you find stressful and to evaluate how stressful each is for you.

Directions   Listed below are 10 stressors that often surface in work organizations. (There is also room to add additional stressors that you may have experienced.) They also sometimes occur in other types of organizations, such as voluntary or community organizations, athletic teams, or social organizations. Most can occur whenever there is work to be done and people must interact with others in deciding how the tasks are to be carried out. Choose an organization in which you spend a good deal of time, preferably a work organization. If you are not currently actively involved in such an organization, think back to a previous one.

1. Lack of clarity regarding your role in the organization
2. Feeling that you are overqualified or underqualified for the job
3. Too much work to do in the time you have
4. Too much responsibility for task completion
5. Not enough information to make necessary decisions
6. Too much responsibility for others' actions
7. Not enough authority to make decisions
8. Poor interpersonal relationships with others
9. Organizational politics

10. Conflict between organizational needs and personal needs

11.

12.

13.

Think for a moment about each of these potential stressors and ask yourself the following questions:

1. On a scale from 1 to 10, to what extent do you experience this type of stress (1 = not a stressor; 10 = creates much stress)?

2. On a scale of 1 to 5, to what extent do you feel you have control over this stressor (1 = no control; 5 = full control)?

3. When faced with this type of stressor, what do you do to cope with it?

Discussion Questions   1. Which of these stressors are you experiencing? What is your total level of stress in this organization?

2. Of the stressors you experience, over which do you feel you have the most control? The least control? What influences the level of control you have?

3. When you have experienced stress in an organization, what have been your most effective coping strategies? Your least effective coping strategies?

4. Have you ever helped others (e.g., friends, coworkers, peers) cope with organizational stress? If so, what differences are there in coping with stress yourself and helping others cope with stress?

Reflection   Many of the stressors listed are reflective of being too far out on the extremes of a continuum. For example, lack of clarity is stressful, but so (for many people) is working in a job where there is no chance to be creative or solve problems on your own. Not enough information is a problem, but so is having too much information—as we discussed in Chapter 4. Research on performance and stress supports the notion of an optimum point—enough stress to keep us focused but not so much stress that we collapse under its pressure. As noted earlier when discussing the best places to work, that optimum point may be very different for different individuals.

LEARNING   Managing Time and Stress/Balancing Competing Demands

We begin this section with a discussion of a model (i.e., line of sight) that will help you make choices and resolve dilemmas presented by the competing demands we all have to resolve on a daily basis. We then turn to a discussion of stress management, briefly examining the sources and organizational consequences of stress. We then present several stress-management methods—some that you can do easily, some that will take practice. Then we move on to time management, examining some of the current thinking about time management and suggesting some techniques to help you manage your time better consistent with your application of the line-of-sight model. We conclude with a practical set of strategies for ensuring the alignment of personal line of sight with an organization's critical path—the best way to optimize time management and minimize the need for stress management.

BALANCING COMPETING DEMANDS: KEEPING OUR LINE OF SIGHT FOCUSED ON CORE PERSONAL VALUES, VISION, AND GOALS

In our discussion of Competency 1, Working Productively, we discussed Thomas's (2000) model of self-management, which involves:

1. Committing to a meaningful purpose
2. Choosing activities to accomplish the purpose
3. Implementing the activities
4. Monitoring implementation for competence
5. Monitoring progress toward the purpose

We focused on Thomas's model of self-management as a way of increasing our experience of the key intrinsic motivators of meaning, competence, self-determination, and impact. Here we introduce a model that we believe will supplement Thomas's approach—particularly the second step, choosing activities to accomplish the purpose. The model involves keeping clearly focused on one's own core purpose, vision, and values while productively working in one's organization. The model involves maintaining your "line of sight," and it is an adaptation of Kelley's notion of the "critical path." In *How to Be a Star at Work,* Kelley (1998) talks about initiatives that are crucial to the success of the organization as those that improve the company's flow on it's "critical path," which he defines as "the line that moves all the efforts of workers and managers toward a delighted customer, where, in turn, profitability and increased shareholder value are sent back down the path" (pp. 66–67). Maintaining your personal line of sight involves aligning your personal purpose, vision, values, and goals with the critical path your organization is pursuing. We demonstrate this process by first discussing an exercise that focuses on articulating an individual's version of critical path and then linking it to a set of practices that integrate the personal version of critical path with the organization's critical path—resulting in the "line of sight."

CRITICAL PATHS AND LINE OF SIGHT

In his classic work on time management, *The Time Trap,* Alec Mackenzie (1997) asks the vexing question: "Why is time management still a problem?" Mackenzie observes:

> . . . *after all these years, and with all these innovations (e.g., books, magazine articles, seminars, workshops, paper and electronic organizers, etc.), we are still caught in the time trap. With this mountain of information, these dazzling new tools, we still groan and say, "There just isn't enough time!" Why is this? Why is it that we still find ourselves making some of the classic time management mistakes, even though we know better? The answer is simple—and very complex: human nature. (pp. 4–5)*

Mackenzie elaborates his answer to the persistent dilemma of a time shortage by essentially agreeing with Thomas (2000) and Kelley (1998) that time management is essentially self-management. Each of us has the same 24 hours each day. Just as organizations pursue their critical path by constantly trying to wisely manage their critical resources of human and physical capital, information, and time, so must we constantly try to manage our critical resources—with the most critical, of course, being time. But "managing time" may not be the best way to frame this dilemma, for we cannot manage time—the sun continues to rise and set each day. We can, however, manage ourselves—how we use the time we have been given—for once time has been spent (or wasted), it is gone forever.

In *Coming Up for Air*, Beth Sawi (2000) recounts an incident that provided her with the name for her book:

> *A Zen student comes to his master and complains that he can't concentrate on his meditation exercises. "Think of your breath," says the master. "Concentrate on that." "But my breathing is so uninteresting," says the student. "Can't you give me another assignment?"*
>
> *With that, the master seizes the student and forces his head into a tub of water. The student struggles, but the master doesn't let him up until he is half drowned. "Now," says the master, "Is breathing still so uninteresting?" (p. 20)*

Sawi takes her readers through a very important exercise that very much parallels several we have asked our readers to engage in throughout this work. Sawi first gives individuals a set of phrases to review (e.g., being financially independent, getting to the top, achieving goals) and asks them to copy those they find appealing onto an index card or small piece of paper. She then asks each person to choose only five from the total. Forcing the choice of only five may seem arbitrary, but Sawi sees it is as critical. She points out that we already have too much going on—that's why we all struggle with time management. By limiting ourselves to a more reasonable number of priorities, we increase the probability that each is likely to happen. The prioritization process also forces us to make those hard choices about what really does matter to us. This step, Sawi observes, is a critical one on the way to balance because it clarifies the fact that rather than trying to do everything and finding our schedules and lives overburdened with commitments, we need to focus and concentrate on our own priorities—that is, our personal critical path. This clarification and prioritization will support not only the second step in Thomas's model of self-management, but also the fifth and last steps, which is monitor progress toward our ultimate purpose.

STRESS IN ORGANIZATIONS

The issue of stress (and stress management) has become an increasingly important one for organizations and their managers. Research over the past three decades has linked stress to a vast array of illnesses, including tension headaches, various forms of heart disease, cancer, ulcers, and even arthritis (Dossey, 1982; McGee-Cooper, 1994). Beyond affecting their physical health, stress can affect employees' ability and willingness to do their jobs by reducing their cognitive abilities, level of energy, and motivation, as well as their ability to relate interpersonally with coworkers. The costs of individual stress to organizations can be measured in terms of increased absenteeism, turnover, and accident rates; low quality of performance and low rate of performance; and stress-related disability claims. While we may be tempted to think about stress as uniquely American, it is in fact a global phenomenon. In Japan, medical expert Tetsunojo Uehata coined the term *karoshi,* which literally means death from overwork, to refer to a "condition in which psychologically unsound work practices are allowed to continue in a way that disrupts the worker's normal work and life rhythms, leading to a buildup of fatigue in the body and a chronic condition of overwork accompanied by a worsening of pre-existent high blood pressure and a hardening of the arteries and finally resulting in fatal breakdown" (quoted in Metcalf and Felible, 1992, pp. 151–152).

Given the potential impact of stress on individuals' physical and mental health, as well as on individual and organizational performance, it is important for the manager to be aware of how the work environment creates stress for individuals. Hans Selye, often considered the father of current research on the health effects of stress on human beings, argued that stress is a nonspecific response to demands placed on the body (1976). Here, the term "nonspecific response" is used to differentiate reactions to specific stimuli—for example, changes in temperature that cause the body to shiver or sweat in order to restore equilibrium—from the more generalized reaction to a stimulus that forces the body out of equilibrium. Thus, stress is within the person; it is the person's response to a change in the external environment.

Selye further posited a *general adaptation system* to describe how the body responds to a stressor. This theory identifies three stages of reaction to environmental demands. In the first stage, the *alarm stage,* the body's defense mechanisms are triggered. When the body senses a threat, it releases adrenaline, cortisone, and other hormones, thus raising both heart rate and blood pressure; this is often referred to as the fight-or-flight reaction. If the situation allows the stress to subside, the body will return to equilibrium. Alternatively, if the demand continues, the person enters the *resistance stage.* In this stage, the body attempts to return to equilibrium, essentially focusing full attention on the stressor. By definition, this results in decreased attention to any other stressors. Thus, an individual who is experiencing large amounts of stress caused by workload, financial problems, or personal concerns may be more susceptible to colds or other illnesses than one who is experiencing less stress. The final stage is the *exhaustion stage.* In this stage, the person has experienced intense and/or prolonged stress, and the body is no longer able to resist. In this stage, the physiological reactions that occurred during the alarm stage may likely reappear and the body is not able to return to its normal state. The result may be psychological, as with depression or other mental illness, or physiological, as with heart disease, ulcers, and so forth. It should be noted that not all stress is negative in its source or in its consequences. Selye argued that "complete freedom from stress is death" (1974, p. 20). The key is to keep the body from entering the exhaustion stage of the general adaptation system. A useful analogy is the tension on the strings of a tennis racket: If they are either too loose or too taut, they will keep the player from playing at peak performance.

SOURCES OF STRESS

While the discussion about the relationship between stress and illness raises issues about the nature of the work environment and its influence on people's stress, you are probably aware that different people react differently to different situations. Some people like to work under tight time pressures and would argue that they become most efficient and even creative as the deadline approaches. Others find working under tight deadlines to be too stressful and prefer to pace themselves so that everything is completed ahead of time. Similarly, when traveling, some managers like to plan to get to the airport early. In order to avoid the stress associated with getting caught in traffic on the way to the airport, they schedule enough slack into their schedule so that they will still catch the plane if delayed by traffic. Other managers find the waiting time to be stressful and prefer to time their arrival at the airport so that they avoid the crowded waiting area. Are deadlines and traffic inherently stressful? Why do some people react to certain situations in a very intense manner while others seem to take these situations in stride? Are there stressors that affect all people consistently?

Psychologists have identified two major categories of sources of stress related to illness and disease: *stressful life situations* and *personality characteristics* (Cohen, 1979). Stressful life situations are those events that cause major changes in (daily) life patterns, thereby creating strain or atypical emotional states. Much research during the late 1960s and early to mid-1970s focused on these stressful life situations. Perhaps the best-known work in this area is built around the Holmes and Rahe (1967) *Social Readjustment Rating Scale.* Based on a series of research studies that examined the relationship between stressful life events and the onset of illnesses of all types, this scale assigns a "life change unit" score to a number of major life changes, both positive and negative, such as death of a spouse (100 points), divorce (73 points), marriage (50 points), retirement (45 points), and gaining a new family member (e.g., through birth, adoption, older relative moving in) (39 points). Individuals identify which events they have experienced within the previous two years and add up their scores. Those who score very high on this scale are said to have an increased likelihood of becoming ill or injured. While the scale has become quite popular, it is somewhat controversial and has been criticized on both methodological and theoretical grounds. In particular, a number of researchers have argued that the relationship between stressful life events and illness is not a direct one; rather it is mediated by other variables, such as biological predispositions to illness, the person's appraisal of the situation, the person's resources for dealing with the situation, the degree of social support from others, and the degree of change in daily activities (Cohen, 1979).

The second category of sources of stress, personality characteristics, comprises those characteristics that predispose individuals to appraise and react to similar situations in different ways. The best-known research in this area is probably Friedman and Rosenmann's (1974) work on the Type A behavior pattern, described as "a particular complex of personality traits, including excessive competitive drive, aggressiveness, impatience, and a harrying sense of time urgency. Individuals displaying this pattern seem to be engaged in a chronic, ceaseless, and often fruitless struggle—with themselves, with others, with circumstances, with time, sometimes with life itself. They also frequently exhibit a free-floating but well-rationalized form of hostility, and almost always a deep-seated insecurity" (p. 4). In contrast, individuals who are categorized as exhibiting Type B behavior have a more relaxed approach and are not as driven by time. Research in this area has shown a strong link between Type A behavior and coronary heart disease (CHD), even after controlling for such factors as parental history of CHD, smoking behavior, blood pressure, and cholesterol levels. This work is particularly important in the context of this chapter because it provides evidence that trying to do more in less time is not effective time management. People who exhibit Type A behavior build their lives around goals, objectives, and deadlines but "are unable to approach a task in a healthy, balanced way" (Dossey, 1982, p. 50).

As noted earlier, organizational researchers have added work-related stressors to the list of sources of stress. Work overload and time pressures, role conflict (see Chapter 3), work relationships, and office politics are, to a large degree, external factors that can lead to stress, regardless of an individual's personality or predispositions. On the other hand, there are a variety of stressors in the work environment that individuals can learn to manage in an effective way. In the producer role, managers must be proactive in helping their units and departments to maximize positive stress (without physical, psychological, or emotional strain), minimize negative stress, and effectively manage those situations in which negative stress cannot be minimized. But first, managers must be effective in managing their own stress. In the next section we provide several tools and techniques for managing individual stress.

STRATEGIES FOR MANAGING STRESS

As noted, stress is not an event; rather stress is a reaction based on one's perception of the event. Although some situations are arguably more inherently stress-provoking than others, many day-to-day experiences are more subjective in nature. Thus two people can experience the same objective situation and have two different reactions—one will feel stressed and out of control, while the other will approach the situation with a sense of composure and perhaps even with a sense of humor. For example, when the boss calls and says that the report you took all of last week to prepare for upper management needs to be expanded and delivered by the end of the day, you can expect the adrenaline to start flowing. The big issue is, What happens next?

In order to reduce or eliminate the negative effects of the resistance and exhaustion stages of stress, you have three options. First, remove yourself from the situation. Second, alter the situation or environment that is causing the stress. Third, teach yourself to respond differently to the situation by altering your evaluation of the situation. Given that you cannot avoid or alter all situations you find stressful (indeed, as noted above, this is not a recommended strategy), this third strategy, which focuses on altering your reactions to situations in order to reduce the negative effects of stress, is considered to be the most effective. Below we focus on five strategies for managing stress. Note that, in general, these are *long-term* strategies that focus on building your personal resources for approaching potentially stress-provoking situations, rather than instantaneous strategies that will help you reduce the stress at the moment the boss calls to ask you to expand the report. The strategies can be seen as investments that require regular attention. Just as you would not expect to be able to go out and run a marathon if you have not been training for this activity, you cannot maintain a Type A behavior pattern approach to work and expect that with a few deep breaths you will be ready to face a difficult task with a sense of calmness. The strategies that work best for managing stress are those that focus on how you approach life in general.

clarify values

CLARIFY YOUR VALUES

The first step in learning to manage stress is to figure out what is important to you in life and then to empower yourself to follow these beliefs. We have already devoted considerable discussion to this issue: in Chapter 6, Competency 1, Developing and Communicating a Vision, where we discussed the criticality of the personal element of communicating vision; in Competency 1, Working Productively, in this chapter, specifically the discussion of intrinsic motivators and empowerment; and earlier in this competency, in our discussion of line of sight. Here we suggest that self-awareness also includes being aware of the needs and expectations that accompany our goals.

physical health

PAY ATTENTION TO YOUR PHYSICAL HEALTH

There is considerable research showing that individuals who are in good physical condition are better able to deal with stressful situations than are those who are in poor physical condition. There are a number of key elements that contribute to your physical health, with the three most important being diet, exercise, and rest. Maintaining healthy diet and nutrition habits is vital to maintaining your physical health. Healthy nutrition includes maintaining a balanced diet, as well as avoiding fad diets and not skipping meals on a regular basis. Indeed, some nutritionists recommend eating several small meals a day, instead of three large ones.

A second key to maintaining physical health is regular aerobic exercise, such as running, swimming, rowing, rope skipping, bicycling, and dancing. Aerobic exercise inoculates the body against stress in a manner similar to medical vaccinations. If the cardiovascular system is exposed to a small amount of stress on a regular basis, it can better cope with other stresses it encounters.

A third key to maintaining good physical health is to get enough rest. While, on average, people tend to feel best with six to eight hours per night, what is enough rest varies by individual. Some people require eight hours of sleep a night; others do quite well with less. In addition, while most people tend to get their sleep at night, others prefer to take short, 15- to 30-minute catnaps during the day and sleep fewer hours during the night. Research has also shown that people who engage in daily aerobic exercise need less sleep. A good way to figure out how much sleep you need is to listen to your body (McGee-Cooper, 1992).

relaxation techniques

TRY USING A RELAXATION TECHNIQUE

The term "relaxation technique" is used here to include a wide variety of stress-management approaches that involve using mental exercises to help you gain greater control over your physiological functioning—and therefore over your stress reaction. Relaxation techniques, like aerobic exercise, should be practiced on a regular basis, usually once or twice a day. Most of these techniques involve increasing one's self-awareness by training the mind to focus attention on a single object or experience, thus allowing both the mind and body to relax. As David Fontana (1989) notes, "The mind has got into the habit of flitting from one thought to another, of following first this chain of associations then that, of existing in a state of almost constant distraction while our thoughts chatter away at us like a cartload of monkeys" (p. 89). Relaxation techniques make you more aware of your body's internal processes and your feelings, and they increase your ability to reproduce these feelings so that you can alter your reaction to a stress-provoking situation.

Three types of relaxation techniques are meditation, muscle (or progressive) relaxation, and imaging (or visualization). Meditation techniques commonly focus on mental relaxation through breathing exercises. Like relaxation techniques in general, there are many different types of meditation. Muscle relaxation techniques, like meditation, emphasize self-awareness. Unlike meditation, muscle relaxation exercises focus on gaining an awareness of the whole body. Muscle relaxation exercises are designed to allow you to gain a better sense of your internal processes, so that you can be aware of and then release the tension when it arises. Finally, imaging is a technique that takes advantage of the brain's ability to create images that are real to the body, in the sense that it can release hormones and other chemicals as if the body were actually having the experience. In recent years, imaging has become popular among athletes as a way to help them visualize winning performances (McGee-Cooper, 1992).

CREATE A PERSONAL SUPPORT SYSTEM

support system

Humans are social animals. We thrive on positive relationships with others. When we are experiencing stress, the need for personal relationships becomes even more important. Several research studies point to social support as being among the most important factors in stress management (Farnham, 1991; Quick, Nelson, and Quick, 1990). In considering your own social support system, think about your friends and decide whom you can count on, who will listen to you when you need to let off steam, who will both respect you and challenge you. Let these people know that you are also available to support them when they need it. Nurture the relationship by sharing positive as well as negative feelings. Keep in mind that while having a personal support system has been shown to be one of the most important elements in coping with stressful life events, you do not want to be seen by your friends as a negative stressor.

TAKE ENERGY BREAKS TO HELP YOU RESTORE YOUR ENERGY

energy breaks

You may not want to think of your body or mind as a machine, but the fact is that they need to be refueled regularly. In general, you can only work for about five hours before your performance starts to deteriorate, you have trouble concentrating, your level of creativity diminishes, and/or you feel less motivated. While you can certainly occasionally maintain performance for longer periods of time, if you consistently exceed your limit, you will feel stressed. If, however, you find time during the day for relaxation and/or play, you give your body and mind a chance to rejuvenate. McGee-Cooper (1992) states that "a good general tip when deciding what type of break to take at a given moment is to choose an activity, and possibly a location, that is different from your current task and site" (p. 71). For example, if you have been sitting for a long period of time, it may help you to stand up, stretch, take a walk, use your muscles. If you have been doing close, detail work, try to sit back and stare out the window or close your eyes and do an imaging exercise. If you have been working intensely for an extended period of time on something that requires a great deal of mental energy and creativity, do something that allows your brain to relax. If you have been working alone, find someone who also needs an energy break and enjoy each other's company for 10 minutes.

TIME MANAGEMENT

We now turn to the topic of time management. Many traditional tips, tools, and techniques of time management assume that managers function in a rational, logical, orderly world in which the only thing about which they must be concerned is doing their own work for eight hours each day. Thus they focus on monitoring activities and keeping track of appointments, on "getting the job done," and on avoiding interruptions. Managers do not, however, live in a rational, logical, orderly world.

Rather, they are usually in the midst of transactions and operations. They need to be able to use their time efficiently, but they also need to allow time for unscheduled encounters and, as noted, they need to be able to stop for an energy break. Most managers listen and talk far more than they read, and they share far more information through the spoken word, via plant tours, telephone and doorway conversations, and meetings, than they do through written reports. Managers need to keep in touch with colleagues and customers so that they know what is going on within their organization, their industry, and the world. Much of their important work is accomplished in bursts of collaborative encounters with others, the average duration of which is about 11 minutes (Alesandrini, 1992). This suggests that time management techniques need to accommodate managers' need for a more fluid approach to time (Deutschman, 1992), one that focuses more on identifying priorities and concentrating on the critical tasks than on mapping out each minute of the day.

Here we present three strategies for managing your time. They reflect the notion that, ultimately, managing your time means managing yourself. Thus, like the strategies for managing stress, the strategies presented for managing time tend to be for the long term. They build on the notion that what you want to accomplish in life should determine how you use your time each day, rather than vice versa. As a result, most of the advice presented here is relevant whether you are a CEO, a middle-level manager, or a front-line employee.

CLARIFY YOUR VALUES

You are probably not surprised to see this advice again; by now it should be apparent to you that the number-one strategy for managing stress should also be the number-one strategy for managing time. The challenge is to prevent the urgent, but less important, tasks from diverting us from important, but less urgent, ones. How do we decide what is important? Important tasks are those that are driven by long-term goals and values. Covey, Merrill, and Merrill (1994) present a *time management matrix* that can help you think about your tasks. The matrix is divided into two dimensions—importance and urgency—and includes four boxes (quadrants): important and urgent, important but not urgent, urgent but not important, neither important nor urgent. In quadrant I, urgent and important, are crises, pressing problems, and projects with deadlines. You could also include interpersonal crises with close friends, relatives, or coworkers in this quadrant. Quadrant II, important but not urgent, includes long-term planning and prioritizing, professional development, relationship building, taking care of yourself (physical health, relaxation, energy breaks, etc.), and working on long-term projects that do not have imminent deadlines. Covey and colleagues refer to this quadrant as the quadrant of quality. These two quadrants are where you should spend most of the time, with quadrant I of necessity taking precedence over quadrant II. Note, though, that the more time you spend on the activities in quadrant II, the less time you are likely to have for dealing with the crises and imminent deadlines in quadrant I.

Quadrant III includes those items that are urgent but not important. These are some of the phone calls, pieces of mail, meetings, and drop-in visitors you respond to. This is where you spend a lot of time meeting other people's expectations and demands, rather than your own. A corollary to the strategy of clarifying your values is, Learn to say no! This does not mean that you are never available to help others; but keep in mind that saying yes to others means that you are saying no to yourself. Ask yourself: Is this request as important as the items in my own quadrants I and II? Finally, quadrant IV includes those items that are neither important nor urgent. These are the real time wasters—junk mail, busywork, some "escape" activities that do not help to reenergize you. In the Practice exercise, you will get a chance to look more closely at how you spend your time.

PLAN AND PRIORITIZE ON A REGULAR BASIS

In line with the first strategy, it is important that you plan your time to maximize the amount of time you can spend in quadrants I and II. Hyrum Smith (1994) suggests that you should spend 10 to 15 minutes each morning planning your day. This does not mean that you plan out every minute. Rather, it means that you examine the list of all the things you could do, decide which have the biggest payoffs, and schedule your time accordingly. In addition, try to keep in mind your own personal rhythms. No doubt you are aware of which times during the day you have the most creative energy and which times you are at a low ebb. Wherever possible, work on the items that are most important during the times when you have the most energy. Also, remember that most top managers leave time on their calendars for the unexpected. If you schedule yourself for back-to-back meetings, and one of the meetings runs longer that expected, there is no built-in slack. If, on the other hand, you have extra time between appointments, you can always fill in that time with activities from the first three quadrants. Note that this all assumes two key elements of time management. First, you need to keep a calendar, preferably one calendar so that you don't "lose" appointments by failing to transfer them from one calendar to the other. Second, you need to keep a master list of things you need to do. From this list, you can make your daily to-do list or schedule, based on your priorities.

REGULARLY REVIEW HOW YOU ARE SPENDING YOUR TIME

The first two strategies focused on looking forward in time. This last strategy suggests that every few months you need to take a look backward and assess how well you are doing in maintaining your time management system. Many time management experts suggest that you should keep a log for a week. Note how you spend your time. Are you working on those things that are important, or just on those things that are urgent? Are you making progress toward meeting your intermediate and long-term goals? As we indicated at the beginning of this section, managing your time essentially means managing yourself.

PERSONAL LINE OF SIGHT, THE ORGANIZATION'S CRITICAL PATH, AND BALANCING COMPETING DEMANDS

In *How to Be a Star at Work,* Robert E. Kelley (1998) links the concept of an organization's critical path (discussed above) with a "star's" effectiveness at self-management. We believe what Kelley describes as core self-management skills will serve as a fitting capstone to this competency as well as to this role. Kelley's core skills are consistent with our discussion of intrinsic motivators and empowerment, as well as our framing of time and stress management and ultimately balancing competing demands. They take both the individual and organizational challenges of being an effective "producer" equally into account:

- Stars identify the organization's critical path and get on it by learning how they personally can add value.

- Stars choose activities at work that allow them to leverage their personal purpose (who they are. . .and what they want), talents, experience, satisfaction, and "flow."

- Stars regularly and frequently monitor and review their personal productivity and consider ways to increase personal effectiveness and efficiency.

- Stars "borrow" shamelessly—not ideas and content, but technique and methods for better self-management. Stars carefully observe others' work processes and adopt innovative techniques into their own approach.

- Stars are not afraid to vary, experiment, and change their work routine in order to develop even more productive practices.

- Stars will make a compelling case to organizational leaders for altering job descriptions and regulations that limit or restrict their productivity or the work at which they excel.

- Stars adopt work processes that allow them to minimize distractions and interruptions in their work without alienating themselves from the group.

- Stars work to avoid time-killer crises by planning for glitches and problems—and building mistake-recovery time into projects.

- Stars develop procrastination-busting work habits—to-do lists, priority plans, and building fun work assignments around drudgery-like tasks.

- Stars also learn to accept the occasional unproductive workday, even several weeks' work slump. They recognize the cyclical nature of productivity.

- Stars get to know their own productivity patterns. Some individuals are most productive when they give their all in a defined burst of intensive activity—obsessive immersion. Other stars schedule their projects with a steady and more consistent rhythm (adapted from Kelley, 1998, pp. 118–119).

ANALYSIS Wasting Time[4]

Objective   This exercise is intended to give you an opportunity to analyze how a manager uses (and misuses) his time. As you respond to the discussion questions, be sure to think not only in terms of making claims about problems, but also providing grounds and warrants to justify those claims.

Directions   Read the case of Frank Fernandez. Discuss the case in your small group using the questions below as a guide. A large group discussion will follow.

Wednesday morning Frank Fernandez, a unit manager in the Human Resources Management Department, reported to the office promptly at 8:30 A.M. After washing out his coffee cup, Frank poured a fresh cup and walked over to Bonnie Wiczarowski's desk. As one of the new employees, Bonnie had been at a training session the last few days, and they spent about 15 minutes reviewing how the course had gone and what had gone on at the office while Bonnie was away.

Leaving Bonnie's desk, Frank stopped by the washroom before heading to his desk. Back at his desk was a memo detailing new policies concerning personal use of state vehicles while on state business. The policy basically stated that state vehicles should be used only for official state business and that employees using these vehicles could not provide transportation for friends or relatives while driving the state vehicle for official state business. Frank was surprised by this news, and he went to ask Ralph Larrowe whether he had read the memo. Although Ralph was a good colleague and well liked in the office, he did have a reputation for talking; once he started it was hard to get him to stop. It was 9:30 before Frank finally told Ralph he had other work to do and would have to return to his desk. In fact, Frank needed to get started on his section of the quarterly progress report. The branch chief wanted the first draft to be completed by close of business on Friday.

When Frank got back to his desk, he found a note from Bonnie. She had wanted to ask him about one of the issues that had come up while she had been out of the office at the training session. Frank went to answer Bonnie's question, but she was away from her desk.

At 10:30 the branch chief telephoned and asked Frank to find a report detailing program expenditures over the last three years. The branch chief also expressed her disgust with the new vehicle policy and discussed (at length) the absurdity of the policy, given its low potential for saving money or improving image and its likely negative impact on employee morale. Clint Thompson, the administrative assistant, would usually be the one to locate the report, but he was upstairs attending a meeting of the Employee Assistance Program's peer counselors. Frank decided he would try to locate the report himself, but trying to understand Clint's filing system confused him, and after 20 minutes he decided to wait until Clint returned to the office. It was now almost 11:00, and there was not enough time to begin any major project before lunch. Frank cleaned up his desk instead, preparing himself for an efficient afternoon.

Returning to work at 1:00, Frank took a few minutes to glance over the departmental newsletter and then started to take out the material he would need to work on the quarterly report. As he was taking out the material, he remembered he had a few telephone calls to make regarding the survey that the interagency task force subcommittee on which he served was planning on conducting. He decided he would take care of the telephone calls and then begin working on the quarterly report promptly at 2:00. It was 1:30 before Frank remembered to ask

---

[4]*Adapted from* training material for *Getting Work Done Through Others: The Supervisor's Main Job,* Advanced Human Resources Development Program, New York State Governor's Office of Employee Relations and CSEA, Inc., 1987. Adapted with permission of the New York State Governor's Office of Employee Relations.

Clint to find that report. About 15 minutes later Clint came back with two reports. One report listed program expenditures over the past two years; the other report listed expenditures over the past five years. There was no three-year report, and Clint said he was pretty sure there had never been one. Frank did not want to question the branch chief's authority and so asked Clint to look again.

At 2:00, Clint returned and this time insisted that there was no three-year report. When Frank called the branch chief, her secretary said she was in a meeting and didn't know when she would return. After Frank left a message, he and Clint returned to what they were doing.

When Frank looked at his watch, he noticed it was almost 3:00 (actually it was 2:45). He felt that he needed to get to the quarterly report, but then he had second thoughts. He had barely gotten halfway through his telephone calls and he felt that two hours would probably not be enough time to really get a good start. The quarterly report is the type of project that is best accomplished when a large block of time is available. Frank knew that by the time he gathered up the materials he needed and laid them out on the desk in such a way that he could look them over all at once, it would be time to put them away. Frank decided he would take some of the material home and work on it in the evening so that he would be ready to start first thing in the morning. Then he turned to his master to-do list and looked it over to see what other tasks he could work on until the end of the day.

Discussion Questions
1. What are some of the problems Frank has in managing his time? To what extent is he accomplishing what is important as opposed to what is urgent?
2. If his productivity today is typical, what may happen to his level of stress in the coming months?
3. What could Frank do to improve his use of time? What specific steps would he need to take?

Reflection
Personal characteristics play a major role in how we manage our time, but organizational culture can also have an impact. Think back to the descriptions of the Clan, Adhocracy, Market/Firm, and Hierarchy cultures and consider how Frank's behavior might also have been influenced by the culture of his organization. For example, cutting off his conversation with Ralph might be seen very differently in a Clan organization compared with a Market/Firm culture.

PRACTICE Clarify Your Values

Objective
The first strategy for managing both time and stress is to clarify your values. This is generally an activity that could take you days or even weeks to fully complete. This exercise gives you an opportunity to get started.

Directions
1. Make a short list (no more than five items) of those things that are most important to you in life. Try to stay focused on the end state. For example, if you think it is important to get a good education, think about why you want to have a good education. What could you accomplish or what would you have if you were well educated?
2. Take one or two of the items from your list and identify one or two long-term goals that derive from your governing values. Next, take one or two of your long-term goals and identify one or two intermediate goals that derive from the long-term goals.
3. Review your activities over the past week and think about how much time you spent on these goals.
4. Decide on how you can devote a little more time to accomplishing a goal that is derived from your governing values.

Reflection As you think about your values, think back to the Anchors and Oars Assessment in Chapter 2 to see how the personal characteristics you identified in that exercise relate to the goals and core values that you identified.

APPLICATION   Improving Your Stress and Time Management

Objectives This exercise has two objectives. First, to apply what you have learned about improving your productivity by trying some of the techniques discussed in the text. Second, to keep a log of your behaviors and outcomes to allow you to modify the techniques in ways that you find most helpful.

Directions 1. Review the strategies for stress and time management.

2. Pick one key thing you could do over the next week to improve your productivity. For example, you may want to watch your diet, try a relaxation technique, or start keeping a master to-do list and beginning each day with a planning session. Keep track of what you do each day to implement this strategy.

Reflection Ideally, the techniques that you implement to improve your time and stress management will become ingrained habits so that you no longer need to think about them. In reality, it always seems to be much more difficult to develop good habits than bad ones. Try to find ways of reminding yourself that you have made a commitment to the practices that you selected. For example, put a magnet on the filing cabinet that says "Breathe" or tape a fortune cookie slip to your computer reminding you that "the secret to getting finished is getting started."

REFERENCES

Alesandrini, Kathryn. *Survive Information Overload: The 7 Best Ways to Manage Your Workload by Seeing the Big Picture.* Homewood, IL: Business One Irwin, 1992.

Babcock, Charles. "Hewlett-Packard: It's Not Just Printers." *Interactive Week* (July 10, 2000): 82–86.

Bowen, David E., and Edward E. Lawler. "What, Why, How, and When." *Sloan Management Review* (Spring 1992): 31–39.

Boyle, M. "Tough jobs make for great workplaces" *Fortune,* January 11, 2006 (accessed online at http://money.cnn.com/magazines/fortune/bestcompanies/).

Charan, Ram. "How to Hire a CEO. Inside or Out? That's Question No. 2." *Fortune* (Sept. 6, 1999): 288.

Charam, Ram, and Geoffrey Colvin. "Why CEO's Fail." *Fortune* (June 21, 1999): 69–78.

Cohen, Frances. "Personality, Stress, and the Development of Physical Illness," in George C. Stone, Frances Cohen, Nancy E. Adler, et al. (eds.), *Health Psychology,* San Francisco: Jossey-Bass, 1979.

Collins, Jim. *Good to Great.* New York: Harper Business, 2001.

Collins, Jim. "Beware the Self-Promoting CEO." *Wall Street Journal* (November 26, 2001): A17.

Colvin, G. "The 100 Best Companies to Work for in 2006" *Fortune,* January 11, 2006 (accessed online at http://money.cnn.com/magazines/fortune/bestcompanies/).

Corcoran, Elizabeth. "The E-Gang." *Forbes* (July 24, 2000): 145–172.

Covey, Stephen R., A. Roger Merrill, and Rebecca R. Merrill. *First Things First.* New York: Simon & Schuster, 1994.

Csikszentmihalyi, Mihaly. *Flow: The Psychology of Optimal Experience.* New York: HarperCollins, 1990.

Deutschman, Alan. "The CEO's Secret of Managing Time." *Fortune* (June 1, 1992): 135–146.

Dossey, Larry. *Space, Time & Medicine.* Boulder, CO: Shambhala, 1982.

Farnham, Alan. "Who Beats Stress Best—And How." *Fortune* (October 7, 1991): 71–86.

Fontana, David. *Managing Stress.* Leicester, England: British Psychological Society, 1989.

Friedman, Meyer, and Ray H. Rosenmann. *Type A Behavior and Your Heart.* New York: Knopf, 1974.

Gagne, M., and E.L. Deci. "Self-determination and Work Motivation." *Journal of Organizational Behavior* 46 (4) (2005): 331–362.

Garfield, Charles S. *Peak Performers.* New York: Avon Books, 1986.

Hackman, J.R., and G.R. Oldham. *Work Redesign.* Reading, MA: Addison-Wesley, 1980.

Hardy, Quentin. "All Carly, All the Time." *Forbes* (December 13, 1999): 138–144.

Herzberg, Frederick. "One More Time, How Do You Motivate Employees?" *Harvard Business Review* (January–February 1968): 57.

Holmes, Thomas H., and Richard H. Rahe. "The Social Readjustment Rating Scale." *Journal of Psychosomatic Research* 11 (1967): 213–218.

Kang, Celia. "New HP Chief Helps Revitalize Company." *The Times* (San Ramon) (July 20, 2000): C1, 3.

Kelley, R.E. *How to Be a Star at Work: 9 Breakthrough Strategies You Need to Succeed.* New York: Times Business Books, 1998.

Ladika, S. "Decompressing Pay." *HRMagazine* 50(12) (2005): 79–82.

Larson, Mark. "Culture Shock." *Portland Business Journal* (August 17, 2001): 14.

Lashinsky, Adam. "The Wired Investor: HP Can't Easily Spin Off Its Problems." *Fortune* (April 12, 1999): 182.

Lawler, Edward E. *Rewarding Excellence.* San Francisco: Jossey Bass, 2000.

Levering, Robert, and Milton Moskowitz. *The 100 Best Companies to Work for in America.* New York: Currency Doubleday, 1993.

Levering, Robert, and Milton Moskowitz. "The 100 Best Companies to Work for." *Fortune* (January 10, 2000).

Livingston, J. Sterling. "Pygmalion in Management." *Harvard Business Review* 47(4) (July–August 1969).

Mackenzie, R. Alec. *The Time Trap,* 3d ed. New York: American Management Association, 1997, pp. 4–5.

Maslow, A.H. *Motivation and Personality.* New York: Harper & Row, 1954.

McClelland, David C. *The Achieving Society.* New York: Van Nostrand Reinhold, 1961.

McGee-Cooper, Ann, with Duane Trammell and Barbara Lau. *You Don't Have to Go Home from Work Exhausted.* New York: Bantam, 1992.

McGee-Cooper, Ann, with Duane Trammell. *Time Management for Unmanageable People.* New York: Bantam, 1994.

Metcalf, C.W., and Roma Felible. *Lighten Up: Survival Skills for People Under Pressure.* Reading, MA: Addison-Wesley, 1992.

Morgan, L.M., and D.C. Feldman. "Underemployed Human Resources: Revealing the Secret Dilemma of Untapped Potential," in R.E. Quinn, R.M. O'Neill, and L. St. Clair (eds.), *Pressing Problems in Modern Organizations.* New York: AMACOM, 2000, 77–96.

Nadler, David A., and Edward E. Lawler (eds.). "Motivation: A Diagnostic Approach," in J.R. Hackman, E.E. Lawler, and Lyman W. Porter, (eds.), *Perspectives in Behavior in Organizations.* New York: McGraw-Hill, 1977.

Nee, Eric. "Open Season on Carly Fiorina: The CEO of HP Has Had a Brutal Ride as Her Promises Outpaced Performance." *Fortune* (July 23, 2001): 114+.

Perone, Joseph R. "Fiorina Remaking Hewlett-Packard." *San Francisco Examiner* (August 20, 2000): C1.

Quick, James Campbell, Debra L. Nelson, and Jonathan D. Quick. *Stress and Challenge at the Top: The Paradox of the Successful Executive.* Chichester, England: John Wiley & Sons, 1990.

Sawi, Beth. *Coming Up for Air: How to Build a Balanced Life in a Workaholic World,* New York: Hyperion, 2000.

Selye, Hans. *Stress Without Distress.* Philadelphia: Lippincott, 1974.

Selye, Hans. *The Stress of Life,* rev. ed. New York: McGraw-Hill, 1976.

Smith, Hyrum W. *The 10 Natural Laws of Successful Time and Life Management: Proven Strategies for Increased Productivity and Inner Peace.* New York: Warner Books, 1994.

Spreitzer, G.M. "When Organizations Dare: The Dynamics of Psychological Empowerment in the Workplace." Unpublished dissertation, University of Michigan, Ann Arbor, 1992.

Spreitzer, G.M. "Individual Empowerment in the Workplace: Dimensions, Measurement, Validation." *Academy of Management Journal* 38(5) (1995): 1442–1465.

Spreitzer, G.M., S.C. DeJanasz, and R.E. Quinn. "Empowered to Lead: The Role of Psychological Empowerment in Leadership." CEO Publication, May 1997. Center for Effective Organizations, U.S.C. School of Business, Los Angeles, CA.

Thomas, K.W. *Intrinsic Motivation at Work.* San Francisco: Berrett-Koehler, 2000.

Thomas, K.W., and B.A. Velthouse. "Cognitive Elements of Empowerment: An Interpretive Model of Intrinsic Task Motivation." *Academy of Management Review* 15 (1990): 666–681.

Vroom, Victor H. *Work and Motivation.* New York: John Wiley & Sons, 1964.

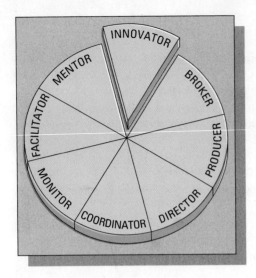

8

THE
INNOVATOR
ROLE

■ COMPETENCIES

Living with Change

Thinking Creatively

Managing Change

The **innovator role** is one of the most compelling, yet least understood, of the eight leadership roles. As one of the two roles of the open systems model, it focuses on adaptability and responsiveness to the external environment. The innovator role involves the use of creativity and the management of organizational changes and transitions, and it provides a unique opportunity for managers to affirm the value of individual employees within the organizational setting.

When people think of the words *"innovator"* and *"innovation,"* they tend not to think in terms of large, established organizations. Rather, they associate the terms with new entrepreneurial business endeavors or with specific corporate divisions related to such things as new product development, new design, or new advertising lingo. In fact, given the many rules and procedures that must be followed in large organizations, people often assume that managers in these organizations have little opportunity to be innovative or to create flexible, risk-taking environments. This chapter aims to debunk the myth that innovation is limited to a few creative people or departments. In describing the benefits of studying the competencies of the innovator role, one student wrote, "Over the past five years I've been working at a toy company. The research and development, creative services, and marketing people are those I considered innovative, surely not someone in the Treasury Department. However, I now realize that being open to new experiences, pioneering in thought practices, and resilient to changes are key characteristics of an innovative person, all of which I am."

The reality is that change is inevitable in all aspects of organizational life today. The action imperative of the open systems model—Create—focuses attention on initiating change, as well as responding to change. Resistance to change is not a viable option. In many cases change and innovation are indispensable to the function, growth, and survival of organizations. The issue today is not whether organizations will experience change, but how they will manage that change.

Innovation and managed change make readiness and adaptability possible in society's increasingly changing conditions and accompanying demands. Today, managers play an important role in both the initiation and the implementation of organizational change. In this chapter the three key competencies of the innovator are:

Competency 1   Living with Change
Competency 2   Thinking Creatively
Competency 3   Managing Change

Each of these competencies requires the manager to be flexible and open to new ideas, new ways of thinking, and new challenges that the managerial role presents.

Competency 1   Living with Change

ASSESSMENT   Personal Acceptance of Change

Objective   The following questionnaire will help you assess your personal acceptance of change.

Directions   Consider carefully the following list of changes. List any others that are applicable. Which of these changes have occurred in your life in the past five years? As you consider each change, recall your resistance to change when it happened.

In column A, place a number reflecting your resistance at the time of the change. Next, in column B, place a number reflecting your current level of acceptance of that change. If you did not experience the change, place a 0 in both blanks.

Scale A	No resistance				Strong resistance
	1	2	3	4	5

Scale B	No acceptance				Strong acceptance
	1	2	3	4	5

A	B	
_____	_____	1. You were married or engaged.
_____	_____	2. There was a death in your immediate family.
_____	_____	3. You moved to a new location.

_____ _____ 4. You enrolled in a college or university.

_____ _____ 5. You had a personal health problem.

_____ _____ 6. You began work at a new job.

_____ _____ 7. An important relationship in your life changed.

_____ _____ 8. Your income level changed by more than $10,000 a year.

_____ _____ 9. You were divorced or separated.

_____ _____ 10. A close friend or relative was divorced or separated.

_____ _____ 11. Other (List):

Reflection   What do your responses reveal about how you deal with change? As you look at each item, note the difference between the number you placed in column A (resistance to change) and the number in column B (acceptance of change). A large difference (4 is the maximum possible) indicates that your ability to accept change is strong.

1. Which changes did you strongly resist at first, but now accept? Think of as many reasons as possible why you now accept these changes. Identifying these reasons may help you identify your strengths in acceptance of change.

2. Based on your responses, do you consider yourself to be open to change, or do you find change difficult to deal with?

3. Are there any events that you strongly resisted and that you still have difficulty accepting? Seek to identify the reasons for your nonacceptance. As you compare strongly resisted events that you accept with those you do not, you may find valuable clues to your ability to cope with change in your life.

LEARNING Living with Change

One of the greatest challenges to the manager in the innovator role is that of living with changes that are unplanned and sometimes unwelcome. As a manager you must often deal with a difficult dilemma when experiencing such change: On the one hand, you need personally to adjust to an unplanned change that you may not welcome, and at the same time you must present the change to your employees in a manner that helps them to make the adjustment as well. Both cases may require a shift in attitude toward change and a conscious effort to eliminate psychological resistance to change.

In studying change in organizations, it is helpful to recognize that people do not just work in organizations—people live in organizations. In fact, people who work full time generally spend more time at work than they do engaged in any other activity.

CONFORMITY IN A CHANGING WORLD

Living with change is a challenge. As humans we are constantly socialized by the groups in which we live. This process of socialization shapes what we believe about ourselves. We then act on those beliefs and, in doing so, we help to create the world in which we find ourselves. That world can be viewed as a place of comfort or imprisonment. Graham (1998) provides an example from the training of elephants. The process begins by placing a huge chain around the leg of a young animal. The chain is then staked to the ground. The elephant begins by fighting this constraint but eventually gives up and accepts that it can only move within the radius of the constraining chain. The trainer then begins to reduce the size of the chain and eventually switches from a chain to a large rope. Finally, the constraint is reduced to a rope no bigger than one's little finger that the elephant could easily snap, except for its prior conditioning.

In our lives we often undergo a similar process. The socialization process teaches us that there are things we can do and things we cannot do. We accept these beliefs and act as if they are true. Our actions are then accommodated and reinforced. Like the elephant, we conform. This conformity serves many positive functions and is actually a good thing. Having routines makes life more efficient. We do not have to think about every decision. On the other hand, our routines tend to blind us to possibilities outside our belief systems. They make it difficult for us to live with change.

PERSONAL CHANGE AND NEGATIVE EMOTIONS

Change leads to negative emotions

Since we live in a world of change, we need to change continually. Yet change threatens conformity, and real personal change always means experiencing some kind of negative emotion. We know this and we fear this. We therefore try to deny the signals that our present reality is different from the reality we have already experienced, a reality that feels comfortable. We insist on the validity of our past beliefs, meaning systems, or scripts. We start to rationalize the need for change. We point fingers and blame others. Doing this often leads us deeper into the process of denial until some disaster occurs.

Mark Youngblood (1997) provides a graphic example. He gives an account of having his business fail. He spent a year trying to launch a company. He spent his life savings, went into debt, and exhausted himself trying to make the business successful. Finally he had to admit that the business was not going to make it. He writes:

> With it went everything that defined who I was to the world. I could no longer say that I "was" my job, because I had none. I couldn't rely on my wealth to create a sense of worth and identity, for I had no money and loads of debt. I could not look to social standing, for a failed entrepreneur has no social standing. And the failure of my love relationship, a month earlier, ensured that I could not find myself through the love of another. I had nothing, therefore I was nothing. I had died. (Youngblood, 1997, p. 208)

As we read Youngblood's words, we can feel his emotion. We clearly understand and empathize. No one would ever want to enter such an emotional space. Yet one of Youngblood's single greatest lessons emerged from living through those negative emotions. Consider his observation:

> Until that point, I had lived my life through the eyes of other people. I had defined myself through object-reference—my sense of identity and my feelings of self-worth were tied directly to the outer circumstances of my life—all of these external references were stripped away. When I looked in the mirror, I did not know who I was. For me, the ego-death and subsequent "rebirth" was a wonderfully and powerfully transformative event. I experienced a sort of "awakening" in

which I realized in a flash of insight that "I" was not my ego or the external trappings of my life. "I" was still all that had ever been, my true self. Nothing that was real and certain had changed, just superficial aspects of my environment. (Youngblood, 1997, p. 208)

Youngblood learned that he had lived his life through the eyes of others. We all do this. We constantly ask, How do they see me? What image must I portray? Who must I pretend to be? Youngblood learned that he had been defining himself through object reference; that is, his assessment of himself was always dependent on how people in his world responded to him. Honors and objects were of exaggerated importance in his world. He was constantly asking, Am I impressive? Are they willing to give me more status? Am I managing my status? Do I own the right things? Am I ready to buy things that convey a higher power and status? Do the objects around me carry status and create the kind of reactions I want? Am I transacting well in the social realm?

Once Mark Youngblood's sources of status and power dried up, he discovered what he had always feared: He was a nobody; he was a zero. This, of course, is what we all fear. Underneath it all, perhaps we are of no value. We all, therefore, greatly fear what Youngblood experienced: the stripping away of all the external props. What could be worse than the death of the ego? Yet his ego death was followed by an event of greater revelation. He says his "subsequent rebirth was a wonderfully and powerfully transformative event." He does not report consciously doing anything to make this rebirth happen. It just occurred in an instant. What was it? He awakened to the fact that his life was much more than the accumulation of honors and material objects. He was not an object. Other people are not objects. Underneath it all, he had a lasting self. The only things that had really changed were the "superficial aspects of his environment." Here a great reversal had occurred. What he was sure about was this: What had seemed to be the most important thing in his life, the foundation of his life, had turned out to be inconsequential and artificial.

CLARITY OF PURPOSE

All of us are socialized like the elephants. In the process we become adapted to an object-reference world in which we come to believe that the real self exists only in the eyes of others and that reality is transactional, dependent on our ability to make compacts and swing deals with people who matter. We strive for power and for objects of status. We judge other people as means to our ends. Yet as the Mark Youngblood story suggests, it is possible to move to another perspective. Chatterjee states it well:

We can practice the law of transcendence by progressively letting go of our urge to hold onto things, objects, addictions, and our urge to be important or powerful. Letting go does not in any way diminish ourselves, it does not make us less influential or less powerful. On the contrary it extends our human capacity for action in infinite ways. (1998, p. 180)

We all want to be important and powerful. We all want to possess things of external value. Note that the problem is not having them, but holding onto them. Being important and powerful is a potentially good thing. The honors and things of the world are to some degree necessary. Holding on to them is not. The paradox is that if we hold on to the scripts that got us to our present level of wealth and status, we will lose wealth *higher purpose*

and status. The key to living with change is to be clear about who we are and where we are going. When we possess a higher purpose, status and power become servants of that higher purpose. It is then that we can not only live with change, we can even become initiators of change.

THE CAPACITY TO LIVE WITH CHANGE

How do we find the higher purpose that will allow us to more effectively live with change? The answer has to do with the concept of fundamental choice. Robert Fritz (1989) is a leading thinker on creativity and innovation. He identifies three kinds of choices:

1. *Primary choice.* These are choices that involve specific results (e.g., I want my child to go to a top university). Primary choices often involve external goals.

2. *Secondary choice.* This kind of choice supports the primary choice (e.g., I will require my child to study for two hours every night). Secondary choices usually involve means to the end represented in the primary choice.

3. *Fundamental choice.* This has to do with our state of being or basic life orientation (e.g., I will pursue education at great personal sacrifice so as to model what I value). Such a decision might change my primary and secondary choices. I might, for example, study with my child for two hours a day. A fundamental choice tends to be about our integrity, our being state, who we are at the core.

Fritz notes that when we make a fundamental choice, doing so changes our outlook and our behavior. Fritz argues, "When people make a fundamental choice to be true to what is highest in them, or when they make a choice to fulfill a purpose in their life, they can easily accomplish many changes that seemed impossible or improbable in the past (1989, p. 193–194)." Here we suggest that when we do the first—make a fundamental choice to be true to the highest in ourselves—then we are far more likely to "make a choice to fulfill a purpose." When we align ourselves with our values, we know where we need to go. The purpose we need to fulfill becomes clear. Whatever suppressed or hidden purpose we may have had rises into our consciousness. Quinn (2000) provides an illustration of a primary choice:

> I remember a man—I'll call him Garret—who attended my Leading Change Course in the Executive Education Program at the Michigan Business School. He was a company president. During the first three days of the course, he said very little. On Thursday morning, he asked if we might have lunch together and I agreed. Over lunch he told me that if he had attended my course any time in the last five years, he would have been wasting his time. He had successfully turned around two companies and felt he knew everything there was to know about leading change.
>
> Today, he told me, he was now a lot more humble. There were five companies in his corporation. He had turned two of them around and was seen as the shining star among the presidents. He had earned the right to lead the largest company in the corporation. The current president of that largest company still had, however, eighteen months left until his retirement. In the meantime Garret had been asked to try his hand at one more turnaround. There was a company in the corporation that was considered hopeless. It had once commanded a large

market share for its product. Today, it had only a small percent of the market and was still shrinking. Nobody believed this company could be turned around, so if Garret failed in his efforts, no one would hold it against him. It had now been twelve months since he took on the challenge. He felt defeated. Everything that had worked for him before, everything his past had taught him, failed in the present situation. Morale was dismal. The numbers were dismal. The outlook for the future was dismal.

I asked Garret what he thought he would do next. On a paper napkin he listed his short-term objectives. He began to draw an organizational chart. He described the people in each of the senior positions and described the assignments and/or changes he was going to make in regard to each person on the chart. I found his answer unexciting. There was no commitment or passion in what he was telling me. Yet it was clear that Garret was a man of character with a sincere desire to succeed. I took a deep breath and asked a hard question.

"What would happen if you went back and told those people the truth? Suppose you told them that you have been assigned as a caretaker for a year and a half. No one believes the company can succeed and no one really expects you to succeed. You have been promised the presidency of the largest company, and the plan is to put you into the plum job. Tell them that you have, however, made a fundamental choice. You have decided to give up that plum job. Instead, you are going to stay with them. You are going to bet your career on them and you invite them to commit all the energy and goodwill they can muster into making the company succeed."

I was worried that I might have offended Garret. I half expected an angry response. He looked at me for a moment, then it was his turn to take a deep breath. To my surprise and relief, he said, "That is pretty much what I have been thinking." He paused, and in that moment I watched him make the fundamental decision. Almost immediately, he picked up the napkin and started doing a re-analysis. He said, "If I am going to stay, then this person will have to go; this person will have to be moved over here; and this person. . . ."

As he talked, there was now an air of excitement in Garret's words. Once he had made the fundamental decision to stay, everything changed. His earlier plans to move on to the larger company were suddenly scrapped. Garret had made a fundamental choice, and now he had a new life stance, a new outlook, and a new way to behave. The organizational chart that made sense a few moments before now made no sense at all. None of the original problems had changed, but Garret had and this made all the difference in the world. (Quinn, 2000, p. 62)

We live in a world of pressures for conformity. Conformity makes us comfortable, but it also imprisons us. We do not want to see the present reality that signals the need for change. When we make fundamental decisions, when we increase our integrity, our purpose becomes more clear, we increase in courage, and we are more willing to make the changes necessary in our lives. Once we make a fundamental choice, our primary and secondary choices begin to change automatically.

ANALYSIS Living with Change and the Power of Purpose

Objective Change comes in many different forms and results from many different experiences. In analyzing this scenario, consider both the changes that the protagonist had experienced prior to the incident, as well as the changes that occurred to the protagonist as the result of the incident.

Directions   Read the following case. Using the concepts that were just covered, write a paragraph that explains what happened in this surprising incident. How was the protagonist able to "live" with change?

The Power of Purpose

Joseph Jaworski was a successful lawyer who gave up his practice to establish an institute that would increase ethical leadership. He called it the "American Leadership Forum." Once he made his courageous decision, his sense of purpose intensified. Then, one night, he had a terrifying experience. He walked to a parking lot and slipped into his car. As he was about to shut the door, he felt a hard object pressing against his body. He looked up to see a young man with a fierce look. He was pressing hard with a huge knife. Through clenched teeth the man said, "I don't want to hurt you, but I will. Now you move over from behind that steering wheel."

Jaworski held up his key and told the man to take the car, but to leave him alone. The man pressed the knife harder and said, "I don't want the car, I want you."

Jaworski noticed that there was a second man outside the car. He felt an intuition that, if he cooperated, he would die. Jaworski reports:

> *I remember thinking for an instant, I'm not going to let this man kill me. I'm doing something too important, and I've got to finish it. With that, I grabbed his wrist with both hands before he could shove the knife any further into me, and I pulled it away, slamming his hand against the door jamb, and causing the knife to fall on the ground. In that instant I was able to swing my feet around outside and hold them up as barriers. By that time, he had the knife again and began thrusting and trying to slash through my feet. I remember kicking him in the face, landing a powerful blow. He backed off with the knife in his hand and was ready to come at me again when I began yelling at him at the top of my voice. He had the knife in his hand, thrust out toward me, and he was ready to come at me, and I screamed at him, "You dirty son of a bitch, you touch me again and I will kill you, I will kill you with my bare hands, God damn you! Come on, come on, just try it."*
>
> *He took a step backward and looked. I screamed even louder, "Come on, you filthy son of a bitch." I felt like a crazed animal. He stood there and looked at me for what seemed like a long while and then turned away and ran, and his partner ran with him. As he ran away, I was still screaming at him at the top of my lungs. (Jaworski, 1996, p.132).*

After the men ran away, Jaworski says the adrenaline wore off and he began to shake uncontrollably. He was amazed at his capacity to defend himself against that knife. But he knew that his power to do so was a function of his commitment to his purpose. He recognized that bringing about the American Leadership Forum was not an external intention. He and his purpose were one. Over time, he came to consider this incident a defining moment in his life. It was then that he had realized a primal part of himself. He had experienced a form of pure energy unlike anything he had previously felt and he began to understand the kind of commitment that is necessary to bring about the "unfolding generative order."

Reflection   Although we hope that you never experience the type of situation that Jaworski suffered through, his experience of a "defining moment" was clearly a positive outcome in his eyes. Having a clear sense of purpose not only helps us develop the capacity to live with change, but it also helps us develop the courage necessary to create change.

PRACTICE   The Power of Purpose Revisited

Objective   Sometimes we become so caught up in the distractions of everyday life that we don't notice how much we depend on having the power of purpose. By reflecting on our past experiences, however, we can often find examples of how having a clear purpose helped us cope with, or even embrace, change.

Directions   Review the paragraph you wrote for the Analysis exercise. Now search for an incident in your own life or the life of another that involved the power of purpose and allowed the person to successfully adapt to changing conditions. Write a paragraph that describes this incident.

Reflection   You may have had difficulty coming up with an incident from your own life that involved the power of purpose. Don't assume that the power of purpose only comes into play in life-threatening situations or "eureka!" moments. The power of purpose is also at work when you stay up late to work on a project to help a coworker who is ill and still commit yourself to meeting your MBA team at seven A.M. the next morning to work on the final version of a class presentation. The power of purpose is reflected, not in the magnitude of the goal, but in the commitment of the individual.

APPLICATION   Providing Help

Objective   Everyone occasionally needs help living with change. This exercise asks you to reach out to someone and offer them encouragement and insight as they attempt to cope with change.

Directions   Using the material from this competency, write a letter to someone in your life who is currently having a difficult time living with change. Provide specific advice that will help that person live with the change more successfully.

Reflection   Sometimes actions that we think are frivolous may turn out to be profound. One example: workshop participants were asked to write a letter to someone expressing their appreciation for that person. Feeling somewhat foolish, Susanna wrote a letter to her sister Leona. Susanna began by saying that she was being forced to write the letter, but being highly conscientious, she also wrote about how much she appreciated Leona and identified some of the things that made Leona so special. Susanna thought nothing more about the letter, but some time later when she was visiting her sister, Leona told her, with tears in her eyes, how much the letter had meant to her.

Competency 2   Thinking Creatively

ASSESSMENT   Are You a Creative Thinker?

Objective   What behaviors and attitudes do you think characterize creative people? This exercise is designed to help you understand how you think about creativity.

Directions   Read each of the statements below. If you think that the behavior or attitude characterizes what creative people are like, put a check in the first column. If you think that the behavior or attitude characterizes what you are like, put a check in the second column.

Creative people
do this   *I do this*

Creative people do this	I do this	
✓	✓	1. In a group, voicing unconventional but thought-provoking opinions
____	✓	2. Sticking with a problem over extended periods of time
____	____	3. Getting overly enthusiastic about things
✓	✓	4. Getting good ideas when doing nothing in particular
____	____	5. Occasionally relying on intuitive hunches and the feeling of "rightness" or "wrongness" when moving toward the solution of a problem
✓	✓	6. Having a high degree of aesthetic sensitivity
✓	✓	7. Occasionally beginning work on a problem that could only dimly be sensed and had not yet been expressed
____	✓	8. Tending to forget details, such as names of people, streets, highways, small towns, and so on
✓	✓	9. Sometimes feeling that the trouble with many people is that they take things too seriously
✓	✓	10. Feeling attracted to the mystery of life

Reflection   In fact, all of the 10 statements above describe individual behaviors or attitudes that have been found to be related to creative thinking ability. For any statements that you did not check in column one, think about why you don't associate that behavior or attitude with being creative. In looking at the second column, did you find that you checked a number of statements even though you never considered yourself a particularly creative thinker? Sometimes, like the student we quoted at the beginning of this chapter, people fail to see their own creativity until they are encouraged to recognize it.

LEARNING   Thinking Creatively

When we think about who is creative, we tend to think of individuals we regard as singularly unique, gifted, talented, and just different from the rest of us. In the arts and sciences, we think of people like Bach, Handel, Einstein, and Rembrandt. In business, we think of people like Steve Jobs (cofounder of Apple Computers), Jack Welch (General Electric), and Anita Rodick (The Body Shop). People rarely think of creative ability as existing in the general population. More important, we are rarely encouraged to think or learn about being creative. It is not surprising, then, that many people underestimate their creative abilities.

In fact, a very wide range of behaviors and personality traits have been found to be associated with creative ability. More important, creative thinking is a skill that each person can develop. Not everyone, of course, can paint a Mona Lisa or derive $e = MC^2$. But creativity and innovation have an important role to play in far more places than Renaissance art or the development of scientific theories. For example, in his book *Explaining Creativity: The Science of Human Innovation,* R. Keith Sawyer (2006) considers creativity in hypertext fiction, computer technology, and business innovation. He emphasizes that creativity is not a sudden "magical" burst of insight that differs from our everyday thinking. "We find that creativity happens not with one brilliant flash but in a chain reaction of many tiny sparks while executing an idea" (quoted in Russo, 2006, p. 89).

Creativity is a way of thinking that involves the generation of new ideas and solutions. More specifically, it is the process of associating known things or ideas into new combinations and relationships. Illustrations of this definition of creativity are found in many diverse areas, from science to humor.

Louis Pasteur's discovery of vaccines against disease provides a good example of creative thinking. The idea of vaccination had been widespread since the mid-1700s, but it had been associated only with cowpox and smallpox. It was not until 1879 that Pasteur discovered the prevention of infectious diseases by inoculation, quite by accident. Previously no one had applied the idea of vaccination to other diseases because it involved two different frames of reference: vaccination and the concept of disease being caused by microorganisms. Pasteur, who had knowledge of both, brought the two together.

In much the same way, researchers at 3M, who know about adhesive and also know that people often use small pieces of paper for notes, brought the two together to create Post-it notepads.

These two examples illustrate how creative thinking often involves utilizing information that is already known and discovering new associations, rather than, as many people think, generating new ideas out of nothing. In Pasteur's words, "Fortune favors the prepared mind."

How can we increase our ability to engage in creative thinking? First, we need to recognize that all of us have assumptions and thought patterns that we use but do not question. As we learn to think more creatively, we break away from these thought patterns. In a classic and telling statement, Koestler (1964, p. 96) referred to creativity as "an act of liberation: the defeat of habit by originality." Many exercises in creative thinking are designed to assist us in developing different ways to look at things and, specifically, to look beyond our assumptions.

Second, we need to recognize that the information used in generating new relationships among things and ideas is already in the mind. Creative thinking is the act of combining those pieces of information in new and unique ways. Thus, although there is a great deal of evidence that creative thinking is not linked to intelligence, creative ability in certain areas is often linked to knowledge and expertise in those areas. For example, one could say that any biologist could have invented penicillin, but not any person.

How does creative thinking differ from critical thinking? It would be useful to compare them briefly. Generally, critical thinking is analytical, logical, and results in few answers; creative thinking is imaginative, provocative, and generates a wide variety of ideas. Critical thinking is often described as vertical, logically moving upward until you arrive at a correct answer. In contrast, creative thinking is described as lateral, spreading out to find many possible solutions (de Bono, 1970). Figure 8.1 summarizes these differences.

For example, suppose that you, as a marketing specialist, have been assigned to join a special citizen's task force in your community. The task force is considering the

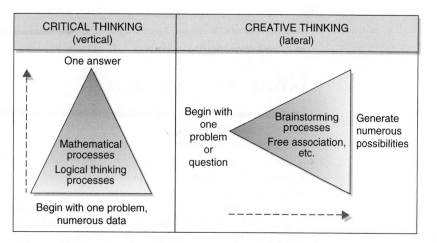

FIGURE 8.1 *Critical and creative thinking.*

problem of how to persuade families and tourists to take their vacations in your home state this year. Notice that there is not merely one answer to this; there are perhaps hundreds or thousands of ways to persuade people to take their vacations in your state. Notice, too, the need for imagination and the prospect of generating many ideas.

By contrast, consider any mathematical problem whose solution has a single answer. Such a problem involves critical thinking; information is analyzed to determine the one best or correct solution. If your task force has generated a large number of suggestions, it will need to use critical thinking in order to decide which ones would be best to implement. Further, critical thinking skills will be necessary in order to arrive at a viable plan of action.

The two modes of thinking are complementary; the findings of the creative thinking process can be analyzed for usefulness by critical thinking. Although Western culture has traditionally emphasized critical thinking skills, the value of creative thinking has become increasingly recognized—within organizations and in society as a whole. Moreover, there is a growing assumption that both creative and critical thinking skills will be needed to meet the challenges of the twenty-first century.

DEVELOPING CREATIVE THINKING SKILLS IN YOURSELF AND OTHERS

People often underestimate their own creative ability. Research indicates, however, that there is one major difference between people who exhibit creative tendencies and people who don't: personal belief in creativity. That is, those who engage in creative thinking tend to regard themselves as creative; the others see themselves as noncreative.

Although many people simply do not see themselves as creative, the manager has an opportunity to affirm employees as individuals by recognizing their creative potential and encouraging the use of creative thinking. In this way subordinates are strengthened both on the job and as individuals. By empowering employees to think creatively, managers increase the probability that new and better ways will be found to do things.

Three dimensions of creativity

To focus on developing creative thinking skills, both in yourself and in others, consider the three dimensions of creativity: domain-relevant skills, creative-relevant skills, and task motivation (George T. Geis in Kuhn, 1987).

DOMAIN-RELEVANT SKILLS

Increase knowledge base.

Domain-relevant skills are associated with the basic and expert knowledge that is essential to creative thinking. Increasing your domain-relevant skills primarily involves increasing your knowledge base. Again, not just anyone could have discovered penicillin, but perhaps any biologist with the requisite expert knowledge could have. Remember that creative thinking is largely knowledge-based, using information already in the mind.

Within organizations, some knowledge differs from area to area. For example, knowledge required for financial planning differs from that required for personnel management. Alternatively, knowledge of organizational and management skills is relevant across various areas of an organization. In reading this textbook, you are increasing your domain-relevant skills for creativity in the managerial role. You can also increase your domain-relevant skills by learning how other organizations in the United States, in other Western cultures, and in non-Western cultures structure their work environments. For example, Japanese management differs in how manager–employee relationships are regarded, in the role of management in organizations, and in the role of organizations in society. Although the extent to which it is either possible or desirable to implement concepts of Japanese management in the United States will vary across organizations, exposure to these ideas may help you to think creatively about your own work environment and relationships with employees.

CREATIVE-RELEVANT SKILLS

associate previously unrelated concepts

Creative-relevant skills are those that enable individuals to associate previously unrelated concepts and to think differently. A vast array of techniques, often called "creativity heuristics," ranging from use of analogies to mental imagery, are available to enhance your creative-relevant skills. These techniques are individual strategies that will help you as an innovator to develop your personal creative thinking skills.

One key to enhancing your creative-relevant skills is to learn to break away from commonly held assumptions regarding the relationships between ideas and things, so that you are able to consider new relationships. It is especially important to recognize cultural barriers to creativity, those commonly held assumptions that are a part of our societal or organizational culture. For example, Western culture traditionally has embraced reason and logic to the exclusion of feeling and intuition. This emphasis on reason and logic has created several barriers to creative thinking, including the following:

1. A negative value on fantasy and reflection as a waste of time, a sign of laziness, or even a bit crazy

2. The belief that only children should play and that adults should be serious

3. The assumption that problem solving is serious and, therefore, humor is out of place

4. A negative value on feeling and intuition, which are regarded as illogical and impractical

Although we cannot change these societally based cultural barriers, we can guard ourselves against their influence. If we are able to diminish our cultural barriers to creative thinking, we enhance our abilities to think differently and develop skills for creativity.

In addition to the barriers presented by our societally based cultural assumptions, individuals often make assumptions that hinder their attempts to become more creative. Like cultural barriers, individual barriers can be overcome if we consciously seek change.

Individual barriers frequently have an emotional basis. These barriers result from personal beliefs and fears associated with taking risks, trying out a new idea, or trying to convince others of the value of our new ideas. The following are 10 of the most common individual barriers to creative thinking:

1. *Resistance to change.* It is natural to become secure in the way things are and to resist change.

2. *Fear of making a mistake and fear of failure.* To counter this fear, the Limited clothing stores encourage mistakes by evaluating buyers on their failures as well as on their successes. They believe that if employees do not make mistakes, then they may not be taking initiatives and trying new ideas. Somerset Maugham once said, "You'll win some. You'll lose some. . . . Only mediocre people are always at their best" (quoted in Miller, 1987, p. 17).

3. *Inability to tolerate ambiguity.* Our need for predictability nurtures our inability to tolerate ambiguity. We like to know the way things are and to be able to categorize things, events, and people in our lives. Creativity requires flexibility in our thinking; inability to tolerate ambiguity is an inability to tolerate flexibility.

4. *The tendency to judge rather than to generate ideas.* This is an expression of the culturally based preference for critical thinking over creative thinking. Many of us are trained to be critical in our thinking and judgmental in our approach. To some extent, we may feel better about ourselves if we are able to critique another's work or action.

5. *Inability to relax or to permit any new idea to incubate.* Many of us find a perverse comfort in having too much to do and, as a result, find relaxation uncomfortable and difficult. Some people report that they do not know how to relax. Others relax by engaging intensely in another demanding project. Research has shown, however, that freeing our conscious minds, through relaxation or repetitive activity (e.g., cutting the grass or cleaning the house), increases our ability to seek associations amid old ideas.

6. *The tendency toward excessive self-criticism.* Many of us are taught to be excessively self-critical. In this respect, some people are kinder to people they actively dislike than they are to themselves. Efforts to eradicate this self-defeating tendency can increase your creative abilities.

7. *Fear of looking foolish.* This is the biggest barrier of all and the hardest to remove. No one likes to appear foolish to others. We find, however, that often we think we appear foolish when we actually do not. The development of a "so what?" attitude can be helpful in these instances (Rawlinson, 1981).

8. *Conformity, or wanting to give the expected answer.* This is very apparent in groups and organizations. Individuals may not want to rock the boat or present an unpopular argument (see the discussion of groupthink in the section, Using Participative

Decision Making in Chapter 3). Managers should actively encourage employees to present different ideas or perspectives (Rawlinson, 1981).

9. *Stereotyping, or limiting the possibilities of objects and ideas to their "known" use.* The inability to see a problem from various viewpoints is a function of mental stereotyping (e.g., a chair is for sitting).

10. *Lack of information, or too much incorrect or irrelevant information.* Lack of information may limit the creative handling of data.

Are you afflicted by any of these barriers? The extent to which you are is an indicator of how much your creative ability is hampered. Equally important for managers is that the encouragement of these barriers in employees will hinder employee creativity as well.

TASK MOTIVATION

Task motivation refers to the existence of a nurturing organizational environment for employee creativity. All individuals have the potential to be creative. The issues are (1) will they and (2) what can managers/innovators do to increase the opportunities for their employees to use their creative thinking abilities?

The task of providing an environment that is conducive to creativity has many challenges. Individual and cultural barriers often decrease our ability to create such environments. Managers must be aware of these barriers as they strive to enhance creativity in the workplace.

There are two types of organizational barriers that managers must overcome to increase employees' opportunities and abilities to use creative thinking. The first is inherent in the definition and structure of organizations; the second is associated with managerial style and attitudes and affords more of a chance to make changes.

Hierarchical, highly structured organizations inevitably create barriers to creative thinking. Set procedures, rules and regulations, specialization of work, criteria for employment evaluation, formal channels of communication, and the preference for the status quo over change are inherent characteristics of large organizations. Since these organizational characteristics are unlikely to change, it is helpful for managers to recognize these barriers for what they are and to anticipate that resistance to creative endeavors may take root in them.

Other barriers, however, are within the manager's realm of influence. These barriers are attributable to managerial style, which is itself often fostered by the hierarchical highly structured organization. Bradford and Cohen (1984) describe the "manager-as-conductor" style as one that regards the manager as "boss." Inherent in this style are several characteristics that create obstacles to creativity in employees, including authoritarianism (an inflexible, closed attitude) and "functional fixedness" (the attitude that there is only one way to do things). Alternatively, they describe the "manager-as-developer" style as one that empowers employees and helps them to do their jobs better. This style is conducive to innovation and creativity.

Table 8.1 is a checklist that may help you to assist your employees to become more creative. Review this checklist monthly, and assess yourself on each item. Ask yourself: (1) To what extent is change needed to help my unit be more creative? (2) To what extent is this within my control?

TABLE 8.1 Task Motivation Checklist for Managers

1. Do not overdirect, overobserve, or overreport.
2. Recognize differences in individuals. Have a keen appreciation of each person's unique characteristics.
3. Help subordinates see problems as challenges.
4. Ask your employees about ways in which they think they are most creative—or would like to be most creative—and what sort of creative contribution they would most like to make.
5. Allow more freedom for individuals to guide their own work.
6. Train yourself and others to respond to the positive parts of proposed ideas rather than react to the often easier-to-spot negative ones.
7. Develop greater tolerance for mistakes and errors.
8. Provide a safe atmosphere for failures.
9. Be a resource person rather than a controller, a facilitator rather than a boss.
10. Act as a buffer between employees and outside problems or higher-up demands.
11. Enhance your own creative ability through special workshops and seminars, specialized reading, and practice of creative exercises and games. This sets an excellent example employees will want to emulate and makes it easier for you to recognize and relate to the creative ability of others.
12. Make sure that innovative ideas are transmitted to your boss with your support and backing; then insist on a feedback mechanism. Without feedback, the flow of creative ideas dries up because innovators feel that their ideas are not given a fair hearing or taken seriously.

Adapted from Eugene Raudsepp, President, Princeton Creative Research, Inc. in R. L. Kuhn, *Handbook for Creative Managers.* New York: McGraw-Hill, 1987, pp. 173–182. Used with permission.

BRAINSTORMING AND THE NOMINAL GROUP TECHNIQUE

One of the most effective strategies for finding and encouraging employee creativity is **brainstorming.** Marshaling the skills, thinking, and knowledge of employees, brainstorming is a technique used for generating new ideas. In brainstorming sessions, group members are encouraged to contribute ideas, without regard for quality. Evaluation of ideas is withheld until all have been expressed. Nominal group technique (Delbecq, Van de Ven, and Gustafson, 1975) is a process that uses brainstorming to generate new ideas and then uses group discussion and systematic voting to choose from among the ideas generated by the group. It is often used when the problem has a large number of potential alternative solutions.

Assume that 10 professional employees who depend very heavily on secretarial and clerical support report to you. Two secretaries have just left for higher-paying jobs and one clerk will be out for several weeks for surgery. As time progresses, it is apparent that conflicts are about to develop over the need for support staff time. You have several options: you may devise a plan and issue memoranda to your employees regulating the use of the available secretarial and clerical resources (and hope they are pleased enough with your solution to happily go about their work in order to finish before the deadline); you may go to your boss for direction (risking, perhaps, the judgment that you cannot handle this yourself); or you can plan a nominal group technique session during which you will get ideas from your employees and, with them, arrive at a workable solution.

Before you hold a brainstorming session, you must first settle in your own mind that you genuinely want the ideas from your employees. Brainstorming sessions can be inadvertently sabotaged by well-meaning managers who have hidden agendas and use the session as a way to manipulate employees to accept an already formulated plan. You must resolve that all ideas should be heard; you must provide a safe environment for the free flow of ideas from employees. You have to be able to accept good ideas from employees and not feel that you have to be the one to generate all of the good ideas at work.

The following steps should be used for planning a nominal group technique session.

1. *Make sure that everyone agrees on the problem definition.* If there is not agreement on the problem definition, you may find that different members of the group are solving different problems.

2. *Have participants write down all their ideas.* Even ideas that do not seem feasible may give other people ideas. During this time no one should talk, except to ask questions about the problem definition. This step may take anywhere from 10 minutes to half an hour.

3. *Use a round-robin procedure to allow participants to share their ideas.* Have each participant give one idea at a time. Record the ideas on a flip chart so that all ideas are visible to all participants. Again, do not allow discussion as the ideas are being recorded.

4. *After all ideas are recorded, review each idea one at a time.* Allow participants to ask questions and share reactions regarding the feasibility and merits of the idea. Use your meeting management skills (discussed in Chapter 3, Competency 2) to ensure that you stay on track and that people are contributing appropriately.

5. *Have participants vote on their preferred alternative solution.* Generally, the voting should be secret, and a rank vote should be used. That is, have participants individually identify their top five ideas, and then assign a score of 5 to their first-ranked idea, 4 to their second-ranked idea, and so forth.

6. *Review the voting pattern.* If one alternative stands out as the obvious preferred choice, then you are ready to decide how to implement that choice. If not, choose the top five to 10 alternatives and return to step 4, this time rank-ordering only the top three choices.

THE IMPORTANCE OF CREATIVE THINKING IN ORGANIZATIONS

The use of creative thinking in problem solving allows organizations to access human resources that often go untapped. In comparing Japanese and American organizations, Deming (1986) has argued that "the greatest waste in America is failure to use the abilities of people." Managers should recognize that employees' abilities are a free resource.

Although most resources have extra cost factors involved, creative thinking does not. From this perspective, one could argue that no organization—public or private—can afford to waste this resource.

Beyond the overall organizational benefits, managers should recognize the personal benefits of encouraging creative thinking among their employees. Creative thinking can increase the effectiveness of the unit through better problem solving. In addition, creative thinking can be used as a motivational tool. In the work environment of large organizations, it is sometimes easy for employees to see themselves as a replaceable cog in the giant wheel and to become unmotivated. When individuals are encouraged to be creative in their thinking and problem solving, they are more likely to feel unique, valued, and affirmed as important employees of the organization. Thus, not only are there benefits from the employees' good ideas, but individuals feel better about themselves as employees. In sum, the encouragement of employees' creative thinking can result in substantial benefits to the organization, to the work unit, and to the individuals who exercise their creative skills.

ANALYSIS Creativity and Managerial Style

Objective   Creative problem-solving skills are not always tied only to your own thought processes. Often creativity involves knowing how to work with other people who are creative and using techniques that will maximize the probability that those people will generate creative solutions. Managers can either encourage or discourage employee creativity. This assessment is designed to examine how you have responded to different managerial styles in the past.

Directions   Reflect on the managers with whom you have worked. If you have not yet been employed, use this exercise to reflect on the skills of a parent, teacher, or anyone else who has evaluated your work. Choose one person for this exercise and analyze whether that person's style helped or hindered the tapping of your creativity. Check any of the following that applied to your situation:

_____ 1. Were you instructed to do things according to a set pattern?

_____ 2. Did this person seek your opinion regarding matters that affected you?

_____ 3. Did this person ever reconsider a decision in light of your input?

_____ 4. Did you have a tendency to fear that you may appear foolish to this person?

_____ 5. Did this person value your ideas and your thinking?

_____ 6. Did you ever feel that there was a better way to do something but did not bring it to the attention of this person?

_____ 7. Did you feel that it was important for this person to like you?

_____ 8. Did you feel that this person would like you more if you tended to agree with him or her?

_____ 9. Did you feel as if this person was always evaluating you?

Discussion Questions   1. How did you feel about yourself in that situation?

2. From your responses, identify specific behaviors that helped you feel affirmed as a valued person and those that did not.

3. How would you answer Question 2 focusing on two other persons: one with whom you had a very positive experience and one with whom you had a negative experience?

Reflection Our creativity in organizations can be encouraged or stifled by the people around us. Think about your own managerial style—does your behavior encourage creativity in others? There is little argument that providing too much structure and direction can inhibit creativity. It is also true, however, that too little structure can also be a problem. The three dimensions of creativity covered in the learning section (domain-relevant skills, creative-relevant skills, and task motivation) all work together to provide a strong foundation for creative thinking.

PRACTICE Creative-Relevant Skills

Objective The activities in this practice are intended to encourage you to move out of traditional ways of thinking.

Directions **Breaking Established Thinking Barriers**

1. *The paper clip.* To assist in thinking differently about objects and concepts, list on a separate piece of paper as many uses as you can think of for a paper clip.

2. *The restaurant.* A new restaurant is opening adjacent to your campus. It will feature vegetarian food. Think of as many possible names for this restaurant as you can.

Developing Mental Imagery

One of the ways to develop one's creativity is to practice mental imagery. The following exercises are designed to assist you in improving your imagination. Translate each of the following descriptions into a mental image. As you do, rate its clarity according to the following scale:

Scale | C = Clear | V = Vague | N = No image at all |

Can you visually imagine:

_____ 1. A familiar face

_____ 2. A rosebud

_____ 3. A body of water at sunset

_____ 4. The characteristic walk of a friend

_____ 5. A newspaper headline

The following descriptions are intended to evoke other modes of sensory imagery. Can you imagine:

_____ 1. A bird twittering

_____ 2. Children laughing at play

_____ 3. The prick of a pin

_____ 4. The taste of toothpaste

_____ 5. An itch

Don't be discouraged if you were not able to create clear images. This was a skill-developing exercise designed to fine-tune your mental imagery processes. Test yourself again in several months and note the improvement.

Using Analogies

Identify three pressing problems that you currently have at school or work. Describe each one briefly in writing. Then review the following list of analogies. Try to apply an analogy from this list, or from your own thinking, to each problem.

1. A snowball rolling downhill, gathering speed, and growing rapidly
2. Finding your way in the fog
3. Trying to start a car on a cold winter morning
4. Taking a bath
5. Frying potatoes
6. Sending a letter
7. Trying to untangle a ball of string
8. Cutting the grass with a pair of scissors
9. A child playing with a new toy
10. A fish out of water

Identify the feelings you have associated with each problem, and describe them with an analogy. The use of analogies should help you to see the problems differently. Describe the different perspectives that you now have on each problem. Use the perspectives to generate possible solutions to the problems.

Reflection   Some people initially respond somewhat negatively to the practice activities above. What is the point of thinking of new uses for paper clips, visualizing rosebuds, or comparing problems at work to untangling a ball of string? The point is practicing changing your perspective. Sometimes when you need a long piece of string you need to patiently untangle the entire ball. If you only need a short piece of string, however, you may find that you can simply cut the string to meet your objective. Perhaps your problem at work can be solved if you are willing to give up something that you initially thought was important but now realize is beyond what you actually need.

APPLICATION   New Approaches to the Same Old Problem

Objective   Now that you have had a chance to practice some creativity-relevant skills, you can apply them to a problem that you are currently facing.

Directions   Develop a plan to approach an old problem in a new way.

1. Start by writing a description of the problem.
2. Restate the problem in several ways.
3. Write down as many facts related to the problem as possible.
4. Identify advantages to this problem—try to see it as an opportunity.
5. Identify as many new ways as possible to approach this problem.
6. Identify people who might be able to help you with this problem.
7. Determine which action you will take first in arriving at a solution to this problem and write down on your calendar the date and time that you will take that action.

Reflection   Identifying something as a "problem" immediately sets up a series of assumptions that may inhibit our ability to be creative. Problems suggest something that is "bad" and needs to be "solved." By reframing problems as opportunities and considering any potential advantages that they may offer, it may be possible to come up with more creative ways of responding. As you go forward, try to remember to use your creative thinking skills when you face a situation that seems to require a problem-solving response. Practice exercising your mind by stretching for alternatives, rather than jumping to conclusions.

Competency 3   Managing Change

ASSESSMENT   Changes in My Organization

Objective   For this assessment you are asked to consider how changes are implemented in your organization. This will help you obtain insights into the differences between successful and unsuccessful approaches to managing change.

Directions   Think about two changes that have taken place in an organization with which you have been involved. The organization may be a work organization, a school-related organization, or a community group. On a separate piece of paper, carefully describe the following:

1. An implemented change which in your view was needed, was implemented, and was successful long after implementation.

2. An unsuccessfully implemented change.

3. From what you have observed, why was the first change implemented successfully but not the second one? If you can distinguish the content of the idea from the methods for implementation, identify the extent to which the success (or lack of success) of the proposed changes was due to content versus the implementation strategies.

4. Write down one change that you would like to make in that organization. If you received approval to make that change, what is the most important thing you would do in your efforts to implement that change? Why?

Reflection   Successfully managing change in organizations is difficult. Although much can be learned by studying how other organizations have managed change, observing successful and unsuccessful change initiatives in your own organization is also important because some roadblocks to change are specific to a particular organization culture.

LEARNING   Managing Change

Our society is currently experiencing change at an exponential rate. Each day, the potential exists for advancements in technology and knowledge that could change the way we live. In addition, national and global social, political, and economic changes affect both our personal and organizational lives.

Changes are necessary in order to accomplish goals and objectives, such as improving efficiency, improving cost effectiveness, competing for money and resources, advancing technologically, meeting government regulations, enhancing services to clients, and addressing public pressure. Although we make these changes to respond to societal changes, these are not necessarily unplanned or imposed changes. Rather, these are changes and adjustments we choose to make in order to fulfill the mission of the organization more effectively as it functions in a dynamic, changing world. In trying to make such changes, it is important to understand the concept of resistance.

UNDERSTANDING RESISTANCE TO PLANNED CHANGE

Resistance to change occurs frequently. Even changes that are necessary and desirable are resisted. For example, if everyone in your work unit enthusiastically agrees that there needs to be more communication with other work units, and you introduce a change that would increase this communication, you might still expect to encounter some resistance to that change simply because it involves changing the status quo.

In addition to resistance from people, you are also likely to meet resistance from the organization. The same barriers that hierarchical organizations present to creative thinking and innovation also operate as barriers to change. Organizational barriers include the power of existing organizational routines and organizational structure, resource limitations, an organizational cultural value that tradition is preferable to change, and so on.

Five types of organizationally related change are likely to provoke employee resistance. These changes cause resistance because employees perceive them as negatively affecting their expected job behaviors. As in the case of planned change, understanding these sources of resistance to change will better equip you to make appropriate changes and to implement them in such a way as to ensure their success.

1. *Changes that affect knowledge and skill requirements.* Employees will resist changes (such as automation) that make their skills seem outdated or unnecessary.

2. *Changes associated with economic or status loss.* Employees will resist changes that result in a demotion or loss of employment. The resisting employee does not have to be the person directly affected by the job changes. Resistance may also come from employees who perceive that the change may somehow negatively affect them. For example, when Kodak's CEO, Colby Chandler, cut 11,000 jobs in his first year, many of the remaining employees were demoralized, fearing that they would be the next to be fired.

3. *Changes suggested by others.* Sometimes good ideas are resisted because they are not our ideas. For example, when one employee is jealous of the success of another employee, or there is the perception that one employee's success diminishes the esteem the manager has for the other employees, or when there is intense competition within a work unit, employees are unlikely to accept others' ideas.

4. *Changes involving risks.* Risk taking sometimes results in mistakes. When an organization's culture does not value risk taking, individuals will not want to take the chance of making a mistake and therefore will probably be reluctant to suggest or embrace changes that involve risks.

5. *Changes that involve disruption of social relationships.* Although organizations have public missions and purposes, they also provide a social environment in which people associate and form friendships. For many people, their work organization is a primary source of social interaction. When these patterns of interaction are disrupted, people often resist.

Resistance to change reminds us that change must be carefully planned. Resistance often forces us to consider carefully the impact of the change so that ill-advised changes may be avoided.

DESIGNING CHANGE AND DESIGNING HOW TO CHANGE

Once the decision has been made that a change in the work processes, procedures, or structure should occur, the manager must focus on two issues: (1) the design of the change, and determining what change needs to occur, and (2) the process of implementing the change.

DESIGNING CHANGE

Designing change involves considering various alternative courses of action, anticipating consequences of such actions, and choosing which specific course of action is appropriate.

The design of the change is the first issue that faces the manager. The manager must ask whether a change is necessary and, if so, what specifically should be changed. Kurt Lewin (1951) proposed a model called **force field analysis.** This model is based on laws of physics: An object at rest will remain at rest unless the forces on the object to move are greater than the forces on it to remain stable. For example, when your car is parked in the driveway with the emergency brake on, it will remain there, in a stable condition, even if your neighbor's nine-year-old son decides to push on the car to move it. The emergency brake is a stronger stabilizing force than is the boy's force. If the car is put into the neutral gear with the emergency brake off, however, the forces for its stability are diminished, and it becomes more possible that the young boy could disrupt the equilibrium.

Similarly, there are forces within organizations that are pressures for change and forces that are resistances to change. When the forces for change are stronger than the resistant forces, change will occur; likewise, when the forces against change are stronger than the pressures for change, change will not occur.

Let's set up a force field analysis list to examine some of the pressures for organizational change, known as **driving forces,** and the pressures against organizational change, known as **resisting forces.**

Force Field Analysis of Change in Organizations

Pressures for Change (Driving Forces)	*Pressures against Change* (Resisting Forces)
Social change in society	Perceived threats to power
Economic change in society	Routine and structure
Improved efficiency	Resource limitations
Improved cost effectiveness	Preference for tradition
Competition for money and resources	Changes in skill requirements
Technological advances	Economic or status loss
Compliance with government regulations	Nonsupport of others' ideas

Pressures for Change	*Pressures against Change*
(Driving Forces)	*(Resisting Forces)*
Public pressure	Reluctance to take risks
Expansion	Disruption of social relationships
Improved effectiveness	
Administrative changes	
Availability of new products	

It is necessary to consider more than the length of the list; you must also look at the importance or relative force of the individual items. Some items may have more impact on a situation than others. To make the list more useful, you would need to assign weights or values to each item.

The following steps are necessary to set up a force field analysis:

1. List the driving forces and the resisting forces.
2. Examine each force and assess its strengths. Note the possible consequences of each force and its value. You may wish to assign a numerical value to each force.
3. Identify those forces over which you have some influence or control.
4. Analyze the list to determine how to implement the change. Your analysis will reveal several natural choices for action:

- Increase the strength of driving forces.
- Add new driving forces.
- Decrease the strength of resisting forces.
- Remove some of the resisting forces.
- Determine whether any of the resisting forces can be changed into driving forces.

Research has shown that the last three strategies, which involve diminishing the effect of resisting forces, are more effective than the first two strategies. Increasing the effect of the driving forces often serves only to increase the resistance.

Once you have worked through this process, you have a chart of the driving and resisting forces to the proposed change, the relative weight of each force, and an assessment of which forces you can influence. Identifying the items over which you have some influence should tell you where to direct your efforts and planning when implementing your changes.

IMPLEMENTING CHANGE

Implementing the change—designing how the change should occur—is just as critical for innovators as the process of designing what change should occur. Although a proposed change might objectively be the very best thing for the organization or for the work unit, careless implementation could potentially make the proposed change look foolish, resulting in the ultimate failure of the idea.

Unfortunately, the process of designing how to change is often given less attention than is necessary. Once we have determined that a proposed change is necessary, appropriate, and beneficial, we are inclined to see its value as so obvious that we expect others to endorse it and work for it with vigor and enthusiasm! Since we have worked so hard at the analysis, we often assume that the hard part is over. A poorly implemented change, however, will reflect on the credibility of the proposed change, and careless attention to implementation of even the best idea will, more often than not, result in failure. Assuming that a given change is seen as desirable and beneficial to the organization, implementing the change will require the same thoughtful effort and consideration as the design of the change.

Lockheed's ambitious attempt to transform itself from a manufacturer to an integrator, as described in the *Wall Street Journal* (Karp, 2006) provides a cautionary tale. Like many companies, Lockheed recognized that manufacturing margins were declining while profits for developing and integrating software were rising. The driving forces were strong enough to move the company to bid on and win a contract in 2004 for an army spy-plane with Lockheed as the lead integrator. Trouble, however, soon followed as problems with the weight of components to be included in the spy plane were found to exceed to capacity of the airframe selected. Lockheed's existing routines and structures played a part in undermining the project. Senior aeronautical engineers were largely excluded from the development team because they were not seen as being necessary for an electronic integration project (Karp, 2006).

FOUR APPROACHES FOR BRINGING CHANGE

In the first section of this chapter, we discussed conformity. We pointed out that over time groups and the people in them often tend to become disconnected from present reality. To be in touch with present reality is to be responsive to things as they are. Because present reality differs from past reality, it requires new behaviors that the actors in a normal group are not yet ready to embrace.

Present or emerging reality tends to threaten deeply held values and suggests the need for taking a risk by plunging into the unknown. At such times we may become self-deceptive because we want to avoid the risk of losing what we presently have. A key assumption of normal life is self-interested survival. In most group settings the leader and the members will put self first. That is only natural. Most theories of leadership and change make this assumption. Some do not.

avoid risk of losing what we have [handwritten margin note]

THE FIRST THREE APPROACHES

Here we will examine some theories that are used in day-to-day life. The first three approaches were identified some years ago by Chin & Benne (1976). Here, for simplicity, we have given them straightforward titles. The three strategies are Telling (making logical arguments for change), Forcing (using forms of leverage such as the threat of being fired or being ostracized), and Participating (using open dialogue and pursuing win-win strategies).

Telling.   The telling strategy assumes that people are guided by reason. If they decide it is in their best interest to change, they'll gladly do so. It is further reasoned that any resistance to change could only be the product of ignorance and superstition. To counter that resistance, the change agent just needs to educate the people to the truth and their resistance will dissolve.

The telling strategy is most effective for normal situations. Someone tells me my tire is going flat and that I need to get it changed. I can verify this by looking at the tire. I can make a clear cost-benefit assessment; I must have a good tire to drive my car. I am not emotionally tied to not getting the work done and I am quite certain that when it is done I can drive safely again. I know what to do and no learning is required. That is normal or "in-the-box" change. It is relatively easy. But what if someone were to tell me that I must change the way I drive because it is causing undue wear and tear on my car. It will be a good investment, I am told, and all I have to do is attend a weekend conference. Now I am out-of-the-box. I have no way of assessing immediately if that person is right or wrong. Besides, I would have to attend classes and learn a whole new way of driving. It does not sound like a good idea for me.

Telling is not as effective in out-of-the box contexts because it has a narrow, cognitive view of human systems. It fails to incorporate values, attitudes, and feelings. Thus, while people may understand why they should change, they are often not willing to make the painful changes inherent in more complex situations. They simply want and expect to get conformity.

Forcing. The forcing strategy persuades people to change or face some kind of punishment or sanction. This strategy often involves money and politics. Political power is exerted by applying sanctions when others fail to align themselves with the change agent. Economic power is exerted by controlling the flow of resources, either within an organization or in terms of salary increases to the person who is resisting change. When political power comes to bear, those with more power apply sanctions upon those with less power. Hence, the strategy is: Identify and apply levers of power, thus forcing the change target to comply.

The forcing strategy tends to work in the short term, but it usually evokes anger, resistance, and damage to the fundamental relationship. Thus, it is not likely to result in the kind of voluntary commitment that is necessary for healthy and enthusiastic change that will sustain the system.

The way for the normal person, acting as a change agent, to behave is to engage in the following two step process:

1. Tell the target why he or she needs to change.
2. If telling fails, figure out a way to force the person to change.

This two-step process is so normalized that most of us do it over and over again. Since we are seldom interested in changing ourselves, we repeat this process while refusing to recognize that in using force we damage the relationship and seldom obtain our desired long-term outcome. The fact that we seldom obtain our desired end seems to make no difference, however. We refuse to learn. For this reason, the reader might find hope in our third strategy.

Participating. The participating strategy involves a more collaborative change process. It is often associated with the facilitator role. (The interested reader might look back at Chapter 3.) Change targets are still guided by a rational calculus; however, this calculus extends beyond self-interest to incorporate the meanings, habits, norms, and institutional policies that contribute to the formation of human culture. The participative change agent welcomes the input of others as equals in the change process. Change does not come by simply providing information, as in the telling strategy. Rather, it requires the change agent to focus on clarifying and reconstructing values. In this model, the change agent attempts to bring to light all values, working through conflicts embedded in the larger collective. The emphasis is on communication and cooperation with the change target. The motto might be: Involve the change target in an honest dialogue, while mutually learning the way to win–win solutions. Yet this strategy is difficult to understand and implement. Consider the following illustration.

As an undergraduate, I took a rigorous course entirely devoted to learning a single skill. The skill was active listening, whereby the listener is not just passive as another person speaks but actively watches his or her own behavior so that he or she can accurately hear what the other person is trying to communicate. The supporting philosophy was the essence of the Participating strategy.

For the rest of my life, that course had provided me with a source of power for both myself and others. I have been able to use the Participating strategy to move through many seemingly impossible situations. Yet I know that not everyone left that course with the same abilities. During the last week of classes a student raised his hand and asked, "Professor, what if I do all these listening things, and the person still will not do what I want?" The deeply disappointed professor shrank behind his podium. After all we had been through, this student could not comprehend the most basic point of the Participating strategy; he could not comprehend the notion of reducing control enough to join with another human being in learning and mutual creation of a win–win solution. This notion remains a mystery to many people, even those who claim to be experts at active listening.

There is still another mystery associated with the participating strategy. Here we are reminded of a story told by Steven Covey. A disbelieving CEO told Covey, "Every time I try win–win, I lose." Covey replied, "Then you did not do win–win." The paradox is that this strategy calls for the reduction of control while remaining clear and strong about one's underlying values and intent. It is not a strategy of weakness, but of strength—the kind of strength that many people lack. Participatory strategies and active listening both require that each person allow others to express their truth while insisting that his or her own truth be heard.

Because participating strategies and active listening are so difficult to understand and implement, they are seldom used as they are intended, but are used instead to manipulate. The change agent determines a solution and then asks a group to join in a discussion. Any answer they come up with is acceptable, as long as it is the "right" one. Because so many people experience the participating strategy as a manipulative technique, they become deeply cynical. The participating strategy thus becomes a politically correct rhetoric, but everyone is quite certain it will not work. We thus get back only what we put out: distrust of the system and what passes for "proof" that the participating strategy does not work. This is most unfortunate because it prevents us from benefiting from a strategy that is indeed most powerful.

A FOURTH STRATEGY

In a recent book, Quinn (2000) has suggested a fourth strategy that complements the above three. It is called the transforming strategy, and it is a part of something he calls Advanced Change Theory, a set of action principles for effectively introducing change.

It is rooted in the teachings of such people as Jesus, Thoreau, Gandhi, and Martin Luther King Jr. It returns us to the notion of fundamental decisions and striving to increase integrity, as discussed in the first section of this chapter.

One of the formative voices of the nineteenth century was that of Henry David Thoreau, a friend of Ralph Waldo Emerson's. Both men were concerned about transcending the pressures for conformity in an industrialized society. Thoreau was born in 1817 and entered Harvard at 16 years of age. After his graduation, he briefly taught school, but after some time he gave up teaching and other professional pursuits. Eventually, he built a simple cabin and lived alone on Walden Pond. His writing about this experiment in solitude would later become renown. In his essay, *Civil Disobedience,* he wrote:

> *Action from principle, the perception and the performance of right, changes things and relations; it is essentially revolutionary, and does not consist wholly with any thing which was. It not only divides states and churches, it divides families; aye, it divides the individual, separating the diabolical in him from the divine.*

Reflecting on this statement, Quinn (2000) suggests that altering our behavior to reflect what we really value is revolutionary because principle-driven actions tend to be outside the normal boundaries of exchange and transaction. When someone engages in a new behavior based on principle, it challenges the norms. The person with a moral purpose is usually willing to endure punishment in order to pursue the purpose. Such principled behavior sends the dreaded signal that perhaps "the emperor has no clothes." It questions whether the present system is moving toward stagnation and decay or toward new levels of life and complexity and productivity. People in the system split into camps, one embracing the new behavior and the other condemning it—hence, the division of humanity into states, churches, and families.

Yet Thoreau's statement suggests that even the individual is split. In the face of principled behavior, the individual observer is constantly required to chose between preservation of the current self and the creation of the new self. When we discipline the self in the pursuit of higher purpose, a new self emerges. This process is exhilarating because it makes us aware of the profound power we each hold within us. On the other hand, when we know that we should be walking a higher road and we do not, we acknowledge the diabolical that also lurks within. We become divided. We lose psychic energy. We become flat, dull, and without enthusiasm, easy prey for those who would dominate or manipulate us. We become like the elephants discussed in the first section of this chapter.

Thoreau's statement about principle suggests that moral power plays a major role in the transformational process. All change theories are rooted in assumptions of morality, but the assumptions differ greatly. Before we take any action, we ask ourselves: What is the right thing to do in this situation? The name for this process is "moral reasoning." There are different levels of moral reasoning. The moral reasoning we see most frequently is based on the assumption that people are externally driven and self-interested. Quinn argues that the transformational strategy only works when we become internally driven and focused on others. It is thus at a higher level of moral reasoning. It is based in principle, not in situational pressures.

So most of the time most of us witness and enact change strategies that reflect and support the norms and expectations of the group. We are driven by the external conditions in which we find ourselves. Very few theories include the role of internalized principles; few theories suggest the need for a transformational change agent who is willing to sacrifice self in the pursuit of the collective good.

In order to observe transformational ability, we cannot observe normal people doing normal things. We must observe people who are outside the box. In order to develop transformational capability, we cannot be normal people doing normal things. We must stand outside the box. To do that we need to go inside ourselves and ask who we are, what we stand for, and what impact we really want to have. Within ourselves we find principle, purpose, and courage. There we find the capacity not only to withstand the pressures of the external system but to actually transform the external system. We change the world by changing ourselves.

Table 8.2 presents a set of questions that a person who wants to bring about change might ask of him- or herself. Each set of questions is reflective of one of the above four approaches to change.

TABLE 8.2 Four Strategies for Changing Human Systems and the Questions Change Agents Should Ask Themselves

Level 1: The Telling Strategy
Method: Telling others to change
Objective: Align change target with established facts
    Am I within my expertise?
    Have I gathered all the facts?
    Have I done a rigorous analysis?
    Will my conclusions withstand criticism?
    Are my arguments logical?
    Do I have a forum for instruction?
    Do the people understand my argument?

Level 2: The Forcing Strategy
Method: Leveraging others to change
Objective: Align the change target with established authority
    Is my authority firmly established?
    Is the legitimacy of my directives clear?
    Am I capable and willing to impose sanctions?
    Is there a clear performance–reward linkage?
    Am I controlling the information flow?
    Am I controlling the design of the context?
    Are the people complying?

Level 3: The Participative Strategy
Method: Engaging others in conceptualizing change
Objective: Alignment of the actors in a win–win dialogue
    Is there a focus on human process?
    Is everyone included in an open dialogue?
    Do I model supportive communication?
    Is everyone's position being clarified?
    Are the decisions being made participatively?
    Is there commitment to a "win–win" strategy?
    Are the people cohesive?

Level 4: The Transformational Strategy
Method: Modeling change for others
Objective: Alignment with changing reality

> Am I aware of the realities of the emergent system?
> What are my patterns of self-deception?
> Are my values and behaviors aligned?
> Am I freed from external sanctions?
> Do I have a vision of the common good?
> Do I operate at the edge of chaos?
> Do I maintain reverence for others?
> Do I inspire others to enact their best self?
> Am I engaging in unconventional or paradoxical ways?
> Have I changed myself as a model for the system to change?

Adapted from Robert Quinn, *Change the World: How Ordinary People Can Accomplish Extraordinary Results.* San Francisco: Jossey-Bass, 2000. Used with permission.

ANALYSIS   Reorganizing the Legal Division

Objective   This exercise asks you to analyze a change process in a series of steps. It is important to take time to respond to the questions as you read through the scenario, as each set has a different purpose. For example, the first set of questions gives you an opportunity to practice some of your creative-thinking skills.

Directions   Read the following case study and answer the questions that follow each section.

The Relocation and Reorganization Begins   As part of a new relocation and reorganization plan for the legal division of a large corporation, the director, Paul Lindford, decided to set up a central paralegal pool. This pool would handle all of the research reports for the entire office, which consisted of 20 attorneys. In the old location, the paralegals had been located in offices adjoining those occupied by the attorneys for whom they worked. Several paralegals even had their own small private offices.

The nature of the firm was such that many of the attorneys traveled a considerable amount and consequently were away from their offices for extended periods. During these absences the paralegal assistants had little to do.

Stop Reading   Respond to the following questions.

1. Based on the limited information, what advantages of the change approved by Paul Lindford can you identify?

2. What might be the response of the paralegal assistants to this change?

3. What might be the response of the attorneys to this change?

4. If you were Paul, what problems would you anticipate at this point?

The Case Continues   For some time, Paul had felt that establishing a central paralegal pool would result in a saving of personnel as well as more efficient use of the paralegal staff. Paul had been reluctant to make this change in the old location, where the attorneys and paralegal assistants were accustomed to working in adjoining offices. But now, with the new office, he felt the time was right to try out the new arrangement.

Two weeks before the move, Paul asked Ashley Ricci to coordinate the move for the paralegal assistants, even though she was not the most senior paralegal. There were two others of higher rank, with more experience than Ashley, but Paul felt good about his choice. Ashley had a lot of energy and was well liked by her coworkers. She seemed to best fulfill the requirements for the job as he saw it. She had worked on some special projects for Paul in the past, and she had been exceptional. At this point, Paul had not really given any thought to who would be directing the paralegal assistants when the move was complete.

Stop Reading   Respond to the following questions.

1. Paul has chosen to implement this change when the general office moves into a new location. Why does he see this timing as advantageous? Do you agree?

2. If you were Paul, would you have chosen Ashley to coordinate the move? Why or why not?

3. What mistakes do you believe Paul has made so far in the implementation process?

The Case Continues   Paul announced his plans for the new central paralegal pool one week before the move. It was received with little enthusiasm. Several assistants objected and threatened to leave rather than accept the change. Some insisted they could not work for more than one person; others complained they would be unable to work in a small cubicle office in a large room. Many of the attorneys affected by the new policy were resentful as well. They believed that a personal paralegal assistant was essential for efficient conduct of their business.

Although Paul knew this change was unpopular, he believed the feelings of the attorneys would change as the benefits of the more efficient service became apparent. Although many of the attorneys probably felt the loss of a personal paralegal assistant as something in the nature of a "demotion," Paul felt they should understand and help make the new plan work. He felt that the few diehards should not be pampered.

During the first few weeks after the move, Ashley did everything she could to maintain the workload at a high level and hoped that, as a result, the complaints from the attorneys would decrease. Their complaints centered around (1) errors made by paralegal assistants who were unfamiliar with the attorneys' caseloads, (2) the slowness of the paralegal staff in bringing back final drafts of the reports that had been assigned to them, and (3) the excessive time they themselves had to spend in minor research efforts that had previously been handled by their personal paralegal assistants.

Stop Reading   Respond to the following questions.

1. What are the specific sources of resistance from the paralegal assistants and the attorneys? Do you see these resisting forces as unreasonable or legitimate?

2. Do you think that Paul is correct in his prediction that the complaints will decrease after the change has been in operation for a while and its benefits are noted? Why or why not?

3. What type of change strategy is Paul using? How well is it working? What should Paul do at this time?

The Case Continues   Ashley also listened to complaints from the paralegals. They felt very strongly that (1) the work they were getting was neither challenging nor generally very interesting; (2) they were not able to consistently work on a particular caseload, and, therefore, the quality of their work was decreasing; and (3) they were tired of taking abuse for the changes they themselves had not instituted.

After the new system had been in operation for six months, Ashley suggested to Paul that perhaps some of these complaints might be eliminated if each attorney were allowed to have priority claim on the time of one paralegal assistant. This arrangement would allow the paralegal to become familiar with the particular work of one attorney, including the issues and current caseload of that attorney.

The paralegal could then be asked to work elsewhere when not busy with the work of the attorney. Paul, however, felt that such a move would defeat the very purpose for which the central paralegal pool had been established.

Stop Reading   Respond to the following questions.

    1. What are Paul's sources of resistance? Are they legitimate?

    2. If you were Paul, what would you do at this point? Why?

The Case Continues   After much prodding by Ashley, Paul finally agreed that something had to be done to make things run more smoothly. Paul admitted that he shared some of her doubts about the success of the new arrangement and wondered whether perhaps the change had not been managed well. More important, he wondered whether something could be done to regain the full support and cooperation of the attorneys and paralegals. He even considered returning the office to its old method of operation, allowing each attorney to work solely with one paralegal assistant.

Discussion Questions   1. What do you think Paul may have learned about this experience regarding implementation of change?

    2. Do you think the change was well designed? Why or why not?

    3. What strategies could Paul have used in the beginning to help him sort out the aspects of the proposed change and to help him plan?

    4. If you were a consultant and Paul commissioned your professional expertise, what advice would you give him about what he should do now and how to do it?

Reflection   Although this case has focused on resistance to change, using some of the competencies that we have discussed in other roles can be useful for understanding and overcoming resistance to change. For example, what impact would acting as a facilitator and using participative decision making (Chapter 3, Competency 2) have had in this situation? Once complaints began, how could Paul have benefited from the suggestions for communicating effectively in the mentor role (Chapter 2, Competency 2)? How might understanding of the concepts of designing work (Chapter 5, Competency 2 in the coordinator role) have helped avoid some of the problems that Paul encountered? In fact, each of the eight roles in the competing values framework is important for Paul, or for anyone interested in planning and implementing change in an organization.

PRACTICE   Force Field Analysis

Objective   Now that you have had a chance to analyze a change situation, practice using the force field analysis technique to estimate the driving and resisting forces in that case and to identify some ways to increase the driving forces or reduce the resisting forces. Recall when developing your plan of action that increasing driving forces is typically less effective than reducing resisting forces.

Directions   Examine the Analysis case study and pretend that you are Paul. Do a force field analysis, listing the driving forces and the resisting forces of the case. Assign the value of each force a number from 1 (least forceful) to 10 (most forceful). Also, identify your level of influence over those forces using the following scale:

Scale

IS = able to influence strongly	IM = able to influence moderately	NI = unable to influence

Discussion Questions   1. What forces for change did you identify? What are the forces against change?

2. Which are the strongest forces over which you have the most control?

3. How could each force be altered?

4. Which actions are most feasible?

5. What should be the plan of action?

Reflection   Performing a force field analysis can be a valuable way to identify potential unintended consequences of an action because it requires that you look at the proposed change from the perspective of all of the impacted parties. This type of creative thinking exercise, sometimes referred to as "perspective taking," may also help you identify innovative approaches that had not previously occurred to you.

APPLICATION   Planning a Change

Objective   Hindsight, it is said, is always 20/20. This exercise asks you to plan a change of your own, without the benefit of hindsight.

Directions   In the assessment activity at the beginning of this competency you were asked to write down one change that you would make in an organization in which you have been involved.

1. Do a force field analysis for this situation, listing the driving and resisting forces. Estimate the strength of the driving and resisting forces, as well as your level of influence over those forces.

2. On a separate sheet of paper, write today's date. Then describe the change you wish to make. Determine when you would like to begin implementing the change. The format should be as follows:

> *Today, write:*   Today's date
> Description of a change you wish to make
> Implementation target date
> Design of the change
> Strategies for implementing the change

Discussion Questions   1. How did you feel once you identified the change and the implementation date? Many people feel vaguely dissatisfied with themselves when they want to change something and often think the dissatisfaction will remain until the change is completed. However, as you probably experienced in this activity, when we take action toward change, the dissatisfaction with ourselves often diminishes, and we are thereby encouraged to continue our plans.

2. What difference did you note in writing down your proposed change, with its accompanying dates, rather than merely having these ideas in your head? Writing down the proposed change is a clarifying effort, and by so doing you tend to increase your belief that it will happen.

Reflection   As you were writing up your change plan, did you think about this in terms of setting goals and objectives (Chapter 6, Competency 2)? If not, go back and review your plan to see if it can be improved by including "SMART" objectives.

REFERENCES

Bradford, David L., and Allan R. Cohen. *Managing for Excellence.* New York: John Wiley & Sons, 1984.

Chatterjee, Debashis. *Leading Consciously.* Boston: Butterworth-Heinemann, 1998.

Chin, Robert, and Kenneth D. Benne. "General Strategies for Effecting Changes in Human Systems," in Warren G. Bennis, Kenneth D. Benne, Robert Chin, and Kenneth E. Corey (eds.), *The Planning of Change,* 3d ed. New York: Holt, Rinehart & Winston, 1976.

de Bono, Edward. *Lateral Thinking: Creativity Step-by-Step.* New York: Harper & Row, 1970.

Delbecq, Andre L., Andrew H. Van de Ven, and David H. Gustafson. *Group Techniques for Program Planning.* Glenview, IL: Scott, Foresman, 1975.

Deming, W. Edwards. *Out of the Crisis.* Boston: Massachusetts Institute of Technology Center for Advanced Engineering Study, 1986.

Fritz, Robert. *The Path of Least Resistance: Learning to Become the Creative Force in Your Own Life.* New York: Fawcett Columbine, 1989.

Graham, G. *Change Is an Inside Job.* Seattle: Gordon Graham & Company, 1998.

Jaworski, Joesph. *Synchronicity: The Inner Path to Leadership.* San Francisco: Berrett-Koehler, 1996.

Karp, J. "Airborne Incident: As It Adapts to Information Age, Lockheed Fumbles Key Project." *Wall Street Journal* (January 26, 2006): A1.

Kiel, John M. *The Creative Mystique: How to Manage It, Nurture It, and Make It Pay.* New York: John Wiley & Sons, 1985.

Kimberly, John R., and Robert E. Quinn. *Managing Organizational Transitions.* Homewood, IL: Richard D. Irwin, 1984.

Koestler, Arthur. *The Act of Creation.* New York: Macmillan, 1964.

Kuhn, Robert Lawrence (ed. in chief). *Handbook for Creative Managers.* New York: McGraw-Hill, 1987.

Lewin, Kurt. *Field Theory in Social Science.* New York: Harper & Row, 1951.

McKim, Robert H. *Experiences in Visual Thinking.* Monterey, CA: Brooks/Cole, 1972.

Miller, William C. *The Creative Edge: Fostering Innovation Where You Work.* Reading, MA: Addison-Wesley, 1987.

Nierenberg, Gerald I. *The Art of Creative Thinking.* New York: Cornerstone Library, 1982.

Pascale, Richard T., and Anthony G. Athos. *The Art of Japanese Management.* New York: Simon & Schuster, 1981.

Peters, Tom. *Thriving on Chaos.* New York: Harper & Row, 1987.

Quinn, Robert. *Change the World: How Ordinary People Can Accomplish Extraordinary Results.* San Francisco: Jossey-Bass, 2000.

Rawlinson, J. Geoffrey. *Creative Thinking and Brainstorming.* New York: John Wiley & Sons, 1981.

Russo, F. "The Hidden Secrets of the Creative Mind." *Time* 167(3) (January 16, 2006): 89–90.

Sawyer, R.K. *Explaining Creativity: The Science of Human Innovation.* Oxford: Oxford University Press, 2006.

Thoreau, Henry David. *Civil Disobedience and Other Essays.* New York: Dover Publications, 1993.

Walton, A. Elise. "Transformative Culture: Shaping the Informal Organization," in David A. Nadler, Robert B. Shaw, A. Elise Walton, and Associates (eds.), *Discontinuous Change.* San Francisco: Jossey-Bass, 1995.

Whetten, David A., and Kim S. Cameron. *Developing Management Skills.* Glenview, IL: Scott, Foresman, 1983.

Youngblood, Mark D. *Life at the Edge of Chaos: Creating the Quantum Organization.* Flower Mound, TX: Perceval Publishing, 1997.

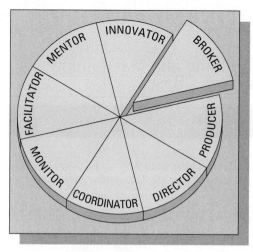

THE
BROKER ROLE

■ COMPETENCIES

Building and Maintaining a Power Base

Negotiating Agreement and Commitment

Presenting Ideas

The competing values framework helps us see that leadership at any level is a social activity as well as a technical one. It is a job that requires the human relations competencies of the coach and mentor as well as the analytic and take-charge competencies of the monitor and director. With its focus on social skills, this chapter discusses the broker role. With the innovator, the broker occupies the upper-right quadrant of the competing values framework. While the innovator envisions change and a better way of doing things, the broker presents and negotiates those ideas effectively. In organizations, good ideas work only if people can see a benefit to adopting them. Consistent with the Create action-imperative of the open systems quadrant, the broker creates relationships and agreements that result in moving the organization forward.

This chapter focuses on the broker role and the core competencies associated with it.

Competency 1   Building and Maintaining a Power Base
Competency 2   Negotiating Agreement and Commitment
Competency 3   Presenting Ideas

Competency 1

Building and Maintaining
a Power Base

Objective   One of the best ways to understand the concept of building and maintaining a power base is by thinking about the people who have greatly influenced your life. This exercise gives you the opportunity to assess your personal beliefs and expectations about power and influence.

Directions   1. Select someone who has greatly influenced your life. Who was this person? How did she or he influence you? What did she or he specifically do and how did it affect you? Did this person have formal authority over you? Write down five to 10 things that this person did to influence you.

2. Now consider your own personal power base. Who is within your circle of influence? Why are you able to influence them? What have you done recently to increase your ability to influence others? Have you done anything recently to add people to your circle of influence? Why or why not?

3. Finally, think about how your attempts to influence people compare with how you were influenced by the person you selected in the first part of this exercise. Are the tactics that you use to influence people similar or different? Can you think of ways to improve your ability to influence others by adopting some of the tactics that helped influence your life?

Reflection   Sometimes the people who influence us the most are not those with formal authority over us. In fact we may be greatly influenced by people whom we have never met. Perhaps we heard them speak at a conference or read a book that they wrote. We may not think of these examples of influence as being related to power, but in fact, they are—the power of ideas, the power of effective communication skills, and the power to attract an audience.

POWER: WHY ARE WE AMBIVALENT?

Our perceptions of power are very revealing. They tell us as much about ourselves as they do about power. How do you feel about the role power plays in the organizations you have observed? When you think of power, what people, experiences, and memories are called to mind?

All of us have power, and all of us are influenced by others who have it. Some of our most painful memories revolve around someone else's misuse of the power and influence they held over us. As teenagers, the authority of our parents may have collided with our need for freedom. As employees, we have all seen supervisors with authority but little ability to motivate followers. To handle power is to make mistakes, often at the expense of others. But to be powerless is to be frustrated and defensive. Thus, most of us have mixed feelings about power.

In an organizational setting, the term "power" is most often defined as essentially "the ability to produce; the capacity to mobilize people and resources to get things done" (Kanter, 1983, p. 213). People often say power is a "necessary evil" in organizations. That statement assumes that power, in all its manifestations, is evil in itself. Power in organizational life is inescapable, but is it inherently bad? Organizations exist in order to get things done. Power clusters around the most important things an organization has to do and around the people who have the greatest access to the resources required to do those things.

Working for an overbearing leader may be frustrating, but working for a weak leader can also be a liability. Leaders with little influence cannot represent the needs of their people, promote their ideas, or acquire the resources they need to do their jobs (Handy, 1993, pp. 123–127). Box 9.1 highlights some misconceptions about power.

USING POWER AT THREE LEVELS

There are three levels from which to study power:

- The macro or organizational level
- The group or team level
- The individual or personal level

On the organizational level, power can be viewed as the ability to influence the flow of available energy and resources toward certain goals. This kind of power shows up in activities such as legislating policies and laws, setting rules and procedures, bestowing rewards and punishments, and making goals and plans. On the group or

BOX 9.1 MISCONCEPTIONS ABOUT POWER

1. *I am the manager. I can do what I want.* Authority and power are not the same thing. People do not do what you want simply because of the position you hold. It takes more than position to effectively influence people. When are you going to do a better job on a project? When your manager forces you to work overtime to finish ASAP, or when you feel personally committed to a project out of respect for the manager?

2. *Power is something people in higher positions exercise upon people in lower positions.* Managers exercise power and influence on subordinates, but subordinates also exercise power and influence on managers. Power is something that exists when people are dependent on each other.

    Some people have more power in organizations than others, but no one is completely powerless. Think, for example, of how an organization depends upon the discretionary effort of each employee. The discretionary effort is the difference between the level of effort required to hold down a particular job and the maximum level of effort the person is capable of putting out. In many jobs, the range of discretionary effort is immense. In most cases, people cannot be forced to exert this extra effort. They only choose to do so.

3. *Supervisors and middle managers are powerless.* This statement is partially true. Some are powerless. However, supervisors and managers are never powerless unless they choose to be. Often supervisors and middle managers claim to be powerless as a way to reduce responsibility. Because the organization is dependent on supervisors and managers, they do, in fact, have latent power.

team level, power can be seen as the ability to influence your peers through the strength of expertise and experience, and the ability to build coalitions of those who share your views and goals. On the personal level, power can be seen as person A's capacity to influence person B's behavior so that B does something he or she would not do otherwise. This focus on power and influence stresses interpersonal relationships and the resources we bring to bear in those relationships. In this chapter we will deal primarily with power and influence at the individual level, because it's the level we can influence the most.

GOOD POWER, BAD POWER, AND NO POWER

The moral or immoral use of power is the product of motives, decisions, and thinking—not the fault of power itself. Power is necessary in using resources to meet goals and to get things done. Not using power when you need to can be as bad as abusing it.

When we commit ourselves to a cause or a project, we want strong, solid people in our corner. We don't want to entrust the things we cherish to weak and passive leaders. Managers who have no power base are not doing their jobs. Part of their job is to effectively and appropriately build a base of legitimacy, information, and influence from which to serve the needs of their unit and their organization (Cohen and Bradford, 1990).

FOUR SOURCES OF BROKER POWER

Where does power come from? First, and perhaps most obvious, **position power**, which is attached to formal roles and authority in an organization. If you are director of finance for a large firm or a state supreme court judge, you have considerable power by virtue of that position. Position power typically has three elements. The first, and often weakest element, is **legitimate authority**—the position gives the holder the right to direct the activities of subordinates. In addition to legitimate authority, position power often includes an ability to reward employees (**reward power**) or penalize them (**coercive power**). Related to a formal role, which may carry considerable authority, is the fact that some situations create opportunities for having influence. This source of power relates to being in the right place at the right time. We have seen many people of equal ability and motivation who have not been equally successful, because some were in work units or organizations that offered more opportunity and challenge than others. Where you are is sometimes as important as who you are. Of course, not all people in similar positions, or confronted with similar opportunities, do equally well. The differences can be explained by the other power sources listed below.

Personal power, sometimes referred to as referent power, comes from the shape and impact your presentation of self has on others—the personal characteristics that people find attractive or influential or persuasive. These resources include attributes such as eloquence, physical stature and appearance, dynamism and spontaneity, intelligence, wit, and the ability to empathize with others. Your personal power is also rooted in the overall impressions you generate in other people—impressions of being trustworthy, reasonable, modest, or courageous.

Too often people think the fastest way to increase their personal power is to be more aggressive. In many ways, increasing your level of aggressiveness will allow for some short-term gains. However, people who are too aggressive often find that others will begin to avoid them. Humility and kindness will increase your long-term personal power.

Your effectiveness as a broker will hinge on your level of trustworthiness and your ability to trust others. There are two essential elements of trust. The first element of trust is your competency—that you can do what you said you'd do. The second element of trust is your commitment—that you will actually do what you said you'd do. The absence of trust complicates the brokering process.

Expert power is based on the expertise that you may have in a special field or knowledge area. Notice that expert power is not the same as the personal resource of intelligence. It is tied to valuable, specialized skills or abilities. Increasingly, expert power is playing a greater role in determining the influence people have in their organizations. For example, a young computer programmer who is proficient in writing code for a new software application may have as much power as the CEO or owner of that firm. When the United States suddenly has vital interests at stake in a certain region of the globe, people who speak the languages of that region and understand its history and culture have more power and influence than they had before.

Network power is a kind of influence also known as "social capital." Social capital is gained through the information and influence you can access through the people who know and trust you—and through all the people those people know. This grand total of all the knowledge and influence wielded by the people you know who are willing to make their knowledge and influence available to you is your social network. This last source of power and influence is becoming increasingly vital. The primary reason is complexity. Because the contemporary world is so complex, we need to be embedded in a vast web of people who know things we don't know and who know people we don't know.

Finally, one needs to go **beyond the myth of individualism.** Wayne Baker, an expert on the influence of social capital on individual and organizational productivity, says that many people cling to the belief that "everyone succeeds or fails on the basis of individual efforts and abilities" (Baker, 2000, p. 2). The problem with that belief, says Baker, is that it grossly undervalues the role social capital plays in our work and personal lives. Though individualism is a trait we cherish, particularly in American society, Baker insists that professional success and even personal fulfillment depend on our relationships with others as much as they depend on our own ability and motivation. The web of relationships and contacts that we weave throughout our lives is a huge factor in determining our effectiveness.

In this description by Ford Harding, an international expert on sales training, we see a person who understood instinctively how to build a network. It was a natural process for him because he saw himself as a helpful broker, a person who could match one person's needs with those of another.

Osgar Megerdichian grew up in the rough and tumble moving industry in New York City and never went to college. Combining social skill with business acumen, he built a consulting firm specializing in move management. A self-educated, intelligent man, he liked people. He liked talking and was always on the phone. He honestly cared about his business friends and tried to help them whenever he could. He knew thousands of people. I once introduced him to a client. As we toured the building we met five different people. During five-minute conversations, he identified mutual friends with each. "What a small world" he would say each time with a quizzical smile. When this happened a month later at another company, I knew I was dealing with something special.

Once you met Osgar, he didn't forget you. He would call periodically to see how you were doing. Better still, he often offered useful pieces of information. His real help came from introductions. He was always introducing people who could help each other. He introduced me to several people who later gave me large consulting assignments. His calls, needless to say, were always welcome, though they did sometimes make me a little uncomfortable that I had not done enough for this nice man who was working so hard for my benefit. I sought ways to return his help in kind.

By the time Osgar died, he had built a substantial firm. More importantly, his life had been warmed by many friendships, and those of us who knew him reflect on him often with affection. (Harding, 1994, p. 43)

When we think of networking, we often think of social activities and gestures engaged in for self-serving reasons—and we assume that these activities are contrived and "phony." We hear about networking in the context of trying to get a job through friends, or doing lunch to get someone's attention, or asking for leads on new business. These are important activities, but, in a larger sense, effective networking is a process of helping other people who, over the long term, can also be a resource to us.

Take, for example, the process of looking for a job. The classic study on the role networks play in the job search was done by Mark Granovetter (1973) in the 1970s. His study confirmed what most people already knew from their own experience: Most people get jobs through personal contacts, not through formal channels. Often job opportunities come through what Granovetter called "weak ties," which is a connection to a person the job seeker didn't know but who was known by a friend or acquaintance of the job seeker. But Granovetter also learned that social networks are also the key channel used by employers. Most employers find people by mining their networks of personal contacts. Many companies today have made it a practice to ask their employees to refer people they know to the company.

Networking is a vital skill not only because it helps you succeed professionally but also because it makes you a more effective resource in your personal life. Networking is a crucial subskill of brokering. Brokering includes the ability to persuade people that your ideas, projects, values, and assumptions are valid and urgent. But the information and talent necessary to put your ideas into motion are usually delivered by good networking. A good broker knows where to go for answers and whose support is necessary to carry the day. If you have a mission in life, you'll need help fulfilling it. Box 9.2 describes some core networking activities to get you started.

Daniel Goleman, a best-selling author on the importance of influence skills in the workplace has this to say about networking:

This talent for connecting [networking] epitomizes stars in almost every kind of job. For instance, studies of outstanding performers in fields like engineering, computer science, biotechnology, and other "knowledge work" fields find the building and maintenance of networks crucial for success. Even in fields like technology, the networks are linked the old-fashioned way, face-to-face and by phone, as well as through e-mail.

But what cements a connection is not physical proximity (though it helps) so much as psychological proximity. The people we get along with, trust, and feel simpatico with, are the strongest links in our networks. . . . People who work a network well have an immense time advantage over those who have to use broader, more general sources of information to find answers. One estimate indicates that for every hour a star puts into seeking answers through a network, an average person spends three to five hours gathering the same information. (Goleman 2000, pp. 206–207)

BOX 9.2 CORE NETWORKING ACTIVITIES

Networking usually involves these core activities (adapted from Harding, 1994, pp. 45–47):

- *Sharing information.* This is the information age. We can share ideas, tips, names of helpful experts, Web sites, suggestions on places to look for something. The list is infinite. Brokers spend most of their time brokering information.

- *Introductions, referrals, and references.* Brokers put one person in contact with another person. Good brokers are great matchmakers: They match the needs of one person with the needs and abilities of another. If you can't actually introduce one person to another, you can at least "refer" one to another, allowing the person who has the need to use your name in making the contact.

- *Ideas and advice.* When people call you frequently for advice or just a listening ear, you know you're well on your way to having a large network. What if most of the information seems to flow *from* you rather than *toward* you? That's not necessarily a problem, but you may want to consider enriching your network with some people who are knowledgeable in areas where you are not. Typically, we tend to associate with people with whom we have a lot in common. This practice, however, can constrict your "knowledge network" too tightly.

Here are some questions to consider as you think about your own brokering and networking skills.

- Are you making an effort to get to know instructors in your classes as well as people you interact with at work? What are you doing to increase your network power? Are these people aware of your interests and abilities? Would you feel comfortable asking some of them to write letters of recommendation for you?

- Think about the network you are building from the perspective of being a current or future job applicant. Is your network broad enough? Do the people you know seem to know the same group of people, or do some of your contacts link into other networks that can provide information and resources you may need?

Networking is not just playing political games. It can make a dramatic difference in your ability to contribute to the organizations you work for. At the executive level, people are often hired because of the strength of their networks. Of two candidates with comparable talent, experience, and ability, the one with the most powerful information and influence network will probably be offered the position.

INFLUENCE STRATEGIES AND TACTICS

The master broker knows that effective influence requires a broad base of approaches and strategies. Too many leaders are assertive or insistent when they need to be open and flexible. Others are passive and deferential when they need to be confrontational and firm.

Traditional research on power and influence has identified a number of different tactics that can be used to influence others. Different tactics may be appropriate in different situations, depending on the circumstances. Many common influence tactics depend on the elements of position power (legitimacy, reward, and coercive power). For example,

- ***Legitimate Authority***—giving directives with the expectation that they will be carried out

- ***Upward Appeal***—giving directions and indicating that they are what higher management wants done

[handwritten: position power]

Position power {

- *Co-optation*—inviting a recalcitrant individual into a group to attempt to change their perspective (e.g., giving a union agitator a seat on the board of directors)
- *Bargaining/Exchange*—offering a reward or incentive for following a directive
- *Pressure/Coercion*—threatening a punitive action if the directive is not followed

Other influence tactics can be linked to personal (referent) power.

personal power {

- *Inspirational Appeal*—appealing to core values to encourage cooperation
- *Personal Appeal*—appealing to personal relationships to encourage cooperation
- *Ingratiation*—attempting to increase positive feelings as a way to increase referent power and thus persuasiveness

For individuals with expert power, rational persuasion can be a very effective influence tactic.

Expert power

- *Rational Persuasion*—using logical arguments as a justification for cooperation

Finally, individuals with a great deal of social capital and strong networks may find success by building coalitions, particularly if they are able to obtain support from a broad base of different constituent groups.

Network power

- *Coalition Formation*—gathering additional stakeholders to support a proposal

INFLUENCE VERSUS MANIPULATION AND CONTROL

There is often a fine line between perceptions of what is considered an acceptable influence tactic and what is seen as an inappropriate attempt to manipulate or control others. Effective brokers recognize that winning a short-term concession with manipulative or coercive tactics but losing an important relationship in the process is not a good trade-off. Influence tactics that undermine trust should be avoided.

INCREASING POWER AND INFLUENCE WITH SUPERVISORS, PEERS, AND SUBORDINATES

If you consistently appeal, even in subtle ways, to the authority of your position in order to get people's cooperation, you should probably try strategies that will increase your interdependence on your subordinates or offer them more personal support by expressing appreciation or taking time to listen carefully to how things are really going for them. A common belief in U.S. management philosophy is that learning from subordinates is a sign of weakness. But learning from others is really a sign of being secure and authentic, and so is the habit of listening carefully. The master broker knows what other people need and how they feel. Most of that information comes from listening and observing, not from talking.

When we work as consultants with managers who are accused by peers and subordinates of being "overcontrolling," these managers often defend their style by saying, "I'm results oriented more than people oriented." But that response assumes that there is only one way to get results: my way. Many of these managers are not results oriented as much as they are control oriented (Fisher, 2000, p. 109–110). They feel a great need to be in charge, and they assume that if they are not in control, the work unit is "out of control." Not surprisingly, they encounter immense resistance from the people they work with.

Here is a list of specific modes of increasing power and influence tailored to the role and level of the person you are trying to influence. These methods must, of course, be adapted to your situation.

Supervisors

- Look for ways to solve problems that your superiors are facing.

- Show appreciation to superiors for things they do to help.

- Encourage superiors to discuss their problems. Ask them about their biggest worries or most important goals and how your role connects to those worries and goals. Listen carefully. Give understanding and support.

- Provide constructive feedback on things supervisors do. Be specific. Demonstrate how their efforts led to concrete outcomes. "Your training session on securing clear commitments from suppliers has helped us reduce our costs by over 10 percent."

- Point out new ways superiors can use your skills. "I've done a lot of work on Web site design in my spare time. If I can help with this project, I'm available."

- Be loyal, even when it's difficult (unless some ethical principle or legal issue is at stake). Don't fall into the trap of bad-mouthing a boss. If the relationship is insupportable, get out of it.

- Take the initiative if you feel you are being used or exploited. Try bargaining and negotiating. "When you put restrictions on me as you did with the Fenlow project, I feel like I can't help the client and I can't help us avoid problems with the account. How do you see the situation?"

These are powerful and practical modes of increasing power and influence. However, there are roadblocks to using them. A major roadblock is the norms of the organization. Norms are unwritten expectations about how work will be done, how people will act, and so on. Your work unit may have a "them and us" norm about relating to superiors. It may not be socially acceptable to show appreciation to your manager or to be loyal to or give encouragement to the people you manage. Suggesting new methods or solutions may be taboo. If so, you may want to consider how much these norms are costing you in your professional and personal development. You may not only need a new manager—you may also need a more positive work climate. Moreover, as a leader in your work unit, you may have to address those norms specifically and try to change them for everyone's benefit. Think about what modes of influence you could use in that effort. Here are some other modes of increasing power and influence for working effectively with peers.

Peers

- Find ways to help peers reach their goals and look and feel successful.

- Try to understand their problems and share useful information.

- Look for common goals you can mutually pursue.

- Form informal problem-solving groups between units.

- If you are working with a large number of people, don't try to influence everyone at once. Identify the people you think are the most respected opinion leaders and recruit their support individually or in small groups. In most cases, wherever the opinion leaders go, others will follow.

Influencing peers is a tremendous challenge. Often organizations have norms that prohibit rocking the boat or going beyond the job description. Efforts to become more influential can be mistaken for power plays or a vote of nonconfidence toward your colleagues. Building power and influence with peers takes a long time and a lot of patience. But people ultimately respond when they see that you are determined to do good work and want to share the credit and stimulation with them. Remember, credit is not a zero-sum commodity. Stephen Covey, an author and management consultant, encourages people to create a "mentality of abundance," an attitude that there is plenty of credit, opportunity, and knowledge to go around (Covey, 1990, pp. 289–290).

This attitude is often self-fulfilling. When people are generous and encouraging, opportunities increase in an organization. The paradox of selfishness is that it usually results in a net *loss* of resources. When people start hoarding and hiding information, recognition, physical resources, and their own energy, the work unit begins to wither. If you have people reporting to you, here are some additional influence strategies for motivating good performance.

Direct Reports

- Consciously try to increase their trust in you by listening to their concerns and encouraging them to share ideas. Sometimes people "test" your patience and trustworthiness with little issues before coming to you with important ones.

- Make certain they know exactly what is expected of them in their role.

- Give them recognition for good performance, and point out how their performance has been helpful. For example, an orderly in a hospital works especially hard to prepare a patient's room. The supervising nurse can point out: "You got the patient's room ready in less than an hour. This usually takes two hours, and the patient often waits in the emergency room. This was a big help to him, and to the treatment team." There usually isn't enough recognition in the workplace, and when praise or recognition come, they are often too vague and indirect to be meaningful.

- Give them credit for their ideas when talking to your superiors. Good managers are generous in recognizing others' ideas and contributions.

- Do everything necessary to give them the tools and resources necessary to do their job.

- Help them solve problems that may be beyond their ability or experience. Keep current on new information and trends in your field. Good managers are good teachers. You don't have to know everything your subordinates know, but you need to be continuously learning.

- Provide training. Champion the cause of professional development even if resources are scarce. You can do a lot informally.

- Never pretend to know something you don't know. The more you manage "knowledge workers," the greater the likelihood that they know a lot of things you don't know. That's to be expected.

- Hold regular performance appraisals, but go beyond the formal "rating sheet" that so many organizations require once a year. Hold candid, detailed conversations with your people on how they are doing and what they need. Take a personal interest in their development, not just in their productivity.
- Do not be afraid to talk about the ways you depend upon each other.
- Clarify your responsibilities to them and theirs to you. "Here's what I most need from you. . . . What do you need from me to do your job effectively and feel good about your work?" Another question we've coached managers to ask frequently is: "Have I made any commitments to you that I haven't followed through on?"

ANALYSIS   "I Hope You Can Help Me Out": Don Lowell Case Study

Objective   For this exercise, you will practice identifying different sources of power and evaluating what types of influence tactics might be successful in the particular situation described in the case.

Directions   Read the following case study and answer the discussion questions.

Don Lowell is a mental hygiene therapy aide in a psychiatric center. He has been in his present position for 13 years, having worked his way up from the bottom. He thoroughly enjoys his job, but he missed being chosen for a promotion twice in the last two years. He was one of the top three on the list but was not able to get the promotions he wanted. He has been working very hard to make himself known in the right circles and has volunteered to serve on various county and private committees, boards, and task forces over the past few years.

Don also works three nights a week and weekends at the Rosewood Home, a well-known, highly rated nursing facility. Don serves as one of the two part-time activity coordinators. With his oldest daughter about to enter college, he can certainly use the money. He also enjoys the work and gets to meet a number of people in the community. He's been thinking for some time now that at some point in the future he would like to return to school and complete the degree, which he began years ago. Right now, however, he enjoys working with the patients and feels the added experience will help him in the future.

Last week Don received a phone call from Frank Calvin, the chief of service in his division at the psychiatric center. Frank's 79-year-old mother is in the hospital recovering from a broken hip. Frank has applied to the Rosewood Home primarily because of its reputation in the area of physical therapy and rehabilitation. The home, however, has a very long waiting list (from three to six months) and Frank understands that unless his mother receives physical therapy immediately upon release from the hospital, her chances of returning to her former mobility level are quite low. Moreover, Frank's sense of the situation, after meeting with the home's intake social worker, was that his mother was not going to be given priority consideration.

Frank discussed his situation with Sarah Anderson, his assistant. She reminded him that Don was still working as a part-time activity director at the Rosewood Home. Frank remembered Don's name from some paperwork that came across his desk. Frank called Don to see if there was any way around normal procedures and asked if Don could help.

During the conversation, Frank mentioned that if Don were able to assist him with this, he (Frank) would try to help him when he could. In addition, Frank said that he would put a note in Don's file mentioning the cooperation he had received from Don in placing his mother in the appropriate health facility. "I just don't know where to turn with this problem," said Frank, "and I really hope you can help me."

Don told Frank that he would see what he could do. He told Frank that he didn't know all that much about the admissions process and really didn't have that kind of "pull" at the facility but that he would give it his best shot.

Don made some informal inquiries around the home concerning the admissions procedures (of which he indeed knew very little). He found out that the director of the intake department, Sheila Hogan, was someone he knew slightly because he had worked with her on a couple of committees. He remembered her as being very focused and knowledgeable and someone who usually played everything by the book. However, he had found her to be accommodating when necessary.

He also remembered an item in the Rosewood newsletter stating that the intake department was severely short staffed and was looking for volunteers or other staff coverage. Don had some ideas that he thought would work very well at providing coverage at no additional cost to the home. He decided to arrange a meeting.

Discussion Questions

1. What sources of power and influence tactics does Don have available to him?

2. If you were Don, what action would you take?
   a. Would you decide not to try to influence the admission process? If not, why?
   b. Would you decide to help only by clarifying the mother's need for admission?
   c. Would you decide to do everything within your power to get the mother admitted?

3. Using the concepts and skills presented in the Learning activity, describe the consequences of how you would handle this situation. What do you think would happen?

4. What strategy and techniques is Frank using on Don?

5. What options or strategies should Don use with Frank?

6. What should Don's next steps be?

7. Have you ever encountered a similar situation? What strategies, if any, did you use? What steps did you take? Did these steps increase your power base? How do you know?

Reflection

It should come as no surprise that opportunities to exercise power and influence are sometimes linked to ethical dilemmas—situations where two values come into conflict. These types of situations are also complicated by cultural differences. For some people, helping a family member or friend would be the paramount value; people who view equity as the overriding value, however, might consider any attempt to influence the admission procedure to be unethical.

PRACTICE   The Big Move

Objective

This role-play will give you an opportunity to practice using and/or identifying different influence tactics.

Directions

Before class, read the situation background for this role-play.

1. Think about the situation background using the force-field analysis technique described in Chapter 8 to be sure that you understand the basic driving forces for this proposed change.

Situation Background

Department X, a financial services unit of a large health care system, is currently located in Albany, New York. The department has come under pressure to move its headquarters from Albany to Westchester County, an area closer to New York City. Many of the hospitals and clients served by the unit are located around Westchester County, and the system has recently acquired a building large enough to house the entire financial services unit under one roof. The relocation would allow the system to cancel a very expensive building lease in Albany. The current offices in Albany are now inadequate, and expansion would be very expensive and pose some legal difficulties with zoning. The board of directors has created an interunit task force to discuss the possibility of the move. This task force has to come up with a recommendation to the board. The department must move as a whole or not at all.

The task force consists of managers from the following areas:

1. Kim Ingo: Client Financial Services
2. Robyn Pinegar: Accounting
3. Carlos Armando: Stock and Bond Transfer
4. Lynn Stott: Personnel
5. Chris Jacobs: Facilitator

2. If your instructor provides you with a role description, read it carefully and develop a plan to try to influence the other members of the task force to agree with your position about the move. Come to class prepared to play a role if one has been assigned to you. If you have not been assigned a role, be prepared to analyze the power and influence attempts used by other students as they act out the role-play.

Each role description outlines an initial position or opinion as to the advisability of the move: for, against, neutral. This is only an initial position, however, and you should feel free to switch sides and/or be influenced by the others. Assume and display the power-personality characteristics outlined in your role description.

A secret-ballot vote will be taken at the end of the meeting, and the results will be announced. The board has asked for a recommendation from a task force of managers. You should assume that the recommendation of the group will strongly influence the board's final decision of whether or not to relocate. At the conclusion of the role-play, you will all be asked to complete a questionnaire on your assessment of each character's ability to persuade and influence the other managers.

3. In class, your instructor will provide directions for how the role play will be performed. If you are assigned a role, you should attempt to influence the other members of the task force. If you are part of the audience, you will be observing the role-play and providing feedback after it is completed, so make notes on the influence attempts you observe. After the role-play is finished, identify the primary sources of power for each participant and evaluate the degree of power you felt each person had on a scale of 0 to 10, with 0 = No Power and 10 = Very Powerful.

Observation Sheet: Assessing and Improving Influence Attempts

Task Force Member	Influence Tactics Attempted	Sources of Power	Degree of Power
Kim Ingo: Client Financial Services			
Robyn Pinegar: Accounting			
Carlos Armando: Stock and Bond Transfer			
Lynn Stott: Personnel			
Chris Jacobs: Facilitator			

Reflection   Each of the role descriptions provided for this exercise included information on the "power personality" of the character because individuals have different preferences in terms of using power and influence tactics. Effective brokers recognize, however, that different situations may call for different influence tactics. Having a clear understanding of the interests of the people you are trying to influence as well as their preferences for using power and influence can be very helpful for selecting the most effective influence tactics.

APPLICATION   Building Your Power Base by Changing Your Influence Strategy

Objective   This activity is designed to help you further develop and maintain your own power base with your subordinates, colleagues, and superiors, if applicable, in your organization.

Directions   Think about the personal power analysis you did in the Assessment exercise at the beginning of this chapter.

1. Identify someone that you would like to add to your circle of influence and consider how you could go about creating an interdependent relationship with that person. Be sure to have a clear idea of why adding them to your network would be helpful both to you and to them.

2. Identify someone who is currently in your circle of influence but who does not seem to value your abilities or contributions. What influence strategies have you used with that individual in the past? Why do you think they have been unsuccessful?

3. What are the similarities and differences between your strategies for expanding your circle of influence and your strategies for improving your power within your existing circle of influence?

4. Building on your responses from parts 1–3, write a brief memo to your instructor outlining a plan to help you expand and strengthen your power base. Be sure to identify the challenges you anticipate in implementing your strategy and discuss the costs of trying to make these changes compared with the costs of just settling for the status quo.

Reflection   Expanding your circle of influence takes time and energy. But unlike typical investments, when investing in your circle of influence it is just as important to think about what you can contribute to others as it is to consider your potential gains.

Competency 2   Negotiating Agreement and Commitment

ASSESSMENT   How Effective Are You at Negotiating Agreement?

Objective   Some people approach bargaining with a sense of dread, others with gleeful anticipation. This exercise will help you assess your own feelings about bargaining and evaluate how effective you feel you are at negotiating.

Directions   Think about some experiences you've had with negotiating—as a consumer, an employee, or a partner in a relationship you value. Ask yourself questions such as those listed, and add any you think are significant.

1. How well are you able to communicate with others? Do you easily understand what others are thinking and feeling? Do you express yourself clearly? How well are you able to deliver arguments and counterarguments?

2. Have you ever bargained for a shift change, a raise, or an adjustment in working conditions with a manager or employer?

3. How well can you cut through the information to objectively discuss facts?

4. Do you press for more information or clarification when listening to a sales pitch, a lecture, or another person's explanation, or do you hesitate to ask questions for fear of appearing uninformed or unsophisticated?

5. In a personal relationship, do you ever tolerate negative behavior in the other person because (a) you feel incapable of broaching the issue effectively, (b) you fear being misunderstood, or (c) you don't want to hurt the other person's feelings, even though the behavior is causing you serious problems?

6. As a rule, do you feel you have a reputation among your peers and family members for being a tough bargainer or as someone who is easygoing and deferential in presenting his or her needs and conditions?

7. Are there certain situations in which you feel more comfortable at negotiating? What are these situations, and why do you feel more comfortable in such negotiations?

Based upon your responses to these questions, indicate your comfort level with negotiating agreements and commitment.

Very comfortable _____

Comfortable _____

Somewhat uncomfortable _____

Uncomfortable _____

Very uncomfortable _____

Reflection   Even people who dread negotiating can become more effective negotiators. Sometimes simply reframing the situation can help. For example, Mary may feel that asking for a day off is selfish, and she does not want people to think of her as a selfish person. If, however, she recognizes that she is getting burned out from working too many hours and that taking some time off will improve her productivity, she may find it easier to assert herself when negotiating with her supervisor for that day off.

LEARNING Negotiating Agreement and Commitment

The balancing act between looking after the needs of others and getting the things we need ourselves leads us to the topic of negotiation. Negotiation is not limited to formal sessions across the desk with "the other party." We negotiate anytime we need something from someone else. William Ury, an associate at Harvard Law School's Program on Negotiation, reminds us that most of the important decisions we make in life are not made unilaterally. Most are negotiated. "Negotiation," says Ury, "is the preeminent form of decision making in personal and professional life" (Ury, 1993, p. 5).

HOW IS YOUR SOCIAL CREDIT RATING?

The first competency in this chapter dealt with building and maintaining a power base. However, we can't exert influence in an organization or a group without knowing what kinds of influence people are ready to accept. This competency will deal with negotiating agreement and commitment.

All members of an organization or group have a social credit rating. That rating goes up or down depending on how supportive, cooperative, and competent people perceive us to be. We do a balancing act. We have to be concerned about the needs of others, and we have to get our jobs done as well. Support is not automatic. Ineffective brokers believe that their assigned duties guarantee them support. Expert brokers never take such support for granted.

THE VITAL ROLE OF DIALOGUE

An important preliminary dimension to effective negotiation is "dialogue," a process of working things out through a thoughtful sharing of viewpoints. Our colleagues at Vital Smarts, a consulting firm that specializes in building communication effectiveness, define dialogue as "the free flow of meaning in an atmosphere of mutual trust and respect." We don't learn from people we don't respect, and we seldom make commitments to people we don't trust. Our colleagues focus on improving the ability of clients to establish and maintain the conditions of dialogue. These conditions include three elements: mutual purpose, mutual meaning, and mutual respect. If one or more of these elements are not present, dialogue will elude us (Patterson, Grenny, McMillan, and Switzler, 2002).

THE CONDITIONS OF DIALOGUE: MUTUAL PURPOSE, MEANING, AND RESPECT

The first condition, mutual purpose, is an "entrance condition" for dialogue. Without a clear and agreed-upon purpose, there is little point in investing in dialogue to begin with. When people and groups disagree, the disagreements are often about means or strategies, not about fundamental purposes; however, the purposes must be spelled out clearly from the beginning.

We once saw a group of environmentalists and developers (two groups who often fail to come to dialogue) come together effectively because they had found a common purpose. Several people in each group had mentioned that as children they had learned to fish with parents and friends in the area whose future was now being hotly debated. They wanted to maintain that possibility for their own children. With that mutual purpose established, the group effectively moved to a constructive dialogue on how to achieve it while still meeting other needs.

Mutual meaning involves each party knowing what the other is actually saying. Do we share the same definitions of terms, words, and expressions? Do I feel, as a participant in this dialogue, that my interests and opinions have been heard? "People never change without first feeling understood" (Stone, Patton, and Heen 1999, p. 29). But how do we know we really have mutual meaning? When we can describe the other person's opinions, position, and feelings to his or her satisfaction (recall reflective listening from

Chapter 2). Another way to say this is, "To get anywhere in a disagreement, we have to understand the other person's story well enough to see how *their* conclusions make sense within it" (Stone et al., 1999, p. 30).

Mutual Respect

Mutual respect is also essential but fragile, especially if two parties have already had a disagreement or conflict. At least one party has to have the courage and wisdom to not resort to name-calling and blaming. When you watch two people in a heated argument, you're usually seeing a game of "tit-for-tat." I call you a name, you call me one; I threaten you, you threaten me. To create and maintain mutual respect, someone has to swallow hard and break the cycle of tit-for-tat. Nor can two parties move to silence, or even partial withdrawal, and hope to reach a constructive agreement. We demonstrate respect by listening respectfully, speaking candidly, and focusing more on solving problems than on placing blame.

AN EXAMPLE OF DIALOGUE IN THE FIELD

William Peace is a former executive with Westinghouse and United Technologies. He is currently director of Doctus Management Consultancy in Great Britain. Peace does not apologize for being a tough-minded, soft-hearted leader. For Peace, soft leadership does not imply weak leadership, and a desire to consider many sides of an issue and listen to the recommendations of others does not imply indecisiveness. He learned a lot about establishing mutual respect from a manager named Gene Cattabiani, a vice president in the Steam Turbine Division of Westinghouse. Cattabiani faced a huge challenge with labor–management relations. The hourly employees in the division were fiercely loyal to their union leaders and convinced that management was out to get them. Managers, on the other hand, were equally convinced that the union leaders were turning employees against management at the expense of the company and even the employees themselves. "Most of these people are just plain damn lazy" was a comment often heard in management team meetings. "We need discipline more than we need negotiation" was another popular comment.

Cattabiani knew things had to change. The division was losing money, costs were climbing, and other companies were eating up market share. But how could he push for improvements and better performance when there was so much anger in the air? He came to the conclusion that he had to communicate with everyone in the plant. If dialogue were going to begin, he would have to step out and make the first move. Because of the size of the plant and the presence of three shifts for each working day, he would have to give the same presentation several times on the huge shop floor to hostile audiences. His management team tried to dissuade him. "You don't have to submit to bad treatment," they said, "we'll give people the news in smaller groups." Another, stronger argument was that the risk was too great: "This will become a massive gripe session that may get out of control." But Cattabiani insisted and the meetings were held. Here's how Bill Peace describes what happened.

> The initial presentation was a nightmare. Gene wanted the workforce to see that the business was in trouble, real trouble, and that their jobs depended on a different kind of relationship with management. But the workers assumed that management was up to its usual self-serving tricks, and there, on stage, for the first time, they had the enemy in person. They heckled him mercilessly all through the slide show. Then, during the question-and-answer period, they shouted abuse and threats.

At this point, Bill Peace was convinced that Cattabiani had made a serious strategic error. The management team worried that this "weakened" leader had lost all credibility and would now be bulldozed by employees who were really flexing their muscles. But Peace and others began to notice some subtle changes in the days that followed the meetings.

> *When Gene went out on the factory floor for a look around (which his predecessors never did unless they were giving customers a tour) people began to offer a nod of recognition—a radical change from the way they used to spit on the floor as he walked by. Even more remarkable was his interaction with the people who had heckled him at the meetings. Whenever he spotted one, he would walk over and say something like, "You really gave me a hard time last week," to which the response was usually something like, "Well, you deserved it, trying to pass off all that bullshit." Such exchanges usually led to brief but very open dialogues, and I noticed that the lathe operators and blading mechanics he talked to would listen to what Gene said, really listen. (Peace, 1991, p. 46)*

This division made steady progress over the months and years that passed, and Gene Cattabiani was largely responsible for it. Not every person came "on board" and supported the changes Cattabiani proposed. Some were moved to another job, and a few were let go. Others were put in leadership positions and were given more authority to make changes. Throughout the process, Cattabiani had a purpose greater than protecting his ego. He knew that people needed some opportunity to ventilate, and they needed to be convinced that he meant what he said about wanting their input and suggestions. He was willing to put himself on the line and not return insult for insult. With mutual respect in place, people could build the other conditions of dialogue: mutual meaning, and purpose. Without respect, meaning and purpose don't really matter.

Cattabiani also understood that leadership can be a lonely spot. He did not expect the plant employees to love him or admire him. He knew that his position required tough choices at times. His goal was to build the overall capability of the organization, not to gain the personal approval of everyone in it. He wasn't seeking popularity or personal approval. He was trying to improve performance so his division could "live to fight another day." He eventually gained the approval of most people, and the organization's performance improved significantly, but that gain was a by-product of being a reasonable, consistent leader who was willing to listen and learn as well as teach.

Cattabiani's experience helps us learn another important principle about dialogue: Dialogue is usually a separate process from decision making. Dialogue is an excellent preliminary process to actually making decisions because (1) it enlarges the pool of information available to decision makers and (2) it builds a great sense of mutual respect and understanding among those who have to implement and live with the decision.

In many cases trust is destroyed not by bad motives but by ineffective strategies. We may have needs and goals very similar to those of a roommate, spouse, colleague, or team member; however, an ineffective approach to filling those needs could trigger distrust in the other person. Once distrust or defensiveness sets in, confrontation or withdrawal follows. Once we're in either of those boxes, it's very tough to get out.

In the next few pages we will present some principles that we have found very helpful in avoiding the traps of confrontation. The negotiation style recommended in this book is somewhat on the soft and "reasonable" side, but it also recognizes the need for tough-mindedness. This reasonable approach tries to be tough on principles and gentle on people.

FOUR PRINCIPLES FOR GETTING TO "YES"

Roger Fisher and William Ury, in their influential book *Getting to Yes* (1991), offer four basic principles they believe should guide any negotiation. These are:

1. Separate the people from the problem.
2. Focus on interests, not positions.
3. Generate a variety of possibilities before deciding what to do.
4. Insist that the result be based on some objective standard.

1 SEPARATE THE PEOPLE FROM THE PROBLEM

Separate problem from personalities

The natural tendency when there are misunderstandings or bruised egos, or struggles over credit or blame, is to focus on personalities. This is a mistake. The problem is the thing that needs solving. The tougher we have to be on the problem, the softer we need to be on people.

Once people feel personally threatened or embarrassed, their energy goes into defending their self-esteem, not into solving the problem. Keep the focus on the problem, even if you feel another person is at fault. All relational conflict is destructive. On the other hand, a healthy level of task conflict can help generate diverse ideas.

Remember, the other person may be mentally constructing the situation in a totally different way. Ask yourself, "How does the other party see the situation?" A good way to find out is to ask questions and then lean forward and really listen. Don't assume anything. Talk to the other person about his or her perceptions, and then feed them back to be certain you have heard correctly. Your paraphrase of the other person's position must be accurate in his or her judgment. If it fails, talk some more until you arrive at mutual meaning. Parroting back what someone has already clearly stated is a ridiculous strategy; however, make sure you understand what the other person is communicating.

When you focus on problems, not personalities, you are better able to let people blow off steam without your taking it personally. There's an old German proverb that says, "Let anger fly out the windows." It's good advice because it saves both parties from that chain reaction of one person's anger feeding off the other's. All professional negotiators seem to agree: Don't react too quickly to emotional outbursts.

2 FOCUS ON INTERESTS, NOT POSITIONS

When we negotiate, we often begin by taking a "position." We believe that in the final outcome we can feel good if we have defended that position and not "given too much away." For years, during the Cold War, the Soviets and Americans argued from different positions on limiting strategic weapons. The U.S. team was committed to a position of allowing for at least six missile base inspections per year by each side. The Soviets dug in for a maximum of three. Negotiations were stalemated for weeks over the magic numbers six and three.

The problem was that no one had really thought through the needs and concerns behind the positions they had taken. Both parties had hunkered into their positions.

Someone needed to ask, "What is an inspection? One person walking around a missile site for one day, or a team of eight people spending a week?" The United States was apparently concerned about sufficient frequency and thoroughness in inspections, and the Soviet Union was anxious about how intrusive the inspections would be. But on reflection, it became obvious that the number of inspections was not the major issue. A bigger issue was how much authority the inspection teams would have and how disruptive inspections would be to the military sites where they were conducted (Fisher, Kopelman, and Kupfer-Scheider, 1994).

When we coach executives, we challenge them to put their purpose before their initial position. "You are not your position," we tell them, "so don't become too invested in that position." Focus on the goals and principles behind your position, and separate those goals from your own ego (as best you can). There may be other ways of reaching your goal than those offered by the first position you develop. Thus, the next rule: Generate other possibilities.

3 GENERATE OTHER POSSIBILITIES: MAKE THE PIE BIGGER

When people are arguing over how to divide a pie, most of them never consider the possibility that the pie could be made bigger. Often it can. Good negotiators try to think of options that are of low cost to them but of high benefit to the other party. This strategy is often called "dovetailing" or collaborating. In order to dovetail your needs with the needs of the other party, you have to probe what those needs are and not take the other party's position at face value. When a fellow manager says that he or she must have control of the training rooms in your facility every Friday afternoon, that position may be based more on a need for power and control than on a practical need for those rooms at that time. It may also be that he or she needs guaranteed space over time, but not necessarily every Friday afternoon. The trap is in reacting to that manager's position before uncovering his or her real needs. That act of questioning and probing will usually enable you to come up with alternatives.

For example, in negotiating over price with a box supplier, a purchasing agent from a small company saw an opportunity. The agent learned from the discussion that the supplier was in a cash-flow squeeze after purchasing a very expensive fabrication machine. The supplier had taken a rigid position on price, and now the purchasing agent knew why. Seizing the opportunity, the agent offered to prepay the supplier for the entire job in exchange for a faster turnaround time *and a major price reduction* (Calano and Salzman, 1988). These opportunities for win–win agreements are too often overlooked because negotiators fail to solve the other side's problems first. Dovetailing your needs with those of the other party requires you to separate your needs from your position, but also to separate the other party's needs from its position.

If alternatives don't come to mind right away, don't panic. Take some time. Huddle with a few associates and friends you trust and do some brainstorming (see Chapter 8). Come up with creative alternatives based on everything you know about your needs, the needs of the other party, and the facts of the situation at hand. Finally, make sure you broker agreements and commitments in such a way that both parties "win." Negotiating is not about who can walk away with the best deal. Negotiating is not a zero-sum game. Short-term negotiating will create win–lose agreements and commitments that will actually erode long-term power.

As a manager, you may need to use your negotiating skills in helping others resolve problems or reach compromises. This process is called *mediation*. Expert brokers think twice before intervening in a dispute or disagreement between colleagues or subordinates. It's usually best to wait to be invited, but this is not always possible. For example, if two people have to work together and a disagreement is making it impossible for them to work effectively, their manager may need to become involved. As their manager, you would have to decide whether you want to deal with the people individually or together and determine how willing they are to solve the problem. For cases in which you decide it's necessary to function as mediator, here are some principles to help you develop a strategy:

1. Acknowledge to your people that you know a conflict exists, and propose an approach for resolving it.

2. In studying the positions of both parties, maintain a neutral position regarding the disputants—if not the issues.

3. Keep the discussion issue oriented, not personality oriented. Focus on the impact the conflict is having on performance.

4. Help your people put things in perspective by focusing first on areas on which they might agree. Try to deal with one issue at a time.

5. Remember, you are a facilitator, not a judge. If you assume the role of judge, each person will focus his or her energy on trying to persuade you, rather than on solving the problem and learning something about negotiation. Judges deal with problems; facilitators deal with solutions.

6. Make sure your people fully support the solution they've agreed upon. Don't stop until both parties have a specific plan, and if you sense hesitancy on anyone's part, push for clarification: "Tom, I sense you're less enthusiastic than Carol about this approach. Is there something about it that bothers you?"

4 INSIST ON USING OBJECTIVE CRITERIA

Fisher and Ury (1991) advise us to make negotiated decisions based on principles, not pressure. Often negotiators make the process a contest of wills: It's my stubbornness and assertiveness against yours. Some people call this yes-we-will-no-we-won't cycle "inefficient disagreement." A way around this trap is to find some objective standards or criteria that will help the parties test the reasonableness of a position. For example, your car is totaled in an accident and you refuse to argue with the insurance adjuster over a price based upon sentimental value: "My father gave me that car!" or "I've owned that car since I was in high school!" You would have to refer to some standard, such as market value as indicated in the "blue book," or some other objective that both parties could consider reasonable.

It's smart to look for the theories and assumptions behind the position. Fisher and Ury use the following example from a colleague whose parked car was totaled by a dump truck. It was time to settle with the insurance company through an adjuster:

Adjuster: We have studied your case and have decided the policy applies. That means you are entitled to a settlement of $6,600.

Tom: I see. How did you reach that figure?

Adjuster: That was how much we decided the car was worth.

Tom: I understand, but what standard did you use to determine that amount? Do you know where I can buy a comparable car for that much?

Adjuster: How much are you asking?

Tom: Whatever I'm entitled to under that policy. I found a second-hand car just like mine for about $7,700. Adding sales and excise tax it would come to about $8,000.

Adjuster: $8,000! That's too much!

Tom: I'm not asking for $8,000, or $6,000 or $10,000, but for fair compensation. Do you agree that it's only fair I get enough to replace the car?

Adjuster: Okay, I'll offer you $7,000. That's the highest I can go. Company policy.

Tom: How does the company figure that?

Adjuster: Look, $7,000 is all you get. Take it or leave it.

Tom: $7,000 may be fair. I don't know. I certainly understand your position if you're bound to company policy, but unless you can state objectively why that amount is what I'm entitled to, I think I'll do better in court. Why don't we study the matter and talk again? Is Wednesday at eleven a good time to talk?

Adjuster: Okay Mr. Griffith, I've got an ad here in today's paper offering an '89 Taurus for $6,800

Tom: I see, what does it say about the mileage?

Adjuster: 49,000. Why?

Tom: Because mine had only 25,000 miles. How many dollars does that increase the worth in your book?

Adjuster: Let me see . . . $450.

Tom: Assuming the $6,800 as possible base, that brings the figure to $7,250. Does the ad say anything about a radio?

Adjuster: No.

Tom: How much extra in your book?

Adjuster: That's $125.

Tom: What about air conditioning? (Fisher and Ury, 1991, pp. 92–94)

Half an hour later, Tom walked out with a check for $8,024. Notice how unemotional Tom was. He was working from a need to ground the discussion of price on objective criteria acceptable to both parties. He didn't lose control, and he didn't cave in to personal pressure. He knew his appeal to objective criteria was fair and reasonable. Negotiating can be an emotional ordeal, but good negotiators don't lose control. They keep dragging an emotional discussion back to the issue at hand.

For more information on how to prepare effective arguments, see the discussion of critical thinking in Chapter 1.

ANALYSIS   Your Effectiveness as a Negotiator

Objective   To help gauge your skill as a negotiator, this assessment asks you to focus on a specific example of a past negotiation in which you participated and evaluate your performance in light of the information provided in the learning section for this competency.

Directions   Take an issue or event from your life in which you needed to engage in some negotiation or secure a commitment from another person or party. You can use any situation you found challenging, for example, buying a product you later wanted to return or needing to lodge a complaint about a service. You may have needed to negotiate a change in your shift during a summer job, or perhaps you had to solve a problem in a personal or work relationship. Prepare a brief memo concerning your experience. Describe the issue in terms of the negotiating techniques you have learned in this chapter and perhaps others that you have found helpful. Evaluate your negotiating performance. How could you now improve it?

Reflection   Sometimes our perceptions of our abilities are inaccurate, we base them on flawed recollections or beliefs that don't match up with reality. Identifying a specific example as grounds for a claim makes the argument more persuasive, as noted in the discussion of critical thinking in Chapter 1. Successful negotiators do their homework to make sure that they have as much credible evidence as possible to support their claims and further their interests.

PRACTICE   Standing on the Firing Line

Objective   An important aspect of negotiating is the ability to communicate your own position and views on an issue, but also to understand the other party's position—including the strong emotions and feelings that often accompany that position. Emotions are the footprints of values, values that people feel are under some kind of threat. The purpose of the following exercise is to help you manage the emotional side of a public discussion about a difficult issue.

Directions   In the two cases described below, you read about two people who are in a position which requires them to manage some difficult and negative emotions in a public setting. In groups of six to eight people, count off 1–2, 1–2 . . . so that each person will have the responsibility of playing one of the two roles, either Boyd Sterling or Karen Williams. (The gender of the person playing the role is not important. You can change the name of characters as needed.)

Your instructor can select a couple of you to take a turn standing on the firing line and playing the role of the person in the case. The rest of you will function as highly engaged audience members who have a deep interest in the issues at hand. Each of you will prepare to be on the firing line in one role and to be an audience member in the other role. Take 10 minutes to study the role before your instructor calls on someone to take the firing line.

We have included some sample questions and comments that audience members can use, but, as an audience member, feel free to go beyond these to comments of your own. The idea is not to "destroy" the person on the firing line but to create a realistic and challenging level of pressure. The person on the firing line should try his or her best to apply the principles in the section on "negotiating agreements and commitments" to this situation. Give the person some feedback after each performance and discuss as a group what you're learning about handling such situations effectively. Where are the traps to avoid, and what kinds of responses seem to be most effective?

Role 1: Boyd Sterling, Chief of Police, Roseville

You are the Chief of Police in Roseville, a midwestern community of 36,000 people. Two of your officers have been accused of brutality by a homeless man, David Oakeson. Oakeson came into the area about six months ago. He lives out of his car most of the time but occasionally spends a night in a local shelter provided by the Coalition for the Homeless, a local charity organization.

Oakeson claims that officers Wilson and Ortega pulled him over on a Saturday evening and ordered him out of his car. When Oakeson insisted he had not been speeding, they allegedly began threatening him if he didn't leave town. Oakeson said that an argument ensued and that the officers clubbed him with their flashlights. He claims they threatened his life if he didn't leave.

The incident became more visible when two other homeless people said they were willing to testify that Wilson and Ortega had used unnecessary force with them as well on separate occasions. Consistent with policy in handling investigations into officer behavior, you have suspended the officers, with pay, while you conduct the investigation.

You are meeting at this moment with two members of the Roseville City Council and several local leaders from public interest groups, such as the Coalition for the Homeless. People at the meeting are quite upset and are directing most of their questions and comments at you.

Questions/Comments
1. I think I see a pattern here, and it really has me concerned. I hear people at the shelter complain about the police. They say they are handled roughly. They are sometimes cuffed and pushed, and they are verbally abused. I'm sick of hearing about tough, mean cops. You must know this kind of thing goes on.

2. Last night the article in the paper said these guys had been suspended, but with pay. What kind of a statement is that to the community—that you can manhandle citizens and then get a free vacation?

3. What do you think is the problem here, Chief? What's the cause of this kind of thing really?

4. What kind of training are officers getting about dealing with the homeless or the indigent? I get the impression they aren't getting any kind of training in this area at all.

Role 2: Karen Williams, Executive Director, Cold Harbor Research Center

You are Karen Williams, executive director of the Cold Harbor Cancer Research Institute. With a staff of 47 people, most of them with advanced degrees in microbiology or chemistry, the Center is a significant and prestigious employer in the town of Cold Harbor (population 56,000). The Center has struggled, since its founding twelve years ago, to secure funding from private and public sources. You have been director for only one year, having come to Cold Harbor from Boston, where you worked in hospital administration. It has been an especially difficult year, because both state and federal grants, for which the Center has historically qualified, have been cut.

Last month, you received a visit from the attorney of Robert Knowles, a wealthy entrepreneur who has recently moved into the community. Knowles, now retired, made his fortune in the southeastern part of the country, developing harvesting and processing equipment for tobacco farmers. He has, for over a decade, been an active force in the tobacco industry's lobbying efforts in Washington.

During a brief visit in your office, the attorney informed you that Knowles has decided to offer the Center a $10.8 million endowment to be used for any purpose its board of directors deems appropriate. There is only one stipulation: The Center would have to change its name to The Robert Knowles Cancer Research Institute.

Fearing that the Center is facing financial demise, you made a verbal agreement with the attorney that you would make every effort to secure the approval of the board of directors to change the name and accept the funding.

That evening, you called Knowles and asked him to have lunch with you to discuss the issues. You became more convinced, as you listened to him describe his motives and interests, that it would be appropriate to accept the funding and change the name of the Center. Knowles claimed that he is trying to "give something back" to the country that has made him wealthy. He has a niece who has been diagnosed with a rare form of cancer, and he himself has been diagnosed with prostate cancer.

One week later, having met with a quorum of the board and gaining their approval, you announced the board's approval and held a brief press conference attended by Knowles and several members of the board.

Within hours, members of the Cold Harbor City Council were denouncing the decision through the local press. Citizens have written angry letters to the city newspapers, and the television stations in the state are beginning to carry the story. Under pressure, you have agreed to hold a press conference to discuss the decision.

Be prepared to respond to questions from the press, members of the city council, and local citizens.

Questions/Comments   1. The most obvious question is, "How can the Center justify accepting money from a person who has so aggressively championed the cause of the tobacco industry?" The moral inconsistency seems too obvious to consider, but apparently it needs some more considering.

2. What exactly is Mr. Knowles hoping to accomplish by having the Center carry his name?

3. This Center was created by donations from about half a dozen donors, all of whom were local citizens or at least attached to this community in some significant way. What can you say to the citizens of this community who feel that their memory and contribution are being undermined by this decision?

4. What will you do if the community insists that the name of the Center not be changed? Surely you've considered this possibility.

Reflection   Situations that require negotiation often are linked to fundamental values and thus may have ethical implications. Going beneath surface positions to identify any values that may be in conflict can be an important step toward finding an effective solution.

APPLICATION   Negotiating at Work

Objective   This application exercise emphasizes bringing together competencies from both the innovator and the broker roles to help you develop your skills to meet the Create action imperative of the open systems quadrant.

Directions   In Chapter 8, the application exercise for the third competency asked you to develop a plan for a change that you wanted to make at work. Now it is time for you to practice negotiating to make that change a reality. In thinking about how to approach this negotiation, be sure to take into account both the driving and resisting forces for change, as well as your insights into your power base from the application exercise in the first competency of this chapter.

Prepare a memo describing how you attempted to negotiate agreement and commitment to making the change that you identified. Discuss the result of your negotiation attempt, and analyze why you think it turned out as it did.

Reflection   It is easy to become myopic when addressing challenges in organizations. We may focus only on one aspect of the situation or may apply only one technique in trying to respond to that situation.

Master managers take full advantage of a variety of techniques from all of the competing values framework, both to analyze the situation and to respond to it. In your negotiation did you use effective critical thinking techniques by providing grounds and warrants to support claims (Chapter 1)? Did you use reflective listening to help understand the interests of the party with whom you were negotiating (Chapter 2)? Did you think in advance about how you would handle conflict if it occurred (Chapter 3)? Did you consider any potential cross-functional issues (Chapter 5) or impacts on motivation (Chapter 7) that your proposed change might have? Were you able to identify how the proposed change fit in with the goals and objectives of the organization (Chapter 6) and existing core processes (Chapter 4)?

Competency 3   Presenting Ideas

ASSESSMENT   The Presenter's Touch: You May Have It but Not Know It

Objective   Teachers are constantly discovering students who are competent oral presenters but who have little idea of how good they are. They also find students who can dramatically improve their presenting ability with minor adjustments in their approach. Many of us have the presenter's touch and don't even know it.

Directions   Answer "yes" or "no" to the following questions.[1]

_____Y_____ 1. Do you get a kick out of helping other people solve their problems?

_____Y_____ 2. Can you cut through a rambling, foggy conversation—dig out the main point and re-state it so that everybody understands?

_____N_____ 3. Do you have a high energy level? Do other people seem to you to be talking slowly?

_____Y_____ 4. Do you like to tell people what you've learned? Would you make a good teacher?

_____N_____ 5. Are you a good editor? Can you digest lots of material into simple, clear language?

_____N_____ 6. Can you handle pressure without blowing your top? Can you deal with provocative questions in a public setting without flaring up?

_____Y_____ 7. Do you like to demonstrate what you're talking about? Do you tend to "act out" what you're describing?

_____N_____ 8. Do you look people in the eye when you talk to them and when they talk to you?

_____Y_____ 9. Do people turn to you when it's time for a meeting to be summed up?

_____Y_____10. Do you notice specific things people do that make them effective or ineffective communicators—and then find yourself applying the effective ones?

Reflection   If you answered "yes" to half of these questions, you are probably an effective presenter right now. If you answered "yes" to fewer than half, don't be discouraged. Your honesty will be a great asset in improving your ability to communicate. You need to believe you really can improve. Over the years we have coached many students, managers, and executives. Those with a desire to improve their presenting skills have all made significant progress. In this section we will share some tools and principles for improving your effectiveness at presenting ideas.

---

[1] These questions are adapted from *I Can See You Naked* by Ron Hoff. Copyright © 1992 by Andrew & McMeel.

LEARNING Presenting Ideas

The last, but certainly not least, broker competency that we discuss is presenting ideas, with an emphasis on making effective oral presentations. Although it may seem as though making presentations should come before a discussion on negotiating agreement and commitment, in reality, formal presentations often occur only after significant informal discussion and negotiation has occurred. Certainly, if one is proposing a major change, it is valuable to get input from people who will be affected (see Chapter 3, participative decision making). Even informational presentations not focused on change, however, can benefit from vetting by other members of the organization. Once that foundation has been laid, successfully conveying those ideas serves to reinforce agreements and inspire commitment.

Public speaking has been labeled the number-one phobia of Americans, and our experience tells us that most people in most societies would prefer not to stand up and express themselves in a public speech. For most of us, there is no way around the requirement because our jobs bring us in front of people regularly. In organizational life, we do most of our work in groups. This is why interpersonal and public communication is vital to every role you play as a manager.

In this final section, we will focus primarily on giving effective stand-up presentations; however, most of these principles will also apply to all management communication tasks: writing proposals and brief reports, interviewing, negotiating, mediating, coaching, and so on.

For this brief discussion of effective presentations, we will use Al Switzler's (Vital Smarts, 1994) framework for effective communication. Switzler says that our strategies and choices for how to communicate with a group should be driven by three considerations:

1. Your purpose
2. Your audience
3. Your resources

You must know your purpose and not assume your audience will automatically share it. Try to write a "target statement" that distills your purpose. For example, suppose you are outlining a brief presentation on shop-floor safety to a group of employees in a large manufacturing company. Your target statement might be this: "Every hourly employee will understand our safety requirements and be able to repeat them, feel more committed to keeping them, and be willing to caution other employees who are not complying with them."

You also have to know as much as possible about your audience. You have to understand their perspective so that you can effectively take them from point A to point B. That is, you will be able to create a more audience-specific message when you understand your audience. You certainly wouldn't deliver the same message on a new method for repairing a broken faucet to plumbers as you would to the weekend handyman. Everything from the vocabulary to the amount of detail should be determined by the audience's understanding.

You can learn a lot about an audience just by looking at them and listening to them talk among themselves. This information will then guide your strategy. Do these people know a lot about this topic or very little? Are they likely to agree with the position or advice you plan to present? What kinds of information and messages have they received on this same topic recently? How have they reacted?

Finally, resources are time, money, energy, and information. All are finite and in limited supply, but you often have more than you assume. What resources do you have available in making a presentation? Can you get some additional advice on a topic or some help with graphics? Do you need graphics or some other kind of visual support for your message? How much is the presentation worth to you? How much time can you spare for preparation? Can you spare the time to practice your presentation before one or more people who can be your "red-team" audience? A red-team audience is a group of people who know you, who want you to be successful, and who commit to give you candid and detailed feedback on how to improve your presentation. All these approaches are potential resources, but all take time, money, and energy.

SSSAP

The other elements of Switzler's framework are known as **SSSAP:** Set, Support, Sequence, Access, and Polish.

SET

Set deals with how you handle your audience's initial mood and expectations. When competitive sprinters step up to the starting blocks, the starter says, "On your mark, get set. . . ." "Set" is the perfect position for starting quickly. When you set your audience, you help them get into the right position physically, emotionally, and mentally. Good communicators connect with their audiences early to prepare them for the journey they are to take. Good presentations are audience centered, not speaker centered. Most poor presentations are built on a weak set. Set does three things: (1) It creates a mood and tone favorable to listening and acceptance; (2) it assures the listener that you are worth listening to; and (3) it maps the journey you are asking the listener to take with you. Switzler calls these three functions of set the climate set, credibility set, and content set.

Climate Set: What Mood Do You Want Them In?   **Climate set** is the effort you make to establish rapport with the audience and cue them to a mood or style appropriate to the presentation. *Rapport* is a French word meaning "to bring back or refer." In English it has come to mean having an accord or harmony with another person. We tend to feel a rapport, or lack of it, when we speak to people individually, but rapport is equally important in speaking to groups. Without rapport, your ability to communicate will be severely limited.

As a way of improving your ability at gaining rapport, try to apply some of the following principles at the next meeting you are required to conduct.

1. Be in the room first and greet each person if possible.
2. Make eye contact. Notice the facial expressions and energy level of the people coming in. Does Kay look tired or distracted? Is Craig irritable or bored before the meeting

even begins? Don't ignore these cues. Use them to establish rapport by helping you key in on the group's mood and energy. If you are on the agenda to present at a meeting of a small group, make eye contact with every person present. We call this "taking roll" nonverbally—checking in with people as if to say, "Thanks for being here. I'll try to do my best to hold your interest." Before speaking to a large group, scan sections of the audience. People will feel that you are connecting with them, even though you can't make eye contact with many individuals. Imagine that people are thinking "I can care about your message if I feel like you care about me."

3. Be pleasant and reach out to your audience with a smile and greeting, but don't press too much enthusiasm or energy onto a resistant group, especially at first. If you have watched many infomercials on American cable TV stations, you'll probably agree that some of these people are "over the top" with their forced enthusiasm for the best food processor or window squeegee on the market. Try, in the beginning, to mirror the energy level of your audience, to match it enough so as not to turn them off. You can show more energy and enthusiasm as you go. Most groups will resist abrupt jumps between their own energy level and that of the speaker.

4. Be positive and supportive. Improve your "climate set" by being positive, even if you have unpleasant or difficult business to conduct. If you aren't positive, what is your justification for being in charge? When this advice is given to people, some react, "But this is just another dumb meeting. Everybody knows that. I'd feel like a jerk trying to get people to enjoy it." That's the point. Even perfunctory, routine meetings are much more bearable when the person in charge is positive and professional. Grand occasions are often less challenging to our skills than routine ones. We enjoy working with people who are professional and upbeat. Try it and see. Don't be dramatically different, but push up your level of energy and optimism, and you'll be pleased to see how contagious your mood is.

Credibility Set: Why Should They Listen to You? **Credibility set** is the assurance you provide the audience that you are an informed and legitimate speaker—that you know what you're talking about because of your experience, credentials, interest, special expertise, and so on. Often your credibility set is offered by the person who introduces you, but, in less formal settings, you may need to provide the credibility set yourself. Obviously, when speaking to a group you know very well, you may not need to provide a credibility set at all. Sometimes the briefest comment will suffice: "I had the opportunity last summer to spend three weeks at the FBI's National Training Academy in Virginia. Susan Grace, our bureau chief, asked me to share some of the things I learned at their forensic sciences lab." Here's another example of a credibility set.

The pace of change is accelerating in our industry, and change is very intolerant of comfort. I remember how hard I worked as a student at Penn State to understand the 1989 Tax Code, and then again how hard I labored over each new code as the years went by, first at Ernst and Young, and then at my own firm in Chicago. Now, as a partner at Deloitte Touche, I'm trying to help our people in the firm worldwide maintain our edge in doing business over the Internet. Every time I start to get comfortable with what I know, I get pushed into something I don't know. But I've learned to thrive on change, and that's what I'd like to speak to you about today.

This credibility set gives the audience a lot of information about the speaker's background and gently tunes them in to her message. This is a modest but effective way for the speaker to establish credibility before sharing his or her message.

Don't assume people know why you are qualified to take their time. Without boasting, you need to think about your credibility set every time you address a group that doesn't know you well. Where possible, your credibility set should be specific to the needs of the audience and circumstance you're in.

For the past two months I've been visiting all the branch offices in our company, interviewing customers and suppliers about how they feel about the services we provide. I've learned a lot from the hundreds of people I've listened to, and I hope I've learned some things that can help us move the business forward.

Content Set: Where Are You Taking Them?   **Content set** is the roadmap you provide your audience. Most of us are uncomfortable with ambiguity. We want to know what's going on, what we're getting into. When you talk to a group, let them know where you're about to take them and do it early in your presentation. "I want to talk for 10 minutes about why I think our record in work-related accidents is deteriorating and make some suggestions on how to turn the corner on our safety problems. When I've done that, I would like your questions and suggestions." With that "set," the audience can understand what's coming because you've given them a map to follow.

A good communicator remembers what it's like not to know much about the topic in question (Wurman, 1989). The more we know about a topic, the more inclined we are to overestimate how much our audience knows about it. Ironically, expertise can be a pitfall to effective communication. Define terms and avoid jargon as much as possible. People appreciate a clear and candid style in speaking as well as writing. William Zinsser, a gifted writer and engaging speaker, shares an example of how not to do it:

> *A few years ago, I was shanghaied on to an advisory panel at Time Inc., and at our first meeting someone asked the chairman what our committee had been formed to do. He said, "It's an umbrella group that interacts synergistically to platform and leverage cultural human resources companywide." That pretty much ended my interest in the committee. And when it later experienced "viability deprivation" (went down the tubes) I was overjoyed.* (quoted in Wurman, 1989 p. 118)

Think about what people need to know up front so that they can relax and pay attention to you. Will you give people a chance to ask questions? What major themes will you cover? How does your topic relate to people's jobs or their individual circumstances? Without the answers to these questions, people might interrupt just before you get to the point they are interested in. They might also stop listening because they assume you are not covering the topic they care about. The roadmap you give your audience will keep their understanding and attention on track.

SUPPORT

Support is the substance of your presentation: the facts, the major reasons you offer for doing one thing rather than another. Without support, your claims or recommendations are just opinions (see Chapter 1, critical thinking). Support is the bones of your

ProofProof

presentation. The support you provide in any presentation should be correct, concrete, complete, relevant, and logical. Al Switzler suggests you use these questions to determine how well supported your message is.

1. What do I mean? Do I define things adequately?
2. Am I specific? Do I use specific examples and illustrations that my audience will enjoy and understand?
3. How do I know? Do I appeal to appropriate authorities and other sources of evidence that my audience believes are credible?
4. Do I answer the "so what?" question? Do I demonstrate that my message makes a difference? Do I make my message relevant to this specific audience at this specific moment?

Anticipate Objections and Counterarguments. Try, whenever possible, to anticipate objections and counterarguments to your position, and address them as you go. This strategy is especially effective when dealing with well-informed audiences. For example, the statement quoted below is part of a technical presentation given by a technician in a global construction company. Notice how the presenter anticipates two counterarguments or objections his audience might have to using a new product.

Our field tests have shown that this new compound forms a better bond for broken pipe joints than any we've used. Admittedly it's less effective in very cold temperatures, so we will be limited to three-season use, but new batches are being developed that promise to be effective year-round. Some of you pointed out in your field report that the compound dries much slower—and it does by a factor of two; however, we know from tracking repair costs that we're saving at least 30 percent on repairing leaky joints, not to mention the savings from damage repairs.

The research on persuasion indicates that it's usually more effective to mix your responses to counterarguments with your own position rather than to isolate counterarguments in one section (O'Keefe, 2002).

Frame Your Issue for the Opinion Leaders. If you are speaking to your colleagues or members of a unit attached to your organization, use your knowledge of that culture to help you support your points. For example, how does that organization or group process information? What kinds of data or arguments do they find compelling? This kind of work is done "backstage" long before giving a presentation. You need, to the extent possible, to understand what kind of approach to your topic or proposal the opinion leaders in your audience would find most compelling or relevant. Communication experts refer to this process as effective "framing" in the same sense that you would frame a picture to present it in the best possible light and context.

For example,[2] Jay Conger, an expert on the role of persuasion in managing change, describes the efforts of a healthcare leader in the early 1980s to establish "palliative care"

[2]The following example is taken from Jay Conger, *Winning 'Em Over: A New Model for Management in the Age of Persuasion*, New York: Simon & Schuster, 1998, pp. 77–78.

as a widely practiced method of treating terminally ill patients. This approach uses coordinated teams of professionals and volunteers who address not only the patient's physical needs but also his or her social, psychological, and spiritual needs. When this healthcare professional, Dr. Balfort Mount, began proposing his idea for palliative care, there was not a single hospital in North America using this approach. A terminally ill patient was typically treated by a specialist, and the focus of the treatment was on managing the fatal illness, not the overall needs of the patient. Dr. Mount knew that to "sell" his vision, he would have to persuade a few key opinion leaders and his approach to each one would have to be tailored to his or her interests and motivations. These three people were the chief of surgery at a major hospital, the head of nursing, and the chief of professional services. Each one had a different "hot button," a core value that had to be addressed in Mount's approach.

- To the head of nursing, Mount emphasized that all members of the treatment teams would have a voice in the patient's treatment. He knew the head of nursing was committed to fair and equitable treatment of nurses, who had historically been viewed as the underlings of high-priced and often aloof physicians.

- To the chief of surgery, Mount stressed the importance of scientific rigor and professionalism—that each patient needed a comprehensive and rational plan for treatment.

- To the chief of professional services, a deeply religious man, Mount stressed the indispensable benefit of providing spiritual support to the patient, knowing that this leader valued this dimension of healthcare and human service, and felt that it was often neglected.

Despite major difficulties, Mount was highly successful in securing support for his ideas, and his approach to palliative care became a norm throughout North America.

In any effort at presenting ideas, try to use the two or three reasons or sources of evidence you feel have the greatest relevance, validity, and impact. Don't load too many reasons and angles into your message or it will sound like a laundry list—with no one item having more value than another.

A very helpful strategy is to use the magic number *three.* The number three is a very important number in our culture. Suzette Hayden-Elgin, an expert on the psychology of human communication, says "People are comfortable with things that come in threes" (Hayden-Elgin, 1997). You can capitalize on that comfort by using three elements in your presentations, particularly if you have little time to prepare and little time to make the points you wish to make. Hayden-Elgin recommends this formula:

1. State or present the problem or situation.
2. Provide three supporting items: *a, b,* and *c.*
3. Conclude with a summary.

For example, given the task of introducing a keynote speaker, this person uses a simple but effective three-element approach. It gives the speaker both a credibility set (which answers the question "Why should we listen to her?") and a warm climate set in very few words. Even the content set is at least implied in the introduction, and then left to the speaker to elaborate on.

I'm very pleased to introduce Fawn Ashton to you today because:

1. She is the person who organized the first Concerned Citizens for Clean Air chapter in the state.
2. As a pathologist specializing in pulmonary research, she is recognized as one of the best authorities in the country on air pollution and its effects on children with respiratory disorders.
3. She is a friend whose courage and integrity I have admired for over 20 years.

Fawn, thanks for sharing your valuable time with us today.

This three-element model will seem familiar and comfortable to your audience because they deal with this kind of structure all the time. Four or more items are often too many; fewer than three items may feel too limited, depending upon the complexity of your topic. When you think about support and sequencing, think about the number three, and then decide the best order in which to put those three items.

SEQUENCE

May I Pray While I Smoke?   Certain locations have more prominence in messages than others. For example, beginnings and endings are the more prominent locations. An audience is more likely to remember the opening and closing comments you make in a talk than the things that go in the middle.

While your content set gives the audience a map of the journey, the sequence of the content is more like the journey itself. Do you go to the drugstore first or the bank? Do you talk about the new security policy from the central office or the events that led to the policy? Do you give your recommendation upfront, or do you prepare your audience first with some background information?

Sequence is the order or arrangement of your talk. If you are conducting a meeting, it is the agenda you work from. You may have superb content, but if you present it in the wrong order, you may be misunderstood or ignored. Sequence is vital, but we often pay little attention to it. Look at these two sentences.

Carol is a superb systems analyst, but she is not great at dealing with people.
Carol is not great at dealing with people, but she is a superb systems analyst.

See what a difference sequence can make? These sentences do not mean the same thing. Each gives us a different impression of Carol. In the first sentence, the emphasis is on Carol's purported weaknesses in interpersonal relationships. The second stresses her strengths as a systems analyst, allowing for her poor performance with people. Gordon Allport, a prominent social scientist, used to tell his students a story about two monks who argued often about the appropriateness of smoking and praying at the same time. They decided independently to ask their superior to settle the question. One monk asked, "Father, may I smoke while I pray?" "Heavens no, my son. Prayer is a sacred activity" was the answer. Later, the second priest, knowing the power of sequencing asked, "Father, may I pray while I smoke?" He was told, "My son, it is always good to pray."

Spill the Beans. In most presentations or briefings, the best approach is to "spill the beans." Unveil your most important message first, and then support the point with elaboration and details. This sequence of main point first, followed by details, is often called the "managerial sequence," for writing and presenting. Action-oriented people, always short on time, usually want the gist, or bottom line, of a message first. For example, a good memo tells the reader up front what its main point is. A good presentation spills the beans at the beginning and provides backup later. We love suspense when we're reading a detective novel or watching a film, but not when we're listening to a presentation at work. Here's an example of a written message that spills the beans upfront.

Memorandum

TO: Product Development Management Team
FROM: Information technology task force
SUBJECT: Recommendation to purchase Windows XP

We recommend that our division purchase Windows XP. We base our recommendation on the following criteria:

- Breadth and power of features
- Ease of transition from our current operating system to Windows XP.
- Cost of both software purchase and support
- Quality of technical support offered by vendor

This memo would then continue to provide details of which operating systems were considered and how each one held up against the criteria used to make the recommendation. Many readers of this memo might have no need or desire to read past the opening paragraph. Others might want far more detail and would read the entire document. The point is that no reader would be required to read the entire document to uncover its core message.

There are exceptions to the spill-the-beans rule. If you have bad news, you may need to "buffer" the jolt by verbally placing your arm on your listener's shoulder. In this example a manager has to give her staff some bad news about an upcoming move.

I think most of you know I've been meeting frequently with our director over office space. I've played all the chips I had to win a resource for what I think is the best staff in this agency. I appreciate your support and your patience. Unfortunately, we've lost this one. We won't be moving into the new wing when it's finished. We'll be staying here in the old facility. We need to talk about what that means, and how best to live with it.

The worse the news or the tougher the topic, the more the need for a buffer. However, don't overdo putting off the bad news. People don't want to be coddled. They usually just want to be treated civilly and professionally.

Deciding on Sequence. Sometimes it's hard to decide what sequence to use. Do you present things in the order in which they happened (chronologically)? Do you go from the known to the unknown, or the simple to the complex? Any of these approaches might work, but you have to decide in each particular case. Think about your purpose and the audience's needs. You may need to persuade a group that your approach

[handwritten margin note: Bad news may need "buffer"]

to tracking inventory is most accurate, but your audience may need to be assured that it will not take more time to implement than the current system. Remember, audience-centered communication is your goal.

ACCESS

Some presentations are interesting, but the points they make are hard to pinpoint and remember. **Access** deals with making information visually and psychologically vivid to the listener or reader. When you write, you improve access by using boldface type, white space, headings, borders, numerals, and color. When you give a presentation, you can improve access by using good visual aids and making clear transitions from one point to the next. You can also make things more concise by stating them in fewer words, or summarizing them.

Words, Numbers, Pictures.   Visuals are extremely important to access. We live in a visual age. We are children of the media, and we process most of our information visually. A "talking head" is death in the media industry. Most network programming will not keep the camera on a person talking for more than 15 seconds. They break up the talking head with graphics or footage illustrating what the person is talking about. We know all this from our own experience, but time and again we see people pull their captive audiences through long, tedious presentations, glutted with details and void of visual enrichment.

Too often visuals are ineffective. Either they don't properly convey the important points of the presentation, or they are used as the primary method of communicating throughout the presentation. How many times have you been to a presentation where the presenter has simply read his or her slides and added little value to the actual on-the-spot presentation? When using Microsoft PowerPoint, the audience's focus should be on you. If you find that both the audience and you are staring at the slides, you are relying too much on the presentation software. Audiences do not want an exercise in reading slides. They want to hear you deliver your message. Here are some additional guidelines for using visuals.

1. Visuals are the tail. You, as presenter, are the dog. Don't let visuals control your presentation. Don't use high-tech equipment if you are unfamiliar with the system you are using.

2. Visuals do enhance audience comprehension and improve your credibility. Most speakers need to think more visually. When you have to talk to a group, try to translate from words into pictures. Turn concepts into pictures and numbers into graphs where possible. Consider using models or real objects in place of just pictures and graphs. If you're talking about a product or a three-dimensional object, show the real thing when possible.

3. Visuals and other props help you as a presenter by providing a reason for moving, pausing, and pointing. This movement gives your audience the visual variety they need, and it makes you look and feel more natural. We have videotaped hundreds of MBA student presentations and coached many executives. Virtually all of our students

and clients agree that presentations supported by visuals are much easier to give than the stand-up speech in which the speaker's body is the only visual.

4. Visuals need to be simpler than we usually make them. We should use line drawings, sketches, and photographs more—and be careful about flashing columns of numbers on the screen. A full page of numbers on a screen is as bad as a full page of sentences. Most numeric tables are hard to read as visuals. If you must use lots of numbers, highlight the most significant ones with a colored marker, or bracket the figures in some distinct way.

5. Visuals are primarily for the audience, not the speaker. Make every choice based upon *their* need to understand, not *your* need to dwell on fine points or impress them with how much homework you've done. If you have to introduce any visual by saying, "I know you can't see this very well but . . . ," kill that visual and use something more vivid and coherent.

6. Visuals can make a fool of you if you don't rehearse with them. Practice the pacing and sequence of your visuals, and become comfortable with handling them.

7. Visuals made from reports or other "page-size" documents are usually unreadable. If your audience is 18 feet away, the lettering on your charts or overheads must be one-half inch (as the audience sees it on the chart or screen); from 32 feet, it should be at least one inch.

8. Visuals need lots of white space. For word visuals, use no more than six items per visual and no more than eight words per item.

POLISH

Polish is the finish you put on anything that represents you or carries your reputation with it. It is the added and extra attention to details and little things. It is having your notes in order, having good visuals arranged at the overhead projector, dressing in such a way that you do not draw too much attention to yourself but need not worry about your appearance. Polish is arranging the environment for maximum effectiveness. People can hear you. They can see the screen. The room isn't stifling or chilly. You can't control all aspects of the environment, but you can do some things, and these make a huge difference. Polish is the extra attention to detail that tells the audience that the topic is important, they are worth the effort, and they are not wasting their time.

Practice, Practice, Practice. Last, but certainly not least, is the importance of practice. In many instances, practice is the difference between a great presentation and a mediocre presentation. Too often, students prepare great presentations that effectively use the elements of SSSAP but fail to spend adequate time rehearsing their presentation. A student who has memorized the flow (not exact words) of his presentation has a greater ability to perceive audience understanding. Understanding the audience allows the presenter to modify the presentation accordingly. The student who prepares a great presentation but practices very little will be too busy reading PowerPoint slides or trying to figure out where the next slide will take the presentation to focus on real communication.

ANALYSIS   Applying SSSAP

Objective   One way to reinforce the SSSAP approach is to analyze other people's presentations to see how effectively they use these principles.

Directions   Within the next week, take special note of a presentation in which you are part of the audience. A live presentation would be better than a televised one. Use the SSSAP principles and your own experience and expertise as a communicator to evaluate the presentation. Consider these questions:

1. Was it effective? Why or why not?
2. How could the presenter have improved his or her performance?
3. What do you think the presenter's main purpose was? Was that purpose clear?
4. Did the presenter prepare the audience with climate, credibility, and content sets? Did the presenter seem to understand the audience?
5. Did the presenter provide the support necessary to make his or her stated claims?
6. Would you have organized the presentation in the same way, or do you think the presentation would have been more effective if the presenter had discussed certain things before others?
7. Did the presenter offer a clear and memorable summary?
8. Was the presenter's message accessible visually and psychologically? How effective were the visuals and why?

Reflection   Even great presenters occasionally have an off day—perhaps due to a late night trip to the emergency room with a child running a fever or a missed flight connection that results in getting in late for a meeting. Following the SSSAP principles when preparing for the presentation, however, should help to minimize the consequences of unexpected challenges. SSSAP ensures that the message has been prepared with care, and the practice sessions help ensure that it will be delivered effectively. As an added bonus, the confidence that comes from knowing you are well prepared can also help mitigate the stress associated with last-minute problems.

PRACTICE   SSSAP: A Document of your Choice

Objective   The SSSAP principles can be applied to any written document, not just to oral presentations. This exercise is intended to give you practice at applying those principles to a memo requesting authority to hire an additional employee.

Directions   Redesign the following document, or one suggested by your instructor, using the SSSAP principles. Use your editing and layout skills to make this document more "user-friendly." Make any changes in wording, organization, layout, or design that you think would make the document more effective.

TO: VP of Human Resources   DATE:

FROM: M. Petuous, Senior Mktg. Admin.   RE: Marketing

The marketing department is struggling—we need to hire another person, if not two, very quickly. We currently have 12 full-time staff, but one person is on administrative duty with the strategic planning group, and three or four have not been doing their share of the work in the department lately. I know that money is tight, but even if we can't fire the slackers to free up some resources, we still need to hire someone who is willing to pick up their share of the work.

Another issue is related to the new MBO system for performance evaluations. Although we heard at the division meeting last week that MBO is important to the company, no one has time to work on developing the types objectives that are expected. Hiring an additional person or two would help us address that problem. It is no secret that the president is very enthusiastic about the MBO program, so it is not hard to imagine that failing to get MBO to work will result in a number of heads rolling, including your own.

After ten years of service I am committed to this company, but I can't see how we can retain new employees who have less invested here if we don't do something to take the pressure off them. Expectations continue to climb, but there are no increases in pay or other benefits to make people feel that it's worth it, particularly when you've got the slackers who've been here for 30 years refusing to learn the new technology and insisting on doing things "the way we've always done it."

The Board of Directors meeting is coming up in a few weeks, and I know that they like to micromanage things and may want to review any new authorizations to hire, so I hope that you agree that the marketing department should be given authorization to hire and that you are willing to present that case to the board. It is embarrassing when the chairman of the board's son is working as an intern in a department that is so understaffed that instead of giving him the typical copying and gophering jobs intended for interns but being done by the old-timers, he is getting stuck developing new marketing campaigns.

Finally, you may not have noticed, but the quality of the food in the dining room has gone from abysmal to practically poisonous. I don't know how we can attract new hires if we take them to eat in the dining room before they have signed a contract!

Discussion Questions
1. What are the main flaws in the document as it was originally written? What do you think would happen if the vice president of human resources received the original memo? What would you do if you were in that position?

2. Do you think that anyone would ever write a memo like this one? Why or why not?

3. How does the tone of the memo affect your perception of the credibility of the writer?

Reflection   All types of communication need to create some kind of climate set with the reader, establish the credibility of the communicator, and convey the content of the message. Information in memos and reports needs to be accessible visually through the use of white space, headings, italics, and other highlighting devices. Given the problems that everyone faces with information overload (recall Chapter 4), you can increase the chance that your message will be heard if you take the time to craft it using the SSSAP principles.

APPLICATION   You Be the Speaker

Objective   This exercise will give you practice in preparing and presenting an oral presentation.

Directions   Prepare a six-minute presentation on a topic of your choice. It may involve a problem or project at work, but it may also be taken from another class or your personal experience. Apply the SSSAP principles as you design your presentation.

Focus on creating a coherent message with a crisp beginning, middle, and end. We suggest you deliver the presentation using presentation software, such as Microsoft PowerPoint. Each slide should contain a significant point. Don't spend a lot of time designing visuals. Use "primitive" visuals if you wish, using the chalkboard or overhead projector. Work less on visual polish and more on the "support" and "sequence" elements of your presentation. Primitive visuals can also be very accessible despite their lack of polish.

Here are some suggested topics to trigger your thinking.

1. Talk about the organization you would most like to work for. What makes this organization a good employer?

2. Present a "briefing" on a significant issue or trend in an industry or sector you are interested in. You can take examples from healthcare, high technology, retail, manufacturing, tourism, telecommunications, education, government, transportation, e-commerce, construction—any area in which you have a personal interest. Envision your audience as a group of people who are currently working in that industry and have an urgent need to understand the issue or trend.

3. Offer a consultant's proposal to one of your instructors on how a class you are taking (or have recently taken) could be improved. Be specific in your recommendations. Describe the benefits of implementing your ideas, and the costs of failing to make improvements. Assume that a group of faculty who teach sections of the course are your core audience.

4. Design a brief training module on one of the 24 competencies discussed in this textbook. Teach your classmates a specific skill that will help them be more competent in one of the eight managerial roles.

Reflection   In selecting a topic for your presentation, what influenced your choice? Did you choose something that you were interested in learning more about or a subject that you felt you could address without doing additional research? Was the topic something that you are passionate about or did you choose something that wasn't especially important to you but would satisfy the requirements of the assignment? Why did you make the choices that you did? As we move to the final chapter on integration and the road to mastery, we have come full circle in the competing values framework, so it is appropriate to reflect back on the very first competency, understanding yourself and others. What does the choice you made about how to approach this assignment say about your interests, motivation, and dedication to becoming a master manager?

REFERENCES

Adizes, Ichak. *Corporate Lifecycles: How and Why Corporations Grow and Die and What to Do About It.* Englewood Cliffs, NJ: Prentice-Hall, 1988.

Calano, Jimmy, and Jeff Slazman. "Tough Deals, Tender Tactics." *Working Woman* (July 1988).

Cohen, Allan R., and David L. Bradford. *Influence Without Authority.* New York: John Wiley & Sons, 1990.

Conger, Jay. *Winning 'Em Over: A New Model for Management in the Age of Persuasion,* New York: Simon & Schuster, 1998.

Covey, Stephen R. *The Seven Habits of Highly Effective People.* New York: Simon and Schuster, 1990.

Fisher, Kimball. *Leading Self-Directed Work Teams: A Guide to Developing New Team Leadership Skills.* New York: McGraw-Hill, 2000.

Fisher, Roger, Elizabeth Kopelman, and Andrea Kupfer-Schneider. *Beyond Machiavelli. Tools for Coping with Conflict.* Cambridge, MA: Harvard University Press, 1994.

Fisher, Roger, and William Ury. *Getting to Yes: Negotiating Agreement Without Giving In.* New York: Penguin, 1991.

Goleman, Daniel. *Working with Emotional Intelligence.* New York: Bantam, 2000.

Handy, Charles. *Understanding Organizations.* New York: Oxford University Press, 1993.

Harding, Ford. *Rain Making: A Professional's Guide to Attracting New Clients.* Holbrook, MA: Bob Adams, 1994.

Hayden-Elgin, Suzette. *More on the Gentle Art of Verbal Self-Defense.* New York: Prentice-Hall, 1997.

Hayden-Elgin, Suzette. *The Last Word on the Gentle Art of Verbal Self-Defense.* New York: Prentice-Hall, 1987.

Hoff, Ron. *I Can See You Naked—A Fearless Guide to Making Great Presentations.* Kansas City: Andrews & McMeel, 1992.

Kanter, Rosabeth Moss. *The Change Masters: Innovation for Productivity in the American Corporation.* New York: Simon & Schuster, 1983.

Kotter, John P. "Power, Success, and Organizational Effectiveness." *Organizational Dynamics* (Winter 1978).

O'Keefe, D. *Persuasion, Theory and Research.* Newbury Park, CA: Sage Publications, 2002.

Patterson, Kerry, Joseph Grenny, Ron McMillan, and Al Switzler. *Crucial Conversations: Tools for Talking When Stakes Are High.* New York: McGraw-Hill, 2002.

Peace, William H. "The Hard Work of Being a Soft Manager." *Harvard Business Review* (November–December 1991): 40–47.

Stone, Douglas, Bruce Patton, and Sheila Heen. *Difficult Conversations: How to Discuss What Matters Most.* New York: Viking, 1999.

Tannen, Deborah. *Talking from 9 to 5: How Women's and Men's Conversational Styles Affect Who Gets Heard, Who Gets Credit, and What Gets Done at Work.* New York: William Morrow, 1995.

Ury, William. *Getting Past No: Negotiating Your Way from Confrontation to Cooperation.* New York: Bantam Books, 1993.

Vital Smarts. *Presenting with Power: A Guidebook* (training manual published by Vital Smarts, formerly called The Praxis Group). Provo, UT: 1994.

Whetten, David A., and Kim S. Cameron. *Developing Management Skills.* New York: Harper-Collins, 1995.

Wurman, Richard Saul. *Communication Anxiety.* New York: Doubleday, 1989.

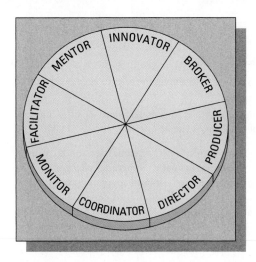

INTEGRATION 10
AND THE ROAD
TO MASTERY[1]

■ CONCLUSIONS

Understanding the Developmental Process

The Profile of a Master Manager

The Possibility of Self-Improvement

We have now presented all eight roles in the competing values framework and discussed how those roles and their related competencies fit with the four action imperatives of Cooperate, Control, Compete, and Create. You have had the opportunity to work on many of the 24 competencies, and you may have experienced some significant change. If you completed the competing values self-assessment instrument at the outset of the course (the assignment at the end of Chapter 1), it may now be useful to return to the instrument and assess yourself again.

ASSESSMENT   Reexamining Your Profile

Objective   People grow and develop over time, so it makes sense to periodically check in to see how we are progressing in our personal development.

Directions   Complete the competing values self-assessment instrument and again examine your profile. Comparing the two profiles, respond to the following questions. (If you did not complete the self-assessment at the outset of the course, answer the questions based on your own understandings of how you have changed.)

1. What were my greatest strengths and weaknesses at the outset?

2. How do I see myself differently at this time?

[1]Portions of this chapter are adapted from Robert E. Quinn, *Beyond Rational Management: Mastering the Paradoxes and Competing Demands of High Performance.* San Francisco: Jossey-Bass, 1988. Used with permission.

3. In which areas do I feel I still need to enhance my skills?

4. To what extent do I feel comfortable in choosing from among the roles to approach group or organizational problems or issues?

5. To what extent do I feel comfortable using several roles in complementary or supplementary ways to approach group or organizational problems or issues?

Reflection   When we step back to assess our personal development, we sometimes see subtle changes; other times the changes we have made may be more dramatic. Sometimes changes we have made move us toward our goals, but sometimes, if we have not been consciously attending to our personal development, we discover that we have allowed ourselves to develop in ways that may hinder our goals. Developing a clear understanding of the developmental process can help you work to develop the competencies you feel are most important for your professional and personal success.

UNDERSTANDING THE DEVELOPMENTAL PROCESS

Using this book, you have had the opportunity to develop skills associated with eight different roles of managerial leadership. The mastery of management, however, requires more than just the development of skills alone. It requires the ability to enter a situation, to see it from contrasting perspectives, and to call upon contrasting competencies. It often requires the blending of contrasting competencies. This is not easy. Consider, for example, the following story that might have been told by the instructor of your own class.

This week in class the topic was building teams. The students were assigned to engage in several group activities outside of class; we also did several in-class exercises. I began the class with a lecture, discussing the differences between groups and teams. I emphasized that when the team is performing at an optimal level, people get inspired and work productively without much need for intervention or control on the part of the boss. I also pointed out that groups evolve through predictable stages before becoming a team and that if this evolutionary process is managed correctly, the team can become one of the manager's most powerful tools. After presenting several concrete examples, I noted that few managers ever experience the phenomenon because managers have a hard time letting go of their control and so the evolutionary process is hindered in its early stages. I presented a list of task functions and a list of process functions that must occur in order for the group to evolve.

As we discussed task functions such as initiating structure, giving information, clarifying, summarizing, and evaluating, they had little difficulty understanding. When we turned to process functions such as processing observations, empathizing, participating, surfacing rather than smothering conflict, and managing interpersonal tension in a positive way, they seemed more challenged. Then we did the exercises.

After class, one of the students wanted to talk. He said he had noticed during the first exercise that one of the members was not involved. He decided that he would try to include that student. This is what he told me: "I totally failed. When you assigned the second exercise, I noticed that this guy was again sitting around and not saying anything. But I decided that I could not do anything about it. We had only so much time and the work had to get done. I do not think it is possible to get the work done and also do those other things you were talking about. You cannot worry about doing both at the same time."

Many managers are like the student in the preceding story. They perform well in some situations, but they have difficulty or feel uncomfortable in others. Or they excel in several of the competencies or roles, but they find that integrating them with other competencies or roles is difficult. The objective of this chapter is to put all the competencies into a dynamic perspective and to show how they are interrelated. Understanding this aspect of the model may help you to avoid some of the pitfalls and to move, with practice, toward mastery. We should note, however, that when we talk about moving toward mastery, we are just as concerned with the journey as we are with the destination. The notion of *becoming* a master manager recognizes that there are always more things to learn and new ideas that will challenge you to enhance your abilities. Moreover, as discussed in Chapter 1, you will find that as you move up the organizational hierarchy, you will need to learn new skills and abilities, as well as unlearn others, to perform well in each of the managerial leadership roles presented in this book. Thus, as you near mastery at one level, you will likely be promoted or moved into a new area where you will be faced with new responsibilities and new challenges, and therefore return to the process of becoming. You will see that as you go through the different stages of your career, you will always need to develop new competencies. The earlier you understand the need for continuous learning, the earlier you learn to value the process of becoming, the more effective you will be as a manager.

THE ROAD TO MASTERY

The road to mastery of an activity is essentially a lifelong learning process that takes place over time. Although this learning can take place at times when you are not consciously aware that you are learning, it generally requires a focused effort at understanding new concepts and practicing new skills. Here is an example to clarify what we mean.

Recently, one of our colleagues told us a story about a conversation she had had with another faculty member in her department. The faculty member was complaining that despite his best efforts to give students group projects so that they could improve their group skills, students were still raising objections to doing these projects because they had trouble coordinating their efforts and found some of their student colleagues to be less willing to pull their weight. When our colleague asked what group management skills he had taught, he looked at her bewildered and said, "I didn't think that I had to teach group skills; I just assumed that they would figure it out by doing it."

Just as you cannot become an expert swimmer by jumping into the deep end of the pool, you are unlikely to become a master manager by taking charge of a large organization. You need to start at a level at which you are comfortable and consciously work at developing your competencies, always challenging yourself to perform at a higher level. Dreyfus and Dreyfus (1986) provide a five-stage model that describes the journey from novice to expert (see Figure 10.1).

Stage 1: The Novice. As a novice, you learn facts and rules. The rules are learned as absolutes, which are never to be violated. For example, a beginning chess player learns the names of the pieces, how they are moved, and their value. He or she is told to exchange pieces of lower value for pieces of higher value. In management this might be the equivalent of learning the various task and group maintenance functions and being

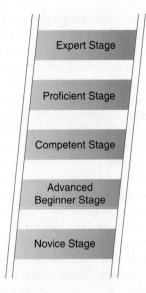

FIGURE 10.1 *Five steps to mastery.*

told that team performance requires attention to both sets of functions. The student in the story was still at the novice stage in trying to perform the maintenance functions in a group.

Stage 2: The Advanced Beginner. In this stage, experience becomes critical. As real situations are encountered, performance improves and you are able to put into practice the stated facts and rules. As you observe certain basic patterns, you begin to recognize factors that were not stated in the rules. A chess player, for example, begins to recognize certain basic board positions that should be pursued. The new manager discovers the importance of understanding the basic norms, values, and culture of the organization. Technical procedures, types of relationships, appropriate dress, and typical career paths are among the things that may vary dramatically from what the novice learned in textbooks. The student in the story at the beginning of the chapter was just beginning to experience real-world challenges as he tried to apply the rules to the specific situation he encountered.

Stage 3: Competence. As you gain competence, you gain a better appreciation of the complexity of the task and recognize a much larger set of cues. You develop the ability to select and concentrate on the most important cues. You are no longer aware of the absolute rules; they are assumed. As your competence increases at this stage, you develop some personal "rules of thumb" that guide, but do not direct, your actions. You engage in calculated risks and complex trade-offs. A chess player may, for example, weaken board position in order to attack the opposing king. This plan may or may not follow any rules that the person was ever taught. The manager may experiment with going beyond the basic tools and techniques taught in school as he or she experiments with new behaviors. Here the manager is more willing to trust his or her intuition and take risks or suggest new approaches. This may occasionally result in successful outcomes; many times it will not. Here the trial-and-error process is critical to continued development. If the student in the original illustration had continued with his group, he might have begun to experiment with stopping the group process to check what quiet members were feeling, or he might have tried to surface conflicts that were being avoided. In this stage we become more at ease with knowing when and how to make such interventions.

Stage 4: Proficiency.   Here, calculation and rational analysis seem to disappear. Unconscious, fluid, and effortless performance begins to emerge, and no one plan is held sacred. You learn to unconsciously "read" the evolving situation. You notice and respond to new cues as the importance of the old ones recedes. New plans are triggered as emerging patterns call to mind plans that worked previously. Your grasp of the situation is holistic and intuitive. Probably only professional chess players achieve the level of play at which they have the ability to recognize and respond to change in board positions intuitively. Managers who reach this stage are seen as highly effective because they are capable of performing in a wide variety of situations and dealing with seemingly contradictory demands. In the proficiency stage our student would be able to manage the various task and maintenance functions in what seems to be an effortless way, but the effort is hidden.

Proficiency does not come easily. It requires practice and an ability to develop one's senses to a point where patterns can be recognized intuitively. Gary Klein studies individuals who make life-and-death decisions to learn about "how people perceive and observe, think and reason, act and react" (Breen, 2000). He has worked with BP Amoco, Duke Power Company, several airline companies, the U.S. Army, and the U.S. Air Force to help these organizations develop faster and better decision makers. What he has found is that individuals who must make critical decisions quickly develop their intuition to draw on previous experiences. In Klein's study of firefighters, Air Force pilots, intensive care nurses and others, he has found that although novices tend to follow classic decision-making models, these individuals abandon these models as their skills and experience grow. Klein talks about a fighter pilot who initially followed all the "rules and checklists in order to fly the plane correctly." At one point, however, the pilot reported that he had a profound breakthrough and that "it felt as if he wasn't flying the plane—it felt as if he was flying. He had internalized all the procedures for flying until the plane had felt as if it was a part of him. He no longer needed any rules."

Stage 5: Expertise.   At this level optimal performance becomes second nature. People at this stage are not consciously aware of the details; rather they use a holistic perspective that gives them a deep understanding of the situation. They have programmed into their heads multidimensional maps of the territory of which the rest of us are not aware. They see and know things intuitively that the rest of us do not know or see. They frame and reframe strategies as they read changing cues. Klein notes that this runs counter to what most people believe. "We used to think that experts carefully deliberate the merits of each course of action, whereas novices impulsively jump at the first option." Thus, many people believe that experts make decisions slowly because they are "weighed down by information, by facts, by memories." Instead, Klein argues, "the accumulation of experience does not weigh them down—it lightens them up. It makes them fast" (quoted in Breen, 2000). This ability facilitates their engagement of the natural flow of events. Here the manager fully transcends any natural blind spots and is able to shift roles as needed. The expert seems to effortlessly meet the contradictions of organizational life.

THE PROFILE OF A MASTER MANAGER

Is it appropriate to apply the notion of mastery to the tasks of management? Certainly managerial leaders progress through stages where we expect them to become increasingly effective in their performance. In the first chapter we discussed three challenges that are associated with effective management. We review them here:

Challenge 1   To appreciate both the values and the weaknesses of the four models of the competing values framework.

Challenge 2   To acquire and use the competencies associated with each of the roles in the framework.

Challenge 3   To dynamically integrate the competencies from each of the roles within the managerial situations that we encounter.

Thus, becoming a master manager requires not only ability to play all eight roles (at least at a competent level), it also requires that the manager have the ability to blend and balance the competing roles in an appropriate way. Recall from Chapter 1 the notion of behavioral complexity, "the ability to act out a cognitively complex strategy by playing multiple, even competing, roles in a highly integrated and complementary way" (Hooijberg and Quinn, 1992, p. 164). This ability involves two components—behavioral repertoire, the number of leadership roles a manager can use effectively, and behavioral differentiation, the ability to use the role they have in their behavioral repertoire differently, depending on the situation (Hooijberg, Hunt, and Dodge, 1997). In the twenty-first century, behavioral complexity will become increasingly important for global leaders whose ability to "generate superior corporate performance . . . [will require them to balance] (1) profitability and productivity, (2) continuity and efficiency, (3) commitment and morale, and (4) adaptability and innovation" (Petrick, Scherer, Brodzinski, Quinn, and Ainina, 1999, p. 60).

As you consider the eight roles and 24 competencies presented in this book, you may question whether it is possible to perform all of these well. During this course, you may have found that you felt very comfortable performing in some of the roles and uncomfortable in others, and you may ask whether it is possible to link the demands of one role with the demands of a role in an opposite area of the framework. In order to approach this issue, we will briefly review a study of ineffective and effective managers.

Using the competing values framework, Quinn, Faerman, and Dixit (1987) found that ineffective organizational leaders tended to have profiles that were badly out of balance. Those leaders might be above average on the top four roles (mentor, facilitator, innovator, broker) and then be well below average on the bottom four (monitor, coordinator, director, producer). Such managers were seen by associates as impulsive and chaotic, spreading disorder everywhere. Some had the opposite profile. They were seen as narrowly focused on control and abrasive toward people. Among the ineffective, there were several other profiles as well, but all were badly out of balance. Four of the ineffective profiles are shown in Figure 10.2.

Interestingly, most of the effective profiles also had some imbalance in them. But here there was a difference. In the effective profiles, people tended to have high scores on more than half of the roles. In addition, the scores on their weaker roles tended to fall near the average. In other words, they did not neglect any of the roles. Nevertheless, they were not free of style. Most tended to emphasize some areas more than others.

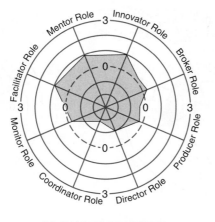

(a) CHAOTIC ADAPTIVES

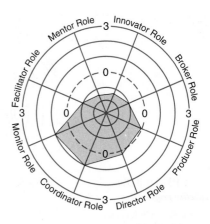

(b) ABRASIVE COORDINATORS

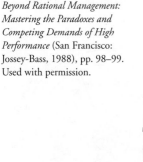

FIGURE 10.2 *Four ineffective profiles.*

Source: Robert E. Quinn, *Beyond Rational Management: Mastering the Paradoxes and Competing Demands of High Performance* (San Francisco: Jossey-Bass, 1988), pp. 98–99. Used with permission.

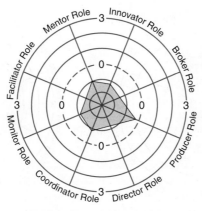

(c) DROWNING WORKAHOLICS

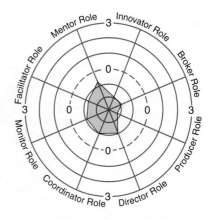

(d) EXTREME UNPRODUCTIVES

Figure 10.3 shows four types of effective profiles, labeled aggressive achievers, conceptual producers, peaceful team builders, and masters. The aggressive achievers tend not to excel in the human relations quadrant. The conceptual producers tend not to excel in the internal process quadrant, and the peaceful team builders are near the average on the two roles on the right side of the framework. Although each of these three clearly reflects a style, all are seen as effective profiles of managerial leadership.

The fourth profile is different from the others—it is big and round. This profile was labeled "masters" because these managerial leaders seem to have transcended style; they seem to appreciate the underlying values in each quadrant and can also employ the behaviors that are represented in each one. What cannot be seen in the profile, however, is that these individuals are not only capable of playing each of the roles; they are also able to integrate the roles and to use the competencies in complementary ways.

How do these individuals come to "round out" their profiles? Part of the answer lies in experience. Masters tend to be in upper-middle and top-level positions. It is reasonable to suggest that these managers did not begin their careers as masters. Although some people have years of experience and are still not effective in all eight roles, masters tend

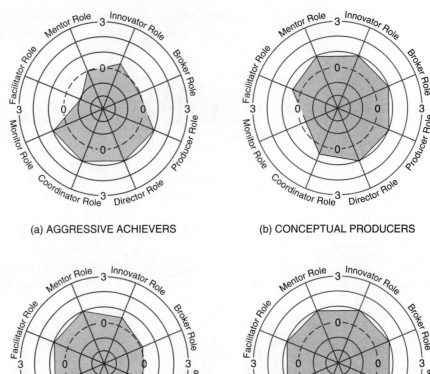

FIGURE 10.3 *Four effective profiles.*

Source: Robert E. Quinn, *Beyond Rational Management: Mastering the Paradoxes and Competing Demands of High Performance* (San Francisco: Jossey-Bass, 1988), pp. 101–102. Used with permission.

(a) AGGRESSIVE ACHIEVERS

(b) CONCEPTUAL PRODUCERS

(c) PEACEFUL TEAM BUILDERS

(d) MASTERS

to focus on personal and professional development. They recognize the need to constantly grow; they welcome transitions that are the most challenging and come out of these transitions with a wider array of competencies, less tied to a particular style. To understand this change process, we now turn to a case illustration.

ONE JOURNEY TOWARD MASTERY

Consider the case of a truly successful organizational leader whose journey toward mastery pivoted around a crucial crisis and transformation (Quinn, 1988).

He had graduated from a five-year engineering program in four years and had taken a job with his current organization. Starting out in a brilliant fashion, he was promoted rapidly. He had an ability to take a complex technical problem and come up with a better answer than anyone else. He was also a hard-driving person who pushed his people to accomplish some impressive tasks.

Initially he was seen as an action-oriented person with a bright future. His profile was that of an aggressive achiever (see Figure 10.3).

After his last promotion, however, everything started to change. He went through several very difficult years. For the first time he received serious negative feedback about his performance. His ideas and proposals were regularly rejected, and for the first time he was passed over for a promotion. In reflecting on those days, he said:

"It was awful. Everything was always changing and nothing ever seemed to happen. They would sit around forever and talk about things. The technically right answer didn't matter. They were always making what I thought were wrong decisions, and when I insisted on doing what was right, they got angry and would ignore what I was saying. Everything was suddenly political. They would worry about what everyone was going to think about every issue. Your appearance, attending cocktail parties, that stuff, to me, was unreal and unimportant. I went through five and a half terrible years. I occasionally thought I had reached my level of incompetence, but I refused to give up."

Finally, a critical incident occurred. Like many critical incidents in the transformational process, it may seem comical to an outside observer. On several occasions, the engineer's boss commented that he was very impressed with one of the engineer's subordinates. Finding the comment somewhat curious, the engineer asked for an explanation. The boss indicated that no matter how early he himself arrived at work, the subordinate's car was always there.

The engineer then went to visit the subordinate and indicated that he had noticed that no matter what time he came in, the subordinate's car was already in the lot. The subordinate nodded his head and explained,

"I have four teenagers who wake up at dawn. The mornings at my house are chaotic. So I come in early. I read for a while, then I write in my personal journal, read the paper, have some coffee, and then I start work at eight."

When the engineer left his subordinate's office, he was at first furious. After a couple of minutes, though, he sat down and started to laugh. He later explained, "That is when I discovered perception." He went on to say that from that moment everything started to change. He was more patient. He began to experiment with participative decision making. His relationships with superiors gradually improved. Eventually he actually came to appreciate the need to think and operate in more complex ways at the higher levels of the organization.

This story represents a learning process. The engineer was very adept in using the skills in the two lower quadrants. Here he was in the proficient or expert stages. Rapid promotions, however, put him into a new and more complex situation. At the higher organizational levels, skills in the top two quadrants—skills that he had not learned as an engineer—were much more important than they had been previously. With respect to the skills in these top two quadrants, he was in the novice or advanced beginner stage. He applied his old assumptions and governing rules only to see them fail. The resulting frustration and panic led him to try even harder and intensify his use of his old skills. This, in turn, resulted in more failure and frustration.

Peter Senge (1990) refers to this phenomenon as "fixes that fail." It is a common occurrence in organizations and stems from the inability to see that short-term successes may have unintended consequences that create new problems. By being successful as an engineer, our protagonist was promoted into a situation where the rules of engineering did not apply. Fortunately for the engineer, he did not quit. With a greater understanding of the power of perception, he was able to examine other assumptions about what it meant to be a truly effective manager. The one event gave him the critical, creative insight that he needed, an insight that led to a reframing of what it means to be successful. As the human and political domains (human relations and open systems models) began to become a part of his worldview, he began to explore and experiment with new skills. This was eventually followed by a marked improvement in performance.

As a manager, this man was not now perfect. Clearly he had his share of bad days. There were occasions when he got discouraged, and there were times when his subordinates felt he was too harsh. Nevertheless, he had widened his range of capacities and most of the time displayed an ability to call upon them in successful ways. Moreover, he had opened himself up to learning about new management approaches and was committed to trying new ideas. For the most part, he had achieved, with considerable effort, a profile resembling those we label as "masters," managers with the capacity to both play and integrate competing roles.

HOW MASTERS SEE THE WORLD

Having examined part of the journey of one master manager, we turn to the broader issue of why some individuals are more successful than others in their journey to become a master manager. What other characteristics differentiate these managers from other managers? Why are some people better able to integrate seemingly opposite modes of behavior? Although we cannot say for certain, our experience has suggested that the answer begins with an understanding of how master managers see (think about) the world. People who become masters of management do not see their work environment only in structured, analytic ways. Instead, they also have the capacity to see it as a complex, dynamic system that is constantly evolving. In order to interact effectively with their work environment, they employ a variety of different, sometimes contradictory, perspectives or modes. In other words, they employ different modes of thinking. Here we will briefly discuss two modes of thinking that appear to be related to behavioral complexity: systems (dynamic) thinking and paradoxical thinking.

Peter Senge describes *systems thinking* as "a discipline for seeing wholes. It is a framework for seeing interrelationships rather than things, for seeing patterns of change rather than static 'snapshots.'. . . [It is] a discipline for seeing the "structures" that underlie complex situations, and for discerning high from low leverage change" (1990, pp. 68–69). One of the key elements of systems thinking is the concept of *feedback,* or the "reciprocal flow of influence" (1990, p. 75). In a situation where there is feedback behavior, if A influences B, and B influences C, C (or something that is influenced by C) will ultimately influence A. Often, when C and A are separated in time, it is difficult to recognize the feedback.

Recall that the engineer's initial superior performance resulted in his promotion into a position for which he was not prepared, a situation in which his performance was poorly evaluated. Thus, as a result of a reciprocal flow of influence, superior performance led to inferior performance. This is an example of negative, or balancing, feedback. Alternatively, positive, or reinforcing, feedback will occur when actions lead to ever-increasing (or -decreasing) levels of behavior. When the engineer intensified his use of his old skills, he received poorer and poorer performance reviews. And the more he failed, the more he tried to return to the old tried-and-true approach.

Most of us, like the engineer in the preceding story, learn to think about organizations in a very static and purposeful way. We see the world in terms of simple one-way cause-and-effect reasoning, believing that events will cause (or are caused by) other events—if you cut expenditures, profits will rise; if you send employees to training, their performance will improve; if you get good grades, you will (at least you should) get a good job. We tend not to notice that actions taken today can result in new problems that we will need to deal with several months (or years) down the line; we tend to believe that a problem addressed in one area of the organization has no consequences for other areas. As noted by Senge, this type of cause-and-effect thinking "distract[s] us from seeing the longer-term patterns of change that lie behind the events and from understanding the causes of those patterns" (1990, p. 21). When organizations exist in stable, predictable environments, this cause-and-effect thinking is acceptable and there is no need to concern ourselves with the larger patterns of action. But few, if any, organizations exist in stable, predictable environments. Instead, organizations exist in dynamic, changing environments, where small changes in the social, political, economic, and technological environment can have a major impact on the organization's future.

Margaret Wheatley (1992) suggests that one reason why we tend to use simple, linear cause-and-effect thinking is that much of our thinking is influenced by seventeenth-century Newtonian physics. "Each of us lives and works in organizations designed from Newtonian images of the universe. We manage by separating things into parts, we believe that influence occurs as a direct result of force exerted from one person to another, we engage in complex planning for a world that we keep expecting to be predictable, and we search for continually better methods of objectively perceiving the world" (1992, p. 6). But, as Wheatley notes, science has changed, and so should our images of organizations. We need to be far more aware of interrelationships. "In a quantum world, relationships are not just interesting; to many physicists, they are *all* there is to reality" (1992, p. 32, emphasis in the original). Recall that master managers and other expert decision makers use holistic recognition in a way that allows them to deeply understand the situation. The ability to see the underlying structures, to see the interrelationships, and to understand that actions have a long-term impact is essentially the basis of systems thinking.

Paradoxical thinking is somewhat related to systems thinking in that both help us deal with apparent contradictions. In Chapter 1 we introduced the notion that organizational leaders spend much of their time living in fields of perceived tensions. They are constantly forced to make trade-offs; there are often no right answers. Moreover, the higher one goes in an organization, the more exaggerated these tensions become. One-dimensional guidelines (care for people; work harder; get control; be innovative) are simply half-truths representing single domains of action. What exist are contradictory pressures. Much of the time the choice is not between good and bad, but between good and good—or bad and bad. In such cases there is sometimes a need for paradoxical thinking, thinking that transcends the contradictions and recognizes that two seemingly opposite conditions can simultaneously be true.

In order to engage in paradoxical thinking, one must be willing to engage in contradiction. This does not simply mean that managers are willing or able to perform different roles at different times. It means that they must be willing to try to resolve the contradiction and to integrate seemingly opposite ideas or behaviors. It means trying to be a mentor at the same time you are being a director, being an innovator at the same time you are being a coordinator, and so on. To do this, managers must be willing to move outside their current level of thinking and attempt to see things from a new perspective. Albert Einstein is often quoted as saying, "No problem can be solved from the same consciousness that produced it" (quoted in Wheatley, 1992, p. 5).

The competing values framework is built around the notion of paradox. It assumes that organizations need to be simultaneously adaptable/flexible and stable/controlled; that in order to perform effectively, they need to focus simultaneously on their external environments and competitive position and on their internal environments and the people and work processes. As a conceptual model, the framework itself suggests that we tend to think of roles on opposite sides of the axes as antithetical. In addition, throughout this book we have mentioned paradoxes that occur within roles, such as the need for individuals to take energy breaks in order to be more productive (producer) and the strategy of creating conflict in order to reduce conflict (facilitator). Implicitly, the model suggests that managers who are most capable of thinking paradoxically would also be most capable of performing in seemingly opposite roles.

One of the most effective ways to increase your ability to engage in paradoxical thinking is to challenge yourself to see the value in areas that are not your strengths, to seek out that which is outside of your comfort zone. Seeking out that which is outside your comfort zone requires several capabilities. First, it requires you to see different points of view. Here we can learn from the words of Martin Luther King Jr.:

> Help us to see the enemy's point of view, to hear his questions, to know his assessment of ourselves. From his view we may indeed see the basic weakness of our condition, and if we are mature, we may learn and grow and profit from the wisdom of our brothers who are called the opposition. (quoted in Phillips, 1999, p. 85)

Second, it requires you to be willing to stretch. In Chapters 2 and 5, we talked about ways in which individuals develop their abilities by taking on new tasks and responsibilities in their jobs. But as Chaleff (1995) notes in *The Courageous Follower,* "We also need external growth opportunities. There is often ample room for growth within our current position if we assertively seek it. . . . At some point, however, it may be desirable to move away from the comfort of our current role to test ourselves in a new, unproven role" (p. 39). Finally, it requires that you be willing to see the many interdependencies that exist between that which one finds comfortable and that which one does not. For example, most people see art and science as very different and are drawn to one or the other. People often ask whether leadership is an art or a science. Leonardo da Vinci, one of the world's greatest geniuses, whose work embraced uncertainty, ambiguity, and paradox (Gelb, 1998), saw the connections between art and science. As Gelb notes:

> For Leonardo, art and science were indivisible. In his Treatise on Painting *he cautions potential adepts:* "Those who become enamoured of the art, without having previously applied to the diligent study of the scientific part of it, may be compared to mariners who put to sea in a ship without a rudder or compass and therefore cannot be certain of arriving at the wished for port." (p. 166)

THE POSSIBILITY OF SELF-IMPROVEMENT

The engineer in the earlier case "stumbled" into a new paradigm. He was both determined and lucky. Many people who encounter his problem are defeated by it; they are not willing to open themselves up to seeing the world in a different way. Although you are also likely to encounter problems in your development, you have some major advantages. First, you have a framework to help you appreciate the necessity of performing in the areas that do not come naturally. Second, you have had the opportunity to practice using different competencies and so should have greater self-confidence in your ability to perform the various roles. Building on the foundation of competencies developed in this course and related experiences, you should be able to continue developing as a managerial leader. Finally, your experiences in this course should have given you an understanding of the necessity to think complexly and to integrate diverse competencies. Thus, you have both cognitive and behavioral (performance) tools to help you improve yourself.

One of the enduring questions asked in the field of leadership is, "Are leaders born or made?" While we do not know "the answer" to this question, or even if there is a simple answer, we are convinced that conscious self-improvement is possible. When a person is willing to put forth the effort required to make a change, and is determined to make a change, that person is likely to succeed.

Many managers, however, excuse themselves from this responsibility. There is an unlimited number of excuses for not trying:

- "I am simply not creative, and there is no way to change that."

- "I hate details, and I will never be a good monitor."

- "Being a hard-driving producer is fine, but it is not worth the effort—life is simply too short."

- "Different people have different talents, and working with people is not my thing."

In each case the statement is an excuse for not making changes. In each case the statement is untrue. It is always possible for someone to make improvements in his or her weak area. He or she may legitimately choose not to, since, as we learned in a previous section, it is possible to neglect some roles to a certain degree and still be effective. However, it is inaccurate to say, "I have a particular style and I am not capable of performing in a different manner." Although sometimes difficult, it is in fact always possible to make improvements in one's weak areas. Here we will outline a procedure for doing so.

AGENDA FOR SELF-IMPROVEMENT

Table 10.1 provides an agenda for self-improvement that involves three general steps: Learn about yourself, develop a change strategy, and implement the strategy. Within each of these steps are some key subpoints. This process has been used with many practicing managers and graduate students. In the beginning of the process, many participants are cynical, and some make only half-hearted efforts. Needless to

TABLE 10.1 Agenda for Self-Improvement

---

1. Learn About Yourself
   - Complete the competing values self-assessment instrument.
   - Do a written self-evaluation of each role.
   - Have others evaluate you.
   - Discuss your skills with people who will be honest.
   - Keep a journal.
2. Develop a Change Strategy
   - Identify specific areas in need of improvement and set specific goals.
   - Consider how you can use your strengths to help you develop in your weak areas.
   - Identify positive role models for your weak areas.
   - Identify courses or workshops that you can take to help you develop new competencies.
   - Identify new job assignments.
   - Read relevant books.
3. Implement the Change Strategy
   - Be honest about the costs of improvement.
   - Develop a social support system.
   - Evaluate your progress on a regular basis and modify your strategy, if necessary.

---

say, they show little achievement. But others attack the process with zeal, and they naturally achieve considerably more. The interesting thing is that the people who make progress do so in whatever quadrant they choose. It is possible to learn and to improve in any area.

LEARN ABOUT YOURSELF

There are many ways in which you can learn about yourself. Some focus on looking within; others involve reaching outside to learn about how others see you. You can start by doing a self-assessment. This involves filling out the competing values self-assessment instrument, analyzing your skills in each role, and doing a written assessment of yourself in each role. In the written assessment, you should explain why you believe you are strong or weak in each area. Completing the self-assessment can be a relatively simple task, but it can also be misleading. Often people assess themselves differently, either more positively or more negatively, than do their subordinates, peers, and superiors. This is why it is important to obtain honest feedback from others.

Although many people claim that they want to receive honest feedback from those around them, they, in fact, behave in ways that prevent such feedback. In one class, students were given an assignment that involved not only improving themselves in the course of a semester, but also going out and helping a manager to develop his or her competencies. They arranged to act as consultants to a practicing manager. Over the semester the students analyzed the manager's behavior and worked with the person to improve weak areas. This provided an important mirror that allowed the students to see the flaws and the resistances in themselves by seeing them first in another person. The following is a typical statement about feedback, written by one of the students.

> *Perhaps one of the most amazing things to me is that, not only the manager we worked with, but virtually every manager that was helped by one of the teams in the class, was so deeply interested in feedback from subordinates and others. They were simply unsure about what others thought about them. In every case, it was the first time in their careers that they received such feedback. As I think about it now, it seems incredible that such a simple thing could be so powerful.*

Feedback from others is indeed powerful. In recent years, many companies have instituted 360-degree feedback (Lepsinger and Lucia, 1997), which provides managers with an assessment from his or her employees, peers, and managers. If you are a manager, you might ask your human resources management department whether they have considered instituting such a process in your organization.

Sometimes, however, feedback can be too powerful. Occasionally a person receives feedback that suggests that other people see him or her as less effective in a given area than the person sees him- or herself. Although most people can handle this negative message, some cannot, and this can be a cause of a personal crisis. Some people get depressed and withdraw; others get angry and want to punish those who gave the feedback. Once you ask for feedback, however, it is important that you be willing to reflect on what you have heard and show appreciation to those who have been willing to provide the feedback (Chaleff, 1995).

When you get feedback that comes as a surprise, use it as a springboard for honest exploration and discussion. Marshall Goldsmith (1996), who has been ranked as one of the "top 10" consultants in the field of executive development by *The Wall Street Journal,* argues that one key characteristic that differentiates leaders of tomorrow from leaders of yesterday is their willingness to "ask, learn, follow up and grow" (p. 227). In order to use feedback as a growth experience, you will probably need to wait long enough to get into the proper frame of mind so that you are indeed ready to hear what people have to say. This may take some time and preparation. Go to those who know you best, ask questions, and then listen carefully to what they have to say. This strategy takes a certain level of maturity and self-esteem. If you feel unsure of yourself, you should wait until some future time to seek feedback. Be careful not to behave in ways that would lead people to say only those things that you will find acceptable.

You may feel unable, for whatever reason, to approach particular people for feedback, but that should not be a cause for concern. In fact, it is a common occurrence. People should talk to those few others with whom they have a trusting and caring relationship but who will nevertheless be honest in their feedback.

Finally, we suggest that you keep a journal. Often people have difficulty remembering experiences that occur over a period of time. As you develop a particular skill, you may not be able to accurately recall what your skill level was when you began, what were some of the milestones that signaled progress, or what issues you encountered along the way. Keeping a journal allows you to learn about yourself by providing a written record of your behaviors and thoughts over the time period. If you had been keeping a journal during this course, you would now be able to review your accomplishments and this might give you a better sense of how you have progressed.

DEVELOP A CHANGE STRATEGY

Once you have sought feedback from others, you might then make a final assessment of what you think are your strong and weak areas. As you write a final assessment of your strengths and weaknesses in each role of the competing values framework, pinpoint the ones on which you most need to work. In developing your plan, think about what opportunities are available for taking courses and/or taking on new job responsibilities. Also identify someone who does very well in your weak role. This will help to make concrete the kinds of behaviors that are appropriate in this role. When you are in situations that call for behavior in the role, you can ask yourself, "What would the person do in this situation?"

This step sometimes makes you uncomfortable because you may not like the people who do well in your weak areas. For example, one of our students had a colleague who, in terms of the competing values framework, was an exact opposite in outlook, strategy, and behavior. Working with him was very difficult. There was conflict over nearly every decision they had to reach together. But the student learned to embrace what he found threatening. In a final paper the student wrote:

role models

> Although the costs of working with him have been high, I have also learned a great deal from him. In many situations I have watched him do the exact opposite of what I would have done. It sometimes has been shocking to see his strategies work far better than my own. Over time I have come to recognize certain situations in which his thinking might be better than mine. I am now able to stop before implementing my natural strategy and ask myself what he would do in this case. Often I am dissatisfied with the answer and proceed with my own approach. There are, however, times when I go against my instincts and follow his lead. Thinking about him as a role model in my weak areas enlarges my pool of possible strategies. Sometimes, following uncomfortable strategies results in the development of a wider array of behaviors and skills.

Another key activity is to read literature that is related to your weak roles. After this chapter you will find A Competing Values Reading List. It is organized according to the eight roles in the competing values framework and lists approximately 12 to 15 books under each role. Some are self-improvement books; others are professional management books. Most are very basic. Many managers have used the list as a source of ideas on how to enhance their performance in a particular role. You should not, however, be limited by the list. Take time to browse through the books in the management section in your library or favorite bookstore. You might also consider nonmanagement books that give you a different perspective on life.

In some cases you should select the most relevant books and read them very rapidly. Then briefly record any useful ideas in your notebook, and on a regular basis consolidate these ideas into strategies that you would like to try. In other cases you may find that you want to read more slowly, taking time to self-reflect. Doing so may suggest important modifications to your change strategy. Alternatively, you may just want to skim some books to see whether you want to include reading them in their entirety as part of your change strategy.

IMPLEMENT THE CHANGE STRATEGY

After you finish analyzing your strengths and weaknesses, considering role models, reading for ideas, and consolidating insights into possible action strategies, it is time to implement your strategy. The first step is to be honest with yourself about the personal costs of improvement. Some people are simply not interested in changing; others want to change but are so impatient that they quickly become disillusioned by the setbacks and failures that they encounter. Just as you would not expect to become a master chess player, a master musician, or a master athlete after taking one course, you should not expect to become a master manager too quickly. The improvement process involves a great deal of practice as well as a fair amount of patience.

Because it is not always easy to engage in this process, it is important to develop a social support system. The key is to find someone to talk to—perhaps a friend, a close relative, or colleague—who will be able to provide encouragement and creative insights. Many managers choose their immediate superiors to play this role. When this is a comfortable arrangement, it can turn into a more long-term mentoring relationship. Others feel uncomfortable with their superiors and prefer to select some other person at work or rely on a spouse or significant other. Regardless of whom you select, arrange a schedule that will allow you to meet regularly with that person to discuss your successes and failures.

As you begin to experiment with new strategies, remember that leaving the status quo usually involves some risk. It sometimes means moving into a situation that requires assumptions very different from those with which you are familiar. Instead of trying to avoid failure, you may need to embrace failure and to see it as an indispensable part of the learning process.

As you implement your strategy, try to be aware of your progress. Keep your notebook close at hand. Use it to record and analyze successes, setbacks, and insights. On a regular basis, review your notes, evaluate your progress, and modify your strategies if necessary. You will be impressed with what you will learn if you consistently monitor your own behaviors as well as your reactions to others' behaviors. One manager with whom we worked scored low on the broker role and was very concerned about his inability to make persuasive presentations. He worked through all the steps described here and reported a dramatic improvement in performance. Here is what he wrote about how he monitored his progress:

> I had never before kept a journal. It was very hard for me to get used to the idea. But I was intense about trying to improve, and it was clear that a journal was going to be important. I read everything I could get my hands on, and I made lots of notes. Whenever anyone made a presentation of any kind—a salesperson, a politician, a young kid in my Sunday School class—I would analyze what was effective and what was not. Each time I drew lessons for myself. Whenever I made a presentation, I would immediately find some time to do a self-analysis. I was a tough self-critic.
>
> Every so often, I would make notes of my notes. That is, I would reduce them to a list of those principles that seemed to be most important for me. I was, without knowing it, building my own personal theory of persuasive speaking. The important thing is that it was an applied theory. It told me "how to." After four months or so, I really started to show signs of progress. People told me they were amazed at how much better I was doing.

THE RESULTS

The improvement process is sometimes easier than one thinks it is going to be. While change takes time and perseverance, if you have the patience and the will, you can be successful. Recall from Chapter 7 that the number-one strategy for time and stress management is "clarify your values." If this is an important item on your agenda, if you truly want to improve, you will need to devote the necessary time. We offer here one final example. The competing values profile of one manager suggested that she was very strong in all the roles except that of monitor. She saw herself as a visionary, and she thought that being a monitor was simply "not her style." Hence, it was with some dread that she undertook the implementation of the steps outlined earlier. Here is her report:

I picked a role model, read some books, made some notes, and designed a change program. It was really very simple. Basically it boiled down to setting times to do a whole raft of tasks that I normally ignored. That was all there was to it. I was amazed. It was not a matter of ability; it was actually quite easy. It is now hard to believe that I once thought I was incapable of doing the things in the monitor role.

We close this section by encouraging you to believe in yourself. It is possible to become a better manager, particularly to improve in those areas that seem far from your natural style. If you are willing to follow the steps outlined herein, they can be very helpful in moving you forward along the road to mastery.

ANALYSIS   The Transcendence of Paradox

Objective   In this chapter we discussed the transcendence of paradox in terms of the ability to integrate seemingly opposite approaches to management. Much of the discussion focused on the need to blend several roles (and their associated competencies) when faced with a complex managerial situation. We also mentioned that paradox is evident *within* each of the roles. Here are a few examples:

Broker	When we empower others, we increase our own power.
Producer	We become most effective in our use of time when we learn the value of taking breaks.
Facilitator	In a team, when every person fully understands each individual's role, team members are more willing (and able) to act outside their own role.
Director	Planning increases your flexibility.

Directions   1. Think about each of the eight roles. Try to find the paradoxes within each role.

2. Examine the four pairs of seemingly opposite roles (facilitator–producer, mentor–director, innovator–coordinator, broker–monitor) and try to find similarities between the two roles.

3. Think about the implications of these paradoxes and similarities for increasing your behavioral complexity.

Reflection   Transcending paradox is not a challenge that you achieve once and then never need to address again. Transcendence is often a fleeting state—one day we seem to act easily as both mentor and director; the next day we come across as too harsh a task master. Distinct situations and diverse individuals are likely to respond differently to our actions, constantly challenging us to find new ways to transcend the paradoxes of effective management.

PRACTICE   The Evaluation Matrix

Objective   The matrix (Table 10.2) will help you organize your thoughts about your personal competencies. This exercise serves as a starting point for developing a comprehensive strategy for mastery that you can implement and monitor in the future.

Directions   Based on all you have learned from Chapters 1 through 9, and from the Assessment exercise at the outset of this chapter, complete the matrix shown in Table 10.2.

Reflection   Did you notice as you were completing the evaluation matrix that some of the questions were linked to competencies that you had studied (e.g., #1—Understanding Self and Others; #5 Setting Goals and Objectives; #7 Measuring Performance and Quality)?

TABLE 10.2 Evaluation Matrix

	Mentor	*Facilitator*	*Monitor*	*Coordinator*	*Director*	*Producer*	*Innovator*	*Broker*
1. In regard to this role, what do I know about myself?								
2. How could I more effectively play this role?								
3. Who are some people I could observe?								
4. What books should I read?								
5. What objectives and deadlines should I set?								
6. With whom should I share my objectives?								
7. How will I evaluate my efforts?								

APPLICATION   Your Strategy for Mastery

Objective   With your assessment matrix as a starting point, you should be well on your way to developing a comprehensive strategy for mastery. Rather than organizing your personal strategy in the order that the roles appear in the text, you may find it helpful to focus first on those roles that you have identified as most important to you at this point in your career.

Directions   Review the material in the chapters focusing on the individual managerial leadership roles (Chapters 2 to 9), as well as your personal work (e.g., Assessment exercises, Application exercises, etc.). Based on this material, and the material in this chapter, write a long-term development plan that focuses on enhancing your behavioral complexity. Discuss what specific things you can do to enhance your ability to integrate the various roles.

Reflection   For strategic planning to be worthwhile, the strategy must eventually be implemented. There will undoubtedly be modifications that you need to make to your strategy for mastery as time goes by, so the sooner you get started, the better!

REFERENCES

Breen, Bill. "What's Your Intuition?" *Fast Company* (Issue 38) September 2000. Accessed August 23, 2000 (http://www.fastcompany.com/online/38/klein.html).

Chaleff, Ira. *The Courageous Follower: Standing Up to and for Our Leaders.* San Francisco: Berrett-Koehler, 1995.

Dreyfus, Hubert. L., Stuart E. Dreyfus, with Tom Athanasiou. *Mind over Machine: The Power of Human Intuition and Expertise in the Era of the Computer.* New York: Free Press, 1986.

Gelb, Michael J. *How to Think Like Leonardo da Vinci: Seven Steps to Genius Everyday.* New York: Delacorte Press, 1998.

Goldsmith, Marshall. "Ask, Learn, Follow Up and Grow," in Frances Hesselbein, Marshall Goldsmith, and Richard Beckhard (eds.), *The Leader of the Future,* pp. 227–237. San Francisco, Jossey-Bass, 1996.

Hooijberg, Robert, James G. Hunt, and George E. Dodge. "Leadership Complexity and Development of the Leaderplex Model." *Journal of Management* 23(3) (1997): 375–408.

Hooijberg, Robert, and Robert E. Quinn. "Behavioral Complexity and the Development of Effective Managers," in Robert L. Phillips and James G. Hunt (eds.), *Strategic Leadership: A Multiorganizational Perspective.* Westport, CT: Quorum Books, 1992.

Lepsinger, Richard, and Antoinette D. Lucia. *The Art and Science of 360°; Feedback.* San Francisco: Pfeiffer, 1997.

Petrick, Joseph A., Robert F. Scherer, James D. Brodzinski, John F. Quinn, and M. Fall Ainina, "Global Leadership Skills and Reputational Capital: Intangible Resources for Sustainable Competitive Advantage." *Academy of Management Executive* 13(1) (1999): 58–69.

Phillips, Donald T. *Martin Luther King, Jr. on Leadership: Inspiration & Wisdom for Challenging Times.* New York: Warner Books, 1999.

Quinn, Robert E. *Beyond Rational Management: Mastering the Paradoxes and Competing Demands of High Performance.* San Francisco: Jossey-Bass, 1988.

Quinn, Robert E., Sue R. Faerman, and Narendra Dixit. "Perceived Performance: Some Archetypes of Managerial Effectiveness and Ineffectiveness." Working paper, Institute for Government and Policy Studies, Department of Public Administration, State University of New York at Albany, 1987.

Senge, Peter. *The Fifth Discipline: The Art & Practice of the Learning Organization.* New York: Currency Doubleday, 1990.

Wheatley, Margaret J. *Leadership and the New Science.* San Francisco: Berrett-Koehler, 1992.

A COMPETING VALUES READING LIST

This resource contains a reading list organized according to the competing values framework and designed to help you identify books that address areas in which you need improvement. It is meant to suggest a few of the many readings that can expand your knowledge in each area. Readers are encouraged to send the authors additional suggestions of books for inclusion.

Mentor Role

Bell, Chip R. *Managers as Mentors: Building Partnerships for Learning,* 2d ed. San Francisco: Berrett-Koehler, 2002.

Bolles, Richard Nelson, and Dick Bolles. *What Color Is Your Parachute? 2006.* Berkeley, CA: Ten Speed Press, 2005.

Bolman, Lee G., and Terrence E. Deal. *Leading with Soul. An Uncommon Journey of Spirit,* San Francisco: Jossey-Bass, 1995.

Bolton, Robert. *People Skills: How to Assert Yourself, Listen to Others, and Resolve Conflicts.* Englewood Cliffs, NJ.: Prentice-Hall, 1979.

Bolton, Robert, and Dorothy Grover Bolton. *People Styles at Work: Making Bad Relationships Good and Good Relationships Better.* New York: AMACOM, 1996.

Covey, Stephen R. *The Seven Habits of Highly Effective People: Powerful Lessons in Personal Change.* 15th Anniversary Edition. New York: Free Press, 2004.

DePree, Max. *Leadership Is an Art.* New York: Currency Doubleday, 1990.

Ensher, Ellen A., and Susan E. Murphy. *Power Mentoring: How Successful Mentors and Protégés Get the Most Out of Their Relationships.* San Francisco: Jossey-Bass, 2005.

Hall, Douglas T., and Associates. *The Career is Dead—Long Live the Career: A Relational Approach to Careers.* San Francisco: Jossey-Bass, 1996.

Hargrove, Robert. *Masterful Coaching: Extraordinary Results by Impacting People and the Way They Think and Work Together.* San Francisco: Jossey-Bass, 1995.

Johnson, W. Brad, and Charles R. Ridley. *The Elements of Mentoring.* New York: Palgrave Macmillan, 2004.

Kouzes, James M., and Barry Z. Posner. *Credibility: How Leaders Gain and Lose It, Why People Demand It.* San Francisco: Jossey-Bass, 1995.

Kreiff, Allan. *Manager's Survival Guide: How to Avoid the 750 Most Common Mistakes in Dealing with People.* Englewood Cliffs, NJ: Prentice-Hall, 1996.

Rhode, Deborah L. (ed.). *Moral Leadership: The Theory and Practice of Power, Judgment and Policy.* San Francisco: Jossey-Bass, 2006.

Richards, Dick. *Awakening Joy, Meaning and Commitment in the Workplace.* San Francisco: Berrett-Koehler, 1995.

Rogers, Carl R. *On Becoming a Person.* Boston: Houghton Mifflin, 1961.

Sashkin, Marshall. *Assessing Performance Appraisal.* San Diego: University Associates, 1981.

Schein, Edgar H. *Career Anchors: Self Assessment,* 3d ed. San Francisco: Pfeiffer, 2006.

Schein, Edgar H. *Career Dynamics: Matching Individual and Organizational Needs.* Reading, MA: Addison-Wesley, 1978.

Sinetar, Marsha. *The Mentor's Spirit: Life Lessons on Leadership and the Art of Encouragement.* New York: St. Martin's Griffin, 1998.

Zachary, Lois J. *Creating a Mentoring Culture: The Organization's Guide.* San Francisco: Jossey-Bass, 2005.

Facilitator Role

Bens, Ingrid. *Facilitating with Ease!: Core Skills for Facilitators, Team Leaders and Members, Managers, Consultants, and Trainers.* San Francisco: Jossey-Bass, 2005.

Buchholz, Steve, and Thomas Roth. *Creating the High-Performance Team.* New York: John Wiley & Sons, 1987.

Cox, Taylor, Jr. *Cultural Diversity in Organizations: Theory, Research and Practice.* San Francisco: Berrett-Koehler, 1993.

Dyer, William G. *Team Building,* 3d ed. Reading, MA: Addison-Wesley, 1995.

Ghais, Suzanne. *Extreme Facilitation: Guiding Groups Through Controversy and Complexity.* San Francisco: Jossey-Bass, 2005.

Harrington-Mackin, Deborah. *The Team Building Tool Kit: Tips, Tactics and Rules for Effective Workplace Teams.* New York: AMACOM, 1994.

Harrison, Lawrence E., and Samuel P. Huntington (eds.). *Culture Matters: How Values Shape Human Progress.* Basic Books, 2000.

Jenkins, Jon, and Maureen Jenkins. *The 9 Disciplines of a Facilitator: Leading Groups by Transforming Yourself.* San Francisco: Jossey-Bass, 2006.

Johansen, Robert, David Sibbet, Suzyn Benson, Alexia Martin, Robert Mittman, and Paul Saffo. *Leading Business Teams: How Teams Can Use Technology and Group Process Tools to Enhance Performance.* Reading, MA: Addison-Wesley, 1991.

Katzenbach, Jon R., and Douglas K. Smith. *The Wisdom of Teams.* New York: HarperCollins, 1993.

Larson, Carl E., and Frank M. J. LaFasto. *TeamWork: What Must Go Right/What Can Go Wrong.* Newbury Park, CA: Sage Publications, 1989.

Loden, Marilyn, and Judy B. Rosener. *Workforce America! Managing Employee Diversity as a Vital Resource.* Homewood, IL: Business One Irwin, 1991.

Martin, Don. TeamThink: *Using the Sports Connection to Develop, Motivate, and Manage a Winning Business Team.* New York: Penguin, 1993.

Quinn, Robert E. *Deep Change: Discovering the Leader Within.* San Francisco: Jossey-Bass, 1996.

Quinn, Robert E. *Change the World: How Ordinary People Can Accomplish Extraordinary Results.* San Francisco: Jossey-Bass, 2000.

Ray, Darrel, and Howard Bronstein. *Teaming Up: Making the Transition to a Self-Directed Team-Based Organization.* New York: McGraw-Hill, 1994.

Rees, Fran. *The Facilitator Excellence Handbook,* 2d ed. San Francisco: Pfeiffer, 2005.

Tjosvold, Dean. *Learning to Manage Conflict: Getting People to Work Together.* New York: Lexington Books, 1993.

Weisbord, Marvin R. *Productive Workplaces Revisited: Dignity, Meaning, and Community in the 21st Century,* 2d ed. San Francisco: Pfeiffer, 2004.

Wilson, Jeanne M., and Jill A. George. *Team Leader's Survival Guide.* Bridgeville, PA: Development Dimensions International, 1994.

Monitor Role

Bounds, Gregory M., Gregory H. Dobbins, and Oscar S. Fowler. *Management: A Total Quality Perspective.* Cincinnati, OH: Southwestern, 1995.

Currid, Cheryl. *Reengineering Toolkit: Fifteen Tools and Technologies for Reorganizing Your Organization.* Rocklin, CA: Prima, 1994.

Davenport, Thomas H., *Process Innovation: Reengineering Work Through Information Technology.* Cambridge, MA: Harvard University Press, 1993.

Eckerson, Wayne W. *Performance Dashboards: Measuring, Monitoring, and Managing Your Business.* New York: Wiley, 2005.

Flood, Robert. *Beyond TQM.* West Sussex, England: John Wiley & Sons, 1993.

Frame, Davidson J. *The New Project Management: Corporate Reengineering and Other Business Realities.* San Francisco: Jossey-Bass, 1994.

Gabor, Andrea. *The Man Who Discovered Quality: How W. Edwards Deming Brought the Quality Revolution to America: The Stories of Ford Xerox and GM.* New York: Penguin, 1990.

Goldratt, Eliyahu. *The Haystack Syndrome: Sifting Information out of the Data Ocean.* Croton-on-Hudson, NY: North River Press, 1990.

Handy, Charles. *Understanding Organizations: How Understanding the Ways Organizations Actually Work Can Be Used to Manage Them Better,* 4th ed. New York: Penguin Global, 2005.

Harrington, James S. *Total Quality Improvement: The Next Generation in Performance Improvement.* New York: McGraw-Hill, 1995.

Kaplan, Robert S., and David P. Norton. *Strategy Maps: Converting Intangible Assets into Tangible Outcomes.* Cambridge, MA: Harvard Business School Press, 2004.

Kaplan, Robert S., and David P. Norton. *The Balanced Scorecard: Translating Strategy into Action.* Boston: Harvard Business School Press, 1996.

Lachotzki, Fred, and Robet Noteboom. *Beyond Control: Managing Strategic Alignment Through Corporate Dialogue.* Chichester, West Sussex, England: Wiley, 2005.

Roberts, Harry V., and Bernard F. Sergesketter. *Quality Is Personal: A Foundation for Total Quality Management.* New York: Free Press, 1993.

Shapiro, Carl, and Hal R. Varian. *Information Rules: A Strategic Guide to the Network Economy.* Boston: Harvard Business School Press, 1998.

Silver, Susan. *Organized to Be Your Best: Simplify and Improve How You Work,* 4th ed. Los Angeles: Adams-Hall, 2000.

Coordinator Role

Cleland, David I. (ed.). *Field Guide to Project Management.* New York: Van Nostrand Reinhold, 1998.

Englund, Randall L., and Alfonso Bucero. *Project Sponsorship: Achieving Management for Project Success.* New York: Wiley, 2006.

Frame, Davidson J. *The New Project Management: Corporate Reengineering and Other Business Realities.* San Francisco: Jossey-Bass, 1994.

Frame, Davidson J. *Project Management Competence: Building Key Skills for Individuals, Teams, and Organizations.* San Francisco: Jossey-Bass, 1999.

Galbraith, Jay R., Edward E. Lawler III, et al. *Organizing for the Future.* San Francisco: Jossey-Bass, 1993.

Hammer, Michael, and James Champy. *Reengineering the Corporation: A Manifesto for Business Revolution.* New York: HarperBusiness, 2001.

Heldman, Kim. *PMP: Project Management Professional Study Guide,* 3d ed. New York: Wiley, 2005.

House, Ruth Sizemore. *The Human Side of Project Management.* Reading, MA: Addison-Wesley, 1988.

Kerzner, Harold. *Project Management: A Systems Approach to Planning, Scheduling, and Controlling,* 9th ed. New York: Wiley, 2005.

Kimmons, Robert L. *Project Management Basics: A Step by Step Approach.* New York: Marcel Dekker, 1990.

Lawler, Edward E., III. *The Ultimate Advantage: Creating the High-Involvement Organization.* San Francisco: Jossey-Bass, 1992.

Means, Janet A., and Tammy Adams. *Facilitating the Project Lifecycle: The Skills & Tools to Accelerate Progress for Project Managers, Facilitators, and Six Sigma Project Teams.* San Francisco: Jossey-Bass, 2005.

Meyer, Christopher. *Fast Cycle Time.* New York: Free Press, 1993.

Parker, Glenn M. *Cross-Functional Teams: Working with Allies, Enemies, and Other Strangers.* San Francisco: Jossey-Bass, 2003.

Rummler, Geary A., and Alan P. Brache. *Improving Performance: How to Manage the White Space on the Organization Chart,* 2d ed. San Francisco: Jossey-Bass, 1995.

Sarason, Seymour B., and Elizabeth M. Lorentz. *Crossing Boundaries: Collaboration, Coordination, and the Redefinition of Resources.* San Francisco: Jossey-Bass, 1998.

Spinner, M. Pete. *Improving Project Management Skills and Techniques.* Englewood Cliffs, NJ: Prentice-Hall, 1989.

Director Role

Collins, James C., and Jerry I. Porras. *Built to Last.* New York: HarperCollins, 2002.

Galbraith, Jay, Edward E. Lawler III, et al. *Organizing for the Future.* San Francisco: Jossey-Bass, 1993.

Goldratt, Eliyahu, and Jeff Cox. *The Goal,* 3rd ed. Croton-on-Hudson, NY: North River Press, 2004.

Hammer, Michael, and James Champy. *Reengineering the Corporation: A Manifesto for Business Revolution.* New York: HarperBusiness, 2001.

Kaufman, Roger. *Strategic Planning Plus: An Organizational Guide.* Newbury Park, CA: Sage Publications, 1992.

Keidel, Robert W. *Corporate Players: Design for Working and Winning Together.* New York: John Wiley & Sons, 1988.

Lakhani, Dave. *Power of an Hour: Business and Life Mastery in One Hour a Week.* New York: John Wiley & Sons, 2006.

Lawler, Edward E., III. *The Ultimate Advantage: Creating the High-Involvement Organization.* San Francisco: Jossey-Bass, 1992.

Maxwell, John C. *The 21 Irrefutable Laws of Leadership: Follow Them and People Will Follow You.* Nashville, TN: Thomas Nelson Publishers, 1998.

Meyer, Christopher. *Fast Cycle Time.* New York: Free Press, 1993.

Mintzberg, Henry. *Mintzberg on Management: Inside our Strange World of Organizations.* New York: Free Press, 1989.

Nanus, Burt. *Visionary Leadership: Creating a Compelling Sense of Direction for Your Organization.* San Francisco: Jossey-Bass, 1992.

Schwartz, Andrew E. *Delegating Authority.* Hauppauge, NY: Barron's Educational Series, 1992.

Seybold, Patricia B., with Ronni Marshak. *Customers.Com: How to Create a Profitable Business Strategy for the Internet and Beyond.* New York: Random House, 1998.

Treacy, Michael, and Fred Wiersma. *The Discipline of Market Leaders: Choose Your Customers, Narrow Your Focus, Dominate Your Market.* Reading, MA: Addison-Wesley, 1995.

Tregoe, Benjamin B., J. W. Zimmerman, R. A. Smith, and P. M. Tobia. *Vision in Action: How to Integrate Your Company's Strategic Goals into Day-to-Day Management Decisions.* New York: Simon & Schuster, 1990.

Trout, Jack, and Steve Rivkin. *Differentiate or Die: Survival in Our Era of Killer Competition.* New York: John Wiley & Sons, 2000.

Producer Role

Alesandrini, Kathryn. *Survive Information Overload: The 7 Best Ways to Manage Your Workload by Seeing the Big Picture.* Homewood, IL: Business One Irwin, 1992.

Carpenter, Phil. *eBrands: Building an Internet Business at Breakneck Speed.* Boston: Harvard Business School Press, 2000.

Covey, Stephen R., A. Roger Merrill, and Rebecca R. Merrill. *First Things First: To Live, to Love, to Learn, to Leave a Legacy.* New York: Simon & Schuster, 1994.

Evans, Gail. *Play Like a Man, Win Like a Woman: What Men Know About Success that Women Need to Learn.* Broadway Books, 2000.

Goldratt, Eliyahu M., and Jeff Cox. *The Goal: A Process of Ongoing Improvement,* 3d ed. Croton-on-Hudson, NY: North River Press, 2004.

Grove, Andrew S. *High-Output Management,* 2d ed. New York: Random House, 1995.

Grover, Ron. *The Disney Touch.* Homewood, IL: Business One Irwin, 1991.

Jensen, Bill. *Simplicity: The New Competitive Advantage in a World of More, Better, Faster.* Perseus Books Group, 2000.

Johnson, Spencer, and Kenneth H. Blanchard. *The One Minute Manager.* Berkley Publishing Group, 1993.

Latham, Gary P., and Kenneth N. Wexley. *Increasing Productivity Through Performance Appraisal,* 2d ed. Reading, MA: Addison-Wesley, 1994.

McCall, Morgan W., Jr., Michael M. Lombardo, and Ann M. Morrison. *The Lessons of Experience: How Successful Executives Develop on the Job.* Lexington, MA. Lexington Books, 1989.

McGee-Cooper, Ann, with Duane Trammell. *Time Management for Unmanageable People.* New York: Bantam, 1994.

McGee-Cooper, Ann, with Duane Trammell and Barbara Lau. *You Don't Have to Go Home from Work Exhausted.* New York: Bantam, 1992.

Neuhauser, Peg, Ray Bender, and Kirk Stromberg. *I Should Be Burnt Out by Now . . . So How Come I'm Not?: How You Can Survive and Thrive in Today's Uncertain World.* New York: Wiley, 2004.

Prentice, Steve. *Cool Time: A Hands-on Plan for Managing Work and Balancing Time.* New York: Wiley, 2005.

Stalk, George, Jr., and Thomas M. Hout. *Competing Against Time: How Time-Based Competition Is Reshaping Global Markets.* New York: Free Press, 1990.

Tichy, Noel M., and Stratford Sherman. *Control Your Destiny or Someone Else Will.* New York: HarperCollins, 2001.

Innovator Role

Buckingham, Marcus, and Curt Coffman. *First, Break All the Rules: What the World's Greatest Managers Do Differently.* New York: Simon & Schuster, 1999.

Christensen, Clayton M. *The Innovator's Dilemma: When New Technologies Cause Great Firms to Fail.* New York: HarperBusiness, 2000.

de Bono, E. *Lateral Thinking: Creativity Step-by-Step.* New York: Harper &ampersand; Row, 1970.

Goldratt, Eliyahu. *Theory of Constraints.* Croton-on-Hudson, NY: North River Press, 1990.

Johnson, Spencer. *Who Moved My Cheese?: An Amazing Way to Deal With Change in Your Work and in Your Life.* New York: Putnam, 1998.

Kanter, Rosabeth Moss. *The Change Masters: Innovation for Productivity in the American Corporation.* New York: Simon & Schuster, 1983.

Kelly, James N., and Francis J. Gouillart. *Transforming the Organization.* New York: McGraw-Hill, 1995.

McCarthy, J. Allan. *The Transition Equation: A Proven Strategy for Organizational Change.* New York: Free Press, 1994.

Ogilvy, James. *Living Without a Goal: Finding the Freedom to Live a Creative and Innovative Life.* New York: Currency–Doubleday, 1995.

O'Toole, James. *Leading Change: Overcoming the Ideology of Comfort and the Tyranny of Custom.* San Francisco: Jossey-Bass, 1995.

PriceWaterhouse Change Integration Team. *Better Change: Best Practices for Transforming Your Organization.* Homewood, IL: Irwin Professional Publishing, 1994.

PriceWaterhouse Change Integration Team. *The Paradox Principles: How High-Performance Companies Manage Chaos, Complexity, and Contradiction to Achieve Superior Results.* Homewood, IL: Irwin Professional Publishing, 1996.

Senge, Peter M. *The Fifth Discipline: The Art and Practice of the Learning Organization.* New York: Currency—Doubleday, 1990.

Senge, Peter M., Art Kleiner, Charlotte Roberts, Richard Ross, Geroge Roth, and Bryan Smith. *The Dance of Change: The Challenges to Sustaining Momentum in Learning Organizations.* New York: Currency—Doubleday, 1999.

Shefsky, Lloyd E. *Entrepreneurs Are Made: Secrets From 200 Successful Entrepreneurs.* New York: McGraw-Hill, 1994.

Tapscott, Don. *Digital Capital: Harnessing the Power of Business Webs.* Boston: Harvard Business School Press, 2000.

Tidd, Joe, John Bessant, and Keith Pavitt. *Managing Innovation: Integrating Technological, Market and Organizational Change,* 3d ed. Chichester, West Sussex, England: Wiley, 2005.

Tracy, Brian. *Change Your Thinking, Change Your Life: How to Unlock Your Full Potential for Success and Achievement.* New York: Wiley, 2005.

Trompenaars, Fons, and Peter Prud'Homme. *Managing Change Across Corporate Cultures.* New York: Wiley-Capstone, 2005.

Whyte, David. *The Heart Aroused.* New York: Currency—Doubleday, 1994.

Broker Role

Baker, Wayne E. *Networking Smart: How to Build Relationships for Personal and Organizational Success.* New York: McGraw-Hill, 1994.

Bolton, Robert. *People Skills: How to Assert Yourself, Listen to Others, and Resolve Conflicts.* Englewood Cliffs, NJ: Prentice-Hall, 1979.

de Bono, Edward. *Six Thinking Hats.* Boston: Little, Brown, 1999.

Deep, Sam, and Lyle Sussman. *What to Ask When You Don't Know What to Say: 555 Powerful Questions to Use for Getting Your Way at Work.* Englewood Cliffs, NJ: Prentice-Hall, 1993.

Evans, Philip, and Thomas S. Wurster. *Blown to Bits: How the New Economics of Information Transforms Strategy.* Boston, MA: Harvard Business School Press, 1999.

Ferrazzi, Keith, with Tahl Raz. *Never Eat Alone and Other Secrets to Success: One Relationship at a Time.* New York: Doubleday, 2005.

Fisher, Roger, and Daniel Shapiro. *Beyond Reason: Using Emotions as You Negotiate.* New York: Viking, 2005.

Fisher, Roger, and William Ury. *Getting to Yes: Negotiating Agreement Without Giving In,* 2nd ed. New York: Penguin, 1991.

Friedman, Thomas L. *The Lexus and the Olive Tree: Understanding Globalization.* New York: Bantam Doubleday Dell, 2000.

Gillette, Jonathon, and Marion McCollom. *Groups in Context: A New Perspective on Group Dynamics.* Reading, MA: Addison-Wesley, 1990.

Hoff, Ron. *Say It in Six: How to Say Exactly What You Mean in Six Minutes or Less.* Kansas City: Andrews and McMeel, 1996.

Jeary, Tony, with Kim Dower and J.E. Fishman. *Life Is a Series of Presentations: 8 Ways to Inspire, Inform, and Influence Anyone, Anywhere, Anytime.* New York: Simon & Schuster, 2004.

Lipnack, Jessica, and Jeffrey Stamps. *The TeamNet Factor: Bringing the Power of Boundary Crossing into the Heart of Your Business.* New York: Wiley, 2003.

McKay, Matthew, Martha Davis, and Patrick Fanning. *How to Communicate: The Ultimate Guide to Improving Your Personal and Professional Relationships.* New York: MJF Books, 1983.

Mooney, William, and Donald Noone. *ASAP: The Fastest Way to Make a Memorable Speech.* Hauppauge, NJ: Barrons, 1992.

Moore, Geoffrey A. *Living on the Fault Line.* New York: HarperBusiness, 2000.

Patterson, Kerry, Joseph Grenny, Ron McMillan, and Al Switzler. *Crucial Confrontations: Tools for Resolving Broken Promises, Violated Expectations, and Bad Behavior.* New York: McGraw-Hill, 2005.

RoAne, Susan. *How to Work a Room: The Ultimate Guide to Savvy Socializing in Person and Online.* New York: HarperCollins, 2005.

Stross, Randall E. *Eboys: The First Inside Account of Venture Capitalists at Work.* New York: Crown Publishing, 2000.

Weissman, Jerry. *Presenting to Win: The Art of Telling Your Story.* New York: Prentice Hall, 2003.

Wiener, Valerie. *Power Communications: Positioning Yourself for High Visibility.* New York: New York University Press, 1994.

Zucker, Elaina. *The Seven Secrets of Influence.* New York: McGraw-Hill, 1991.

INDEX